Praise for *Swami in a Strange Land*

"*Swami in a Strange Land* is a timely volume, auspiciously marking the fiftieth anniversary of A.C. Bhaktivedanta Swami Prabhupada's arrival in the West. It offers an attractive narrative of this most interesting and surprising pilgrim and pioneer, the devotee and teacher who brought Krishna to the West. It will edify insiders to the ISKCON tradition, and inform those who know of him only from a distance; and it is a solid contribution to our understanding of this notable religious movement and of Hinduism's emergence as a truly global religion."

—DR. FRANCIS X. CLOONEY, SJ

DIRECTOR, CENTER FOR THE STUDY OF WORLD RELIGIONS, HARVARD UNIVERSITY

"In 1965, Prabhupada stepped off a cargo ship in New York Harbor after thirty-eight days at sea. A lone saint from India, seventy years in age, with neither money nor a single acquaintance, he wandered the streets of Manhattan in his saffron robes. Yet, overflowing from his heart was a treasure of spiritual love that he yearned to share with the world. And miraculously, he did—within a few years Prabhupada had inspired a movement that spread across the planet. Let us open our hearts as Joshua Greene tells us this story of timeless love."

—RADHANATH SWAMI

AUTHOR, *THE JOURNEY HOME* AND *THE JOURNEY WITHIN*

"*Swami in a Strange Land* is a moving account of Prabhupada's bold challenge to the dominant discourses of our time. Joshua Greene is an accomplished storyteller, a diligent historian, and a dedicated bhakta. His biography of Prabhupada pays careful attention to historical context while honoring the transcendent power of bhakti."

—DR. RAVI M. GUPTA

CHARLES REDD CHAIR OF RELIGIOUS STUDIES, UTAH STATE UNIVERSITY

"Not only was Prabhupada a saint who lived on the highest level of devotion, but he was also an organizer, manager, and inspiration to a worldwide movement. He embodied that rarest of combinations: common sense and uncommon love for God. *Swami in a Strange Land* will be a revelation for all who seek to foster a spiritual awakening in the world."

—HRISHIKESH MAFATLAL
CHAIRMAN, MAFATLAL INDUSTRIES, LTD.

"Joshua Greene makes an enchanting historical addition to our understanding of the early days of the Hare Krishna movement and its founder, Srila Prabhupada. Whether the reader is searching for an uplifting biography, insight into religious movements, a glimpse into cross-cultural experiences, or a deep drink of the elixir of spirituality, it can be found in this book."

—DR. EDITH BEST
PROFESSOR, SOCIOLOGY OF RELIGION

"In *Swami in a Strange Land*, Joshua Greene relates the unprecedented, remarkable story of Prabhupada's life and mission in vivid detail, with intelligence, wit, compassion, and love."

—GIRIRAJ SWAMI

"How could it be possible that a seventy-year-old, penniless, little Indian man, wrapped only in a thin piece of orange cotton cloth, all alone, was able to step off a freighter ship from Calcutta in New York City in 1965 with no one to greet him, carrying nothing in his suitcase but humility, passion, and unshakable faith in God's Holy Name, and start a worldwide revolution that spread like wildfire in a few short years, attracting millions of devotees to Krishna consciousness? Master storyteller Joshua Greene reveals the magical rise to international celebrity status of a "Swami in a Strange Land"—the true, thrilling adventure story of Srila Bhaktivedanta Prabhupada, a modern-day spiritual giant."

—SHARON GANNON
CO-FOUNDER, JIVAMUKTI YOGA; AUTHOR, *YOGA AND VEGETARIANISM*, *JIVAMUKTI YOGA*, AND *SIMPLE RECIPES FOR JOY*

"Joshua Greene's affable yet masterful writing style makes *Swami in a Strange Land* a pleasure to read. Reading this book not only instilled in me an uncanny feeling of closeness to Srila Prabhupada, but also gave me a stockpile of valuable lessons with which to improve my life."

—VAISESIKA DASA

"*Swami in a Strange Land*, by Joshua Greene, is a major contribution to our understanding of Prabhupada. The author strikes a powerful balance between his roles as devoted participant and detached observer, and is thus able to balance Prabhupada's own divine and human nature. This balance makes the book unique and important. The author neither mythologizes nor demythologizes. Rather he wisely and sensitively presents Prabhupada just as thousands experienced him during his life on earth. Countless future generations will thank the author for his contribution, just as we thank him today."

—HRIDAYANANDA GOSWAMI

"Joshua Greene's beautiful book *Swami in a Strange Land* introduces me to Prabhupada in a most intimate and delightful way. Seeing his struggles, his commitment, his deep devotion and compassion, and his absolute disregard for his own comfort or well-being in the service of Krishna consciousness is a great inspiration and wake-up call to all of us aspiring bhaktas. Sometimes the path seems too difficult and our passion becomes dulled, but Swamiji's life story reminds us to not waste a moment, a single breath, in our journey back to Godhead. I loved reading this and I'm sure I'll read it again and again."

—JAI UTTAL
GRAMMY-NOMINATED MUSICIAN

"Welcome to the age of spiritual globalization. Bhaktivedanta Swami Prabhupada trans-nationalized an otherwise local, provincial sect into a global movement with massive publications and a benevolent social-services understructure. This timely biography by Joshua Greene reveals how a single Hindu ascetic achieved this humongous global feat and how his legacy continues to inspire the sustaining work of ISKCON across the world."

—DR. PURUSHOTTAMA BILIMORIA
CORE FACULTY, GRADUATE THEOLOGICAL UNION; VISITING PROFESSOR,
UNIVERSITY OF CALIFORNIA, BERKELEY

"Who could have predicted it? An impoverished, retired pharmacist in his sixties travels from India to the United States, sets up shop in 1966 on the Lower East Side of New York City, and begins to teach young hippies to chant the names of Krishna. The hippies become initiated Brahmins, and Krishna consciousness spreads from America around the world and back to India. Joshua Greene tells this remarkable story with an insider's perspective, enhanced by anecdotes and memories from many who were there at the beginning. *Swami in a Strange Land* is a real pleasure to read."

—RICHARD H. DAVIS

AUTHOR, *THE BHAGAVAD GITA: A BIOGRAPHY*; PROFESSOR OF RELIGION, DIRECTOR OF THE RELIGION PROGRAM, DIRECTOR OF THE ASIAN STUDIES PROGRAM, BARD COLLEGE

"Little remains to add to [Greene's] great accomplishment in the way of praise; the work speaks louder than any secondary eulogy. A masterful storyteller, an elegant speaker, a consummate artist in his own right, Joshua has transmitted to us a lucid account and a vivid portrait of this spiritual giant, Srila Prabhupada."

—BARADRAJ MAREK BUCHWALD

FOUNDER, ART CENTER FOR TRANSCENDENCE

"*Swami in a Strange Land* by Joshua Greene will not just be a new item in a list of interesting biographies about Bhaktivedanta Swami Prabhupada, founder of the ISKCON movement; it will be recognized as one of the most accurate and reliable among them. Greene's material for this biography stems from thorough historical research, the consultation of previous biographical accounts, newspaper articles, and direct testimonies of the times—and mainly, on his experience as a disciple serving his teacher. Besides documenting the beginnings and development of the religious movement called ISKCON, *Swami in a Strange Land* allows readers to reexperience the extraordinary transformations that Prabhupada fostered in the lives of so many others."

—MARCO FERRINI (MATSYAVATARA DASA)

FOUNDER AND PRESIDENT OF THE ACADEMY OF TRADITIONAL INDIAN SCIENCES, ITALY

Appreciations for A.C. Bhaktivedanta Swami Prabhupada

"The thing that always stays is his saying, 'I am the servant of the servant of the servant.' I like that. A lot of people say, 'I'm it. I'm the divine incarnation. I'm here and let me help you.' You know what I mean? But Prabhupada was never like that. I liked Prabhupada's humbleness. I always liked his humility and his simplicity. The servant of the servant of the servant is really what it is, you know. He just made me feel so comfortable. I always felt very relaxed with him, and I felt more like a friend. I felt that he was a good friend. Even though he was at the time seventy-nine years old, working practically all through the night, day after day, with very little sleep, he still didn't come through to me as though he was a very highly educated intellectual being, because he had a sort of childlike simplicity. Which is great, fantastic. Even though he was the greatest Sanskrit scholar and a saint, I appreciated the fact that he never made me feel uncomfortable. In fact, he always went out of his way to make me feel comfortable. I always thought of him as sort of a lovely friend, really, and now he's still a lovely friend . . . Srila Prabhupada has already had an amazing effect on the world. There's no way of measuring it. One day I just realized, 'God, this man is amazing!' He would sit up all night translating Sanskrit into English, putting in glossaries to make sure everyone understands it, and yet he never came off as someone above you."

— GEORGE HARRISON (1943–2001)

"Swami Bhaktivedanta came to USA and went swiftly to the Archetype Spiritual neighborhood, the New York Lower East Side, and installed intact an ancient perfectly preserved piece of street India. He adorned a storefront as his Ashram and adored Krishna therein and by patience and good humor singing chanting and expounding Sanskrit terminology day by day established Krishna Consciousness in the psychedelic (mind-manifesting) center of America East. . . . To choose to attend to the Lower East Side, what kindness and humility and intelligence! . . . The Hare Krishna Mantra's now a household word in America. . . . The personal vibration set up by chanting Hare Krishna is a universal pleasure: a tranquility at realization of the community of tender hearts; a vibration which inevitably affects all men, naked or in uniform. . . . This rare fortune (as Thoreau and Whitman our natural-hearted forefathers prophesied) is our heritage, our own truest Self, our own community of selves, our own true America."

— ALLEN GINSBERG (1926–1997)
FROM HIS INTRODUCTION TO *THE BHAGAVAD GITA AS IT IS*

"Christians are taught to respect and admire those who are willing to pay the heavy price of leaving comfort and security behind to go somewhere else to carry a message of liberation. . . . At what almost anyone would consider a very advanced age, when most people would be resting on their laurels, he harkened to the mandate of his own spiritual master and set out on the difficult and demanding voyage to America. Srila Prabhupada was, of course, only one of thousands of teachers. But in another sense, he is one in a thousand, maybe one in a million."

— HARVEY COX
EMERITUS PROFESSOR OF DIVINITY, HARVARD DIVINITY SCHOOL

"Swami Bhaktivedanta brings to the West a salutary reminder that our highly activistic and one-sided culture is faced with a crisis that may end in self-destruction because it lacks the inner depth of an authentic metaphysical consciousness. Without such depth, our moral and political protestations are just so much verbiage."

— THOMAS MERTON (1915–1968)
CATHOLIC THEOLOGIAN, MONK, AUTHOR

"I certainly honor Srila Prabhupada as one of India's preeminent scholars. As a translator of many of India's important religious texts, he gave special attention to the spirit and beauty of the texts. . . . Srila Prabhupada, in his translations, really captured their essential spirituality. A literal translation which lacks sympathetic reverence for the text itself can obscure rather than elucidate its profound inner meaning. I find that Srila Prabhupada's translations bring these works to life. . . . Due to his unstinting and diligent labors, the whole world now has been made aware of the devotional essence of the Indian spiritual tradition, as well as of one of India's great saints, Sri Chaitanya, and of Gaudiya Vaishnavism, whereas before they were scarcely known outside India except by specialists in Hindu religious tradition."

— J. STILLSON JUDAH (1911–2000)
PROFESSOR OF THE HISTORY OF RELIGIONS
GRADUATE THEOLOGICAL SEMINARY, BERKELEY, CALIFORNIA

SWAMI
~ in a ~
# STRANGE
# LAND

SWAMI
∽ in a ∽
STRANGE LAND

THE BIOGRAPHY OF
A.C. BHAKTIVEDANTA
SWAMI PRABHUPADA

Joshua M. Greene

JAICO PUBLISHING HOUSE

Ahmedabad Bangalore Bhopal Bhubaneswar Chennai
Delhi Hyderabad Kolkata Lucknow Mumbai

Published by Jaico Publishing House
A-2 Jash Chambers, 7-A Sir Phirozshah Mehta Road
Fort, Mumbai - 400 001
jaicopub@jaicobooks.com
www.jaicobooks.com

Originally published by Mandala Publishing in 2016
Mandala Publishing
P.O. Box 3088, San Rafael, CA 94912
www.mandalaeartheditions.com

SWAMI IN A STRANGE LAND
ISBN 978-93-87944-09-1

First Jaico Impression: 2018

Printed by
Thomson Press (India) Limited

To the Bhakti Yogis

The Swami's followers, Achyutananda (at left) and Brahmananda (1943–2015) (right), danced in Tompkins Square Park as the Swami looked on while leading the chanting. These outdoor kirtans became part of the fabric of 1960s New York life.

"Swami Bhaktivedanta came to USA and went swiftly to the Archetype Spiritual neighborhood, the New York Lower East Side, and installed intact an ancient perfectly preserved piece of street India. He adorned a storefront as his Ashram and adored Krishna therein and by patience and good humor singing chanting and expounding Sanskrit terminology day by day established Krishna Consciousness in the psychedelic (mind-manifesting) center of America East. . . . This rare fortune (as Thoreau and Whitman our natural-hearted forefathers prophesied) is our heritage, our own truest Self, our own community of selves, our own true America."

— ALLEN GINSBERG
FROM HIS INTRODUCTION TO THE *BHAGAVAD GITA AS IT IS*

A.C. Bhaktivedanta Swami Prabhupada arrived in New York in 1965, without resources or contacts. Over the next twelve years, he built an international institution that would spread to every country in the world.

CONTENTS

FOREWORD

JOSHUA M. GREENE'S *Swami in a Strange Land* narrates the truly amazing story of how sixty-eight-year-old, penniless Swami Bhaktivedanta came from India to America to begin an international movement, relying on nothing but his faith in the mission he had received from his guru decades back. It is one of those stories that one would not believe if it were not fact.

I met Swami Bhaktivedanta quite often in Vrindavan between 1962 and 1964, but I had no idea of his future world mission and certainly would not have thought that one day I would be asked to write a foreword to his biography. Swami Bhaktivedanta was a fairly regular visitor at The Institute of Oriental Philosophy, founded and directed by his *guru-bhai* Swami Bon Maharaj, to which I was attached as "Research Guide in Christian Philosophy." For me he was one of the many pious elderly men who spent the eve of their life in this holy place, and I was really taken by surprise when he emerged as the founder of ISKCON, triumphantly coming to Mumbai in 1975—where I was then located—with a group of enthusiastic American devotees.

Swami in a Strange Land chronicles the development of ISKCON from its small beginnings in New York to its present worldwide presence. Penniless and without any connections when he arrived in New York in 1965, Swami Bhaktivedanta passed on as highly revered Prabhupada in 1977, surrounded by an international assembly of disciples who had built a temple in Vrindavan, where he was to find his *samadhi*. What impresses me most in Greene's biography is the emphasis on the universal character of Swami Bhaktivedanta's teachings. The Swami had not come to make America Hindu or to establish another esoteric cult but to bring God-consciousness into the lives of a lost generation and to awaken the deepest reality in them. The book is a fitting contribution to the celebration of the fiftieth anniversary of ISKCON. It reads very well and will be of great interest not only to the members of ISKCON but to all students of contemporary religion.

Klaus K. Klostermaier
Distinguished Professor Emeritus
The University of Manitoba

The author and his teacher, Prabhupada, in Paris, 1973.

PREFACE

A CHALLENGE in writing Prabhupada's biography for general readers was portraying his humanness, which risked making him seem like an ordinary person who became extraordinary. That impression would be at odds with his esteem in the devotional community. Devotees of Krishna (the Sanskrit name for God in personal form) revere Prabhupada as a *nitya-siddha*, an "eternally liberated" being, a person sent by God to save humanity, someone who never knew material life as the rest of us do. Some scholars use the term "doubling" to describe this dual citizenship of eternal and temporal worlds. My task was facilitated by a simple fact: Throughout his life, Prabhupada loved Krishna. He never had to convert to Krishna worship, nor did his faith ever waiver. In that sense, it does not matter whether one views him as descending into the world by God's will or as rising through the world to become an exalted teacher. His life stands on its own merit. If, on occasion, the narrative veers overly toward the human, for the sake of making his life story accessible to readers, I assume the responsibility and thank my devotee colleagues for their patience with such literary license.

The Vaishnava tradition honors senior devotees with honorific titles such as Sri, Srila, His Divine Grace, or His Holiness, and during his lifetime Prabhupada was often called "His Divine Grace" or "Srila Prabhupada." To simplify the reading, I chose to use the one-word title Prabhupada and eliminate longer forms of address. Prabhupada's spiritual master was also addressed by lengthy honorific titles, such as Sri Srimad Bhaktisiddhanta Saraswati Goswami Maharaj or sometimes Srila Bhaktisiddhanta Sarasvati Thakur Prabhupada. Here, he is referred to as Bhaktisiddhanta or Bhaktisiddhanta Saraswati. No disrespect is meant in abridging these formal titles. For similar motives, the suffix Das (awarded to initiated men) and Dasi or Devi (awarded to initiated women) have often been left out.[1]

PROLOGUE

IT WAS FOUR O'CLOCK ON A CHILLY MORNING when I stepped off the train from Calcutta. The one-story brick station was empty, and a breeze swept down dusty aisles between rows of weathered wooden benches. Outside, a dozen bicycle-rickshaw drivers in weary cotton shirts and stained pants casually blew smoke from cheap *beedi* cigarettes.

"ISKCON," I said, mounting the nearest three-wheeler. By 1977, more or less everyone in India knew the acronym for the International Society for Krishna Consciousness. For more than a decade, ISKCON followers—young people like myself dressed in Indian robes and chanting the ancient prayer "Hare Krishna" in public—had been profiled in newspapers and magazines around the world. The rickshaw driver nodded confidently, and off we went.

A half hour later, we glided to a stop by an open field. The driver pointed into the void, then pedaled away, leaving me standing in darkness. To one side of the road, a bare light bulb hung from a tree and glowed weakly, as though powered by a trickle of sap. Beneath the bulb was a foot-long wooden sign nailed to the tree: ISKCON, with an arrow pointing off into the distance. I walked for a while through grasses and wild growth, clutching the bottom of my robes and hoping to avoid snakes and open holes. Morning peeked out from behind a serrated edge of hills in the distance. A dim haze limned a series of thatched huts. Off to the side of the first hut, a heavyset Indian with a big smile methodically stirred something thick and sluggish in a large pot over an open flame. His *dhoti*—a length of orange cotton cloth—was tied high around his waist to avoid the fire, and steam from the pot encircled him like a translucent veil. I entered the hut, and my teacher, Prabhupada, looked up from behind a low bamboo desk.

"Ah, Yogesvara, you are here," he said, calling me by my initiated name, meaning "servant of Krishna, the master of all mystic powers." In 1969, when I was nineteen years old, I left university studies in Paris to become his initiated disciple. It would take too long to explain why. The short form is that French existentialism was taking me nowhere, and Prabhupada was taking me everywhere. I began traveling with him as his translator in French-speaking countries.

I prostrated myself on the floor before him, then sat up and examined his humble quarters. The room was spare. Rattan mats covered a hard-packed cow-dung floor. The walls were made of exposed bricks, and the ceiling of braided straw. Through a cutout window in the wall behind his desk, I saw grassy fields. Dawn was breaking in the distance. On the desk were objects familiar to me from times we had traveled across Europe. Large volumes of scriptural commentaries in Bengali and Sanskrit. A dictating machine with a handheld microphone. Stacks of airmail letters awaiting reply. A wooden box housing the ink pen he used for signing his name, A.C. Bhaktivedanta Swami, which he always did in one continuous motion without lifting the nub from the page. A stainless steel pitcher and cup next to a small framed photo of his spiritual master, circa 1930. A space heater kept the fifteen-by-fifteen-foot enclosure warm, and his chest was bare. Prabhupada was thinner than I remembered. Every day since his arrival in American twelve years before, his routine had included a brisk walk and vigorous massage, but he had a seasoned athlete's disdain for physical training, and rumor had it his health had deteriorated. Circling the globe fourteen times in a dozen years was finally catching up with his physical body. He turned from me and looked at the spackled walls and thatched ceiling as though assessing whether they would hold up as well as he had.

"Sometimes my disciples put me up in a fancy apartment," he said, "and sometimes in a mud hut." He shrugged his thin brown shoulders. "What's the difference? The sensations are all the same."

Before leaving India for New York in 1965, he had lived in similar simplicity: a tiny brick room in a deteriorating medieval temple in Vrindavan, a village two hours southeast of Delhi. Vrindavan is the holiest of holies for Vaishnavas, worshippers of Krishna. He had achieved modest success earlier in life as a pharmacist, but in the 1950s, he gave up all predictable sources of income, moved to Vrindavan, and for the next decade wrote scriptural commentaries, lived like a pauper, and ate whatever food the locals provided. It took several years to secure the official papers and government clearances needed to travel out of the country. When he finally left India and arrived in America, he was unknown and without contacts. What a startling contrast with his life now, twelve years later. By 1977, he had thousands of followers and more than one hundred centers around the world.

I had come from Paris to ask his permission to write children's books about Krishna. Stories about Krishna found in ancient scriptures such as the Sanskrit *Srimad Bhagavatam* were not intended for young people but for advanced practitioners of *bhakti* or devotional yoga. Still, children in India grew up hearing stories about Krishna the way kids in the West heard stories from the Brothers Grimm or Hans Christian Andersen, and now that many of Prabhupada's disciples had children of their own, such books would be important. Were there risks in adapting Krishna's *lilas* or pastimes for young minds? Might Krishna's identity as the Supreme Being be misconstrued as a fairy tale if his activities were retold in children's book form? Did our Vaishnava tradition approve of such simplification?

To my relief, Prabhupada thought children's books were a good idea. "What is learned early in life is never forgotten," he said with a nod. He never wrote books for young people himself, but he was a prolific author. Spurred by his late guru's order to see devotional books distributed around the world, Prabhupada had written dozens. Books were still a popular source of knowledge in the 1970s—cable television and Internet cafes were at least a decade away—and disciples distributed his works with mission-ary zeal. In 1976, ISKCON's publishing office had ordered what was then the largest single print-run of any book in history: one million copies of the *Bhagavad Gita As It Is*, his edition of India's essential wisdom text. Ninety-five flatbed railcars were needed to deliver the paper to the printer's warehouses in Kentucky. The procession of cars extended nearly two miles. Just before my visit to Bhubaneshwar, the publishing office announced that the number of his books and magazines distributed worldwide had surpassed 100 mil-lion. I remember blinking my eyes when reading that number and trying to imagine 100 million of anything, let alone books about Krishna. Despite the preeminence of his own publications, Prabhupada wanted his students to also write, and I was glad he liked the plan for a library of children's books.

THERE WAS ANOTHER REASON I had made the trek from Paris: to see him once more before it was too late. I wanted to burn into my memory a final impression of this extraordinary spiritual leader who had dedicated his life to convincing the world that consciousness existed separate from matter. The Vedic viewpoint[2] asserts that consciousness is not produced by combinations of chemicals or physical laws as most hard sciences claim, and he urged his stu-dents to speak out strongly on this point. I do not recall him ever encouraging us to be peaceful or tranquil. Rather, he made frequent reference to fighting a war with *maya*, by which he meant working diligently to expose the fallacy that consciousness has a beginning or an end. Life, he insisted, was eternal.

Prabhupada conducted his mission in the 1960s and 1970s when spiritual teachers were expected to be peaceniks. He turned that image upside down. For example, he was not anti-science, but he called scientists who presumed to eliminate God from creation "demonic." He also praised hippies for being dissatisfied with consumer culture, and he condemned the U.S. government for sending young people off to be killed in war while failing to provide them with spiritual direction. One of his more controversial acts was to award his students formal Brahminical initiation—essentially bringing "low caste" Westerners into the "high caste" priesthood—an innovation that had India's religious hierarchy up in arms. By such spiritual activism, he set the stage for a whole new breed of holy man.

Prabhupada was innovative in technique, but when it came to teaching bhakti yoga, he faithfully represented a lineage that dated from Chaitanya Mahaprabhu, the sixteenth-century *avatar* of Krishna. The word *avatar* as used in bhakti texts refers to a scripturally predicted incarnation of the Supreme Being who comes into the world with a particular mission. These bhakti texts identify Chaitanya Mahaprabhu as Krishna himself—the *avatari* or source of all avatars— whose mission was to propagate the chanting of God's names. Before Mahaprabhu, Prabhupada's lineage extended back through cosmic time to the first being, Brahma, and, before Brahma, to Krishna himself. As the current link in that line of preceptors, Prabhupada created a language with which to convey millennial teachings to a contemporary audience.

Bhakti practice begins and ends with the chanting of the Hare Krishna mantra: "Hare Krishna, Hare Krishna, Krishna Krishna, Hare Hare, Hare Rama, Hare Rama, Rama Rama, Hare Hare," which translates as, "O Hare (Radha, the feminine Godhead), O Krishna (the male Godhead), O Rama (another name of Krishna, meaning the source of highest bliss), kindly engage me in your service." No one ever did as much as Prabhupada to popularize the chanting of Hare Krishna. He could look out from an airplane window, down onto Paris or Nairobi, Moscow or Hong Kong, and know that people in nearly every country had heard the chanting of Krishna's names as a result of his mission. Paradoxically, few people knew anything about him.

THE BRIEF MEETING IN BHUBANESHWAR was the last time I saw Prabhupada. He passed away ten months later. In our final moments together, the sun rose and burst through the window of his hut as if on cue. His parting words still ring in my ears.

"These books are important," he said. We were discussing children's books, but I had the impression he was referring more generally to all books about Krishna. "When people see the books, they will understand Krishna consciousness is here to stay." The unspoken part of his message was obvious: He would not be around forever, but the knowledge contained in scripture would survive for ages to come, just as it had for thousands of years before.

As of this writing, we have entered the fourth generation of Western Krishna devotees. That alone marks a historic turning point: Hardly anyone in the West knew about Krishna before Prabhupada arrived. Still, it is only within the past few years that followers have begun exploring the connections between Krishna's teachings and issues of global concern. We humans want happiness for ourselves and others, yet without factoring consciousness into our equations, happiness has no fertile soil in which to grow. Consciousness—the life force which animates the body—is as fundamental to reality as time, space, or gravity. The challenge Prabhupada left his followers was to define the role of consciousness in progressive human society, and ever since his departure in 1977, that has been a work in progress.[3]

The Vedic texts reveal consciousness at work in every detail of creation. Prabhupada's mission was to make that vision, obscured for centuries by the intricacies of Sanskrit and the biases of science, accessible. Here, then, is an attempt to describe someone whose teachings ranged from the dawn of time to the end of time, from the tiniest particle to the largest of cosmic scales. It is an epic life, the stuff of legends.

In Prabhupada's case, it is an epic that has the advantage of being utterly true.

PART ONE

INDIA

His Divine Grace A.C. Bhaktivedanta Swami Prabhupada (1896–1977), Founder-Acharya of the International Society for Krishna Consciousness.

CHAPTER ONE

*Whenever and wherever there is a decline in dharma
and a rise of a-dharma—at that time I descend.*

—SRI KRISHNA IN THE BHAGAVAD GITA, 4.7

CALCUTTA, 1912

The scaffolding of metal bars and bamboo poles spiraled 200 feet into a moonlit sky. Soon the Victoria Memorial—Britain's architectural declaration of dominance over India—would be finished in white marble, and the cobweb of supports would be dismantled. Before that happened, sixteen-year-old Abhay Charan could not resist scaling it to the top.

Streets were quiet at this late hour. Do Not Enter signs lined the construction site, but rules had never held Abhay back before. He ducked under the barricade, climbed the crisscross of beams hand over hand, reached the wood-planked summit, and stared out over the city to the Hooghly River, a tributary of the mighty Ganges. The Hooghly's tides ran rapidly, sometimes producing head waves that capsized small boats.

Abhay gazed out over Bengal. From his classes at the local Higher Secondary School, he knew that 150 years before and about eighty miles upstream there had been a great battle to determine India's future. There, at the town of Plassey, the last Nawab of Bengal, Siraj Ud Daulah, attacked British forces commanded by Robert Clive. Unknown to the Nawab's men, Clive had bribed their commander-in-chief, and the British quickly won the day. Clive's victory at Plassey was followed by a rapid expansion of British power, and by the mid-nineteenth century Great Britain ruled India.

To maintain control over such a massive nation, the British fomented hostility between Hindus and Muslims by forcing them to live apart. On October 16, 1905, Abhay's home province of Bengal was split into segregated neighborhoods. The British appointed Muslim governors in Hindu provinces, Hindu magistrates in Muslim districts, and positioned the Crown as the central government ruling them all. The division succeeded in creating tension between neighbors but also an outburst of anger against British domination. Young Indians, including Abhay, rallied to calls by nationalists to fight for India's freedom. Anti-British riots broke out almost daily in Abhay's teen years. His participation in the volatile independence movement had his father, Gour Mohan De, worried, particularly since Abhay's mother had recently passed away, and Abhay was needed at home more than ever.

From atop the Victoria Memorial, he watched the Hooghly's tides flow swiftly out of the city, down to the Bay of Bengal, and beyond to Europe and America. His image of the United States was shaped by photos in India editions of *Look* and *National Geographic* that revealed mountainous skyscrapers under construction, Model Ts cruising down paved highways, airplanes setting speed and distance records, electric vacuum cleaners and washing machines, and other miracles of technology—all blending into what Brahmin priests called *maya*, the illusion of materialism. That was America: *maya's* capital across the ocean at the other end of the globe.

It would take more than fifty years before Abhay set sail across those waters. He was not impatient. For now, India was in trouble. His own people needed him. He climbed down from the scaffolding, waves crashing in the distance, and headed home, back to school and family and the tumult of a nation awakening to an uncertain future.

IN THE EARLY YEARS OF THE TWENTIETH CENTURY, the British Raj controlled India with a firm hand, and separation between rulers and ruled was strictly enforced. The only Indians allowed in British restaurants or officers' clubs in those days were servants who entered by side doors, donned white jackets, ladled soup out of antique silver dishes, and kept their thoughts to themselves. Abhay's family, the Des, had made their peace with British rule. They lived on Harrison Road in the north end of Calcutta, away from the urban center, where British administrators dictated India's affairs. The north district, home to Chaitanya Vaishnavas[4]—Krishna worshippers such as Abhay's family, who followed Chaitanya's example of constantly chanting Krishna's names—bordered several Muslim neighborhoods. Despite the embarrassment of this segregation, Hindus and Muslims did business together, and their children played as friends. Harrison Road included a block of buildings owned by the aristocratic Mullik family, a mercantile clan that had traded gold and salt with the British for more than two hundred years. In a previous generation, one of the Mullik men had married a De woman, and on Harrison Road their descendants built homes.

Abhay and his family lived across from the Mullik community temple, and the temple deities were Abhay's first vision coming into the world. After he was born, his father, Gour Mohan (1849–1930), and his mother, Rajani (c. 1866–1912), recited mantras for his body and soul. They dabbed his tongue with a drop of date sugar and carried their son to the temple so he could gaze at the brass deities of Radha and Krishna, God in female and male forms. Sweet sensations and divine visions: a good start in life. The family's astrologer drew up Abhay's chart. At age seventy, he predicted, this child will become a religious leader and build 108 temples around the world. There are no records describing how the family reacted to this prediction, but it must have delighted Gour Mohan, who was an orthodox Vaishnava determined to see his son cultivate the habits and character of a devout Krishna worshipper.

Gour Mohan was a hardworking man whose cloth shop generated enough income to keep his middle-class home stocked with *ghee*, rice, and potatoes, and provide dowries for his four daughters. Abhay's mother cared for the family's six children and filled their home with the spicy aromas of traditional cooking. Once the curried vegetables, milk sweets, and other dishes were ready, she placed portions on a brass tray and carried it across the road to the Mullik temple, where she bowed and offered the food with prayers. By age three, Abhay was reciting prayers along with her and thinking the deity of Krishna had beautiful slanted eyes. If a grain of rice fell on the ground, he picked it up and touched it to his forehead as a gesture of respect for *prasadam*, God's mercy in the shape of food.[5]

Abhay had a high forehead, doe-like eyes, large ears, and flared nostrils. When provoked, he furrowed his eyebrows and pursed his full lips, and Rajani would supplicate this or that divinity to spare him from evil. Sometimes the young boy's haughty nature took over. In response to a rebuke from his teacher, five-year-old Abhay picked up a kerosene lamp from her desk and threw it to the ground. When Abhay spied a toy gun in an outdoor market, he insisted his father buy it. Gour Mohan obliged, then Abhay insisted on having a second—"one for each hand"—and lay down in the street kicking his feet until Gour Mohan acquiesced. His parents grew alert to their son's moods. They had named him Abhay Charan, wanting him to be both *abhay*, fearless, and *charan*, surrendered to the *charan*, or feet, of God. The fearless part seemed to come naturally, as though he understood, even as a child, that obstacles were to be expected in the material world.

To nurture Abhay's devotion, Gour Mohan hired a musician to teach him the *mridanga*, a two-headed drum used in temple ceremonies. The three-foot-long clay cylinder hung from the musician's neck by a thick cord, and he beat the large and small heads with rapid hand movements. Abhay could barely reach both ends of the drum at the same time, but he took to the mridanga like a professional. "What's the point?" Rajani asked her husband. "He's just a child." But Gour Mohan looked to the future, to a time when Abhay would fulfill the astrologer's predictions and make a sound the world would hear.

GOUR MOHAN FOLLOWED A STRICT SCHEDULE. He woke before 7 a.m., bathed, set out on morning chores, and returned home by 10 a.m. For the next three hours, he recited prayers, read scripture, and worshiped the family deities with incense, flowers, and prayers. This *puja* or worship was his father's real business, Abhay would comment in later years. After a light lunch, Gour Mohan walked to his shop for an afternoon of meetings with customers. At 10 p.m., he put a bowl of rice on the floor for rats that would otherwise eat his merchandise, locked the front door, and returned home to continue his worship. The gentle murmur of mantras and the tinkling of a handheld bell woke Abhay. He tiptoed downstairs, not wanting to disturb his mother, and soon father and son were in the kitchen cooking up puffed rice as a snack before sleep.

Electricity had not yet been installed in Calcutta, and motion pictures would not become an industry in India until 1912, so there was little to distract Abhay from creating his own adventures. On sunny days, he took his younger sister, Bhavatarini, by the hand and climbed to the flat roof of their home to launch paper kites into the air.

"Pray to Krishna," Abhay told her, "pray the kites will fly."

Abhay pretended to be their family physician, Dr. Bose, and cured Bhavatarini of imaginary troubles with potions and poultices made of garden soil. They acted out stories learned from their grandmother: the story of Prince Rama rescuing Princess Sita from demon king Ravana, or the story of sage Viswamitra defeating envious King Vasistha with the power of his devotion. Abhay's favorites were stories about Krishna, the mischievous child of Vrindavan village, who stole his mother's yogurt and made jokes at everyone's expense and demonstrated mystic powers by lifting a hill or bringing down ogres who occasionally attacked the village.

Five-year-old Abhay dreamed of one day traveling to the town of Puri on the Orissan coast, 300 miles to the south. He thrilled to his father's descriptions of the annual festival there called Rathayatra—the "journey of the chariots"—that drew millions of pilgrims. On this day only, Gour Mohan explained, *pujaris* or attendants in Puri's renowned Jagannath temple were allowed to lift the three massive wooden deities of Krishna from their altars. So heavy were the deities of Krishna and his brother and sister that it took twenty men to place them on the forty-foot-tall Rathayatra chariots. Thousands of pilgrims then pulled the chariots through the streets with long, thick ropes. Everything sprang from Krishna, Gour Mohan told his son, and if he chose to appear before his devotees in the form of a wooden deity, was that not his right? And if from time to time he wished to parade through the streets to see his devotees, no matter how big or heavy he was, who could stop him?[6]

Abhay wanted a cart of his own, but when Gour Mohan took him to the market he found the cost of a good quality miniature prohibitive. Abhay stood on the street crying, which prompted an elderly woman walking by to ask what the problem was. Gour Mohan explained his son's wish. "I have such a child's cart," she said and escorted them to her nearby home, where Gour Mohan paid a nominal sum for her three-foot-tall chariot. Father and son bought paint and screws, and back home they restored the colorful columns, reinforced the wooden wheels, and installed six-inch wooden Jagannath deities on the bridge. Abhay rallied the neighbors, and Harrison Road held its own Rathayatra festival. Not unlike how they are today, Bengali communities at that time were very much like a village with a deep sense of community. Arms raised, he instructed his friends to pull the chariot down the street, beat miniature mridangas, and play little brass *kartal* hand cymbals while he led the chanting: "Hare Krishna, Hare Krishna."

The procession ended at the Mullik temple, where parents added to the festivities by handing out fruits and sweets.

That night Abhay slept with the wooden cart next to his bed and woke from time to time to touch it, amazed that he possessed a Rathayatra chariot of his very own. Gour Mohan expected great things from his son, but even he could not have imagined that one day Abhay would lead ten-ton Rathayatra carts down the streets of cities around the world.

At age six, Abhay asked his father for Radha and Krishna deities to worship—a rewarding moment for Gour Mohan. He and his wife had performed *samskara* rituals of passage for just this time when their son would see the rightness of devotion to God. Yes, of course, Abhay could have his own deities. Particularly now, in the opening years of the twentieth century with Christian missionary activity at its height, Abhay's faith had to be strong. The missionaries were polite for the most part, but beneath the veneer of cordiality lay a harsh message: Hindus were not truly civilized. If ever they wished to rise to a respected place in the world, they had to renounce their backward religious practices, especially worship of "idols." And of all "idols," missionaries condemned Krishna as the worst of all.[7] In the words of British Supreme Court judge Sir Joseph Arnould, "It is Krishna the darling of 16,000 Gopees [cowherd women]; Krishna the love-hero . . . who . . . tinges the whole system with the stain of carnal sensualism or strange, transcendental lewdness."[8]

Gour Mohan did not discuss such things with his children, but he worried that they would succumb to the propaganda. The compulsion to do so would be strong, since his children heard the condemnation of deities not only from the missionaries but from school teachers, neighbors, and the British administrators who controlled their lives. Vaishnavas were "uneducated natives," the message went. Worshipping statues of Krishna made of marble and wood embodied everything the Europeans found distasteful about India. The stigma of idolatry hung like an invisible placard around the necks of the faithful.

Of the Europeans' many complaints, "idolatry" was by far their main objection to Hinduism. "Whatever plausible argument may be advanced for image-worship," one missionary wrote, "we believe if history teaches anything, it teaches that such worship materializes and debases the human mind, gives most unworthy views of God, and in the case of the vast majority leads to a fetishism which in principle is identical with that of the most barbarous tribes. Till India rises above this idolatry, she will never have her proper place in the world."[9]

Not only Europeans, but the Hindu intelligentsia, too, favored moving the nation away from its "idolatrous" past through English education. Reformist Rammohun Roy and other eminent leaders approached the chief justice of the Supreme Court, Sir Edward Hyde East, to tell him of their desire to form "an establishment for the education of their children in a liberal manner as practiced by Europeans." Abhay's mother wanted her son to have such an education and learn the ways of the world.

"Our son should become a British lawyer," she told her husband, "even if it means he must go to London to study." Gour Mohan would hear nothing of it, since living in England would expose their son to European habits.

"He will learn drinking and woman-hunting," Gour Mohan said, and the topic never came up again.

Those were days when such allurements tempted an entire generation of young Indians, and Gour Mohan was determined that at least this one child would learn to resist. Attaining adulthood as a Vaishnava meant walking away from the pleasures that seduced weaker minds. He felt responsible for fostering a higher standard in Abhay than the "pounds-shillings-pence" materialism of the British. He would see to it that his son grew up knowing there was a God behind the miracle of creation, a God who lived in Abhay's heart, ready to guide him and provide whatever he needed in life. The society of English barristers had nothing to offer.

TO ALL APPEARANCES, Abhay Charan's early life was comfortable and headed toward the predictable future of a middle-class Bengali Vaishnava. When he was eight, his father enrolled him in Mutty Lal Seal Free School at the end of Harrison Road. Abhay dressed in traditional dhoti and *kurta* and walked with other boys in a group, carrying schoolbooks and lunch in a stainless steel tiffin. Occasionally, they stopped to let British officials pass by in horse-drawn carriages, the boys' world on one side of an invisible line and the British on the other.

In 1916, at age twenty, Abhay entered Scottish Churches College, where he majored in English, philosophy, and economics. When he was twenty-one, his father arranged for him to marry a girl from their neighborhood: eleven-year-old Radharani Datta, although they would not live together for several years, as was the custom. Abhay did not find her appealing and wanted to marry another young woman. Gour Mohan had ambitions for Abhay, whom he envisioned one day becoming a great spiritual figure, and he discouraged the idea.

"My dear boy," he said, "I advise you not to do this. It is Krishna's grace that your fiancée is not to your liking. This will help you to avoid becoming attached to wife and home, and that will be beneficial in the matter of your future advancement. Don't be worried about her. If she wants to remarry, she can do so. I shall arrange for you to become a sannyasi, and you will be free to preach."[10]

Because he wanted to encourage his son to focus on his own spiritual path and not become overly involved in family life, Abhay's father decided to take matters into his own hands. Gour Mohan proposed they visit the girl's family and saw that she was indeed very beautiful, the kind of girl who risked becoming an anchor for his son. So he insulted her.

"Does your daughter dance?" Gour Mohan asked the girl's father. In conservative Vaishnava circles, implying that a girl "danced" equated to calling her a prostitute. The girl's father was outraged.

"Sir, we are not like that," he replied with suppressed anger. "We do not teach our girls dancing." With that, the interview was at an end. Gour Mohan had effectively quashed any hopes Abhay might have had for another wife. It was a Machiavellian strategy: better his son marry a plain girl, someone from whom separation, when it came, would be less stressful.

Gour Mohan's ambitions for his son reflected the esteem in which the Vaishnava community held their spiritual leaders. No more revered citizens existed in traditional India than the sannyasis, the holy persons whose interest was the well-being of others. Part priest, part educator, part life counselor, sannyasis had served as advisors to emperors. They had brokered peace between warring kingdoms, functioned as court of last appeal for civil and religious disputes, and exemplified a holy life. As far back as could be traced, sannyasis had determined the course of India's history.

"I accepted my father's advice," Abhay described in his later years. "Consequently, I was never attached to my wife or home, which resulted in [the freedom to] devote myself fully to Krishna consciousness."[11]

ON APRIL 13, 1919, a crowd of Sikhs gathered in a garden in Amritsar, Punjab, to celebrate a traditional religious festival. Convinced an insurrection had begun, British soldiers opened fire with rifles and machine guns. Ten minutes later, a thousand civilians lay dead. The massacre provoked riots, which led to further government retribution. Gandhi appealed to the nation for a nonviolent response. Twenty-three-year-old Abhay answered Gandhi's call to nonviolent protest by refusing to accept his degree from Scottish Churches College. He also followed Gandhi's example of replacing British shirts and pants with domestic handspun *khadi* clothes. For the next three years, Abhay volunteered as a local organizer for Gandhi's campaign. At age twenty-five, he began working in the laboratory of his family's physician, Kartick Chandra Bose.

In 1922, one of Abhay's closest friends, Narendra Mullik, met monks from the Gaudiya Math, a Vaishnava institution, and the monks invited him to meet their guru. Like other well-to-do residents of Calcutta, Narendra was willing to support religious organizations if they were honorable, but honor was not always obvious. Many sannyasis came knocking at his door looking for donations. Who could tell what their motives were? *Maths*, religious schools, abounded, and the monks charged with raising funds looked more or less alike. There was every chance his money would be wasted supporting a place for loafers who sponged off innocent Hindu families. The greater danger was inadvertently giving money to monks who indulged in sex or ate meat. Celibacy and a meat-free diet were behavioral requirements for Vaishnavas. Narendra's friend, Abhay, always had good advice to offer, and Narendra asked that he accompany him to the math and provide a second opinion.

Abhay declined. From childhood, he said, he had seen cheaters dressed like monks exploit his father's charitable nature. They took Gour Mohan's donations, stepped outside his door, and lit up marijuana cigarettes. Some of his family relations ran a boarding house for single men. Abhay recalled seeing one of these boarders dressed in saffron robes gulp down a cup of tea, finish a cigarette, and then grab his waterpot and staff and head out the door to collect his daily "*sadhu*'s" donations. Abhay had no patience for such people.

"I'm not going," he told Narendra. There were more pressing matters. Orders in Dr. Bose's laboratory were waiting to be filled, supplies needed to be restocked, there were customers to serve, meetings of Gandhi's movement to organize, and simply no time for listening to another so-called guru spout off.

"Come on!" Narendra insisted. As a courtesy to his friend, Abhay agreed to be dragged along.

They arrived at a building on Ultadanga Junction Road in north Calcutta. A sign over the door announced that the one-story structure was headquarters of the Gaudiya Math, "the monastery of Greater India." Abhay and Narendra climbed a worn marble staircase to the roof. Air conditioning was scarce in those days, and public events were often scheduled on rooftops, where evening breezes offered relief from the day's heat. Monks greeted the two guests and brought them to the front of the gathering to meet the head of their mission. Even seated, Srila Bhaktisiddhanta Sarasvati Thakur's stature was obvious to Abhay: This was not another pretend sadhu. He seemed at least six feet tall and sat with perfect posture. His forehead was broad and high, his color fair. He wore the traditional robes of a Vaishnava sannyasi: two lengths of saffron-colored cloth, one wrapped around the waist, the other draped across his shoulders and chest. Three strands of small wooden *tulasi* beads looped around his neck. Two stripes of white clay ran from the bridge of his nose to his shaved head—the full uniform of a devout Krishna worshipper and, in Bhaktisiddhanta's case, *acharya* of the Gaudiya Math.

Vaishnava community elders elevated a candidate to the exalted position of acharya, head of a recognized lineage of teachers, based on mastery of scripture and personal character.[12] Historically, some acharyas received their appointment as a result of family affiliation, for there was a sentiment that virtue and ability were inherited. If, for instance, a man's father and grandfather had served with distinction, it was assumed he possessed comparable talents. In Bhaktisiddhanta's case, both criteria applied. He was son of the late Bhaktivinode Thakur, respected former head of the Vaishnava community and prolific author and poet, and in his own right, Bhaktisiddhanta demonstrated the character and wisdom of a true acharya.

Abhay and Narendra touched their foreheads to the ground in the traditional way of greeting a holy person. Something about Abhay must have impressed itself upon Bhaktisiddhanta, as barely had Abhay stood up when Bhaktisiddhanta said, "You are an educated young man. Why don't you take Chaitanya Mahaprabhu's[13] message and spread it in English to the Western world?"

IN YEARS TO COME, A.C. Bhaktivedanta Swami Prabhupada would describe that he hesitated when his guru issued the instruction that changed his life. Leave everything and travel to the West? How could he do that? Of course, Abhay knew quite a bit about Chaitanya Mahaprabhu. His father and mother had raised him as a Chaitanya follower, and since childhood he had been chanting Hare Krishna as Mahaprabhu had taught, but aside from an astrologer's questionable prediction, nothing in the profile of Abhay's life suggested he would become a religious leader. He and his wife, Radharani, had a one-year-old daughter and were planning to have more children. He earned an honest living and paid his bills and left the religious grandstanding to others.

More to the point, Abhay followed Gandhi and believed the real key to moving India forward was freedom from British rule. For hundreds of years, Bengal's Hindus and Muslims had lived in relative peace. It was the British who set one religion on the other and turned neighbors into enemies. When it came to choosing between religion and nationhood, to Abhay's twenty-six-year-old mind, Gandhi's movement came first. Rid India of the Raj, and her millennial wisdom will have a platform for expression.

"Sir," Abhay said. "Who will hear Chaitanya Mahaprabhu's message as long as we are a dependent nation? Let us first achieve our independence, then we can spread Indian culture."

Bhaktisiddhanta disagreed. Mahaprabhu's message did not depend on politics. Real independence, he said, meant freeing the soul from the shackles of illusion. Doctrines of impersonalism and voidism pervaded India's thinking. These dangerous ideas decrying the personhood of God were the true enemies, not the British. Until people were trained to know the difference between the body and soul and the soul's ultimate fulfillment in love of God, they would never know peace. Chaitanya Mahaprabhu had given the formula: Chant Hare Krishna, follow the teachings of the Bhagavad Gita, and the sun of Krishna will rise to illumine a dark time.

It was indeed a dark time. In 1920, a visit by the Prince of Wales had turned into a four-day riot. Shops were pillaged, and any Europeans seen in public were attacked. Just weeks before Abhay's meeting with Bhaktisiddhanta, a mob stormed a police station in the town of Chauri Chaura, beat twenty-two officers to death, and burned their bodies. Nationalism had released poisonous resentment, and civil disobedience was careening out of control. As much as Abhay had convinced himself Gandhi held the torch of truth, he could not stand by that conviction after hearing Bhaktisiddhanta speak about respiritualizing the world. By comparison with such a global mission, Gandhi's plans for a politically independent country seemed stunted and trifling. Up to that moment, Abhay's perspective had been primarily Indian. Bhaktisiddhanta was proposing something greater, something universal.

And deeply troubling. "The West" implied America, from all accounts a most unpleasant place where everyone ate meat, drank alcohol, and frequented speakeasies where women, it was told, exposed their legs! God only knew what else went on in such places. Americans were the wealthiest, the most heathen, and yet the most influential people on Earth. Certainly if the Americans took up Mahaprabhu's mission, it could spread anywhere. But what were the odds of that ever happening?

Americans had been overtly hostile toward Hindus for more than half a century. Particularly after World War I, America's isolationism intensified, and the nation had little use for foreigners or their strange customs. Over the past thirty years, some teachers had gone there hoping to sway opinion and reverse America's image of Indian religion. Swami Vivekananda had addressed the World's Parliament of Religions in Chicago in 1893 and founded the first Vedanta Society in the United States, but his teachings minimized devotion to Krishna. Bhakti was "a little love," he said, that must be abandoned on the way to higher realization.[14] Paramhansa Yogananda went to America in 1920 and espoused a similar strain of monistic Hinduism. "God's omnipresence is your omnipresence," he told his audiences. Almost without exception, Hindu teachers who had made the journey to America all condemned worship of a personal God as philosophically naïve. American church leaders for their part made little distinction among these teachers. They were all "non-Christians," and everything they said was anathema.[15] Hindus worshiped cows and snakes and topless goddesses, and whatever philosophy they might use to justify such practices was not worth hearing.[16]

Nothing in this grim portrait suggested that the message of Chaitanya Mahaprabhu would find a warm welcome. If America's isolationism and xenophobia were not enough to dissuade Abhay from accepting Bhaktisiddhanta's challenge, he had only to read the daily papers: Gandhi's movement was gaining ground. Was this the moment to abandon his country?

Despite his attraction to nationalism, something in the brief exchange with Bhaktisiddhanta quickened Abhay's pulse. They had not spoken long—maybe an hour—but in that short space of time, Bhaktisiddhanta managed to refute Abhay's assumptions that God took a backseat to politics and that independence offered a lasting solution to India's woes. India suffered from lack of a spiritual revolution, Bhaktisiddhanta argued, and campaigning for political independence merely distracted from the more critical campaign launched by Chaitanya Mahaprabhu to reinstate God in his creation. British rule was irrelevant: Not only India, but all of humanity needed liberating.

Something more had occurred. "It was in my very first *darshan*" or meeting, Abhay later wrote, "that I learned how to love."[17] In his guru's presence, elements of Abhay's Vaishnava training—compassion, a call to service, a vision of divinity in the heart of every creature on Earth—coalesced. It did not take a lifetime of suffering to qualify for such an epiphany. Abhay had seen enough of the material world by age twenty-six to know it was not a hospitable place. He loved his mother but could not stop her from dying. He loved his family, but nothing would stop them from dying eventually. Nothing lasted in this world—but the soul was never destroyed. Only now, in the presence of someone who lived outside material time, did he begin to see the implications of that truth for the entire world.

Abhay's transformation into modern history's greatest missionary of love for Krishna did not occur in a flash: It would evolve over the next forty years. But when he met his guru, something irrevocable occurred that raised the curtain on the rest of his life.

THE NEXT DAY Abhay walked into the office of his employer, Dr. Kartick Chandra Bose, and resigned. Bose had been the De family's doctor for more than twenty years and had watched Abhay grow up. The elder physician appreciated the personal touch Abhay always brought to their customers, such as answering requests for pricing with handwritten letters, but Bose also recognized how headstrong Abhay could be and knew better than to question his plans.

"I understand your attraction to this teacher," Bose said. "Still, you are a family man. I will give you a franchise to my company's products. Sell wherever you like, whenever you like. The commissions will be more than your current salary, and you will still have time for these pursuits."

Abhay weighed his options. What was work or money or even family compared to the instruction he had received on the roof of the Gaudiya Math? Bhaktisiddhanta had opened his eyes to the meaning of Krishna devotion, and taking Krishna's message to the West was no trifling matter. It would not happen between sales calls. Still, Bose had a point. No one travels abroad without funds, and pharmaceuticals had potential. India was ripe for Indian-made goods, and Bose's prices were better than those of the British. Maybe he could save some money and then go West. Abhay agreed to Bose's offer to start a franchise.

The talk with his wife did not go as well. Radharani did not share her husband's enthusiasms, political, religious, or otherwise—and here he was, telling her Gandhi had it wrong and that he would be going to the West. There are no witnesses or diaries from which to assess her reaction to Abhay's meeting with Bhaktisiddhanta, but when they married, it is likely she did not envision becoming a missionary's wife.

BHAKTISIDDHANTA SARASWATI exercised extraordinary influence over his followers. Not only did his erudition and exemplary behavior elicit a large following, he also solidified followers' allegiance with exciting, innovative plans for a global mission. Historically, all Vaishnava acharyas innovated one way or another, usually in response to evolving social and political conditions, but those innovations had taken place inside India. No previous acharya had confronted the role of Vaishnava faith on a global scale, since the world had never before been so interdependent. In the late 1800s, Bhaktisiddhanta's father, Bhaktivinode Thakur, predicted that one day there would be Vaishnavas from every country of the world, but he did not actively pursue creating such an international community, apart from sending copies of a brief Chaitanya biography to literary figures and educational institutions abroad.[18] It was his son, Bhaktisiddhanta, who saw the possibility of an actual worldwide movement.

Not just the possibility but the necessity of such a movement informed his leadership of the Gaudiya Math. The ground rules of humanity were evolving. Cultures were no longer isolated. Now what happened in one place affected the lives of people halfway around the world. Wars were reconfiguring the geography of continents, political theories were revolutionizing the economic structure of nations, and technology was binding people together in accelerating networks of travel and communication.

For the first time in history, ideas had global consequences. The Vaishnava community would either recognize that and evolve with the times or remain irrelevant to the rest of the world.

Consequently, he did things no acharya had ever done before. He traveled in cars, contrary to the tradition of sannyasis only traveling on foot. He sent disciples to Europe, counter to the injunction that no Hindu should cross "the black ocean." He wore a watch, which Brahmins frowned upon as ostentatious; opened city temples instead of forest *ashrams*; and spent huge sums on tented festivals that featured elaborate dioramas and electric lighting to facilitate late night attendance. These public programs drew huge crowds. On October 25, 1930, the newspaper *Liberty* reported that more than 100,000 people attended the Gaudiya Math's Govardhan Puja, the festival that celebrated Krishna lifting Govardhan Hill as an umbrella to protect his village from a torrential rain. To feed the large crowd of attendees, Bhaktisiddhanta commissioned a "hill" to be built from more than 1,008 fresh vegetarian dishes and several tons of steamed rice. Even greater crowds turned out for the Gaudiya Math's annual Theistic Exhibition. Each year between 1928 and 1936, attendance surpassed one million visitors. The Theistic Exhibition took up more than a square mile of tents, displaying nearly one hundred exhibits on developments in medicine, education, agriculture, arts and crafts, child welfare, sports, music, drama, and film. Bhaktisiddhanta used these displays to capture public attention. Then, once guests were hooked, he excited their devotional curiosity with crafted figures (dioramas) of Krishna's incarnations, artifacts belonging to Vaishnava saints of the past, rare devotional books, and a stone-and-brick map of India's holy places—all housed in a half-acre-wide tented museum.[19]

Conservative religious leaders were shocked. They decried the production of such entertainments and accused him of betraying the renounced order. Not so, Bhaktisiddhanta replied, citing Vaishnava commentaries that defined real renunciation as using everything for Krishna's service.[20] "The Ganges shifts," he explained. "Its course changes all the time. If you bathe in a dry bed, arguing, 'This is where we have always bathed,' what can be said for you?" Conservatives were not moved.

Even more objectionable to them: Bhaktisiddhanta initiated non-Brahmins as his disciples. Only men born in Brahmin families, conservatives argued, qualified for initiation. Lower castes had never been allowed to take part in the *diksha* ceremony. The prohibition was purely political, since nothing in India's scriptures supported such discrimination, but it had kept caste Brahmins in power for generations. If a Vaishnava businessman returned from traveling abroad, for instance, he was considered unclean and obligated to pay a Brahmin in gold to perform purifying rituals. The Brahmins kept lists of clients for promotional purposes. "As your family priest," the pitch might go, "I must remind you to perform this rite on the anniversary of your grandfather's death." This had been going on for centuries. In effect, Bhaktisiddhanta threatened their commercial livelihood.

Hostility against Bhaktisiddhanta escalated when he added empowerment of women to his list of outrages. Chaitanya Mahaprabhu taught that all souls were *prakriti*, or female in relation to God. For Bhaktisiddhanta, this meant gender was not a consideration on the path of devotion,[21] and unlike the dominant Hindu orthodoxy, he extended full and equal rights to women and awarded them initiation regardless of their family or caste. Several of these women disciples became scholars who contributed articles to his publications. Bhaktisiddhanta's nondiscrimination policies not only defied caste powerbrokers, they also reversed entrenched social customs and exposed Indian misogyny. Other than outright sedition, he could not have found more contentious issues on which to base his movement.

With each adjustment made to render devotional life accessible to the modern world, Bhaktisiddhanta Saraswati added to his reputation for controversy. On January 29, 1925, at the start of a one-month pilgrimage, he and his followers were attacked by an angry crowd of caste Brahmins wielding bricks, stones, and glass bottles. A disciple, Vinode Bihari Brahmachari (Keshava Maharaj's name prior to entering the renounced order) took his guru inside a building where they swapped clothing. Bhaktisiddhanta, disguised in his disciple's white cloth, escaped. No one was killed, but Bhaktisiddhanta instructed organizers to hire police escorts for subsequent public programs.

HERE, ABHAY REALIZED, WAS A TEACHER WILLING to take risks if it helped modernize Krishna worship, which explained the impressive caliber of his disciples. They were not lost or without a rudder, these men and women of the Gaudiya Math; many had university degrees and challenging careers. Bhakti Pradip Tirtha Maharaj was twenty years Abhay's senior, a graduate of Calcutta University and an initiated disciple of Bhaktisiddhanta's father, Bhaktivinode Thakur. Pradip Tirtha's wife died in 1919, and the following year he became Bhaktisiddhanta's first sannyasi disciple, after which he traveled across East Bengal to spread Chaitanya Vaishnavism. Another disciple, Bhakti Raksak Sridhar Maharaj, studied law prior to joining Gandhi's non-cooperation movement. He began attending Bhaktisiddhanta's lectures in the early 1920s, and after his wife and mother passed away, he joined the Gaudiya Math full-time. In 1930, he, too, was awarded the sannyasa order. Born in 1898, Bhakti Pramode Puri Maharaj was a university student when he first met Bhaktisiddhanta Saraswati in 1915. For the next thirteen years, he transcribed his guru's lectures and conversations, oversaw their publication, and was revered for his meticulous deity worship. Other disciples were medical students and government employees. Two came from Germany. Another joined at age twenty-four after ending his career as a wrestling champion. N.K. Sanyal was a well-regarded history professor whose understanding of Krishna philosophy was so profound that Bhaktisiddhanta remarked, "Although a householder, he is the guru of sannyasis." There were hundreds of these educated, accomplished disciples affiliated with Bhaktisiddhanta's many maths across India.

Abhay spent every free hour in the company of the Calcutta Gaudiya Math community. During evening classes, he participated in conversations about Vaishnava theology. These included topics such as the qualities of consciousness: *sat-chit-ananda* (eternity, self-awareness and bliss); the cycles of *kala* (time) and the *kalpas* or ages of the universe; prakriti, the elements of creation, and *devas*, empowered beings who controlled them. They discussed the structure of matter, from subatomic particles to the outer limits of the material universe as revealed in the Vedas. They compared the three features of absolute truth: all-pervading *brahman*, localized *paramatma* in the hearts of all beings, and *Bhagavan*: Krishna, the Supreme Person. They analyzed how conditioned souls were covered by forgetfulness and the best methods for extracting them from their cosmic slumber.

Conversations in these gatherings included a comparative analysis of the yoga systems, the many types of yogic powers, and the preeminence of bhakti yoga, devotion to God. They discussed foundational texts such as Bhagavad Gita, as well as esoteric texts such as the writings of the Goswamis of Vrindavan and the tenth canto of the *Srimad Bhagavatam*, where Krishna's personal life was summarized. They ventured into esoteric territory, such as the ecstasies experienced by residents of the eternal world. Their deepest discussions entered the inner sanctum of Vaishnava theology to a place even beyond God: to Radha, the feminine Godhead. An understanding of Radha, Abhay learned, was the unique contribution of Chaitanya Mahaprabhu, who embodied her love and devotion.

Along with other students of the Gaudiya Math, Abhay studied *rasa*, the theology of love for God as achieved through the practice of bhakti yoga. The word *rasa* has several meanings. The most common is "taste" or "essence." A traditional Indian dinner, for instance, contains several rasas, or flavors: sweet, salty, spicy, pungent, and so on. When applied to devotion, the word rasa signifies a shade or flavor of loving exchange.[22] Devotees situated in *shanta* rasa, or the neutral stage, appreciate God with a mood of awe and veneration as the merciful deliverer of fallen souls. The aspiration of such devotees is to study scripture, live in a peaceful place, keep company with saints, and always think of the eternal form of Krishna. Examples of these devotees include yogis who meditate on *paramatma*, the Supreme Being present in their hearts. In the eternal world, where everything is sentient, even Krishna's flute and the cows of Vrindavan experience this form of neutral love.

Devotees who feel an active, affectionate attachment to Krishna are described as serving in *dasya* rasa, a reverential mood of servitude. Devotees in this rasa take shelter in and feel protected by God. Some popular personalities in this mood are Hanuman, the monkey-like warrior-servant of Lord Rama, and Arjuna, hero of the Bhagavad Gita. Devotees in dasya rasa can face all kinds of adversity calmly, knowing they are protected by Krishna. In dasya rasa, devotees honor Krishna as their superior.

In *sakhya* rasa, friendship, devotees love Krishna as their equal. The mood of a sakha, or friend, is playful, someone who jokes and shares adventures with the Supreme Being. In this friendly mood, Krishna's identity as the Supreme Being and source of all creation is subdued and secondary to the spontaneous interactions between Krishna and his friends. The cowherd boys of Krishna's village exemplify this form of love.

Devotees who feel a sense of responsibility for God's well-being, who treat him as a parent would a child, are situated in *vatsalya* rasa. Devotees in this parental mood care for Krishna as though he is not self-sufficient, but needs their care and attention. God for these devotees is no longer the providing Father but a dependent Child. Krishna's mother and father, Nanda and Yashoda, embody this mood of parental love.

The devotees that embody these rasas bow before the position of the *gopis*, the cowherd women of Krishna's village, who have no concern for guidelines, responsibilities, or restrictions. Their feelings of conjugal affection for Krishna, *madhurya* rasa, ignore all social constraints. Their love is unfettered, unconcerned with anyone's opinion and without regard for consequences. The gopis belong to Krishna—heart, body, and soul.

IN THE SIXTEENTH-CENTURY TREATISE *Bhakti-rasamrita-sindhu*[23] by Rupa Goswami, Chaitanya Mahaprabhu's chief disciple, Abhay read that the journey to love of God begins with *shraddha* or faith, which aptly described his reaction on meeting Bhaktisiddhanta Saraswati. Faith in a teacher and in the validity of devotional life leads to *sadhu-sanga*, the company of dedicated practitioners. In time and with *bhajana-kriya* or consistent spiritual practice, the aspiring lover of God achieves *anartha-nivrtti* (cessation of unwanted habits), which in turn stimulates *nistha* (firm practice) and *ruci* (a taste for devotional life). Having reached these stages of progress, the sincere candidate rises to *asakti* (attachment to Krishna). From there, the path is open to experiencing *bhava* (ecstatic emotions) and finally *prema* (love of God).

In his discussions with members of the Gaudiya Math, Abhay found not the dry piety of institutional religion but something much more exciting. Krishna consciousness, as presented in his guru's institution, was more like a roiling volcano of the soul's ecstatic love of God, nurtured in stages of spiritual awakening.

AS THE ACHARYA OR CUSTODIAN of this distinguished school of devotion, Bhaktisiddhanta Saraswati taught his students with what he called "aggressive grace,"[24] which included a rigorous daily schedule. At 4 a.m. a large bell rang in each of the dozens of Gaudiya Maths around India to wake students-in-residence from their sleep. They showered, dressed in clean robes, and gathered in the temple room to sing prayers. A disciple then read excerpts from Chaitanya Mahaprabhu's biography, and at 4:30 a.m., they attended morning services. Disciples chanted on their beads until 7 a.m. when a light breakfast was served. After their meal, residents went off to morning duties such as administration, publishing, and programs in local homes and institutions. At noon, all returned for midday services and lunch, which Bhaktisiddhanta sometimes personally supervised. At 2 p.m. residents sat for *ista-ghosti*, a time for questions and answers about issues of philosophy and scriptural interpretation. Then afternoon duties, followed in the evening by another temple service, more singing, and a lecture by Bhaktisiddhanta. Evening programs were attended by guests and visitors, and it was then that married and working disciples such as Abhay arrived.

In his lifetime, Bhaktisiddhanta established sixty-four maths, creating for the first time an institution of Vaishnava culture. Previously, Krishna devotees worshiped in their homes and went on pilgrimages to holy sites where sadhus offered free instruction. Bhaktisiddhanta's institution facilitated the more rigorous education required for missionaries who were expected to travel both inside India and abroad. "There is no use in constructing maths merely to facilitate eating and sleeping," he wrote. "They need be built only for broadcasting *harikatha* [the message of Krishna], which will benefit ourselves and others."[25] So far no one had fulfilled the mandate of bringing Krishna to the rest of the world, but Bhaktisiddhanta had no doubt it would happen.

Gaudiya Math residents vowed to chant 100,000 names of Krishna daily on prayer beads (the equivalent of sixty-four rounds of beads or approximately seven hours of prayer every day). For initiated disciples living and working outside, sixteen rounds was the prescribed minimum. For those living outside but not yet initiated, the minimum was four rounds. All initiates pledged to follow the basic behavioral guidelines: no meat, fish, or eggs in the diet; no sex outside marriage; no intoxicants; and no gambling.

The Gaudiya maths were less retreats per se than monastic army bases for training missionary monks to rescue souls caught up in maya's matrix. "I wish that every selfless tenderhearted member of the Gaudiya Math be prepared to shed two hundred gallons of blood," Bhaktisiddhanta wrote, "for the nourishment of the spiritual body of every individual in human society."[26] When residents of the maths presented themselves in public, Bhaktisiddhanta insisted they dress in traditional Vaishnava fashion for easy recognition. This included neck beads and lines of white clay on foreheads and noses and, for the men, shaved heads.

Life in the Gaudiya Math was a constant intellectual exercise, based on rigorous study and dialogue. Underlying the emphasis on scriptural study was Bhaktisiddhanta's conviction that in the near future devotion to Krishna would expand beyond India—and that books would be the medium of such global transmission. "The Gaudiya literature will be translated into all the languages of the world by the agents of divine mercy at the appointed time," he prophesied.

Abhay's role in helping fulfill that prediction was nearly a half-century away.

IN 1923, ABHAY AND HIS WIFE AND CHILD moved to Allahabad, a twelve-hour train ride northwest from Calcutta. The modern, paved, and well-lit city was home to many affluent European and Indian families. Abhay settled in Allahabad's older section, with narrow streets and a large Bengali population. The city, also known by its traditional name, Prayag, was a popular place of pilgrimage, situated at the confluence of three sacred rivers: the Ganges, Yamuna, and Saraswati. For business, Abhay rented a small shop in the commercial center of town and called it Prayag Pharmacy, specializing in medicines, tinctures, syrups, and other products manufactured by Dr. Bose's Laboratory. He rented an apartment with several rooms for his family. His father, Gour Mohan, now seventy-five, came to live with them. A year later, Abhay's wife gave birth to their second child, a son whom they named Prayagraj.

From Allahabad, Abhay traveled by train to visit customers and solicit new business. He was frugal and had no qualms over sitting in cheaper, unreserved seats. In 1925, he took a sales trip to Agra, renowned for the Taj Mahal and only forty miles south of Vrindavan, Krishna's childhood village. He had heard stories about Vrindavan all his life, and the temptation to visit was irresistible. He boarded the third-class compartment of the Taj Express, crowded with urban civil servants in cotton shirts and pants, Punjabi men wearing colorful turbans, and a swarm of men and women in saris and dhotis. An hour later, he stepped down at Mathura station and paid a *tanga* driver to take him six miles north to Vrindavan.

IN YEARS TO COME, as a result of Abhay's mission, Vrindavan would grow into a thriving city hosting visitors from every country. In 1925, it was still a hard-to-reach village. Cars those days were a rarity in Vrindavan. Pilgrims traversed the village on foot or bicycle or, for longer distances, in oxcarts and horse-drawn wagons. Many of the visitors were Krishna *bhaktas* like himself, for whom Krishna was not a religious figure but a friend living in their hearts. A visit to Vrindavan for such devout souls meant coming home. Well-to-do visitors rented furnished rooms in guesthouses, while pilgrims of more modest means stayed in *dharmsalas*, hostels that provided a rope mattress, a blanket, and a meal for a few pennies per day. Where they stayed mattered little.

Pilgrims were prepared to sleep on the banks of the Yamuna if necessary, since anywhere in Vrindavan was shelter for Krishna's devotees.

Tradition held that Krishna had appeared on Earth 5,000 years before and that, when he descended from the eternal world, his home, Vrindavan, came with him. From a shastric or scriptural perspective, there was no difference between the earthly Vrindavan and the eternal Vrindavan. When Krishna left the world 125 years later, forests and vines took over the earthly Vrindavan and obscured the bathing *ghats* and other sacred sites. Excavation began in the early sixteenth century, when Chaitanya Mahaprabhu sent his chief disciples, the Six Goswamis, to resuscitate the village for future generations. The Goswamis solicited funds from wealthy landowners, rebuilt the holy places, and salvaged Vrindavan from obscurity. In 1570, the Goswamis' reputation inspired Emperor Akbar to pay them a visit. One historian notes that "such a marvelous vision was revealed to him [in the Goswamis' company] that he was fain to acknowledge the place as indeed holy ground."[27] The Goswamis identified the lost sacred sites, oversaw construction of temples and schools, rebuilt roads and public facilities, collected Sanskrit texts, wrote books of their own, and developed what had been abandoned woodland into one of India's most important religious centers.

By the late seventeenth century, the Goswamis had passed away. The temples and roads they built fell into disrepair, and the village's original beauty could be seen only through the eyes of love. "Don't judge Vrindavan by the external manifestation," Abhay would one day write. "When your eyes are smeared with the salve of love, then you can see Vrindavan."[28]

HE ENTERED THE VILLAGE and sprinkled dust from the ground onto his head, as was the custom. He watched stray dogs and cows wander about and noted crumbling stone parapets that lined Vrindavan's dusty roads. Abhay saw through "eyes smeared with the salve of love" and beheld Vrindavan's hidden splendors. "The ponds and lakes are filled with multicolored lotus flowers, swans and water-birds," wrote a seventeenth-century poet-scholar who saw Vrindavan with his own eyes of love. "In some places the ground is made of precious jewels, emeralds and rubies, and the trees are made of gold and crystal."[29] When the sun beat down during Krishna's time 5,000 years before, Vrindavan's trees— including kadamba trees, which blossomed at the sound of monsoon thunder; fifty-foot-tall, medicinally rich neem trees; and peepal trees, whose heart-shaped leaves rustled in the slightest breeze—spread their limbs to shade all who passed.

Brijbasis, as Vrindavan residents were called, caressed them, and the bark of these holy trees was worn smooth from generations of such affection.

The Yamuna River flowed gently around the village. "Yamuna's waters are sweet as grape-sugar-milk," wrote Rupa Goswami in the 1600s. "She is filled with golden lotus flowers. Jewel-fish splash in her waters. Along her fragrant banks wander wide-eyed does."[30] Cows meandered along the banks of the Yamuna, and Abhay recalled the words of *Srimad Bhagavatam* — "The beautiful, fatty cows of Vrindavan are of various colors: red, black, green, yellow, and ash. In their joy over the nearness of Krishna, Vrindavan's cows gush milk that runs in rivulets on the ground, and homes overflow with the bounty."[31]

Krishna was commemorated in every corner of Vrindavan. Here is the place, pilgrims enthused, where Krishna braided Radha's hair and decorated her with red *kunkuma* powder. And there, they announced, is the spot where the creator god Brahma bathed Krishna in apology for doubting his divinity. Ahead is Govardhan Hill, which Krishna lifted like an umbrella to protect his friends from torrential rains. Abhay listened to these many accounts and walked through a forest sheltering long-necked egrets, red-faced sarus cranes, and pheasant-tailed jacanas. When he emerged from the forest, a group of locals were seated roadside, singing songs of praise to Krishna. The lead singer stretched his hand toward heaven, sorrow and yearning palpable in his voice. Abhay had known such prayers all his life, yet here in the place where Krishna lived they came alive. He walked down dirt roads, looking for a place to spend the night.

"Go to the Madan Mohan Temple," a Brijbasi advised. "There are rooms there."

The temple sat on a rise overlooking the village and surrounding forests. A young monk in robes and shaved head brought Abhay a plate of fruits and vegetables from the midday offering. Seventy years later, the monk still lived in Madan Mohan Temple.

"From the time Bhaktivedanta arrived until the time he returned home," the monk recalled, "he did not go shopping. He chanted on his *japa* beads or stood on the edge of our hill and looked out over the Yamuna River."[32]

God is everywhere, but Vrindavan is his home and Abhay was tempted to stay, but he knew he could not, given the urgency of his guru's instruction to bring Krishna consciousness to the West. There was no place in the circumference of that order for early retirement. To sit back and chant for one's own liberation while the suffering souls of Kali Yuga spiraled faster and faster into violence and oblivion—that was not the way of a true Vaishnava. Krishna's devotees were *para-duhkha-duhkhi*, said the sages. Their only suffering was seeing the suffering of others.[33] So he climbed into a horse-drawn tanga, arrived back at Mathura station, bought his train ticket, and returned to Allahabad, where he rejoined family and home and the precarious balance of the material and spiritual. For the next several years, he manufactured medicines and ointments, delivered orders, fixed leaks, bought his growing children new clothes, and contemplated the enormity of his mission.

IN JANUARY 1928, one of Bhaktisiddhanta Saraswati's leading sannyasi disciples, Bhakti Pradip Tirtha Maharaj, arrived in Allahabad and came to Abhay's Prayag Pharmacy. This was the same sannyasi who had convinced Abhay's friend, Narendra Mullik, to meet Bhaktisiddhanta in Calcutta. Pradip Tirtha Maharaj and a group of *brahmacharis* (celibate students) had come to establish a temple, and Abhay offered to help. Together they raised funds and opened a math on South Mallaca Street within walking distance of Abhay's pharmacy.

Each evening, Abhay closed his shop, walked to the math, and spent the evening studying, playing mridanga, and chanting. The ways of math life included memorizing verses from the Bhagavad Gita and *Srimad Bhagavatam* and mastering a repertoire of Vaishnava songs. Consecrating prayers to memory came naturally to him. One of his favorite was by seventeenth-century Vaishnava poet Narottama Das Thakur.

> *O Lord Hari,[34] I have wasted my life.*
> *I obtained a human birth but failed to worship you, O Radha and Krishna.*
> *By this neglect, I have knowingly drunk poison.*
> *Divine love descended from the eternal realm in the form your Holy Names.*
> *Why have I never felt any attraction for chanting?*
> *Day and night my heart burns from the fire of worldliness*
> *Yet I take nothing to relieve the pain.*
> *Dear Lord, please do not push me away with Your reddish lotus feet*
> *For who is my beloved except You?*

Senior members of the Gaudiya Math admired Abhay's singing. His voice carried such sincerity that they may have thought it strange coming from someone so new to their company. It was heartfelt and unguarded and more stirring than a thousand lines of philosophy. He chanted all the time. He chanted when walking to his pharmacy in the morning. He kept his bead bag on his desk and chanted before and after meals. He chanted while traveling to appointments, while running chores, and whenever there was a lull in conversation. Talks with customers and suppliers quickly shifted to talks about Krishna and the chanting of Krishna's names. He would take a conversation with guests and veer into reciting verses in praise of chanting.

> *As soon as I utter Krishna's Name my tongue dances*
> *And I want to possess innumerable tongues.*
> *This Divine Name is so sweet*
> *That it releases all chains within me*
> *And my heart knows no more bounds.*
> *When the Holy Name enters my ears*
> *I long for millions of ears.*
> *I forget all else and am giddy with love of the Name.*
> *Oh! I could never fully describe the sweetness*
> *Of these two syllables: Krish and na!*[35]

O.B.L. Kapoor, a research scholar at Allahabad University, remembered Abhay from those early days. "I saw him playing on mridanga at the time of kirtan," Kapoor recalled. "We became acquainted, acquaintance turned into friendship, and friendship into brotherhood." Kapoor remembered filling a prescription at Abhay's pharmacy. When Abhay handed over the vial, Kapoor joked, "I wish you would give me the tonic *you* take, the tonic of Krishna prema—love for Krishna."

"I have no Krishna prema," Abhay said, "but I do know the formula."

"Let me know," Kapoor asked, "if it's not a secret."

"No, it's not a secret," Abhay replied, and he sang a prayer by Chaitanya Mahaprabhu.

> *In a humble state of mind*
> *Thinking oneself lower than straw in the street*
> *More tolerant than a tree*
> *Devoid of all false prestige,*
> *Ready to offer respect to others —*
> *In such a state of mind*
> *One can chant the Holy Name of the Lord constantly.*

"I shall preach this formula the whole world over," Abhay said.

"At that time, I couldn't understand what he meant," Kapoor admitted years later. "I thought he was making a casual pronouncement without any plan in his mind."

IN A COPY OF THE GAUDIYA MATH'S English-language magazine, *The Harmonist*, Abhay read that Bhaktisiddhanta Saraswati would be leading a pilgrimage to Vrindavan in October of 1932. Prayag Pharmacy demanded every moment of Abhay's time, but he would not pass up a chance to spend a day or two with his guru.

As with all of Bhaktisiddhanta's programs, organization for the pilgrimage was precise. An advance team arrived with hundreds of tents, bedding for at least 1,000 pilgrims and supplies for the equivalent of a small town. The site of the pilgrimage was Koshi, a village outside Vrindavan where Krishna's father, Nanda Maharaj, had constructed his treasury 5,000 years before. The camp was divided into sections arranged in a semicircle. Men and women were assigned their separate quarters, sannyasis were allocated their area, and a deity of Chaitanya Mahaprabhu was installed in the main tent where Bhaktisiddhanta would lecture. At night, gaslights and campfires illumined the campground.

Abhay arrived by train from Allahabad and climbed onto a rickshaw. The road was crowded with pilgrims arriving on camels, horsedrawn wagons, and bullock carts. The rickshaw glided to a halt in Koshi. Abhay received his tent assignment and heard a disciple, Keshava Maharaj, announce that a group would leave soon to visit the famous Vishnu temple named Sesasayi. Pilgrims had their choice of either joining the group and going to the temple, or remaining in Koshi to hear Bhaktisiddhanta lecture. Abhay had no interest in sightseeing. He had come to hear his teacher speak.

He entered the main tent and sat with a small group of disciples who had also stayed back to hear Bhaktisiddhanta's lecture. "It is Krishna who is the only Superlord over the entire universe and, beyond it, of Vaikuntha, the transcendental region," Bhaktisiddhanta began. "As such, no one can raise any obstacle against his enjoyment." It was a sophisticated talk, delivered in scholarly language, and several guests wandered out, leaving a handful of senior disciples and Abhay, the only uninitiated person still in attendance. Bhaktisiddhanta noted his presence, but there was no exchange between them.

Two days later, Abhay returned to Allahabad. In later years, he admitted not having understood all of Bhaktisiddhanta's philosophical points but thinking Chaitanya Mahaprabhu's mission was in the right hands.

IN ALLAHABAD, NAYANANDA DAS, a young brahmachari, made housecalls with other disciples of Bhaktisiddhanta, soliciting donations for their teacher's books and temples. "We would often be out late into the night," he recalled, "but Abhay always opened his door to us. He gave us his own room, and he slept in the living room. He had not yet requested formal initiation, but still he chanted sixty-four rounds each day on his beads."[36]

Nayananda and the disciples reported to Abhay that Bhaktisiddhanta had agreed to lay the cornerstone for a new Allahabad temple and would be awarding initiations at that time. For Vaishnavas, initiation was a transformative moment. The disciple placed his life in the hands of the guru, and the guru agreed to liberate the disciple from further births in the material world. If the disciple fell away, the guru was prepared to come back into the world to save him. To qualify for such a sober promise, the candidate for initiation vowed to study hard and lead a clean life.

It was clear to Abhay that Bhaktisiddhanta did not award initiation casually, as did teachers who wanted to increase their following and the money that came with it. Bhaktisiddhanta was quite capable of turning away candidates for initiation if they failed to grasp its importance. At one lecture, a businessman who had made a monthly pledge to the Gaudiya Math sat down next to Abhay and whispered a question into Abhay's ear. Abhay leaned forward to hear more clearly. Bhaktisiddhanta saw them and stopped speaking.

"Baba," he said, addressing the donor. "Do you think you have purchased me with your monthly one-hundred-fifty rupees?" Then to Abhay he said, "Why don't you come up here and speak instead of me?" Gandhi may have impressed himself at one time on Abhay, but here was a model worth emulating, an acharya whose strength was untrammeled by politics, finances or anything else of this world.

Abhay's reaction to hearing that Bhaktisiddhanta would conduct initiations was immediate. "I wish to be included," he announced to Atulananda, president of the Allahabad Math.

BHAKTISIDDHANTA SARASWATI ARRIVED IN NOVEMBER 1932, and Atulananda listed the many services Abhay had rendered on their behalf, such as raising donations, participating in speaking programs, and leading melodic kirtans.

"Yes, I remember him," Bhaktisiddhanta said. "He came to see me in Kosi. He sat and listened and did not go away. I marked him."

On the day of the initiation ceremony, monks shoveled soil into a four-foot square and decorated the sacrificial mound with colored dyes and incense. Brahmins recited verses from scripture. Bhaktisiddhanta chanted on loops of beads, handed them to his new disciples, and announced their initiated names.

"Your name," he said to Abhay, "is Abhay Charanaravinda: Abhay Charan, who has taken shelter at Krishna's lotus feet."[37] Go on with your devotional studies, Bhaktisiddhanta told his new disciple, but not with the selfish intention of seeing God.

"Rather," Bhaktisiddhanta advised, "act in such a way that God will want to see you."

Some time later, Bhaktisiddhanta lectured to a crowd that had assembled for a *parikrama* or walking tour of Mayapur, the birthplace of Chaitanya Mahaprabhu.

"Guru Maharaj was looking out at the large crowd of devotees," Nayanananda Das Babaji recalled. "Then he turned his head toward the left side where I was standing. He was looking intently at someone behind me and became silent for a long moment. I turned and saw that the person with whom he was making eye contact was Abhay Charanaravinda Prabhu."

"I have a prediction," Bhaktisiddhanta announced. "However long in the future it may be, one of my disciples will cross the ocean. That devotee will bring back the whole world."[38]

IN FEBRUARY 1935, disciples gathered to celebrate Bhaktisiddhanta's sixty-second birthday. The celebration of a guru's birth was called *Vyasa-puja*, since the guru represented Vyasadev, compiler of the Vedic scriptures. Abhay was invited to address the audience assembled in the Bombay math.

"While others were yet in the womb of historical oblivion," Abhay told the crowd, "the sages of India had developed a different kind of civilization, which enables us to know ourselves. They had discovered that we are not at all material entities but that we are all spiritual, permanent, and non-destructible servants of the Absolute."

He continued his Vyasa-puja offering, stressing the importance of cultivating this spiritual dimension of life under the guidance of a qualified guru. He concluded by telling the crowd, "Although we are like ignorant children in the knowledge of the transcendence, still His Divine Grace, my Gurudev, has kindled a small fire within us to dissipate the darkness of empirical knowledge, and we are so much on the safe side that no amount of philosophical argument of the empiric schools of thought can deviate us an inch."

From his years of study and devotional service, Abhay had become an eloquent, philosophically astute devotee, and for this occasion, he had written a poem that was published in Bhaktisiddhanta's newspaper, *The Harmonist*. One verse in particular caught Bhaktisiddhanta's attention:

> *Absolute is sentient*
> *Thou hast proved,*
> *Impersonal calamity*
> *That hast moved.*

The simple couplet captured the essence of Bhaktisiddhanta's campaign to expose the fallacies of *mayavada* or impersonalist philosophy. "Whatever he writes," Bhaktisiddhanta told his editors, "publish it."

WHILE ABHAY'S DEVOTION blossomed, his pharmaceutical company was losing money. "He is a very honest man," Abhay's partner told their employer, Dr. Bose. "In good faith, he extended credit to his accounts, but they are defaulting on payments." The debts had reached 10,000 rupees, a fortune in those days.

"I can't go on giving him money," Bose said. He called Abhay, and they agreed the best solution was for Bose to take over Abhay's accounts and let him go.

Abhay saw the setback as an opportunity to open his own pharmacy in Bombay. It seemed to be the right choice: No sooner did he open his own shop than a larger manufacturer, Smith Institute, requested that he act as their sales agent. Abhay accepted, calculating that he could earn money selling products from both his own company and Smith Institute. Two sources of income would be better than one for financing his journey to America.

Abhay's supervisor envied his successes and lied to company officials, claiming Abhay was stealing their accounts. The accusations were false, but they led to Abhay's dismissal and a transfer of his accounts to the supervisor's son. These constant fluctuations in Abhay's income did not sit well with Abhay's wife. Abhay and Radharani no longer had the expense of maintaining Abhay's father, who had passed away in 1932, but they now had three children, and bills were mounting. From Radharani's perspective, the family's well-being was no longer Abhay's chief concern, and when he hosted gatherings in their home, she did not attend.

In November 1935, Bhaktisiddhanta Saraswati led a pilgrimage to Vrindavan, and Abhay joined him. By now, Abhay had become a respected member of his teacher's institution. They walked together around the periphery of Radha Kund pond, one of Vrindavan's most holy sites, and Bhaktisiddhanta confided a dread he had not shared with others. Frictions had arisen among some of his disciples.

"*Agun jvalbe,*" Bhaktisiddhanta said in Bengali. "There will be a fire."

His students were to be respected for their devotion and hard work, and as Vaishnavas, they were dear to Lord Krishna, but a few had chosen to fight over seniority and the right to live in more spacious rooms and buildings.

"When we were living in a rented house," Bhaktisiddhanta said, recalling the early days of his mission, "we were happier. Then we were given this marble palace in Baghbazar," referring to the Gaudiya Math's new headquarters in the prestigious area of north Calcutta that was home to Bengal's aristocracy, "and ever since there has been this friction between our men: who will occupy this room, who will occupy that room. Everyone is planning in different ways. It would be better to sell the marble from the walls and print books." Then he offered a prophetic instruction.

"If you ever get money," Bhaktisiddhanta told Abhay, "print books."

IN DECEMBER 1936, two weeks before he passed away, Bhaktisiddhanta sent Abhay a letter reiterating his instruction at their first meeting. "I am fully confident," he wrote, "that you can explain in English our thoughts and arguments to the people. This will do much good for you as well as your audience. I have every hope that you can turn yourself into a very good English preacher and convey the novel impression of Lord Chaitanya's teachings to the general public."

A week later, Bhaktisiddhanta issued his final wishes to disciples. "All of you please preach this message. Work together for this single purpose. Do not abandon this goal even in the face of hundreds of dangers, insults, or persecutions. Do not lose your spirit if you see that the majority of people cannot accept the principle of selfless service to the Supreme Lord. The doctrines of Krishna bhakti may at first seem startling, perhaps even perplexing," he said, "but every human being is knowingly or unknowingly struggling to eliminate the dualities which interfere with direct experience of eternity."

In succinct, precise terms the great acharya had summarized for followers the essence of the human condition. What made life worth living? Why should anyone bother getting up in the morning if not because some hope existed for "a direct experience of eternity"? Like the shackled dwellers in Plato's cave who had never seen the multidimensional outside world, embodied souls experienced only a two-dimensional shadow of the glories of creation. Everyone had experiences: How many people actually understood what they meant or what lay beyond sensory limits? Human experience was compromised by imperfect tools of perception and faulty analysis—the "dualities" or shortcomings that came with being eternal souls housed in temporary bodies.

"Our only obligation," Bhaktisiddhanta concluded, "is to help them go beyond those dualities and enter the world of eternal fulfillment. And never abandon your chanting. Please. Always chant the name of the Lord while remaining humbler than a blade of grass and more tolerant than a tree."[39]

Bhaktisiddhanta passed away on January 1, 1937, and the schism among Gaudiya Math leaders widened. The late founder had instructed disciples to form a twelve-man governing body, but soon after his demise, a senior disciple positioned himself to be the successor acharya. Another began signing properties over to himself as trustee, arguing that Bhaktisiddhanta had not been the rightful owner of Gaudiya Math assets. They belonged to God, he told the courts, and their ownership could not be dictated by anyone except the current trustee: himself. The litigation escalated. To cover legal costs, Gaudiya Math officers sold off Bhaktisiddhanta's cherished printing presses. One of the disputants broke his sannyasa vows, took up with women, and the institution splintered even further. Some members left in disgust while others continued serving the cause by founding their own maths and initiating disciples.

Abhay kept out of the politics. His sole interest was executing his guru's instruction to go West, not conspiring for power or position. He respected those godbrothers who worked hard to perpetuate Bhaktisiddhanta's mission, and there were many—only a few of the senior people were causing trouble—but Bhaktisiddhanta had given Abhay a particular assignment. If other disciples were not available to join him on the journey to America, then he would take it alone.

He did not prefer to break away or form his own project. But if necessary, he would.

"Godhead is Light , Nescience is darkness. . . Where there is Godhead there is no Nescience."

BACK TO GODHEAD

(An Instrument for glorifying the Absolute)   *Edited and Founded*   (It revives man's Divine nature)
Under direct order of His Divine Grace Sri Srimad Bhakti Siddhanta Saraswati Goswami Prabhupada
By Goswami Abhay Charan Bhaktivedanta

VOL. III { Annual Rs. 2·25. Price 10 nP. a Copy.   Delhi Thursday 20th November 1958   Fortnightly published. } PART XIV

TRUTH AND BEAUTY

Under caption of LITERARY LAPSES in the editorial column of the *Times of India*, Bombay dated 12/10/58 it was argued whether truth and beauty are compatible terms with one another. The editorial said, while criticising Professor Humayun Kabir's speeches in Calcutta on literary lapses, that one would agree willingly, if it came to that, to express the truth, but since truth is not always beautiful—indeed it is frequently rather startling and unpleasant—how is one to express truth and beauty at the same time ?

In reply to this we may inform all concerned that Truth and Beauty are compatible terms. It is rather emphatically asserted that truth which is Absolute is always beautiful. The Truth is so beautiful that it attracts every one including the Truth itself. Truth is so beautiful that many sages, saints and devotees have left everything for the sake of Truth. Mahatma Gandhi the idol of the modern world dedicated his life for experimenting with Truth and all his activities were targetted towards Truth only.

Why Mahatma Gandhi—every one of us is searching after an urge of Truth only because it is not only beautiful but also all powerful, all resourceful, all famous, all renouncing and all knowledge.

Unfortunately people have no information of the actual Truth and 99·9 per cent men in all ranks of life are following the footprints of *Untruth* only in the name of Truth and its searcing after. We are actually attracted with the beauty of Truth but we are habituated to love untruth from time imm- emorial in the name of Truth. And therefore to the mundaner Truth and Beauty are incompatible terms. The mundane Truth and beauty is explained as follows :

A person fell in love with a beautiful girl (?). The man was very powerful and strongly built but his character was very doubtful. The girl was not only beautiful in appearance but also saintly in character. As such the beatiful girl did not like the pro- posal of the powerful man. The powerful man however insisted upon his lustful desire. And the beautiful girl requested the man to wait for seven days only and after that she fixed up a time when the man could meet her.

The strongman agreed and with high expectations began to count and wait for the zero hour when he was fixed up to meet the girl.

The saintly girl however in order to maifest the real beauty of relative Truth adopted a means which is very instructive. She took up a very strong dose of purgative medicine and for seven days continually she passed only loose stool and also vomitted all that she ate. And all the loose stool and the vomits were stored up in suitable reser- voirs. As a result of this laxa- tive medicine the socalled beautiful girl became lean, thin like a skeleton and turned blackish in complexion and the beautiful eye balls were pushed into the sockets of the skull. And at the appointed hour she was waiting anxiously to receive the man in love.

The man appeared on the scene well dressed and well behaved and asked the waiting girl, who was depressed in appear- ance, about the beautiful girl who called him there. The man could not recognise the waiting girl, as the same beautiful girl whom he was asking for. The same girl however was in a pitiable condition and the foolish man inspite of repeated assertion could not recognise her. It was all due to the acion of the medi- cine only.

At last the girl told the powerful man all the story of her beauty and told him that she had separated the ingredients of beauty and stored them up in the reservoirs. She also told him that he could enjoy the juices of beauty stored up in the reservoirs. The mundane poetic or the lunatic man agreed to see the juices of beauty and thus he was directed to the store of loose stool and liquid vomit which were emanating unbearable bad smell and thus the whole story of beauty liquid was dis- closed to him. The character- less man by the grace of the saintly girl was able to distin- guish between the shadow and the substance and thus he came to his senses.

That is the real position of every one of us who are attracted with the false material beauty. The girl as above mentioned developed a beautiful material body as she desired in her mind but in fact she was apart from such temporary material body and mind. She is in fact a spiritual spark and so also the man in love who was attracted by the false skin of the girl.

Both professor Humayun Kabir and the editor of the Times of India are however deluded by the outward beauty and attraction of the relative truth and are un- aware of the spiritual spark which is both Truth and Beauty at one and the same time. The spiritual spark is so beautiful that on its leaving the so called beautiful body full of stools and vomit—no body would like to touch it even though the same is decorated with costly costume.

And because we are all after a false relative truth therefore the same is incompatible with real beauty. The truth is so permanen- tly beautiful that it maintains the same standard of beauty as it is for lacs and crores of years. Be- sides that such spiritual spark is indestructible. The beauty of

the outer skin can be destroyed in a few hours time only by one dose of strong purgative pill but the beauty of Truth is always the same and indestructible as it is always. Unfortunately mundane editors and professors are ignorant of this beautiful sparks of spirit as well as the whole dry resources of these spiritual sparks and their interrelations of transcendental pastimes. When the same *is* dis- played here by the Grace of the Almighty the foolish persons who cannot see beyond the senses take that pastime of Truth and Beauty in the light of the above store of looses stools and liquid vomit and thus become despaired and de- clare how Truth and beauty can be accomodated at one and the same time.

The mundaners do not know that the Whole spiritual Entity is the beautiful Person attracting everything as the Prime Sub- stance and the Prime source and Fountain Head of everything that be. And the infinitesimal spiri- tual sparks as parts and parcels of the Whole spirit are qualita- tively the same beautiful and eternal entities. The difference is that the Whole is eternally the Whole and the parts are eternally the parts. Both of them are the Ultimate Truth, ultimate beauty, ultimate knowledge, ultimate energy, ultimate renunciation and ultimate opulance.

So far literary lapses are con- cerned any literature which does not describe such Ultimate Truth and Beauty is a store of loose stools and liquid vomit of the re- lative truth may it be described by any mundane poet or thinker of any country. Real literature is that which describes about these ultimate Truth and beauty. Poet Kalidas is as much a mundane liter- atuer as professor Humayun Kabir or the editor of the Times of India. Such a mundane literatuer like poet Kalidas went to see a learned queen of his time and sent his card.   *(To be Continued)*

From 1944 to 1956, Abhay wrote and published *Back to Godhead* and walked the streets of Delhi, selling one copy at a time. By the mid-1970s, more than one million copies were distributed per month in the United States alone.

CHAPTER TWO

*Whatever behavior great souls exhibit, others follow. Whatever acts they do,
whatever standards they set by example, the world pursues.*

—SRI KRISHNA IN THE BHAGAVAD GITA, 3.21

CALCUTTA 1938

With his Bombay business in decline, Abhay moved back to Calcutta and
rented a two-story house at 6 Sita Kanta Banerjee Lane, a narrow street
lined with three-story houses. He turned the ground floor into an office and
moved his family into rooms on the second floor. He rented the adjoining
building and built a small chemical laboratory for manufacturing distilled
water, De's Pain Liniment ("Good for Relieving Gout, Rheumatism & All
Pains"), and other medicines. He hung a signboard out front, ABHAY
CHARAN DE & SONS, featuring a painting of himself, the mustachioed
proprietor. Business stabilized, but his heart was elsewhere. In the evenings
he read his guru's books and spoke with neighbors about his future mission
in the West. Abdullah, his bottle merchant, was receptive to discussions
about philosophy and religion. The Muslim businessman had started out
poor, worked hard, and now earned a sizeable income.

"How are you going to use your money?" Abhay asked.

"My dear sir," Abdullah said, "I would like to build a mosque." Abdullah
was a man after Abhay's own heart.

Some of Sridhar Maharaj's disciples met with Abhay at his Banerjee Lane
residence. Like Abhay, Sridhar Maharaj had also distanced himself from contentious elements in the Gaudiya Math, and now he and his disciples hoped
to open an ashram in Calcutta. For twenty rupees a month, Abhay leased

them four rooms above his chemical laboratory. Whenever Sridhar Maharaj and other Gaudiya Math monks such as Puri Maharaj and Bhakti Saranga Maharaj visited Calcutta, the rooms in Abhay's place served as their base of operations. The sannyasis cooked, performed their morning puja, and held classes and kirtans. Abhay lived downstairs with his family, but when the day's work ended, he mounted the stairs to chant Hare Krishna with his godbrothers.

IN SEPTEMBER 1939, the viceroy of India announced that England—and by extension India—was at war. By April 1942, Japanese forces had routed the British in neighboring Burma and occupied India's eastern border. The Port of Calcutta, Howrah Bridge, and the city's Dum Dum Airport all lay within range of Japanese bombers, and throughout 1942 and 1943, constant air attacks created panic among the population. Walking down the city's streets swarming with soldiers and army trucks, Abhay sidestepped debris from bombings and the impact of a population fleeing danger. Looking up, he saw shattered windows taped over with paper. Gone were the days when children flew kites from rooftops as he had done with his sister, Bhavatarini. Gone, too, were the pigeons that used to fly across the city's skies. Calcutta was a ghost town. Abhay's neighbors had packed their bags and left. Native Bengalis with their children in tow, Anglo-Indian families that had proliferated under the Raj, Jewish and Muslim merchants who had prospered in happier days—all had gathered their belongings and departed for shelter in outlying villages. Howrah and Sealdah stations were packed with people trying to get out.

Abhay arranged for his family to relocate to Navadwip four hours north, but his wife refused to leave, saying she preferred to be bombed at home and insisting that Abhay stay with her. When sirens sounded, the few remaining city-dwellers grabbed water jars and took shelter in basements. After the all-clear siren, they surfaced and surveyed the damage. Not far from Abhay's house was Jamaat Khana, a Muslim religious center. The center had been bombed, and its two cows lay dead on the road. Broken glass and shrapnel littered the streets.[40]

Newspapers reported the impact of war on other parts of the world. Half of northern France was in flames. German planes had dropped more than 100 tons of explosives on cities across England. Hundreds of thousands lay dead, and millions were walking the streets of Europe homeless. Someone needed to give a spiritual perspective to the madness. His guru's English-language newspaper, *The Harmonist*, had not been published in years, and the

Gaudiya Math was too steeped in litigation to pursue publication now. Abhay envisioned a magazine that would pick up where his guru's paper had left off. He had no funds or help, but he also had no choice. He had been charged with a mission, and the moment demanded that he do something.

Abhay would later design a logo for his publication: a rectangle around the words BACK TO GODHEAD, with a photo of his spiritual master, Bhaktisiddhanta Saraswati, in one corner and a drawing of Chaitanya Mahaprabhu in the other. Abhay secured donations and purchased enough paper to print 1,000 copies, and a forty-four-page first edition of *Back to Godhead* rolled off the press in the print shop of Surendra Kumar Jain, located in Delhi's Chandni Chowk district.

An analysis of the war received front-page placement. Godhead and individual souls were both by nature deathless, he wrote, but souls in this world had forgotten their connection to Krishna or God. Having become embodied, immortal souls could never achieve true satisfaction, be it through peaceful efforts or warfare. "We may flee the Japanese bombs," he wrote, "but material nature will continue her assault with bombs of old age, disease and death."

In a second edition of *Back to Godhead* eight months later, Abhay wrote that behind hatred and war lay the misimpression that selfhood was defined by place of birth. No one was permanently Indian or American, German or Japanese, he admonished. All beings were spirit souls. When that true identity was lost, people created selfish allegiances based on material crite-ria—political ideology, color of skin, religion, or place of birth—each with its own interests to defend. "The frenzy of hatred," Abhay wrote, "is another side of the frenzy of love. The frenzy of love of Hitler's own countrymen has produced the concomitant frenzy of hatred for others, and the present war is the result of such dual side of frenzy."

THE DAY WORLD WAR II ENDED the streets of Calcutta hummed with trucks carrying allied soldiers from one base to another. Gangs of young Indians whooped and shouted from trams as they crossed and recrossed Howrah Bridge. American officers handed out tins of carrots and other supplies. They were heading home, and the surplus made good parting gifts.

With the war over, India turned its attention back to affairs at home. While united in their determination to expel the British, Indians stood divided over the shape of their post-British future. Gandhi and Congress demanded a unified free nation. The Muslim population, led by Muhammad Ali Jinnah, head of the All-India Muslim League, called for partition and a country of their own. The conflict turned violent in August 1946, when rioting broke out in Calcutta, and four thousand men, women, and children were killed. Violence spread, and British administrators were forced to admit they had lost control over the Indian subcontinent. The time had come for England to cut her losses.

In early 1947, Britain's final viceroy to India, Lord Mountbatten, deployed surveyors to draw a geographic line dividing Hindu India from Muslim Pakistan. The rules laid down for this territorial division excluded any consultation with its population. The arbitrary partition consequently tore villages in half and triggered the largest human migration in history. More than seven million Muslims trekked to the newly formed nation of Pakistan, while as many Hindus and Sikhs walked to their new Hindu homeland. The two rivers of refugees snaked in opposite directions for hundreds of miles. Attacks broke out up and down the human highway. Helpless to deal with such staggering numbers of refugees, officials stood by and watched the slaughter. More than a half-million people died in a matter of weeks.

Abhay noted what others seemed not to see: The dead bodies lying in piles looked alike. Municipal workers carted away the bodies of men and women whose religious or political affiliations no longer mattered. The one hope for reconciliation had gone unexplored: As God's children, all were entitled to share their Father's property in peace. Even Gandhi had minimized a spiritual solution to the conflict, and in Abhay's estimation, the Mahatma now risked being held accountable for the deadly consequences.

"Dear friend Mahatmajee," he wrote in a prophetic letter to Gandhi in December 1947, "I tell you as a sincere friend that you must immediately retire from active politics if you do not desire to die an inglorious death." Abhay reminded Gandhi that he had tried for so many years to achieve freedom for India, but India was now divided. He had wanted to uplift the outcastes, but still they rotted in ghettos and slums. Consider these defeats as a message from God, Abhay advised. Now the illusion of achieving peace through politics has been dispelled. To at last do substantial good, Abhay concluded, "you must give up rotten politics immediately and rise up for the preaching work of the philosophy and religion of Bhagavad Gita." Abhay proposed that Gandhi retire for one month, during which they would discuss the Gita together. There was no reply. One month later, a radical Hindu nationalist, Nathuram Godse, seething over Gandhi's failure to achieve a unified India, assassinated him with an automatic pistol.[41]

THAT SAME YEAR, the sannyasis who resided at 7 Banerjee Lane bestowed on Abhay the honorific title "Bhaktivedanta," signifying a devotee steeped in bhakti or devotion and one who knew the *anta* or conclusion of the Vedas: love of God. It was an apt honor, considering Abhay's unwavering determination to fulfill his spiritual master's order. Yet the new title also underscored the urgency of doing so soon. He was fifty-one years old and could not afford to postpone the journey West much longer.

Still, there was his family to consider, now expanded to five children: two daughters and three sons. In a final effort to secure finances for his family and mission, he rented a building in Lucknow 600 miles from Calcutta and built a factory that he named Abhay Charan De & Sons. It was a 40,000-rupee gamble, bigger than any he had taken before—and one that did not last long. Within six months, the factory started losing money. Costs were high, income in those austere postwar years was minimal, and Abhay fell behind in the rent.

In November 1947, he wrote to his household servant, Gouranga, who was in Calcutta with Radharani and the De children. "I am fighting, practically staking my whole life," he wrote and pleaded with Gouranga to come to Lucknow and help him make the new business a success. Gouranga arrived but saw no future in the failing venture. Besides, he argued, Abhay had been away from home too long and had neglected his family. The moment proved to be a turning point for Abhay. Something in the clash of material and spiritual duties led him to make a firm declaration of his intentions.

"I tried to serve them," Abhay replied, "but up until today they have not become attached to devotional service. So I am no more interested about those affairs. If I see that they are interested about devotional service, then only will I maintain my establishment there. Otherwise, I will not maintain them anymore."

A mission long overdue had forced its way to the forefront of his priorities. It was a mission that obliged him to assess priorities differently than other men of his generation. His spiritual master had instilled in him a vision of humanity's potential, a picture of what the world could be if people were educated to recognize their eternal nature—and that calling trumped the needs of family. He and his wife had long since agreed to live their own lives, joined only as far as necessary to maintain the unity of their home and children. They had succeeded for more than twenty years, and for that he respected her and would always be grateful. But time was running out, and he could no longer deny what had to be done. He would maintain his family as best he could—but that was all. The rest of him belonged to his guru.

Gouranga shook his head and returned to the De family in Calcutta. Abhay and Gouranga never saw one another again. In 1948, Abhay closed his Lucknow factory. With the help of some acquaintances in Allahabad, he opened a small factory not far from where his first venture, Prayag Pharmacy, had operated fifteen years before. With the help of his youngest son, Vrindavan Chandra, he manufactured a line of medicines and made sales calls, but the income was always minimal. In 1950, Radharani took her five children and moved back to her father's house at 72 Mahatma Gandhi Road, Calcutta. Abhay was no longer the man she had married.

"He was always thinking seriously to make more money from business," recalled Abhay's nephew, Sudhir Kumar Dutta, "but that would have meant giving more time for business—and he would never give up his writing for that. People accused him, 'Hey, you are writing religious things and only thinking about God. Who will maintain your family?' Sometimes he argued with them, 'Why should I forget about God? This is the real thing, what I am doing. You cannot realize what I am doing.'"[42]

ABHAY'S FACTORY HAD FAILED, his family was dissolving, and one night Abhay dreamed he saw his guru standing before him. "Leave home," Bhaktisiddhanta Saraswati urged. "Become a sannyasi." Abhay woke in fear. His image of the sannyasa order was "horrible," he later described. Sannyasis had no place in society. They were social and financial outcasts. Sannyasis were celibate, which did not trouble him. That part of his life was over. But Sannyasis were held in highest spiritual esteem, and out of his natural humility he may have questioned his right to such a revered position. Topping the list of hesitations was his ongoing sense of duty to his family. How could he leave his children without a father, without support?

He sent letters to religious leaders, government officials, educators, social activists, and industrialists, urging them to join him. To the Ford

Foundation in Detroit, he proposed creating "an association of the intelligent class of people." The reply stated, "The Ford Foundation has no program in which specific ideas such as you describe might be included." Abhay attended a meeting held by an Indian industrialist who promoted harmonious relations between labor and management. In a letter the following day, Abhay suggested the industrialist convert his employees' lounge into a hall for chanting Hare Krishna. There was no reply.

In February 1952, Abhay responded to an article that had appeared in the *American Reporter*, addressing East-West economic development. When we speak of development, Abhay wrote the editor, it must be for a higher purpose than financial gain. He offered to "present an analytical study of Bhagavad Gita through the pages of your *American Reporter* in order to help the American people." The editor never replied.

ABHAY AGAIN DREAMED OF BHAKTISIDDHANTA, and once more his guru told him to become a sannyasi. The image of himself as a pauper with literally nothing—would that not be a defeat of sorts? What difference was there between failing in a mission and failing to finance such a mission? How many so-called sannyasis had he known in his life who were nothing more than men fleeing a world they were not strong enough to navigate? He refused to become one of those pretend sadhus who used renunciation to cloak their failures. Then, while reading the *Srimad Bhagavatam*, he came upon a verse: "When I feel especially merciful toward someone," Krishna declared, "I gradually take away all his material possessions. His friends and relatives then reject this poverty-stricken and most wretched fellow."[43]

That deserved some deliberation: poverty as a merciful dispensation.

BACK TO GODHEAD acquired a modest number of subscribers. One, a Mr. Dubey, owned the municipal hospital in Jhansi, 180 miles southwest of Lucknow. In October 1952, Dubey invited Abhay to lecture at one of the city's meeting halls. Abhay agreed, and after his lecture several guests offered to help if he decided to bring his mission to Jhansi. It would have crossed Abhay's mind that Krishna may have intended for him to fail in business so that he could build a math in Jhansi from which to launch Bhaktisiddhanta's mission in the West. With the Gaudiya Math in disarray, maybe the plan was for him to have an institution of his own. He wrote to his middle son, Mathura Mohan, authorizing him to take charge of the pharmacy while he concentrated on opening a math in Jhansi.

One of the attendees at the Jhansi talk, an ayurvedic doctor named Shastri, lived in a two-story building. Downstairs was his clinic, upstairs a one-room residence. Shastri invited Abhay to live with him, and they shared the small space, cooking together and discussing plans for establishing a league of devotees. Shastri would later recall Abhay as having an "iron-will determination and self-confidence about his mission"[44] and its prospects: perhaps some day to become a registered political party and support Vaishnava candidates for a seat in parliament or the post of prime minister. In service to Krishna, anything was possible.

In Jhansi, Abhay lectured wherever he was invited: temples, homes, shops, and offices. One day, on a break from his morning writing, he walked the city and found a property that appealed to him. The Radha Memorial, built in 1939, was vacant. Abhay tracked down the owner and convinced him to lease the building and land for religious purposes. Abhay prepared a charter, and the League of Devotees was born.

At first, the project seemed to fulfill Abhay's vision of a place in India from which to grow his mission abroad. He ran an ad in several Calcutta newspapers:

> EDUCATIONAL — Wanted: candidates from any nationality to qualify themselves as real Brahmins for preaching the teachings of Bhagavad Gita for all practical purposes throughout the whole world. Deserving candidates will be provided with free boarding and lodging. Apply: A.C. Bhaktivedanta, Founder and Secretary of the League of Devotees, Bharati Bhawan, P.O. Jhansi (U.P.)

There were no replies.

WHEN HE VISITED HIS FAMILY IN CALCUTTA, Abhay gathered old friends in his father-in-law's home for talks about Krishna. He invited his wife and children to take part, but they preferred to sit in an upstairs room where Radharani would prepare a pot of tea.

"You have to choose," he finally told her, "between tea and me. Either the tea goes or I do."

Under other circumstances, a cup of tea would not have meant much. Although proscribed by Vaishnava custom due to its caffeine content, drinking tea for health reasons was a common practice. Tea as a daily ritual, on the other hand, had begun with the arrival of the British East India Company. There were no four o'clock teas prior to the colonial period, and in the early years of the twentieth century, it was a habit adopted only by Anglicized Indians. Radharani's capitulation to a distinctly British ritual was more than a flaunting of a religious interdiction: It was a red flag, a message that giving up their way of life to become a Krishna missionary in the West was his fantasy, not hers.

"Well," she said, taking the threat as exaggeration, "I'll have to give up my husband then."

THE BREACH BETWEEN ABHAY AND HIS WIFE WIDENED beyond repair on a day of shopping in 1955. In the 1950s, before credit cards and access to global markets, India's shopkeepers sometimes accepted house-hold goods in lieu of money. Buyers brought objects for barter, and if the merchant had interest, the object was traded for an agreed equivalence in produce. Radharani took one of Abhay's books, a volume of his sacred *Srimad Bhagavatam*, and traded it for tea biscuits. On some level she must have known this was sabotage and that their marriage hung in the balance, but for too long she and their children had been relegated to a place behind his many ambitions. If the relationship was going to end, it would be at her instigation. When he asked her why she had sold his book, her explanation was perfunctory: They had run out of biscuits.

And Abhay had run out of patience. Shared memories, a home, and children — none of it was sufficient to hold this relationship together. Why pretend? All that came from pretending was a bitter residue. He had tired of weighing life's chores on one side of his mental scale and his guru's call to arms on the other and knowing in advance which way it would tip. He was fifty-eight years old. They had been married thirty-six years. He had done what he could for his family. Getting his sons and daughters married first, before leaving, had been a consideration, but then he reasoned that if he left his family, would the world stop turning? How would staying at home make any difference to them other than financial? They had their own lives to live, the years were dragging on, and the time had come to fulfill his guru's order. That meant leaving home.

No doubt there would be recriminations. His family would complain bitterly for the rest of their lives, and neighbors and business associates would condemn him. Worldly people would find what he was about to do morally reprehensible, but he no longer had a choice. If others did not agree, that was not his problem. Raising capital, filling out papers, hiring and firing, taking out loans, placating creditors, warehousing goods, paying bills, distributing bottles and jars—for what? Abhay had a higher calling, regardless of his wife's opinion, and his *dharma* was not the same as someone else's. It was not for everyone, what he was about to do. But it was the only path for him.

He packed a small bag. Where to go? He could not return yet to his new headquarters in Jhansi. He first had to get his bearings. He took a brief train ride to the town of Jhargram, where there was a small chapter of the Gaudiya Math. The *mahant* or head of the math, Paramahamsa Maharaj, had been present at Abhay's first meeting with Bhaktisiddhanta Saraswati and remembered him from that day in 1922. Abhay explained to Paramahamsa Maharaj that his efforts to earn money had failed, and that his family had grown hostile.

"This is my situation," Abhay said. "Now let me preach the message of Lord Chaitanya."

FOR THE FIRST FEW DAYS in Paramahamsa Maharaj's math, Abhay did nothing but chant Hare Krishna on his beads. Then, feeling acclimated to this new chapter in his life, he bought a ticket and returned to Jhansi, ready to build the League of Devotees. But he had been gone too long. In his absence, a women's group with allies in the Jhansi government had convinced the owner of the Radha Memorial to evict Abhay and turn the building over to them. Abhay was ready to fight the eviction and took the next train to Mathura to consult with his godbrother, Keshava Maharaj.

Bhakti Prajnan Keshava Maharaj was two years younger than Abhay but had received initiation from Bhaktisiddhanta Saraswati four years earlier, which made him ecclesiastically senior to Abhay. Like Abhay, Keshava Maharaj had also been active in Gandhi's civil disobedience movement. In 1919, Bhaktisiddhanta appointed him manager of press operations and editor of the mission's weekly Bengali magazine, *Jnani Nadia*. After Bhaktisiddhanta's passing, and after the onset of lawsuits, Keshava Maharaj left the Gaudiya Math. He entered the sannyasa order in 1941 and established the Sri Kesavaji Gaudiya Math temple in Mathura. It was here that Abhay traveled on learning he had lost possession of the Jhansi lease.

"Help me recover my headquarters so that I may fulfill our spiritual master's order," Abhay pleaded. Keshava Maharaj accompanied him by train back to Jhansi, but it took only a day to conclude that the location was too remote.

"Our Guru Maharaj's vision was to preach in larger cities," he reminded Abhay, and Abhay admitted that two years of effort in Jhansi had accomplished little. Keshava Maharaj proposed that Abhay return with him to Mathura and that, in exchange for room and board, he take charge of editing the math's newspaper, *Gaudiya Patrika*. Abhay agreed and left the Jhansi project in the care of friends, asking them to continue the good work without him.

When another Gaudiya Math monk, Bhakti Saranga Maharaj, learned that Abhay had left home to take up devotional service full-time, he sent Abhay a letter from his math in Delhi. The senior monk published a Vaishnava journal titled *Sajjana-tosani* ("source of pleasure for devotees") begun by Bhaktivinode Thakur in 1881. If Abhay agreed to move from Mathura to Delhi, Bhakti Saranga Maharaj would provide him living space, and Abhay could edit both his and Keshava Maharaj's publications. Abhay saw possibilities in the arrangement. In particular, he knew that under the direction of Bhakti Saranga, *Sajjana-tosani* had become weighed down by intellectualism. There was Vaishnava truth in its articles, but page after page of truths would not draw readership. Abhay proposed expanding *Sajjana-tosani* so that it would have a real impact on readers. We should make the magazine more exciting, he suggested, "just to the standard of *Illustrated Weekly*," referring to India's most widely read magazine, "with numerous pictures in order to make it a very popular literature." His wardrobe may have been down to two worn-out dhotis, but Abhay's ambitions to spread Krishna consciousness were lavish.

The boldness of Abhay's plans intimidated Bhakti Saranga and his fellow monks, who sent Abhay a polite letter of eviction. "Your project is very lofty," they wrote, while their own plans, they professed, were less ambitious. As a consequence, "we are suspecting that it won't be possible for an able and respectable Vaishnava like yourself to stay long."

Abhay was homeless. He moved about and slept wherever invitations were extended—one week in a local Vishnu temple, the next week at the Kapoor College of Commerce. With his few remaining rupees, he paid for a newspaper ad offering a home study course: "Learn Bhagavad Gita and Become a Strong Man." There were no takers.

TOP: Prabhupada emphasized deity worship as an important part of devotional practice, and very soon after arriving in America established the worship of Radha and Krishna in deity form. To a large extent, daily ISKCON temple activity revolves around various services to honor the deity.

BOTTOM: At the Sri Chaitanya Saraswat Math in Navadwip, Prabhupada met with several of his godbrothers and supporters, including Bhakti Raksak Sridhar Maharaj, Bhakti Prapanna Damodar Maharaja, Bhakti Kamal Madhusudan Maharaj, and Bhakti Sundar Govinda Maharaj.

BIPIN CHANDRA MISRA, a New Delhi Supreme Court judge, admired Abhay's missionary zeal and made modest monthly donations to help cover his living expenses. Abhay collected the funds each month, thanked the judge, and, in lieu of buying food, headed to the local paper merchant where he purchased however much he could afford. Workers loaded the stacks of paper onto a rickshaw, and Abhay set out for Surendra Kumar Jain's print shop. There had not been enough money to print *Back to Godhead* since 1952, and now, four years later, there was just enough money from the judge's donations to go to press once more. Abhay saved a few *paise* by skipping breakfast and walking to Jain's shop to supervise the job.

"Abhay Babu," Jain asked, "did you have anything to eat this morning?"

Abhay shook his head. "I just came to see the proofs."

"That's all right. I will get breakfast for you."

They went through this ritual whenever Abhay came to oversee printing. The ruse was transparent, but it allowed Jain to feed his impoverished client without embarrassing him. They talked for hours, and, like others who knew Abhay, Jain became as much a friend as a supplier. That was Abhay's way. Business or other excuses might bring people together, but the purpose of human interaction was to acknowledge one another as eternal souls, and he spoke with Jain from that level, honoring Krishna in the printer's heart. It was a courtesy that had practical benefits, since Jain preferred to extend payment terms rather than draw attention to his friend's poverty.

After collecting the newly printed edition of *Back to Godhead*, Abhay walked around Delhi, God's paperboy, soliciting people at tea stands and outdoor restaurants to please purchase a copy. Most people ignored him or waved him away with the back of their hand. He delivered copies to his few subscribers and occasionally tried expanding sales by knocking on the doors of their neighbors. Reception was not always warm for an old man wearing worn cloth, in a city where there was no end of beggars.

"Go away!" one man shouted from his veranda. "We don't want you here!"

In November 1956, Abhay sent the latest edition of *Back to Godhead* to Dr. Rajendra Prasad, the first president of the Republic of India. "I beg to submit herewith," he wrote in the accompanying letter, "that by the grace of Shri Krishna and through his mercy personified—my spiritual master—I have realized most thoroughly that going 'Back to Godhead' is the highest privilege of mankind. Unfortunately, the present day civilization is overpowered by sense gratification. Please, therefore, save them from the great fall down," he wrote.

"Believe me or not," he continued, "I have got the clue of going 'Back to Godhead' just after leaving my present material body. In order to take along with me all my contemporary men and women of the world, I have started my paper, *Back to Godhead*, as one of the means to the way."

A close reading of his letters from the years prior to leaving India reveals the depth of Abhay's conviction. Krishna consciousness, as expressed in these many correspondences, was not one plan among others for moving humanity forward: It was *the* formula that would open the door to liberation from birth and death for "all contemporary men and women of the world."

"Please do not think of me as a madman," Abhay's letter to India's president continued, "when I say that I shall go 'Back to Godhead' after leaving my present material body. It is quite possible for everyone and all of us. I am seeking an interview with Your Honor herewith. I am sure your Excellency will be interested in cooperating with me. I am crying in the wilderness at the present moment. So please help me in this noble cause."

Despite the urgent tone of Abhay's letter, there is no record of Rajendra Prasad ever sending a reply.

He persevered with his door-to-door distribution of *Back to Godhead*. The streets of Delhi smoldered in 110-degree summer heat. As the day grew warmer, shopkeepers and apartment dwellers opened their doors and windows, and while delivering his magazines, Abhay became the casual confidant of a hundred conversations. In the midday heat, voices merged, the ground shifted, his head started to spin, and suddenly he keeled over. An acquaintance happened by at that moment. He helped Abhay into his car and drove him to a doctor who diagnosed heat stroke and ordered Abhay to rest.

Something had to change: Nothing was coming of this door-to-door routine in Delhi apart from fainting spells and rejection. He did not have to live in such an expensive and difficult place. He could move to Vrindavan, find a small spot to write his *Bhagavatam* commentary, and continue raising money to print books. Once the first canto of the *Bhagavatam* was printed, he would go to America. He was sixty years old. The clock was ticking.

He boarded the morning train, stepped down at Mathura station, mounted a tanga, and an hour later arrived in Krishna's village.

THIS WAS HIS FOURTH TIME in Vrindavan. His first visit in 1925 had been a brief pilgrimage while on business in nearby Agra. In 1932, he had joined his guru on pilgrimage. Three years later, he again met up with his spiritual master and received the instruction, "If you ever get money, print books." This time was different. He had come here for as long as it took to publish the first canto of *Srimad Bhagavatam*, collect his exit papers, and go where he had been ordered to go more than thirty years before.

Tall trees signaled that the tanga was entering the precincts of the village. Vrindavan was calm, unchanged, as if a pact had been struck between the people and all who lived there—humans and animals, plants and birds—that Krishna's home would forever remain unsullied by the material world. It was as he remembered: somnolent cows and cunning monkeys, white-saried widows making daily rounds of temples, sadhus and *pandits* chanting verses. Peacocks trumpeted, and in the distance, purling waves washed onto the Yamuna's shores. The sounds blended, reassuring one and all there was no reason to worry. The holy land of Sri Krishna was in good order. He walked the dusty streets as in years gone by, and there was always someone to greet, someone to talk to, someone to discuss philosophy with or share a kirtan, always someone who would tell a story or sing a song. At any moment, an old sadhu might sidle up, look him in the eye, and say, "Chaitanya Mahaprabhu was always chanting Hare Krishna!" and move on as though having bid him good morning. Oxcarts trundled along carrying fruits and vegetables to market. Children swam and splashed after school. In the evening, mothers cooked dinner, the men performed puja, pandits wrote commentaries by lantern light, and the temples filled with worshippers arriving for the final *arati* ceremony of the day.

At the end of a dirt road by the Yamuna River stood the small stone entrance to Vamsi Gopalaji Temple, a narrow, three-story building ornamented with domes and arches. Mahant Gopal, a temple pujari whom Abhay had befriended during his last visit, greeted him warmly. He led Abhay upstairs to the roof. From one side of the roof, Abhay saw the Yamuna flowing nearby. From the other, he saw temple spires and domes looming up over the village. Mahant Gopal showed him a small stand-alone room on the temple roof, with narrow double doors and barred windows to keep out monkeys. Gopal presented a government-stamped agreement. Abhay calculated that he could just afford the five rupees monthly rent and signed.

In the morning, he visited Vrindavan's principal temples—those that had been built by the Goswamis—then shopped for groceries in the open-air markets. He returned to his temple-roof quarters and used a kerosene burner and three-tiered brass cooker to prepare *dal* soup, vegetables, rice, and potatoes. With a handful of flour and a splash of water he kneaded a simple dough, tore off small pieces, rolled them into six-inch rounds, flame-roasted a few *chapatis*, offered prayers, and sat down to consume his one meal of the day. He lived on pennies and kept an exact ledger of every expenditure as though still running a pharmaceutical company, noting the cost of supplies, bus rides, and postage. The rest of the day was dedicated to writing.

FROM THE OUTSET, Abhay calculated there were three texts he would have to publish to make a mission in the West successful: two from Sanskrit and one from Bengali. The Sanskrit works were the Bhagavad Gita and *Srimad Bhagavatam*. The Gita was short: only 700 verses summarizing the essence of devotional life. The *Bhagavatam* was long: 18,000 verses divided into twelve cantos exploring Vedic cosmology and the lives of sages in remote times. Vaishnavas referred to the *Bhagavatam* as the post-graduate study of the Bhagavad Gita. The Gita ended with Krishna urging his warrior-devotee, Arjuna, to accept him as the Supreme Being, to set aside all other considerations and fight as an act of devotion. Still, the Gita only hinted at the destination after death of such a devoted soul. The *Bhagavatam* offered specific details concerning the structure of the universe and the migration of souls up and down its many planetary systems. Among all Sanskrit texts, the *Bhagavatam* was unrivaled, the "ripened fruit" of the tree of Vedic wisdom. "If all the books in the universe were burned to ashes," Bhaktisiddhanta Saraswati once said, "there would be no loss if only this one scripture remained."[45]

The *Bhagavatam* was also a prophetic work that described future as well as past events. The twelfth and final canto detailed what life would be like in Kali Yuga, the current cosmic age. People will not live long, the *Bhagavatam* predicted. Qualities of truthfulness, cleanliness, tolerance, mercy, and memory will atrophy. Law and justice will be for sale. Influence will be a matter of personal wealth, and wealth will follow deceit. Humanity during Kali Yuga will experience extreme shifts of cold and hot weather, and as a consequence, fruits and vegetables will shrink in size and lose their nutritional value. With food scarce, people will live in uncertainty and fear. The twelfth canto predicted that Kali Yuga would continue to deteriorate for

1,000 "celestial years," the equivalent of 432,000 Earth years. After that, the Golden Age, Satya Yuga, a time of peace and prosperity, would begin anew.

Stories in the *Bhagavatam* unfolded like layers in a nested Russian matryoshka doll: Tucked into each main narrative were hidden a dozen more. Scholars had given up trying to find the *ur*-text, the authentic original, since no sooner did one Sanskritist determine a date of origin than another found antecedents to a particular *Bhagavatam* story in yet older Sanskrit works. The *Bhagavatam* lacked not only a precise date of origin but a place of origin as well. References within the text suggested the *Bhagavatam* came into being at the dawn of time and existed in thousands of volumes on other planets, yet British scholars discounted the *Bhagavatam* as a later work, no older than perhaps a thousand years, long on sentiment and short on philosophy. "When we were in college," wrote Bhaktisiddhanta's father, the scholar-devotee Bhaktivinode Thakur, "we had a real hatred towards the *Bhagavata*. That great work looked like a repository of wicked and stupid ideas, scarcely adapted to the nineteenth century." In his forties, Bhaktivinode located a copy of Chaitanya Mahaprabhu's biography and found Mahaprabhu's explanations of the *Bhagavatam* to be "of such a charming character that we procured a copy of the *Bhagavata* complete and studied its texts.

"Oh!" he concluded, "What a trouble to get rid of prejudices gathered in unripe years!"[46]

The third text required for Abhay's mission in the West, a Bengali work, was *Chaitanya Charitamrita*, the official biography of Chaitanya Mahaprabhu written by Krishnadas Kaviraj Goswami within a half century of Mahaprabhu's departure from the world in 1533. The title translated as "the characteristics of the living force in eternity." Like the *Bhagavatam*, *Chaitanya Charitamrita* was also an elaborate composition of more than 11,000 verses. Abhay calculated that an English edition would comprise at least a dozen volumes.

Without the *Bhagavatam*, more complex dimensions of the Gita philosophy would be missing, and without Mahaprabhu's biography, no one would understand how to live the teachings of the *Bhagavatam*. Together these three texts would form a sturdy liturgical foundation for launching Krishna consciousness abroad. Creating commentaries would exercise him on several levels. The writing needed to be accessible for Westerners unfamiliar with Bhakti theology. Once printed, the books had to be distributed, and time was short. There was a combined total of more than 30,000 verses to render into English and explain, and he was already in his sixties. The pace would be daunting.

ON DAYS SET ASIDE FOR SELLING *Back to Godhead*, he packed copies in a cloth sack and boarded the morning train. With nowhere to stay in Delhi, he had to return to Vrindavan by evening, which gave him only a few hours of daylight. Sales were minimal, and he did not always collect enough to cover costs. Some days he made appointments with wealthy men to request support. A few responded with token donations for his cause. He befriended an ayurvedic doctor who promised assistance. One day Bhakti Dayita Madhav Maharaj from the local Gaudiya Math was bicycling by and saw Abhay standing at the gate of the doctor's large house.

"What are you waiting for?"

"I am waiting to get a five-rupee donation," Abhay called back.

After some hours, Bhakti Dayita Madhav Maharaj again passed by on his bicycle. Abhay was still standing there. "Did you get the five rupees?"

"No. The gentleman has not yet arrived," Abhay replied, "but I will wait."

"Let it go. I will give you five rupees."

Abhay thought for a moment. "Every month?"

The senior devotee noted Abhay's torn and weary clothes. "Let's make it ten," he said.

LIVING APART FROM HIS FAMILY freed Abhay to pursue support for his mission, and the frequency of his letter writing increased. To a prominent Kanpur industrialist he wrote, "The leaders of India in the name of secular government have engaged themselves in everything foreign. They have carefully set aside the treasure house of India's spiritual assets and are imitating the Western material way of life. So my idea of preaching in the foreign countries means that they are rather fed up with material advancement of knowledge. They are seeking the guidance of the *Vedanta Sutra* and Bhagavad Gita in an authentic way. And I am sure India will again go back to spiritual life when the principle is accepted by the Europeans and Americans."[47]

Abhay's letters demanded much from their readers. What would a businessman in 1950s Calcutta make of such a petition, sent by a stranger, written in awkward English, arguing that Westerners were seeking guidance

TOP: In 1935, Abhay Charan De (far right) attends a reception for disciples of Bhaktisiddhanta Saraswati after their return from Europe. Thirty years later, he would bring Krishna's teachings to the world.

BOTTOM: In the front row, from left to right: Abhay Charan De with his son, Prayagraj; father, Gour Mohan; and sister, Rajesvari, who is sitting holding Abhay's daughter, Sulakshana. Standing in the back row, from left to right: Abhay's wife, Radharani De; nephew, Tulasi; and brother, Krishna Charan. Photo taken in Allahabad, circa 1924.

Bhaktisiddhanta Saraswati Thakur (1874–1937), Founder-Acharya of the Gaudiya Math, leading Vaishnava scholar of his day, and spiritual master of Abhay Charan Bhaktivedanta (later known as Prabhupada).

Bhaktivinode Thakur (1838–1914), author, philosopher, court magistrate, spiritual reformer of Gaudiya Vaishnavism, and father of Bhaktisiddhanta Saraswati.

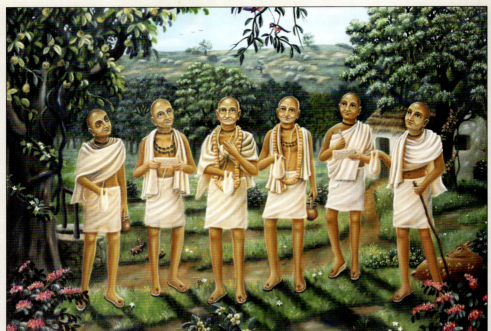

© BBTI

© Mandala Publishing

TOP: The Six Goswamis of Vrindavan, fifteenth- and sixteenth-century devotional teachers, were sent by Chaitanya Mahaprabhu to Krishna's village, Vrindavan, to resurrect places of pilgrimage and codify bhakti teachings.

BOTTOM: Bhaktisiddhanta Saraswati was an innovator who did things sannyasis had never done before, such as use cars in Krishna's service.

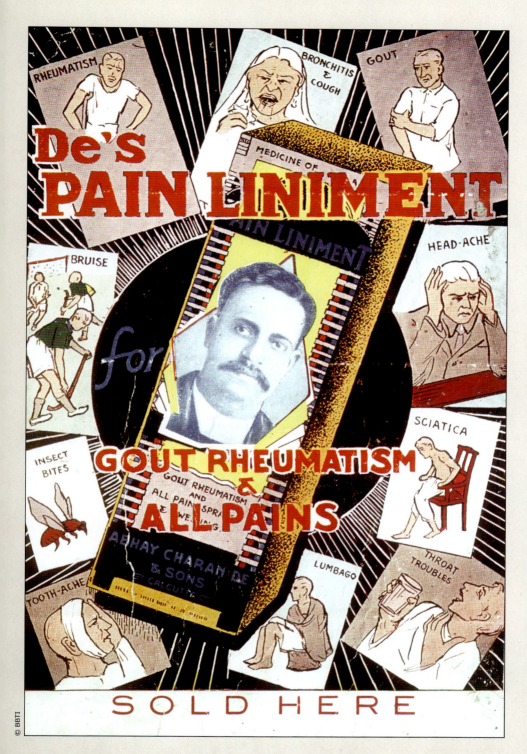

An ad for one of Abhay's pharmaceutical products, circa 1940.

Chaitanya Mahaprabhu (1486–1534) inaugurated the sankirtan movement by leading followers in chanting the Hare Krishna mantra through the streets of sixteenth-century Bengal. In doing so, he brought about a spiritual renaissance and the revitalization of the bhakti tradition.

TOP: Prabhupada attended the opening ceremony of ISKCON's Mayapur temple in 1973 with Bhakti Raksak Sridhar Maharaj (1895–1988), whom Prabhupada honored as a senior godbrother. At the lower left is Sridhar Maharaja's disciple and future successor, Bhakti Sundar Govinda Maharaj (1929–2010).

BOTTOM LEFT: Bhakti Prajnana Keshava Goswami (1898–1968), founder of the Sri Gaudiya Vedanta Samiti and Prabhupada's sannyasa guru.

BOTTOM RIGHT: Bhavatarini De, Prabhupada's sister (d. 1980), affectionately known as Pishima or "Aunti."

TOP: Bhaktisiddhanta Saraswati leads a sankirtan chanting party with disciples, following the example of Chaitanya Mahaprabhu, circa 1930.

BOTTOM LEFT: A painting of Yashoda with her child, Krishna, by renowned artist B.G. Sharma. Rasa theology proposes that when friendly affection for God is enhanced by a sense of responsibility for God's well-being, it resembles the nurturing, attentive love of a parent toward a child.

BOTTOM RIGHT: A painting of Radha and Krishna by B.G. Sharma. Radha and Krishna are described in bhakti texts as the Supreme Being in female and male forms. The love between them (madhurya rasa) is honored by devotees as the pinnacle of divine love.

from ancient Sanskrit scriptures, and concluding that Hindus would revert to their spiritual roots if Westerners did so first? The whole idea was insane.

Then again, so were most revolutionary ideas, but the Kanpur industrialist did not reply.

January 1, 1957, was the twentieth anniversary of Bhaktisiddhanta Saraswati's passing from this world. During the heyday of his mission, printing presses ran day and night in Gaudiya Math centers. Now the presses had been sold, and the institution had divided into many smaller efforts to continue Bhaktisiddhanta's mission—all within India. Was this the end of prophesies of a worldwide movement, of a global spiritual renaissance rising from the ashes of Kali Yuga? If his guru, a monumental devotee, could not make it happen, who was Abhay to presume to do better? You sent your servants door to door, Abhay wrote in a memorial poem, and the preaching then was strong.

"Now, in your absence," he wrote, "everything is darkness."[48]

IN THOSE EARLY DAYS before fame and an international institution, before millions of books and worldwide radio broadcasts of the Hare Krishna mantra, in the days when he was still called Abhay Babu and wore a white dhoti and a shopkeeper's jacket, A.C. Bhaktivedanta was rebuffed and often reviled for his persistence.

"The history of the West," he wrote Prime Minister Jawaharlal Nehru on August 4, 1958, "beginning from the time of the Greeks and Romans down to the modern age of atomic war, is a continuous chain of sense-gratifying materialism. The result is that the Westerners were never at peace within 3,000 years of historical records. Therefore, India may not waste her time in imitating the Western way of life. Do you think that horseless carriages or telephones or radio communications or any other such ephemeral facilities of life can bring real prosperity? No, they cannot. It is spiritual knowledge which makes a man really rich, not radio sets and motor cars. If you can spare a little time, I am sure to convince you."

Nehru did not reply.

If he could not get a reply to a letter sent inside India, how realistic was it to expect a better response in America? Would atheistic foreigners addicted to undignified habits ever accept the Gita's proposal to restrain their senses and live a life of devotion? Still, Mahaprabhu had predicted that the Holy Names would be sung worldwide, so sensible minds must surely be there—but how to reach them? Discussing scriptures and chanting mantras were nothing new for Krishna's devotees inside India: They had been doing so long before the tea-drinking *sahibs* arrived. But America was not India, and even if he did succeed in getting there, it would likely be a lonely visit.

In the fall of 1958, contemplating his poverty and isolation, Abhay wrote a poem.

> *I am sitting alone in Vrindavana-dhama.*
> *In this mood I am getting many realizations.*
> *I have my wife, sons, daughters, grandsons, everything,*
> *But I have no money, so they are a fruitless glory.*
> *Krishna has shown me the naked form of material nature;*
> *By His strength it has all become tasteless to me today.*

He had no idea what lay ahead, only that the past could no longer hold him and that some fundamental rip had occurred in the fabric of his life. His parents had died, his marriage had devolved into domestic nausea, and his commercial efforts had amounted to nil. He recalled the verse in *Srimad Bhagavatam* where Krishna described his way of reciprocating with the faithful, for those whom he would draw nearer to him, and Abhay added it to his poem:

> *"I gradually take away all the wealth of those upon whom I am merciful."*
> *How was I able to understand this mercy of the all-merciful?*
> *Everyone has abandoned me, seeing me penniless—*
> *Wife, relatives, friends, brothers, everyone.*
> *This is misery, but it gives me a laugh. I sit alone and laugh.*
> *In this maya-samsara [material world], whom do I really love?*
> *Where have my loving father and mother gone now?*
> *And where are all my elders, who were my own folk?*
> *Who will give me news of them, tell me who?*
> *All that is left of this family life is a list of names*

DONATIONS FOR PRINTING TRICKLED IN, and he hoarded every penny until there was enough money to print another issue of *Back to Godhead*, the first in two years. In October 1958, 1,000 copies rolled off the grimy letterset press at Kumar Jain's print shop, and Abhay took once more to the streets, a sixty-four-year-old missionary with pointy white rubber shoes and a stack of magazines.

At night, more dreams came of his spiritual master urging him to accept the sannyasa staff, dreams too frequent to ignore. Despite his hesitations, he wrote to Bhaktivilas Tirtha Maharaj, leader of the Chaitanya Math in Calcutta, requesting his blessings to become a sannyasi and travel to America. Tirtha Maharaj responded: Come here and work under me, then we will decide about your going abroad.

Abhay knew Tirtha Maharaj barely had enough money to maintain his math, let alone print books or finance a mission to America. Shortly after receiving Tirtha Maharaj's reply in the mail, Abhay met with him in person. "The discussion was loud," Dr. Verma, Tirtha Maharaj's secretary recalled.

The day after speaking with Tirtha Maharaj, Abhay called a meeting. Since his guru Bhaktisiddhanta Saraswati's movement had now splintered into a number of independent institutions, Abhay decided to confer with his trusted godbrother B.R. Sridhar Maharaj and his disciple B.S. Govinda. Also in attendance were Abhay's son, Vrindavan Chandra, and Abhay's sister, Bhavatarini, whose marriage had not been going well, and who spent a fair amount of time with Abhay's family. The group heard him out and gave their opinions and support.

"Yes, it would be better if you become a sannyasi," Bhavatarini said. "Don't worry about your family. I will take care of them. I have five sons who each have an income. In any case, in your house they do not want that spiritual way of life."

"Because of my close relationship with your family," Sridhar Maharaj said, "it would be better if I did not perform the ceremony. Best approach Keshava Maharaj in Mathura. I can then continue to support them in your absence." Abhay took the recommendation to heart and traveled quickly to Mathura.

"YOU MUST DO IT," Keshava Maharaj said. "Without accepting the renounced order of life, nobody can become a preacher."

"I don't know if I have the strength," Abhay confessed.

"That strength will come from above," Keshava Maharaj said, "from your Gurudev acting on you. He will give you strength to carry out his order. You just be the instrument."[49]

To spread Krishna's teaching abroad required someone who was an exemplar of the bhakti tradition yet flexible enough to adapt its teachings to a world governed by science and technology. Abhay had that balance. He was a devotee raised in strict Vaishnava fashion yet also educated in chemistry and economics, a person with his feet on the ground and his heart surrendered to God. He had no pretenses about being an emissary sent by Krishna, but his determination to do what his guru had asked was unshakeable, and he agreed with Keshava Maharaj: The strength to do the impossible would come from above. He just had to agree to become the instrument. Entering the sannyasa order was the first step.

On September 17, 1959, in a 50- by 25-foot room on the second floor of the Keshavaji Math, B.V. Narayan Maharaj—a disciple of Keshava Maharaj—prepared the sacrificial fire. Abhay's head was shaved, his *tilak* formed impeccable double lines on his nose and forehead, and he was dressed in saffron, the color of those who no longer belonged to the material world. Another disciple of the late Bhaktisiddhanta Saraswati, Akinchana Krishna Das, sang prayers. A handful of math residents were in attendance at the sannyasa ceremony, which began at 8 a.m. and continued until 3 p.m., and when it ended there were embraces and tears of congratulations.

He walked out into the heat of summer and took a boat to one of the islands in the middle of the Yamuna River. There, he dragged the boat up onto the sandy shore and walked for a while. Renunciation, it seemed, was worse in the contemplating of it than in the actual doing. "Have the trees forgotten to create fruits for you to eat?" sage Sukadev declared in the *Srimad Bhagavatam*. "If you are tired, are there no open fields for your bed? And if you are thirsty, are there no rivers to quench your thirst?"

He paused to push sand into the shape of a small hill and stuck his bamboo sannyasa staff in the middle of the mound, like the American flag at Iwo Jima or young King Arthur's sword, Excalibur, set in its stone. He raised his arms to the sky and shouted, *"Haribol! Haribol!"*[50] Then he retrieved his staff and made his way back to shore.

In Vrindavan, no one called him Abhay Babu anymore. He was Swami Maharaj, or Swamiji for short.

In 1959, Abhay resided briefly in a temple in the Chippiwada section of Delhi.
Photo taken by his son Vrindavan Chandra.

On September 17, 1959, Abhay (right) received sannyasa initiation from Keshava Maharaj (center) in preparation for his journey to the West. Also initiated that day was one of Abhay's godbrothers, Sanatana Das (left), age ninety.

CHAPTER THREE

Give up all other duties and surrender unto Me. Have no fear.
—SRI KRISHNA IN THE BHAGAVAD GITA 18.66

VRINDAVAN, 1959

At last he was a member of the renounced order—poorer and older but free from the anchors that had held him back from full-time dedication to his guru's mission. At his age, most men handed in their retirement papers, met up with friends, joined clubs, ate meals, and felt relieved the next morning to discover they had survived the night. Retirees played chess, settled into a routine earned after a lifetime of victories and disappointments, made a comfortable home, and awaited the inevitable.

There would be no such capitulating to the golden years for Swamiji, who felt zero compulsion to mellow with age and had not a drop of self-pity. During his nearly forty years of married life, when answering customer complaints, resolving supplier problems, or tolerating partnership with an embittered wife, not once did he ever mistake the drudgery as a prelude to comfortable retirement. Someone, somewhere, calculated that great innovations were made by pioneers before age thirty. Swamiji defied statistics. Now was the time, at age sixty-five, for a battle plan. He kept no souvenirs, harbored no regrets, and saw nothing now to stop him from taking on the world. He would finish the first canto and then leave for America. He would print three volumes now, and the rest would follow later, somehow. His English prose was not perfect, but this was Kali Yuga, an emergency situation, like a house fire. Even imperfect cries of alarm could save lives.

"Our capacity of presenting the matter in adequate language, specially a foreign language, will certainly fail," he wrote in the opening passages of his commentary on the *Bhagavatam*, "and there may be so many literary discrepancies in spite of our honest attempt to present it in the proper way. But we are sure that with all our faults in this connection the seriousness of the subject matter will be taken into consideration and the leaders of the society will still accept this on account of its being an honest attempt for glorifying the Almighty Great so much now badly needed."

GAURACHAND GOSWAMI, a caste Brahmin and head priest of Vrindavan's famed Radha Damodar Temple, invited him to live in two of the temple's ground-floor rooms, and Swamiji gratefully accepted. His quarters were modest enclosures, with an entrance so low visitors had to duck down. One room served as his kitchen and workspace. In this room he kept a trunk for clothes, papers, and a few pots. He slept in the second room, a few steps across a stone veranda, furnished with a kerosene lamp and wooden bedframe with woven rope mattress. The kitchen window gave onto the courtyard behind the temple. Each morning through the carved lattice came wafts of air laden with a heady blend of many scents: incense, the musky dust from crumbling bricks, the earthy aroma of cow manure, the loamy perfume of vegetables freshly cut, and an undertone of sediment from the nearby Yamuna River. Here, in Vrindavan, were the *samadhis* or tombs of Chaitanya Mahaprabhu's chief disciples. Five hundred years before, Rupa, Sanatan, and the other followers of Mahaprabhu met in this sacred village to analyze Krishna philosophy, write their commentaries on palm leaves, cook together, and sing. Here, Rupa Goswami composed *Bhakti-rasamrita-sindhu*, which traced the development and subtleties of love for God. Here, too, the Goswamis wrote poetry and songs, for ultimately bhakti lifted followers beyond philosophy into the world of devotional music and dance and the heart's spontaneous expressions of love for God. The small stone room, with its close proximity to the places of the Goswamis, was a perfect spot for the Swami to compose his scriptural commentaries.

His life was so impoverished at this time that B.V. Narayan Maharaj, a disciple of Keshava Maharaj, gave him his own wool *chadar*, concerned that he would fall ill without something to protect him from the morning chill. "The walls of his room were crumbling apart, but he was too consumed in the writing of *Srimad Bhagavatam* to care for that,"[51] Narayan Maharaj recalled.

A young man, twenty-one-year-old Gopal Chandra Ghosh, befriended the Swami. Ghosh visited one evening and found Swamiji coughing. Ghosh paid his respects and left quickly so Swamiji could rest. The next morning, he returned to find him stronger and back writing.

"Today you are feeling better?" Ghosh asked.

"At night my Prabhupada came in my dream," the Swami said, referring to his guru Bhaktisiddhanta Saraswati. "He encouraged me, saying that I should write. I have received my guru's mercy. He blessed me and gave me power. I was too much anxious for the *Bhagavatam* commentary. In my dream, he told me, 'You just write, and all six of the Goswamis will help you.'"

In Delhi, the printer who had previously handled his flyers for the now defunct League of Devotees introduced him to Sri Krishna Pandit, proprietor of a temple in the Chippiwada neighborhood of Old Delhi. Pandit admired Swamiji's determination to fulfill his guru's order and offered him use of a room on the roof of his temple. Now the Swami would have a place to work in Delhi when he came to oversee printing or to sell his magazines. The journey from Radha Damodar Temple involved taking a horse-drawn tanga to Mathura, then a train from Mathura to the Old Delhi station near Chandni Chowk, then a walk down the broad avenue that ran through the city, past the famed Red Fort to the Chippiwada neighborhood where streets were so narrow no cars could pass. Balconies overhead, crowded only inches apart, formed a webbed umbrella through which stippled patches of sunlight filtered down.

At Chippiwada, he rose at 3:00 a.m. to translate verses and compose commentaries, which he called "purports." At first, he wrote everything longhand. Eventually, he purchased a used American typewriter, a heavy Corona, old and awkward with keys so weighted it took strong fingers to strike the page. When not typing, the Swami accepted doles of vegetables and rice from his host and cooked them over a small stove fueled with cow dung cakes. Then he offered the humble meal to Krishna with prayers, as he had done since childhood. His modest meal finished, he returned to writing.

He referred to two books for his work. One was a commentary of the *Srimad Bhagavatam* by his spiritual master, Bhaktisiddhanta Saraswati; the

other was a larger volume containing commentaries by Vaishnava acharyas of the past. The acharyas had written with a silver needlepoint stylus
on fragile palm or banana leaves or else on strips of cotton cloth. When
a manuscript was completed, the leaves were pressed between wooden
boards and secured with a cord threaded through holes drilled through the
boards and leaves. A manuscript could last hundreds of years if properly
preserved, but whatever original manuscripts still existed sat on shelves in
museums, temples, and academic institutions, exposed to the elements and
crumbling into dust. Many of these were one-of-a-kind works. Publishers
in 1950s India focused on technical manuals and postmodern fiction and
had no interest in salvaging ancient scriptural writings. Swamiji's volume of
commentaries was one of the few compilations available.

"Every day he came, and we talked," a Vrindavan merchant recalled
twenty years later. "He would tell of his difficulties publishing books. Such
difficulties! But he said, 'I have temples already in America, and many
people worship Krishna there. Only time now hides them from vision.' He
spoke like that, and who was I to question? He had the manner of a *raja*, a
king, and I believed him."

"You say that now," a fellow Brijbasi broke in, laughing, "but back then
you thought he was a beggar. We were thinking, 'Why this old man has
such fancies? He lives as a Vrindavan sadhu, so he has reached life's goal—
why was he bothering with such dreams? Only to disturb his mind?' Of
course, now we say, 'Oh yes, Prabhupada was my good friend for so many
years, I encouraged his mission, I knew he was a *mahatma*,' and so forth.
We were all fools. We could not see this old man was a future *jagaδ-guru*
[world teacher]."[52]

In February 1961, on the birth or "appearance" day of Bhaktisiddhanta
Saraswati, Swamiji attend a gathering of fellow disciples. The custom on
such commemorative occasions was for each disciple to read an appreciation of their guru before the assembly. Bhaktivedanta Swami's offering was
more like an explosion.

"Merely having a festival of flowers and fruits does not constitute
worship," he began. "Actual worship of the spiritual master means to
serve his instructions. Oh, shame, shame, my dear brothers! Aren't we
embarrassed by what we are doing? Our spiritual master has told us
to go out and preach. Let the neophytes remain inside the temples and
ring the bells. Just open your eyes and see the tragedy that has arisen.

Everyone has become a sense enjoyer and has given up preaching. From sea to sea, crossing the Earth, all of us should unite in purpose and flood the world with an inundation of Krishna conscious preaching. Please give up your stubbornness—there is no better time than this. Oh come, all my Godbrothers, this is the auspicious occasion to unite as one!"

His appeal may have impressed attendees, but it failed to inspire their participation. Many of the senior men in attendance had opened maths—some directly instructed to do so by Bhaktisiddhanta—and their priority was to propagate their guru's mission in India. Others were old and lacked the strength to travel. If Bhaktivedanta Swami wanted to take Mahaprabhu's message abroad, he was certainly welcome to try. But he would have to do so without them.

AMONG THOSE WHOM HE APPROACHED for funds to print the first volume of *Srimad Bhagavatam* was Hanuman Prasad Poddar, head of the Gita Press in Gorakhpur. At the time, Gita Press was the world's largest publisher of Hindu religious texts. The company's catalog listed works in a dozen local languages. Publications included several editions of the Bhagavad Gita, the twin epics *Ramayana* and *Mahabharata*. and translations of the 108 *Upanishads* and 18 *Puranas*. Gita Press also published storybooks advertised as "especially for women and children" and transcripts of discourses by popular religious speakers.

Gorakhpur was 513 miles from Delhi, and the trip cost Bhaktivedanta Swami dearly. On August 8, 1962, his daily ledger showed a balance of 130 rupees, and by the time he arrived, his coffers were down to 57 rupees. But the trip turned out to be a well-calculated gamble. Poddar examined the manuscript and pledged 4,000 rupees toward its printing.

With funds in hand for printing volume one, Bhaktivedanta Swami next approached Hitsaran Sharma, owner and operator of Radha Press, whose sole machine printed tiny 10-point type. Bhaktivedanta Swami was an avid reader and objected that the type was too small. So Hitsaran Sharma took the project to a colleague, Gautam Sharma, of O.K. Press.

In the final months of 1962, the Swami traveled to O.K. Press to at last oversee the printing of volume one, first canto, *Srimad Bhagavatam*. Everything at O.K. Press was done by hand. Workers loaded the Swami's supply of paper onto the press's metal feeding platform. Then they smoothed layers of viscous black ink across the machine's feeder well and started the press. As printed sheets spooled off the other end, workers folded them twice into eight-page signatures and collated the folded sheets into a completed book. At the next station, workers stitched the collated signatures together and positioned the book blocks one by one in a vise. Edges of each block were trimmed neat with a handsaw. Thick cardboard covers were positioned front, back, and spine, and a thin brown burlap cloth glued over the whole. Then the finished books were set aside to allow time for the glue to dry. While the rest of the world was advancing to larger, more streamlined methods of printing, India in the 1960s had not moved far past the days of Gutenberg.

Back at Radha Press, Hitsaran Sharma printed dust jackets that would be folded and wrapped around this first volume of *Srimad Bhagavatam*. "Swamiji had a great haste," Sharma recalled. "He used to say, 'Time is going, time is going! Quick, do it!' He would be annoyed with me also, and he would have me do his work first."

When the printing and binding were done, 1,100 copies of the 400-page book sat in stacks. He had done it: one book. The total cost was 7,000 rupees. Swamiji made an agreement with Sharma to take 100 copies at a time, sell them, and pay off the balance.

Setting out from his residence at Radha Damodar Temple in Vrindavan, he traveled each week to Delhi and presented copies to statesmen and scholars, requesting that they write endorsements. Hanuman Prasad Poddar wrote a review. So did the *Adyar Library Bulletin*, which noted the Swami's "vast and deep study of the subject." Fellow disciples of Bhaktisiddhanta offered favorable comments, as did the governor of Uttar Pradesh and India's vice president, Zakir Hussain. With these reviews in hand, the Swami convinced libraries and universities to purchase copies for their collections. The Ministry of Education bought fifty copies. The U.S. Embassy purchased eighteen. He deposited the money and returned to his room in Vrindavan to continue writing.

It took him more than a year, but by January 1964, he had saved enough money to print the second volume of the *Srimad Bhagavatam*. Like the first volume, the second was 400 pages long, bound in heavy cardboard and covered with brick-colored cloth. One Delhi bookseller, Manoharlal Jain, founder of the Munshilal Manoharlal bookstore chain, was happy to see Swamiji return with a new book. Jain had sold more than 150 copies of volume one and expected to sell as many of volume two.

Courteous words, a few books sold—all well and good. But he was still in India. The money from these few sales was negligible, and his mission lay abroad. He was sixty-eight years old. Time had run out.

THROUGH CONTACTS IN DELHI, the Swami secured a meeting with S. Radhakrishnan. A letter of recommendation from India's new president would certainly expedite his visa for America. During his tenure as Spalding Professor of Religion and Ethics at Oxford University, Radhakrishnan had been inspired by the teachings of eighth-century scholar Shankara, whose Advaita Vedanta philosophy defined Krishna as a temporary manifestation of a higher impersonal truth. The Swami knew Radhakrishnan was a Shankarite "Neo-Vedantist" with little sympathy for Krishna worship, but he did not mince words on arriving at the president's office.

"I have been ordered to preach in the foreign countries," he said, "and I need your help."

"What will be the result of preaching in foreign countries?" Radhakrishnan replied skeptically. Religion was not high on his list of exports. Bhaktivedanta took the offensive, critiquing Radhakrishnan for not implementing religious policies.

"You may be president of India, but what are you doing for the nation's benefit? There are so many criminals, yet you are failing to reform them. You should be like Narada with Valmiki," he said, referring to the Vaishnava sage, Narada Muni, who had reformed a murderer by convincing him to chant the names of Rama. "My advice is that you begin yourself hearing the teachings of *Srimad Bhagavatam*," Bhaktivedanta said, "and then teach the public that chanting will cure their materialistic disease."[53]

If the impoverished Swami was bold enough to challenge India's president on his record of social reform, Radhakrishnan was enough of a sport to issue a challenge in return. He proposed that the Swami teach *Srimad Bhagavatam* in a local prison. If, after some time, his efforts had any positive effect on prisoners, Radhakrishnan would provide a letter of recommendation. He arranged for the Swami to teach Tuesdays and Thursdays each week in a Delhi correctional facility, and after two months, prison officials deemed the experiment a success. "I am glad to see that my lectures have brought some changes in the mind of the young offenders," Bhaktivedanta wrote to one of the guards. "The means which I have adopted is spiritual, and it works more quickly than any material means."[54]

Radhakrishnan kept his word, and Bhaktivedanta had his letter of recommendation.

LITTLE BY LITTLE, he navigated the torpid waters of India's byzantine bureaucracy in pursuit of the papers needed to travel to America. Still, before he could leave there was a third volume of the *Bhagavatam* to be printed. Funds remained low. He had heard from godbrothers that Sumati Morarjee, head of Scindia Steam Navigation Company, sometimes helped sadhus and that she had once made a donation to the Bombay Gaudiya Math. He traveled from Delhi to Bombay intending to meet her, but his first attempts through her secretaries were unsuccessful. One hot day he arrived at the Scindia offices and sat on the front steps of the building, prepared to wait however long until Morarjee came out. Late in the afternoon, Morarjee left the building and noticed the elderly man in sannyasa robes. The Swami rose, introduced himself, and showed her the first two volumes of his work.

"I want you to help me print the third volume," he said.

"Come tomorrow," Morarjee said.

SUMATI MORARJEE'S INTEREST in the Swami's proposal reflected her own Vaishnava heritage. She had been born in 1907 to wealthy Bombay parents who named her Jamuna after the sacred river that flowed through Krishna's village. As a follower of the Vallabha *sampradaya* (lineage) of Vaishnavism, Morarjee was a dedicated devotee of Sri Nathaji, a deity of Krishna popular in that line. Apart from their shared religious background, Morarjee may have been impressed with the Swami's determination to break new ground, something she had done in her career as the first woman to head the Indian National Steamship Owners Association, a traditionally male bastion. At a young age, she married the only son of Scindia Steamship Navigation Company's founder, Narottam Morarjee, and by 1946 had become head of the company, managing more than six thousand employees and dozens of ships servicing Germany, the Pacific coasts, Poland, and Canada. During the war years, Morarjee had kept close contact with Mahatma Gandhi and played an active role in the movement for India's independence. "It is not purely for business motives that we today concentrate on shipping," she once commented. "We did business in merchandise for centuries, but our most precious cargo has been ideas of universal brotherhood and deep spirituality."[55]

"WE HAVE MET BEFORE," Morarjee announced when Bhaktivedanta Swami arrived at her office the following day. "I remember meeting you in

Kurukshetra," she said and described seeing Swamiji sitting under a tree at that holy place of pilgrimage and watching him chant on his beads. "I approached you and asked for your blessings," she recalled. Now she would be pleased to reciprocate by providing the money to print his third volume of *Srimad Bhagavatam*.

In January 1965, the third volume was printed, and Swamiji could prepare in earnest for his journey to America. There had never been any question where he would go first. Others wanting to leave India dreamed of London, but that was for selfish considerations: A British education guaranteed a well-paid position back in India. New York was the place for a missionary seeking to convert the world to Krishna worship. Some nights he dreamed he had already arrived and was walking the streets of the city.

"Most of us at that time were quite doubtful he would succeed in going," said a Vrindavan resident, remembering back forty years later. "He was practically penniless, without sponsors or connections in the West. He came one day excited, having just finished his *Srimad Bhagavatam* third volume. 'Now I am ready to go,' he said and asked us to please bless his books so he could cross the ocean and be successful. He passed the books around, and we touched them."[56] The small group understood the risks of such a journey. One of the attendants from Radha Damodar Temple brought him a garland from the deity and placed it around his neck. They embraced and cried.

A POPULAR STORY IS TOLD OF HRIDAYANANDA BABAJI, who lived next door to the Radha Damodar Temple, where Swamiji had his humble quarters. Often, after midnight, Babaji heard a voice crying from inside the temple courtyard. One night he climbed to the roof of his house and peered into the courtyard. There by the light of a full moon, he saw Swamiji kneeling down and sweeping the ground in front of Rupa Goswami's tomb with a small broom.

"Hey Rupa! Hey Sanatan! Hey Gurudev!" the Swami cried through tears. "Please give me your mercy. Without your mercy, I cannot do anything. Give me the strength to fulfill your orders."

Hridayananda Babaji approached him the next morning and offered to help with some of his chores. While Swamiji was out, Hridayananda noticed cobwebs hanging from the ceiling and brushed them away with a broom. Bhaktivedanta Swami returned to his quarters and found spiders crawling across the floor.

"Why have you disturbed them?" he asked.

Hridayananda explained that he had been cleaning but took care not to hurt them. That may be, the Swami replied, "but we are the newcomers to Vrindavan. These spiders and their ancestors have been residents for generations and deserve our respect."

"Never have I seen anyone do *sadhana* like he did," the elder Babaji recalled years later, referring to the Swami's daily meditations and devotional character. "I have lived all my life in Braj [Vrindavan], and I have never seen anyone like him."[57]

FINDING A SPONSOR for his entry into America proved as difficult as getting the money to go. A sponsor had to be a permanent U.S. resident, gainfully employed, and willing to guarantee that all his expenses would be met. A mutual friend introduced the Swami to a businessman named Agarwal. The Swami described his dilemma.

"I have a son," Agarwal said, "an engineer in Pennsylvania."

The Swami thought nothing more of it. Then, three months later, he was contacted by the Ministry of External Affairs and informed that his No-Objection Certificate had arrived from the Indian consulate in New York, signed by Gopal Agarwal of Butler, Pennsylvania.

On June 10, 1965, Bhaktivedanta Swami's passport was ready. Now he needed a ticket. He returned to the Scindia Steamship offices in Bombay and presented the passport and sponsorship letter to Morarjee. Even with all the requisite papers, she refused to book him passage on one of her ships.

"You are too old," she chided, "and New York is too cold for someone your age. Besides, nobody there will listen to you." The Swami assured her that he would be fine and that Krishna would protect him. Reluctantly, Morarjee agreed to book him passage on the *Jaladuta* (*The Sea Messenger*), a cargo ship bound for New York harbor.

"This will be a return ticket," she cautioned. "I fully expect to see you back here very soon. You will need a P-form," she added, referring to a certificate from the State Bank of India declaring that he had no debts and was free to travel. While waiting to get the form, Morarjee invited the Swami to stay at the Scindia Colony, an apartment complex for employees of the company located in a residential suburb not far from Juhu Beach, north of Bombay. Each evening at 6 p.m. during the two weeks of his stay at the Colony, Morarjee sent her car to bring Swamiji to her home, and each evening he read to her from *Srimad Bhagavatam*. You will need warm clothes, she said, and sent her secretary to buy him a wool jacket and new dhotis.

THERE HAD BEEN A TIME when Indians took pride in their spiritual history, knowing India was the destination chosen by avatars and sages to make their appearance, a nation with wisdom to offer the world. After independence, that changed. India in the 1950s and 1960s was a nation preoccupied with factories and technology. Government leaders such as Prime Minister Nehru never invoked India's spiritual past as a rallying point for the people; rather, they advocated training India's children to become the workforce for an industrialized future. "Let Our Factories Be Our Temples" read government signs posted in classrooms across the country. Government money built thousands of schools, colleges, and institutions of advanced engineering with this industrialized future in mind. The funding assured that attention would focus not on the cultivation of devotion but on "progress," meaning the construction of dams, irrigation canals, roads, highways, and hydroelectric power stations, and on retooling India to become a global power. As industry and commerce rose to the top of national priorities, religion sank to the bottom. Marching toward their future, Indians erased their past.

Bhaktivedanta Swami was keenly aware that India was part of his guru's vision for a world Vaishnava culture, but he could never compete with a government hell-bent on modernization. If Indians were so fascinated by Western imports, then he would go to the West, establish his mission there, and bring back something truly worth importing: Krishna, courtesy of the United States of America.

THE *JALADUTA* was scheduled to sail from Calcutta on August 13, 1965. On the morning of Friday, August 6, Bhaktivedanta Swami traveled to Mayapur, the birthplace of Chaitanya Mahaprabhu, to visit the tomb of his guru, Bhaktisiddhanta Saraswati, and consecrate the upcoming voyage to his memory. Most dead bodies in India were cremated, but the bodies of revered teachers were considered sacred by virtue of their lifetime of service and buried in samadhis or tombs that became places of pilgrimage. In a village near the samadhi of Bhaktisiddhanta stood the sixteenth-century home of Advaita Acharya, one of Chaitanya Mahaprabhu's inner circle during those years when the chanting of Hare Krishna made its public appearance. The house was maintained by an attendant.

"In the 1940s and 1950s," the attendant recalled, "a Bengali gentleman used to visit here every month or two. I never disturbed his devotions, but sometimes I noticed his eyes were full of tears and his voice would choke while chanting. After chanting for many hours, he would thank me and leave. Then he did not come for a long time. In August 1965, I saw a saffron-clothed sannyasi sitting in the back, and I recognized him as that Bengali man from before, but that day he was chanting and weeping even more than he used to. Evening came, and he paid his prostrated obeisance for a long time. When he stood up, I told him that I remembered him from long ago and asked who he was.

"'My name is Abhay Charanaravinda Bhaktivedanta Swami,' he told me. 'My guru, Bhaktisiddhanta Saraswati Prabhupada, gave me an impossible mission. He told me to cross the ocean to the Western countries. There are countless souls there who have never heard of Krishna and are suffering greatly. I do not know how this mission will be successful. I want to satisfy my guru's desire, but I am feeling unqualified, so I have come to this place where the *sankirtan*[58] movement began.'

"He had tears falling down his cheeks," the attendant recalled. "Then he said that the following day he was leaving for America. He did not know what would befall him there. So he had come here to pray most earnestly for his guru's help.

"Then he asked for my blessings," the attendant said, "and he left."

FOR THIRTY YEARS the Swami had attempted to launch his mission inside India, but nothing had worked. Contracts for properties fell through, pleas for financing failed, letters to heads of state went unanswered. He had even walked the streets of Delhi with a self-published newspaper, approaching strangers seated at outdoor cafes and politely entreating them to purchase a copy.

Here he was, finally on his way to America, and maybe Sumati Morarjee was right. It was foolish for a man his age to pursue a dream with no money or contacts. He was a strict vegetarian. What would he eat? Winter was coming. How would he survive the cold? Teachers who had gone West before him—Swami Vivekananda, Paramhansa Yogananda, Rabindranath Tagore, and others—were younger and more experienced travelers. Swamiji was about to turn seventy, and he had never been outside India.

He had written to his middle son, Mathura Mohan, letting him know that he was at last leaving on his mission and asking for his help. He offered Mathura Mohan a monthly salary of 100 rupees if he would agree to oversee future printings of his books and magazines while he was in America. Mathura Mohan had not forgiven his father for renouncing their family. He refused the offer of employment and declined to show up at the pier when his father boarded the *Jaladuta*.

The Swami placed a call to his youngest son, Vrindavan Chandra. Please come, he asked, and take me to the ship. Twenty-six-year old Vrindavan Chandra arrived by taxi at the Scindia residences in North Calcutta around 5 a.m. on August 13, 1965. The Scindia freight office had taken responsibility for loading onto the *Jaladuta* 200 sets of the Swami's three-volume *Srimad Bhagavatam* packed in metal trunks, and Vrindavan Chandra found that his father was not carrying much, only a small suitcase, an umbrella, a trunk for personal items, and a bag of dry cereal. If the West provided nothing acceptable to eat, he could soak the cereal in water and live on that. They loaded everything into the taxi and drove off.

The *Jaladuta*'s gangplank was down, ready to receive its crew. Bhaktivedanta embraced his son, turned, and boarded the ship.

"I took it calmly," Vrindavan Chandra remembered, "but psychologically, after all, he was my father. As a child, I had accompanied him on trips to Mayapur and Navadwip. I had stayed with him also in Chippiwada, Delhi, in 1964, but to be very frank, the family had an extremely hard time when he took sannyasa. We suffered from that. And now, going to America—I was simply crying. I was going to miss him."

The crew of the *Jaladuta* knew what lay ahead. They had made the crossing before and were prepared for violent storms and gale-force winds. The trip across treacherous waters was scheduled to take more than a month. They had heard about their elderly passenger and watched him walk up the gangplank, ready to chase an impossible dream. Yet weren't all great journeys just that, impossible dreams? Climbing to the top of the world's tallest mountain with crampons and gloves, diving to the bottom of the ocean in a tin bucket, riding into outer space on a giant firecracker—was it so different, traveling halfway round the globe armed with an umbrella and a bag of cereal, determined to respiritualize humanity? There were only two possible outcomes to such folly.

He would succeed, or he would die trying.

YOUNG KISHANLAL SHARMA grew up in Vrindavan. By age ten, his duties included caring for his father's cows and delivering metal containers of fresh milk to village residents. As a boy in the early 1960s, he watched Bhaktivedanta Swami go from house to house, begging alms. On days when the elder sadhu came to the Sharma home, dressed in his tattered dhoti and wearing dusty sandals on his feet, Swamiji held out a metal cup, and Kishanlal's father filled it with fresh milk. They spoke for some time of the sad shape of the world, of how fortunate they were to live in Krishna's land, and of the Swami's plans to share Krishna with the world. Mr. Sharma smiled indulgently, marveling at how consistently an old man could nurse a dream.

Sometimes Mr. Sharma sent his son, Kishanlal, to bring milk to Swamiji's room in nearby Radha Damodar Temple. One day, with the metal container swinging back and forth on his handlebars, young Kishanlal biked to the temple, but the gates to Swamiji's rooms were locked. Kishanlal knocked on the door of the pujari, the temple priest.

"Where's Swamiji?" he asked.

"Swamiji is gone," the pujari replied. "He has gone to the West."

THE SCINDIA STEAM NAVIGATION CO. LTD.
BOMBAY

№ 774

Place of issue _CALCUTTA_ Date _4. 8._ 19_65_

CABIN CLASS
NON-TRANSFERABLE PASSAGE TICKET

PER Regular Cargo Carrier s.s. _JALADUTA_ embarking about _____ 19__
m.v.

From the port of _CALCUTTA BACK_ to the port of _____

Names	AGE Yrs.	AGE Mths.	Cabin No.	Berth No.	Passage Fare	Taxes
1 Sri. ABHAY CHARAN ARAVINDA BHAKTIVEDANTA	69					
2 SWAMI.		1				
3						
4						
5 (Complimentary		Ticket	with	Food)		
6						
7						

Adults _1_   Children _—_   Infants _—_   TOTAL _one_

IT IS MUTUALLY AGREED that this contract ticket is issued by or on behalf of THE SCINDIA STEAM NAVIGATION CO. LTD. and is accepted by the passenger(s) on the terms and conditions printed or endorsed on the face and back of this ticket.

For The Scindia Steam Navigation Co. Ltd.

(K. B. Mehta)
Senior Deputy Manager

TOP: On August 13, 1965, at age seventy, the Swami left India for America. He sailed on a cargo ship, suffered two near-fatal heart attacks at sea, and arrived in New York City a month later without funds, a home, or contacts.

BOTTOM: The Swami's "complimentary ticket with food" for passage to America.

PART TWO

AMERICA

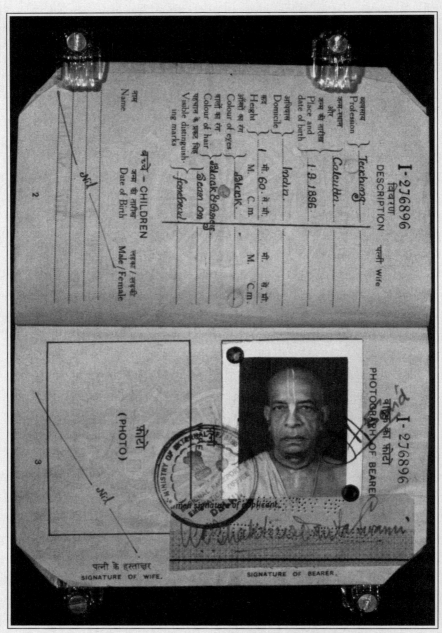

The Swami's passport detailed his profession as "teaching," his height as just under 5'3", and the clay tilak on his forehead as a "visible distinguishing mark."

CHAPTER FOUR

I am victory and adventure.

—SRI KRISHNA IN THE BHAGAVAD GITA, 10.36

ON BOARD THE *JALADUTA*, AUGUST 1965

The first heart attack occurred just days after the *Jaladuta* left port. *The Sea Messenger* crossed the Bay of Bengal, sailed out into the Indian Ocean, and from there, into a foreboding Arabian Sea, where high waves buffeted the 13,000-ton vessel. From the moment the *Jaladuta* left port, the Swami kept a diary. The entry on August 24 noted, "Rain, seasickness, dizziness, headache, no appetite, vomiting." At the height of the storm, a jolt of pain exploded in his heart, and his legs gave way. He staggered back to his bunk, where he collapsed, shivering with fever. He put his right hand in a cloth bag that held his prayer beads and turned the wooden beads between first and third fingers, reciting the Krishna mantra, "Hare Krishna, Hare Krishna, Krishna Krishna, Hare Hare, Hare Rama, Hare Rama, Rama Rama, Hare Hare." A second heart attack struck three days later. The pages of his diary for the following week were blank. He went without food and had no energy to write.

Darkness at sea brought a brittle cold, and the Swami wrapped himself in a regulation steamship company blanket. When the pain in his chest finally began to abate, he slept. In his diary, he wrote that Krishna appeared in a dream, rowing him in a boat toward a distant shore.

Over the next week, the storm dissipated. Sunlight emerged from behind dark clouds, and the waters calmed. The *Jaladuta* steamed into the Atlantic Ocean under clear skies and a crisp breeze. On August 31, the

Swami wrote in his diary, "Passed over a great crisis in the struggle for life and death." This was hurricane season, yet there were no waves. The Atlantic was smooth as glass, placid as a lake. The crew whispered. Their passenger was no ordinary sadhu.

"This kind of quiet Atlantic I've never seen in my life," the *Jaladuta*'s captain marveled.

"It is only by Krishna's mercy," the Swami told him, thinking that if there had been a third attack he would surely have died. There was no choice now but to continue on to whatever Krishna was planning. His guru had inspired him to become a warrior like Arjuna, the hero of India's sacred text Bhagavad Gita. If the Swami was going to die, better to die on the battlefield. So he reached into his small battered suitcase and pulled out an edge-worn copy of *Chaitanya Charitamrita*, the seventeenth-century biography of Chaitanya Mahaprabhu, the avatar who had sung the sacred names of Krishna in the streets of Bengal. Mahaprabhu predicted that one day the names of Krishna would be sung around the world. A.C. Bhaktivedanta Swami passed his remaining days at sea meditating on a prediction he hoped to make come true.

Thirty-five days later, after traveling 12,000 miles, the *Jaladuta* arrived in Boston harbor. The Coast Guard saluted the crew as they disembarked. Sailors unloaded cargo, and the following day the ship departed for New York. At noon on September 18, 1965, Swamiji stared out at skyscrapers lining the horizon like giant concrete teeth, took out his pen and composed a poem in his native Bengali. "My dear Lord Krishna," he wrote, "I guess you have some business here, otherwise why would you bring me to this terrible place? Now it is up to you to make me a success or failure, as you like. I am just like a puppet in your hands. So if you have brought me here to dance, then make me dance—make me dance, O Lord. Make me dance as you like."

On the morning of September 19, he dressed in a saffron-colored dhoti and put on white rubber shoes. He packed his small bag and said goodbye to the captain and crew and thanked them for their hospitality. Then he arranged for the two hundred sets of his three-volume *Bhagavatams* to be stored in a Scindia warehouse. If somehow he were able to sell a few copies, he would use the money to cover expenses for however long he stayed in America. Then he picked up his tiny suitcase and bag of cereal and tucked his umbrella under his arm. Holding the railing as firmly as his recovering muscles would allow, he descended the gangplank, stepped off the *Jaladuta*, and walked into the future.

THE AGARWALS HAD ARRANGED for a representative from Travelers Aid to meet the Swami on his arrival, and together with the agent, he set out for Port Authority Bus Terminal. The Swami had sold a set of his books for $20 to the *Jaladuta*'s captain, enough to purchase a ticket for Butler, Pennsylvania, where the Agarwals lived with their infant son. Along with a letter of sponsorship, the Agarwals had extended an invitation to stay for a few weeks in their home as a way of adjusting to life in America. On the bus, the Swami watched an endless stream of cars fill the highways exiting New York City. He traveled past skyscrapers and slums, past billboards and blackened industrial zones, and miles of factories that lay between New York and Pennsylvania.

America's four hundred-year history revealed itself to him with every passing mile. Pioneers had made their way across the Atlantic seeking religious freedom in a land of their own. They crafted homes of wood, cut and carved with their own hands. They plowed the Earth, offered prayers of thanks, and built a nation like none other in human history. Generations came and went, and descendents swapped their ancestors' noble purpose for the chance to bore through mountains and urbanize vast tracts of land. They spent fabulous sums constructing coast-to-coast highways, soaring skyscrapers, and dense cities that concentrated millions of people into vertical mazes of concrete and glass. Inspired by advances in technology, they evolved a new ethos. Americans were no longer caretakers of the Earth but its masters, competing with one another for profits and goods. They turned their backs on covenants with the natural world, gouged the ground for oil, pillaged forests, built slaughterhouses, churned out weapons, conquered foreign lands, and made of the world one huge market. Money was their God—the same God now worshiped by India.

The Swami looked at the vista of this strange land whizzing past his window and knew there would be a reckoning. Once the Americans exhausted their fantasies about finding contentment in material things, they would emerge from their offices, clubs, shopping malls, and restaurants and wonder what had gone wrong. When the veil of illusion fell away, when the reality of old age and disease and the sad brevity of a lifetime at last penetrated, the meagerness of their lives would become clear—and that would be the moment for Krishna consciousness, the lifeline that could save them from drowning in an ocean of repeated births and deaths. He had come for this purpose, to make the message available. Wake up, the Vedas declared. Don't remain in darkness.

Come up to the light![59]

THE AGARWALS GREETED HIM WARMLY. They arranged for a room at the local YMCA and scheduled lectures for him in schools and church groups. A local paper described him as "a slight brown man in faded orange drapes wearing white bathing shoes" and reported on one of his talks.

The *Butler Eagle*, Wednesday, September 22, 1965

Devotee of Hindu Cult Explains Commission to Visit the West

A.C. Bhaktivedanta Swami, a messenger from India to the people of the West is fulfilling a mission given to him by his spiritual master to enlighten English-speaking people about their relationship with God. "Human life is a stage of perfection in evolution. If we miss the message, back we go through the process again," he believes. A simplified version of his theory is that life progresses from aquatic to reptile, to bird, to beast, to "beastly" human being and finally to civilized man. "After this life, there is still better life on other planets," predicts the visitor. He believes the highest possible state will be to go to God, or eternal life.

The Swami shopped with Sally Agarwal; quizzed her husband, Gopal, about life in America; played with their young child; spoke to a few other local community groups; and formed impressions of this strange land. America was "a very, very expensive country," he wrote to a fellow monk back in India, and he underscored the point by offering examples in rupee equivalents. Laborers earned eighty rupees daily. His room at the YMCA cost fifty-five rupees weekly, and everybody had a motor car costing no less than ten-thousand rupees. There are hundreds of thousands of these motor cars, he wrote, that go no less than fifty miles per hour. Americans never stopped running, even after dark. "At night in the city," he wrote, "the shops are lit up and it appears like daytime." Houses were immensely tall, he described, and television was an amazing thing. "Just staying in one room, they can watch how the whole world is going on." Then, perhaps sensing that converting America to Krishna worship might be more than a one-man job, he concluded by writing, "If you want to come to this country, reply to me."

Sally Agarwal was amused by the Swami's awkwardness when putting coins into the fare slot on buses and his fascination with laundry machines and frozen vegetables, things he admitted never having seen in India. A month later, after teaching at a few local venues and showing Sally how to cook a few traditional Indian vegetarian dishes and with little else to do in their small town, the Swami announced he was ready to go back to New York. There were eight million conditioned souls living there, and they all needed Krishna consciousness, he said. His mission awaited. Sally and her husband gave him an old sweater and coat as protection against the winter cold, watched him board a Greyhound bus, and waved goodbye.

The bus rolled back east on Route I-80 from Butler to Port Authority Station, New York, where the city greeted him with freezing winds, eye-scorching fumes, glaring neon lights, deafening traffic, acrid smells of hot dogs and caustic fried onions, pawnshops hawking bric-a-brac of the dead, billboards of women in various stages of undress—showing their legs!—one sensory assault after another.

The Swami had only one contact in New York City: Dr. Ramamurti Mishra, recommended by a mutual acquaintance in Delhi. He made his way to Mishra's offices at 33 Riverside Drive and rode the elevator. Mishra greeted the Swami warmly and showed him his apartment, which featured large windows overlooking the brackish waters of the Hudson River. The handsome forty-year-old Mishra had been giving yoga classes in New York since the late 1950s and was happy for the company of a fellow teacher. He offered to let the Swami stay in a room adjoining his hatha yoga studio on Seventy-Second Street near Central Park and invited him to speak to his students. In these gatherings, the Swami sang prayers to Krishna, explained verses from the Bhagavad Gita, and led students in dancing: left foot across the right, then right across left, hands raised in the manner of Chaitanya Mahaprabhu's public processions.[60] He was politely received. A few students expressed tentative interest in learning more.

There were other invitations for the Swami to lecture before small gatherings here or there but hardly enough to justify staying on in this expensive and alien city. Donations were negligible, only a few people purchased his books, and he had no place of his own. In a letter to his godbrother, B. R. Sridhar Maharaj, the Swami wrote that if members of the Gaudiya Math agreed to help, then he would extend his visa. If not, he would give up plans for conquering America with Krishna consciousness and return to India.[61]

THE BLIZZARD OF JANUARY 1966 was one of the worst in New York's history. Snowdrifts rose above second-floor windows, and sixty-mile-per-hour winds threatened to knock pedestrians off their feet. The black branches of naked trees whipped against a dark sky. At night, temperatures fell below zero. Another day ended after unsuccessful meetings with foundation officers who saw no value in helping the Swami teach Bhagavad Gita in America. He sat on a park bench and chanted on his beads. The wooden beads rattled gently in their cloth bag as he repeated the sacred mantra, "Hare Krishna, Hare Krishna." Ghostly snow settled on his coat and dissolved into wetness. He closed his eyes, perhaps remembering Vrindavan and the brevity of days and wondered what to do.[62] A man bundled up against the elements sat down next to him. The man inspected the Swami and noted his flimsy rubber shoes and how sparsely he was dressed against the cold.

"I'm a subway conductor," the man said. "What is your situation?"

"I am not a poor man," the Swami said, sensing his concern. "There are temples and books—they are existing. Time only is separating us from them." His words conveyed the depth of his faith, but even he could not envision the full scope of what was to come.[63] If the subway conductor doubted the Swami's word he said nothing.

"Do you know anyone here in New York?" the conductor asked.

The Swami lifted his bead bag slightly. "I am never alone," he said, although in India he had known what it meant to be alone, and again now in such a strange land. He stood, offered the subway conductor a smile and a handshake, and set out on his weekly rounds of bookstores. He placed copies of his precious books on consignment at various shops, but sales were as cold as the weather. "Two sets books taken back from Paragon Book Gallery," he wrote in his diary on January 19, 1966. He returned back to his borrowed room and noted down food purchases for the day: fifteen cents worth of salt and a banana for twenty-two cents. Finances were at a breaking point.

If he returned to Vrindavan, he would not miss this sorry make of a city with its high prices and polluted river. Where he was from, river meant the sacred Yamuna, which lapped Vrindavan's shores with her cleansing waters. The Yamuna smelled sweet. The Hudson was as foul as a sewer.

His visa would soon expire, and he was, despite the audacity of having come to America at age seventy with nothing in his pocket, a practical person. He had spent four months trying to adjust, but conditions were harsh, harsher than he had anticipated, and his energies were spent. He went so far as to travel by bus to Scindia Steamship headquarters in Brooklyn to inquire when the next boat would leave for Calcutta. He noted the date, then bused back to his borrowed space in Dr. Mishra's quarters and resigned himself yet again to carrying on. He knew he could never return to India empty-handed. There would be no life for him back there if he failed. What would his teacher have said about such a useless disciple? To disappoint his guru would be worse than death.

In his diary for Sunday, March 6, 1966, he noted that this day in India was being celebrated as the day Chaitanya Mahaprabhu came into the world. "Devotees are enjoying the celebration," he wrote, remembering the elaborate feasts and blissful chanting that took place in Gaudiya Maths on Mahaprabhu's Appearance Day. "I am here alone without any devotee company," he wrote, "but I have come here to serve the Lord and not for personal happiness. I am prepared to live in hell even, if I am able to serve the Lord. Sri Chaitanya Mahaprabhu wanted that his mission should be propagated all over the world and that is my objective. I do not mind the inconvenience personally felt."

TWENTY-FOUR-YEAR-OLD MICHAEL GRANT had grown up in Oregon with conservative Jewish parents who nurtured his love of literature and music. In 1965, he lived in Greenwich Village with his girlfriend, Jan Campanella, and earned a living as piano sideman for jazz legend Pharoah Sanders. Michael was talented but so were thousands of other musicians in New York, and he and Jan spent their free time exploring the city's spiritual centers. They found little to their taste, least of all classes by what musician friends called the "Uptown Swamis," New York–based Hindu monks who parceled out a smattering of Vedanta for the elderly and well-to-do. Michael and Jan preferred their own readings in Eastern texts, although the writings tended to deliver more questions than answers. Spiritual books popular at the time included Thomas Mann's *The Magic Mountain*, Thomas Merton's *The Seven Storey Mountain*, Swami Vivekananda's *Raja Yoga*, and Paramahansa Yogananda's *Autobiography of a Yogi*. Each book explored journeys to selfhood and recounted fascinating anecdotes of meetings with shamans and mystics. Their authors all seemed to have achieved some level of self-awareness, but the books left a number of readers adrift and unfulfilled.

In June 1966, a drummer mentioned to Grant that "an old guy from India" was holding classes out of a loft at 94 Bowery. The loft's tenant, a seventeen-year-old named Paul, was a student of Dr. Mishra. Paul had offered to let the Swami share his space until the Swami found a place of his own. In years to come, the Bowery section of downtown New York would be gentrified and expensive; in the mid-1960s, it was a derelict outpost of cheap bars and homeless winos panhandling for nickels and sharing cups of "sneaky Pete," wood-grain alcohol filtered through a baseball cap.

Grant walked from his apartment. The door to number 94 was painted black, and the glass panels were reinforced with chicken wire. It opened onto a dark hallway smelling of beer and urine. The lights were out. Grant climbed four flights of stairs, holding the wall to guide himself. At the top, he entered a dimly lit loft, 100-feet long by 25-feet wide, where he found a handful of people sitting cross-legged on the floor before a raised wooden platform. On the platform, twelve feet below a crisscross of unpainted rafters, sat a man in saffron robes and bare feet, his eyes closed, his brow knitted. He sang something in a foreign language while keeping time on half a bongo drum tucked under his left arm. His features were pronounced: an aquiline nose, full lips, and large ears with thin filaments of hair sprouting out like gossamer antennae. His head was shaved but for a few hairs at the back,[64] and his skin glowed golden brown. From the side, he appeared simply foreign. Then he turned and looked at Grant, and the disparate features of his dramatic face came together as a single work, something declarative—*I have come here for you*—projected through deep eyes that seemed to never blink.

The man in saffron robes finished singing and spoke to the small gathering about the soul's immortality and the recitation of Krishna's name, and the urgency in his voice impressed the young musician. Over the course of his talk, the Swami emphasized that people were not their material bodies. "As spiritual beings," he said, "we are pure—no contamination, no disease, no birth, no death, no old age." We have, he explained, forgotten our original identity. From birth, we have misidentified with the body, with family relationships, and with national and ethnic origins—all temporary, illusory. When we die, the illusory selves of this life and their many sorrows and disappointments disappear, and off we go to another life. Reawaken love for Krishna and that cycle of repeated birth and death ends.

"I enjoyed your talk," Grant said after the small group of guests had departed. "How long have you been in America?"

"Almost one year," the Swami replied. It was in 1922, he said, that his spiritual master told him to teach in the Western countries. "I was married then, working and busy with family affairs. So now, forty-three years later, here I am." Then he laughed at his own tardiness and added, "Better late than never." Grant asked how he spent his days. The Swami motioned to a stack of papers sitting on a metal trunk.

"That is my Bhagavad Gita," he said. "Someday it will be published." He pointed to three books stacked on a small table. Those, he said, were the first canto or division of a Sanskrit work called the *Srimad Bhagavatam*, which he described as the post-graduate study of the Bhagavad Gita. The details of creation were revealed in this one text, he explained, and added that he had funded the printing of these first three volumes himself at great pains, and there was a tone in his voice that conveyed just how difficult the task had been. Grant lifted one of the heavy volumes. On the dust jacket was a colorful illustration rendered in a primitive style depicting planets and clouds and four-armed beings. He removed the dust jacket and ran his hand over the book's rust-colored cloth. He opened the book, and the pages felt raw and toothy to the touch and smelled of hand-milled pulp. Grant read a paragraph at random. Typographic errors abounded.

The Swami explained there were 18,000 verses in the twelve cantos of the *Bhagavatam* and that it was his mission to translate and explain them all. Grant did a quick calculation: The old gentleman was talking about nearly sixty volumes of writing. How long did he think he was going to live? Grant bought a set of books for $15. He assured the Swami he would return and headed down the dark stairs.

Back home he opened the first volume. The word "unfortunate" appeared frequently in the opening pages. So did the phrase "Kali Yuga," which the Swami's commentary described as "the current age of quarrel and confusion." That struck Grant as accurate. Americans in the Sixties, caught in a vice of war and racial hatred, were not bad people—just unfortunate victims of an age of quarrel and confusion.

HOWARD SMITH, a writer for the *Village Voice*, first heard about the Swami from a contact who recommended he interview the holy man from India who had set up shop in the Bowery. "I believe he's about to start a major religious movement," Smith's friend conjectured. Smith arrived at number 94 and climbed to the top of the stairs. Shoes lined the hallway outside the door to the loft. Smith walked in. Filling the room were people in hippie garb sitting cross-legged and staring at the walls. Smith tiptoed past them, careful not to disturb their meditations. He noticed an Indian cloth hung like a curtain at the back of the loft. He walked over and peeked behind the curtain and found a man in robes sitting on a cushion and chanting on beads.

"Swami Bhaktivedanta?" Smith asked.

"Yes?"

"I'm Howard Smith. Excuse me, I'll just take my shoes off."

"Why do you want to take your shoes off?" the Swami asked. "I didn't ask you to take your shoes off."

Smith retied his laces and motioned toward the people staring at the walls in the outer room. "What are all those people out there doing?" he asked.

"I don't know!" the Swami admitted with surprise. "And *they* don't know what they are doing. I am trying to teach them, but they seem to misunderstand me. They are very confused people."

Smith sat, and he and the Swami talked for an hour. The Swami candidly explained that he was new to America and asked Smith for his advice about living in New York. The young reporter found him open-minded and practical and appreciated the informality of their chat, but he was doubtful when the Swami mentioned having temples all over the world.

"These temples are there—now?" Smith asked.

"Well," the Swami replied, "we have got a long way to go. But I am very patient. Do you know about Indian culture?" he asked, shifting the focus back to Smith. The Swami was not deceived by a title such as "journalist." Beneath the title lived an eternal soul deserving of recognition. Smith replied that he was not familiar with the culture, and the Swami handed him the three volumes of *Srimad Bhagavatam*. "If you want more background," he said, "you can read these." Smith's article appeared a few days later.

The *Village Voice*, June 1966

The meeting of the mystical West and practical East comes alive in the curious contrast between A.C. Bhaktivedanta

Swami and his American disciples. The swami, a cultivated man of seventy with a distinguished education, is here for a year to preach his gospel of peace, good will, nearness to God. . . . His main teaching is that mankind may come closer to God by reciting his holy name.

THE SWAMI'S STAY in Paul's loft came to an abrupt end when Paul overdosed one night on LSD and chased the elderly teacher down the stairs. The Swami did not know about LSD, but it was evident Paul had become deranged and meant him harm. Was this his reward for risking death at sea to bring Krishna's message to the West—to be cut down by a crazed youth before the mission had even begun? The Swami quickly found his way to the nearby loft of an attendee at his lectures, Carl Yeargens, and tapped persistently on the door. The thirty-year-old Yeargens had graduated Cornell University and was now studying Eastern religions. Perhaps he would agree to help. Carl and his girlfriend, Eva, ushered him in and offered to let the Swami sleep on the couch of their apartment for a few days until he could relocate.

The next day the Swami spoke to Michael Grant about the incident. Grant, sensitive to the plight of a senior citizen traveling outside India for the first time, bought a copy of the *Village Voice* and searched the For-Rent section. A storefront was available on Second Avenue at First Street, along with a small apartment in an adjoining building. A few days later he and a few friends helped the Swami move his belongings from the loft to 26 Second Avenue. The storefront was nothing more than a small ground-floor space in a dilapidated downtown building, but the display window would give passersby a view of classes. Maybe a few would enter to learn more.

After inspecting the downstairs space, they lugged his boxes and suitcases through a long hallway, across a small courtyard decorated with a half-dozen shrubs and two tall elm trees, and up the stairs to apartment 2-C. This would be the Swami's new residence.

ON A HOT AFTERNOON IN JULY, twenty-six-year-old Howard Wheeler, on leave from a teaching post at Ohio State University, was walking from his Mott Street apartment to a friend's place nearby. Wheeler stood over six feet tall. He sported flowing black hair and a thick beard and spoke with a Southern accent acquired growing up in Mobile, Alabama. He crossed the Bowery at Houston Street and spied a diminutive figure on the opposite side of traffic, with his head held high "like a great actor in a famous movie," Wheeler later described. The tall professor had been to India the year before and knew what a Hindu swami looked like. But what was one doing here on the streets of the Lower East Side?

He watched the swami stroll down the street and noted with amusement his pointy white rubber shoes, like those of the genie who popped out of Aladdin's lamp. On the swami's nose and forehead were two vertical streaks of clay that ended at his shaved head, and his right hand was encased in a cloth bag. Wheeler crossed the street, introduced himself, and asked the obvious, not knowing what else to say. "Are you from India?"

"Oh yes," the Swami said politely, his eyes bright. A bus drove by, blowing exhaust around them like a cloud of toxic incense. "And you?"

Wheeler felt sorry for this grandfatherly gentleman so far from home. Why was he here? Where did he live? Was anyone taking care of him? They walked and chatted, and soon they arrived at Second Avenue and First Street. With the one finger not covered by his cloth bag, the Swami pointed to a small storefront wedged between a gas station and a laundromat. Above the door of the storefront hung a wooden marquee with the prophetic words MATCHLESS GIFTS painted in big white letters against a black background. Apparently, the former tenant had run a curio shop. A hand-lettered sign in the window announced, "Lectures on Bhagavad Gita. Monday, Wednesday, Friday, 7 p.m.–9 p.m. A.C. Bhaktivedanta Swami." Wheeler cupped his hands and looked through the window. He calculated the shop was maybe ten feet wide and fifty feet long. A few straw mats, a bare light bulb hanging from the ceiling, and that was about it. He turned to the elderly gentleman and was met with a big smile. Whoever this swami was, he had a child's look of innocent optimism, which struck Wheeler as out of place amid the sadness and filth of the Lower East Side. Yet he also fit in with a seamlessness that was hard to define. A.C. Bhaktivedanta Swami suddenly appeared, Wheeler would later say, "as if the whole chaotic stage had been deliberately, specifically set for him." Wheeler said goodbye and puzzled over the meeting on the walk back to his apartment.

Ever since Wheeler and his roommate, Keith Ham, had returned from India a few months before, their place had become a hangout for young people from the neighborhood keen on sharing the souvenirs—hashish and marijuana—while ogling their posters of four-armed gods and scantily-clad goddesses. Wheeler would occasionally read them poetry by Allen Ginsberg, Walt Whitman, Ezra Pound, or William Blake. Sometimes he quoted to them from works by Edgar Allen Poe or Ernest Hemingway.

"I just met this man on the street," he announced. "He's a swami from India." A friend, twenty-nine-year-old recording engineer Wally Sheffey, rolled his eyes. There were so many swamis showing up in New York these days. The year before, Congress had lifted restrictions on Asians coming to the United States, and a wave of Indian teachers had been flowing in ever since, all claiming to have a handle on truth.

"Just what we need," Sheffey said, "another spiritual master."

"Is he an avatar?" asked Keith Ham, using the Sanskrit term denoting an embodiment of God.

Wheeler shrugged. "Let's find out."

THE FOLLOWING MONDAY the three friends arrived at the storefront around 7 p.m. and took their seats on straw mats. The summer evening was warm, and the storefront's back window and front door were propped open. Apart from the straw mats, the room was bare. There were a dozen other people, most in their twenties. Unlike West Coast hippies who tended to drop out of society, many of the New Yorkers who attended the Swami's classes were educated activists ready to work for a worthy cause. New York hippies did not wear flowers in their hair. They were the serious variety of counterculturists.

A few minutes later, the Swami entered through a door at the rear of the shop. His saffron-colored robe was wrapped around his waist, and he wore a thin shawl over his bare shoulders. He sat down on one of the straw mats and, from a cotton bag, withdrew two brass discs held together by a length of cloth. He tapped the cymbals together gently—ching-ching chinnng, allowing the third beat to extend longer—then closed his eyes and sang, "Hare Krishna, Hare Krishna, Krishna Krishna, Hare Hare, Hare Rama, Hare Rama, Rama Rama, Hare Hare"—simple words and a simple melody, four notes, over and over, something the young audience could imitate and repeat. His was not, to be sure, a conventionally beautiful voice. But he sang unashamed and unrestrained, as though alone and oblivious to the stares of strangers watching him. He opened his eyes briefly, long enough to motion for the group to join in, and attendees stumbled through the lyrics as best they could. Then he closed his eyes again and returned to wherever the singing took him. After several minutes, he ended the chant, opened his eyes, and smiled.

"In my childhood," he said, "I first heard about America in geography and history classes. By hearing, I understood, 'Oh, a very wonderful country, very far away. If I go there, I will see big buildings and many motor-cars.' I had some mental conception—by hearing. Similarly, if you want to see God, you must first hear about God from the proper source, from the lips of a pure devotee."

What's a pure devotee? Wheeler wondered.

"The name Krishna is not a Hindu name," the Swami continued. "It is not sectarian. 'Krish-na' means all-attractive. God is not an old man. Why should he be old? He is eternal, ever fresh, and ever youthful. We are all part and parcel of Krishna, originally Krishna-conscious entities. We share God's qualities, just as a spark has all the qualities of the fire. God is eternal, and we are eternal. God is joyful, and we are joyful. But Krishna, God, is infinite, and we are infinitesimal." Guests smiled at his pronunciation of *infinite-seemal*. "Krishna is the unlimited Supreme Personality of Godhead," the Swami continued. "God is a person, and we are persons eternally."

He spoke clearly, articulating his words, and Wheeler appreciated the effort, but there were ideas here that didn't compute. The idea of souls being "part and parcel" of God sat well with him, for that spoke to a unity he had read about in texts from other traditions. But could the Swami possibly mean what he was saying about Krishna being the Supreme God? In the bedroom of Wheeler's Mott Street apartment was an entire wall of bookshelves. In volumes on Hindu philosophy, he had read descriptions of Krishna as a blue-skinned cowherd with a feather in his hair, playing a flute, "the hero of countless legends." He had always understood Krishna in that way, as an incarnation of Vishnu, the four-armed Supreme Being of Hindu mythology—an amorphous light that trickled down and assumed earthly forms from time to time such as Shiva, Durga, Ganesh—and Krishna was one of them, in essence nothing more than a metaphorical device meant to help beginning yogis envision their deeper impersonal self. The Swami described Krishna not as myth but as the actual source of creation, the Godhead in substantive personal form, the original Supreme Being. Did he really expect people to think God was a blue-skinned boy who played a flute? Throughout the talk, visitors noted that the Swami supported his statements with verses from the Bhagavad Gita and other Sanskrit texts. It was clear he wanted them to know these ideas were not his invention but ancient philosophy with scriptural pedigree.

As provocative as his lecture was, not everyone stayed. By 8:30 p.m. half the guests had left. The Swami stopped speaking, sliced two apples, placed the slices in a wooden bowl, and passed it around. A touching bit of hospitality, Wheeler thought. Maybe more. The Swami's gesture, the courteous sharing of an apple, epitomized something primordial in human nature, something warm and universal. They sat on threadbare mats in this little shop at a troubled moment of American history, and no one would have known, observing the enclave of seekers communing with their teacher and chewing bits of apple, that there were such things as poverty or suffering or a nation on edge from the constant chill of war.

"Have you ever heard of LSD?" Wheeler asked between bites.

"No," the Swami said.

"It's a chemical," Wheeler explained. "Some people claim it can give religious insights or ecstasies. Do you think LSD could be helpful in spiritual life?"

The Swami shook his head. "You don't need to take anything for your spiritual life," he said. "Your spiritual life is already here."

Wheeler nearly choked on his apple. The notion that "you don't need to take anything for your spiritual life" made no sense. As far as he had understood, up to that moment, there could be no spiritual life without taking *something*: the right drug, the right pilgrimage, the right secret teaching. Had hallucinogens not been part of spiritual traditions throughout recorded history? Had seekers not gone to India or Tibet or the mountains of Mexico to find truth? Had mystics not spent years in mountain caves, performing yoga to realize the secrets of their souls? Over his years of experimenting with drugs, Wheeler had assumed that spiritual life was indeed a thing apart, something to be obtained.

But in the darkness of his apartment, when the hallucinogens had failed, and the books stood silently on their shelves along with his college degrees, he confronted a truth he had never shared with roommates or fellow seekers. All that remained from the journeys was a frayed backpack and souvenirs, pieces of a cosmic puzzle collected here and there with no clue what the landscape looked like from above — just a jumble of disconnected bits. Along comes this diminutive teacher with a big smile, and over goes the applecart. "Your spiritual life is already here."

Yes, it certainly is, Wheeler thought, sitting before the most exalted personality he had ever met and feeling a tug in his chest, a crack in his usual intellectualism. Maybe this is what awakening is supposed to feel like, he thought. So weighted was the moment that years later, when looking back on it, the Swami himself would comment, "It was our first meeting. And I think it was eternal."

THE AIR AROUND MATCHLESS GIFTS was thick with the smell of garbage. Up and down Second Avenue, taxis and trucks added fumes to the nauseating mix. The Lower East Side of New York in the mid-1960s was a neighborhood in disrepair. Tenants contended with infestations of rats and cockroaches. There were as yet no organic markets or gourmet food courts. A pound of flour cost fifteen cents, a banana cost a dime, and each morning A.C. Bhaktivedanta Swami walked to a nearby market to purchase tiny portions of vegetables and butter and whatever else his minuscule budget would allow. On returning to his apartment on Second Avenue and First Street, he would often find drunkards sleeping off a bender in the doorway. Wheeler arrived one morning and watched the Swami looking calmly down at a man passed out on the stoop.

"My dear sir," the Swami said softly. "Please get up."

Wheeler froze. The concern and affection in the Swami's voice embodied for the tall New Yorker everything he had ever imagined about sainthood. To love what was broken and scorned and tossed aside, to honor what smelled rank and what nobody else would touch, to know that beneath the appearance of dereliction was a spark of God—what could this poor inebriated soul possibly have done in this life or in others to merit such love? Wheeler had to stay with the Swami. He had to know more.

LATER THAT SUMMER Wheeler crossed the small courtyard that separated Matchless Gifts from the weathered brick apartment building, climbed to the second floor, and knocked on the door to apartment 2-C. Above him, bits of paint hung precariously from a molded tin ceiling. The Swami opened the door and greeted him with a smile. Wheeler parked his shoes outside the door and entered the apartment. To his immediate left, he noted a small kitchen. To the right, a tiny bathroom. In a room on the far left, he saw saffron-colored laundry hanging on a rope that criss-crossed the room. A three-foot-wide wooden table held a small vase of flowers and an incense holder.

He looked into a room ahead and to the right. Morning sun peeked in through the window of the Swami's sitting room. Wheeler noted a faint smell of mustard oil. Apart from a tin footlocker, the only other furniture was a small wooden bookshelf and an inexpensive area rug. Wheeler followed the Swami into his room. The Swami sat behind his footlocker, and Wheeler sat crossed-legged on the floor in front of him.

"I need help spreading Krishna consciousness around the world," the Swami said. "Can you type?"

Wheeler nodded, amused by the notion of the Swami's little group going global. The Swami reached across his desk and handed Wheeler a stack of typed pages. The typing filled the sheets, single-spaced, with no margins. In his frugality, the Swami had squeezed every inch out of the flimsy yellow stock. The top page read, "*Srimad Bhagavatam* of Dvaipayana Vyasa, second canto, chapter one." So, Wheeler noted, the Swami has begun the second canto of his epic work. That left only ten more cantos to go. For the next several hours, Wheeler typed sitting on the floor while the Swami went about his day receiving visitors, reading and translating from behind the tin footlocker that was his desk.

The first manuscript page described a conversation that took place in remote times between a sage and a king.[65] "Swami," Wheeler said, "you have written here 'Oh the king.' This sounds like the king's name is 'Oh'. I'm guessing you want this in proper English, which would be 'O King.'"

"Yes," the Swami nodded. "Change it."

"I can make similar grammatical changes throughout, if you want," Wheeler said.

"Very good," the Swami said. "Put it nicely."

Visitors came and went throughout the morning, curious to speak with the Swami whose presence had residents of the Lower East Side buzzing. Around noon, the Swami leaned over and napped briefly. Then he rose, entered the kitchen, and began cooking. Wheeler smelled butter melting in a pot, and heard the Swami methodically chopping vegetables. By early afternoon, lunch was ready. Wheeler had transposed eight, single-spaced pages into twenty double-spaced, professionally edited sheets with wide margins. He handed them over.

"Is there any more I can do?" he asked.

The Swami smiled mischievously, walked over to his closet, and opened the door. Wheeler stared in disbelief at thousands of pages stacked in columns. The Swami grabbed two more bundles of typed sheets tied in saffron cloth and held them out.

"It's a *lifetime* of typing!" Wheeler protested.

"*Many* lifetimes," the Swami corrected.

IN THOSE EARLY DAYS of A.C. Bhaktivedanta Swami's mission in the West, attendance at his classes was sporadic. Sometimes only one or two new people came. Occasionally, no one came at all, apart from a handful of regulars. Still, he spoke with enthusiasm, as though addressing a full house. One sultry evening in June 1966, he waited to begin class with only Keith Ham and Howard Wheeler in attendance. Through the display window at the front of Matchless Gifts, the Swami noticed a number of drunks loitering on the sidewalk. He motioned for his two students to bring them in for the lecture.

"Swami," Ham cautioned, "they won't be able to understand anything."

The Swami disagreed and shook his head. "The soul will hear," he said.

Ham and Wheeler went outside and came back with a half-dozen vagrants. Some promptly leaned back against the wall and fell asleep. The Swami spoke for an hour, offering a full-out presentation of Krishna philosophy with scriptural references and an outline of devotional practice. After his talk, the young students escorted the men back outside and watched as they stumbled their way into the night. Ham and Wheeler reentered their storefront temple, marveling at the ways of the Swami.[66]

On other occasions, fifty or more people crammed in to hear the Swami speak. One hot humid evening later that month, the subject of the Swami's lecture was dharma, which he defined as the essential nature of a thing. "Liquidity," he explained, "is the dharma of water. Heat is the dharma of fire. What is our dharma? Humanity's dharma is service. It is the soul's nature to serve."

At that moment, a middle-aged drunk staggered into the room. Despite the heat, he wore a heavy black overcoat and exuded an overwhelming smell. Michael Grant wondered whether he should escort the man out but couldn't tell if the Swami had even noticed. The man stumbled forward, then stopped. He groped inside his coat pocket and pulled out a roll of packaged toilet paper. He deposited the roll on the Swami's lectern with a flourish, turned, weaved his way to the center of the room, and plunked himself down. The Swami smiled.

"Thank you very much," he said. It was as if the moment had been orchestrated to fit the class. "Just see," he said to attendees. "It is a natural tendency to give some service. He is not in order, but he thought, 'Let me give some service.' That is dharma."

The point had been made, and he picked up his small drum and led a Hare Krishna chant. Guests rose and danced as he had shown them, one foot crossing over the other. The drunk stood and joined in the dancing. He threw his arms into the air and spun slowly in time to the music. When the chanting came to an end, he collapsed, smiling, back onto the floor. Two nights later, he returned—neatly dressed, hair combed, trousers pressed, face cleanly shaved, and he danced and clapped, a well-turned-out *bon vivant* transformed by this new form of intoxication.

MOST DAYS EIGHT OR TEN STUDENTS showed up at the Swami's apartment for morning class and breakfast. There was Steve Guarino, a social worker, and Charles Barnett who practiced yoga and played flute with notable musicians of the era such as Richie Havens. Another student was a freelance cartoonist, someone else waited tables at a local macrobiotic restaurant. Each of these regulars had a story to tell about their encounter with the Swami, and when one of them told his story, the others all grinned and nodded like a reunion of war veterans. Steve Guarino described wanting to impress the Swami with his appreciation of spiritual India and told him he had read Gandhi's autobiography and thought it was glorious. The Swami was less than impressed.

"What's glorious about it?" he asked, leaning his head slightly back and to the side as though forming a question mark.

Guarino described a chapter in the book where Gandhi reported that, as a boy, he succumbed to pressure from friends to eat meat and how, after eating the meat, he felt like a lamb was howling in his belly.

"That is not glorious," the Swami scoffed. "Most of India is vegetarian. Gandhi called his autobiography *Experiments with Truth*, but that is not the nature of truth. Truth is not to be found by experimenting. Truth is always truth. Gandhi was a great man by worldly estimation and a good man by his character and behavior," he said, perhaps remembering his days as a Gandhi follower. "But he wanted to prove nonviolence from Bhagavad Gita. The Gita was spoken on a battlefield!"

Guarino had not thought of that.

REGULARS ARRIVING FOR THE MORNING PROGRAM knew the Swami had already put in several hours of writing, yet he always looked fresh and alert. Sometimes they entered to find him chanting on his *japa-mala*, his "garland of beads," not the cheap plastic kind that hippies wore but substantial hand-turned wooden beads fashioned from the sacred tulasi plant, strung together with small knots separating each one. Guests sitting nearby noted that the Swami's beads were worn smooth from years of chanting. There was serenity in the way he twirled the beads inside their cloth bag, index finger extended out of a slit in the side, pointing to guests as though saying, "Where are *your* beads? We should chant together."

He began morning class by tapping his small brass kartals, and the group clapped along. "Softly," he said. "The neighbors complain." He closed his eyes. The sun slowly rose through the rear window. In a wavering baritone, he sang an eight-verse Sanskrit prayer to his guru: "Samsara-davanala-lidha-loka . . ." Then he translated, explaining that the spiritual master was compared to a rain cloud that poured down waters of wisdom to extinguish the forest fire of material life. His students appreciated the excursion into Sanskrit prayers and songs. Other gurus sprinkled their talks with a few Sanskrit words, such as yoga, karma, or Vedanta. He was the first they had met who recited entire prayers and complete verses.

The Swami had no hesitation introducing Vaishnava culture into their world the way he had practiced it as a young man in his guru's institution, the Gaudiya Math, with morning services, readings from the Bhagavad Gita, offerings of food, and other practices. He knew the young Americans coming to him were frustrated with materialistic life and that they wanted something more substantial, just as he had when he met his spiritual master forty years before. The traditional way had worked for thousands of years, and it would work for them as well if they gave it a chance.

He ended the chanting and one of the regular guests who knew the routine took Sarvepalli Radhakrishnan's edition of the Bhagavad Gita from the Swami's wooden bookshelf and handed it to him. The Swami was grateful to the former president of India for helping him obtain his visa for America, but he did not endorse Radhakrishnan's commentary of the Gita, which denied Krishna's personhood. Still, Radhakrishnan's English translation of verses was adequate for teaching purposes.

"Today I will prove that Dr. Radhakrishnan is an impersonalist," the Swami told his flock, and he handed the book to one of the students. "Read chapter nine, verse thirty-four." The student flipped through the pages, found the spot, and read, "On Me fix thy mind. To Me be devoted. Worship Me, revere Me and thus, having disciplined thyself with Me as thy goal, to Me shalt thou come."

"Now read the commentary," the Swami said.

"It is not the personal Krishna to whom we have to give ourselves up utterly," the student read aloud, "but to the unborn, beginningless Eternal who speaks through Krishna."[67]

"You see?" the Swami asked the group. "I told you he was an impersonalist. This mayavada philosophy," he said, "is worse than atheism."[68] He explained that impersonalists are called mayavadis because they consider Krishna's transcendental, eternal body to be maya or illusion.

For students with only an outsider's understanding of Indian philosophy, Radhakrishnan's interpretation seemed to make perfect sense. Form was obviously perishable, and so it was an illusion. Spirit, as the opposite of matter, would have to be imperishable and thus a formless, indestructible energy that permeated everyone and everything. "Isn't that the real goal of meditation and yoga," one student asked, "to lose one's individual material identity and merge with that all-pervading energy?"

The Swami shook his head. The student was projecting his material experience into the realm of eternity, he explained, and that was misleading. There was such a thing as spiritual form and individual spiritual identity. If, by definition, spirit was indestructible, he explained, then it could not be cut into pieces. If we are individuals now, then we must be so eternally—not cut off from the brahman whole in the past and then magically glued back on again sometime in the future. That would contradict the indestructible nature of the *atma* or soul. The soul was an individual eternally, as was Krishna. It would be insulting to deny Krishna his individuality or to depict him as the temporary residence of something else, something shapeless and mystical.

"Mystical means misty," the Swami said. "Our concept of Krishna is not misty. It is very clear. Krishna says, 'Here I am. This is what I am.' Our job is not to interpret Krishna but to accept him as he presents himself: the Supreme Person."

Wheeler was not convinced. "Most Western theologians and philosophers would say that God in the form of a blue cowherd boy is imaginary," he commented.

"Devotees do not imagine Krishna," the Swami replied. "They see his actual form. In India, during the British days, there were Hindu-Muslim riots. Men would go into the Hindu temples and break the deity and say, 'We have killed their Hindu God.' Krishna calls such people *mudhas*, fools. They think he assumes a temporary body like we do when we are born.[69] Krishna's body is eternal. He does not take birth like a conditioned soul forced by the laws of nature. He comes here of his own sweet will."

The difference between what Wheeler had read elsewhere and what the Swami taught was dramatic. As a professor of English, Wheeler could quote the Greek and European thinkers, many of whom he admired. "Is Western philosophy all speculative? Socrates, for example."

"Socrates was brahman realized," the Swami said, referring to a level of self-awareness above material but not yet complete—a realization of one's own eternal nature but not yet direct perception of God. "He was a great philosopher convinced of the immortality of the soul. When Socrates was condemned to death," the Swami said, "his jailers said he must drink hemlock poison. But he did not lament. He knew he would not be destroyed when his body was destroyed. 'First, you must catch me,' he told them. 'Then you can put me in the grave.'" He laughed with pleasure over a condemned philosopher's wit, and Wheeler was obliged to admit the Swami understood Socrates better than he did.

"Socrates did speak of God with form," Wheeler acknowledged. "His teacher, Diotima of Mantinea, tried to turn him from the imperfect beauty of earthly forms to the ideal form of beauty."

"Yes, that is real philosophy," the Swami said. "All our senses must be withdrawn from external temporary forms and concentrated on the ideal eternal form of Krishna within our hearts. That is the perfection of both yoga and philosophy."

Wheeler knew Judeo-Christian religions hinted at the notion of a personal divinity, but in all his talks with rabbis and priests, no one had ever suggested that God possessed eternal form. Wheeler's roommate, twenty-nine-year-old Keith Ham, jumped in.

"Radhakrishnan is right when he says it is the unborn Eternal who speaks through Krishna," Ham declared. Along with a smattering of Eastern philosophy, he possessed his Baptist father's missionary zeal, and he rambled on about something higher speaking through Krishna. The more he talked, the deeper the Swami's face turned red.

"Are you finished?" the Swami asked.

"No," said Ham, and on he went. Eventually, he ran out of steam.

"Now are you finished?" the Swami asked.

"Yes," said Ham.

"Do you understand what we have been saying," the Swami asked calmly, "that Krishna is God?"

"Yes," said Ham.

Then the Swami did a most unexpected thing. He slammed his hand on his little tin footlocker. *Wham*! The room shook from the impact.

"Then why do you want to take it away from him!" he shouted. *"It is Krishna! It is Krishna! Not something unborn within Krishna. It is Krishna! IT IS KRISHNA!"*

The Swami stopped, and the room became silent. Ham was having trouble breathing. It was the first time, at least in their experience of such things, that a teacher from India dared speak so strongly. Where was the shanti? Where was the peace and tranquility in such behavior? All the other yogis around town exuded calm and spoke of freedom from anger as the sign of an enlightened being. Well, here was one who roared like a lion.

Still, the students reasoned, he wasn't putting himself on a pedestal, he was just talking forcefully. The strong statement had nothing to do with ego or lack of self-control. He was making a point of philosophy important enough to merit dramatic emphasis. Students witnessing the display were obliged to consider that they themselves probably qualified as mayavadis, as impersonalists who saw themselves as supreme and denied any separate higher authority. The Swami wasn't speaking down to them, but rather making sure they understood that they were not God. Krishna was God, a person separate and distinct from them. Krishna was a person, souls were persons, and personhood was glorious. Personhood was the prerequisite to love. They couldn't love a cloud or a vacuum. Love occurred between individuals, and according to the Swami, the highest love was between the individual soul and the Supreme Soul.

It was refreshing for them to meet a guru who taught what needed teaching, regardless of listener comfort. And what he taught! Chant Hare Krishna, he said. Follow a few simple guidelines, and one day you will see God face to face. Not only will you see God, but God will dance with you.

The more they attended his classes, the more the Swami's intentions for them became clear. He was not offering a course in yoga or a smattering of philosophy, but issuing a challenge to get serious about achieving life's full potential. They had never met anyone so absolutely certain of anything. Krishna was God, and all living beings shared his qualities of eternity, self-awareness, and joy. All beings on that eternal platform were beautiful, perfect, and complete. Now start acting that way and go help others do the same. Become Krishna conscious, then let us join together and change the world. The Swami's missionary spirit was as irresistible as it was unexpected.[70]

"Did you see how red Swamiji got?" Wheeler asked Wally Sheffey, after the class broke up. "Boy, was he angry."

"But he was also right," Sheffey said. "You've read the Bhagavad Gita before. All the commentators try to avoid Krishna. Until meeting Swamiji, did you ever think of worshiping Krishna?"

Wheeler had to admit that it had never crossed his mind.

THAT AFTERNOON, after the startling morning class, students sat in a row in front of paper plates and cups. Another student emerged from the kitchen with a tray of lunch dishes and placed the tray on a table that served as altar. Next to the tray he positioned pots of steaming saffron rice with fresh milk cheese balls, spiced vegetables, and round wholewheat chapati flatbreads. The Swami offered the food to Krishna with prayers just he had done since childhood, and everyone bowed their knees and head to the floor. When prayers were done, the Swami squatted down on his haunches and moved sideways while serving out heaping spoonsful of the hot, nutritious meal. Then he sat with his own plate, and everyone dug in, content to be together, and some might have even imagined that if all the world could be like this, sharing a meal of Krishna's prasadam, that hatred would be only a bitter memory. From time to time, he called out a student's name and chided affectionately, "Why are you not eating more? Take more prasadam," and he surveyed the scene with pleasure.

"When I was coming to your country on the boat," he said between bites, "I was wondering, 'How will the Americans ever eat this food?'"

He chuckled as his crew scoffed down first portions and held out their plates for more.

IN THE QUIET TIMES, after visitors had left and the door to Matchless Gifts was closed for the night, A.C. Bhaktivedanta Swami chanted on his beads, rested a few hours, and rose again by two o'clock in the morning to resume writing. Someday he hoped to open a publishing operation as his spiritual master, Bhaktisiddhanta Saraswati, had done. "The Big Mridanga," Bhaktisiddhanta had proudly called the Gaudiya

Math's four printing operations, since clay mridanga drums could only be heard for a mile or two while books could reach the far corners of the globe. From his printing workshops in Calcutta, Krishnagar, Mayapur, and Cuttack, the erudite Bhaktisiddhanta had produced a library of scriptural commentaries, in addition to weekly newspapers in English, Bengali, Oriya, and Assamese. One of his newspapers, the *Nadiya Prakash*, was published daily. An astonished politician asked him how it was possible to publish a newspaper about God every day. "This planet," Bhaktisiddhanta replied, "is but one of innumerable planets in our universe. This universe is only one among an unlimited number of universes in the material creation. The material creation itself is only one-fourth of the Kingdom of God. On this one insignificant planet, there are so many cities. In each city, there are dozens of newspapers. If people are capable of filling so many papers with mundane news from this minuscule planet, imagine how much more there is to say about the eternal realm. Why only daily? Every second we could publish another newspaper about Krishna."

IT WAS AN EARLY SUMMER MORNING in New York. Seven thousand miles away in Krishna's village, it was closer to midday. A scorching wind called the *loo* would be keeping Brijbasis—the residents of "Braj," Vrindavan—indoors. Brijbasis had improvised an ingenious evaporation system for staying cool. They covered their windows with screens woven from fragrant *khas* grass, used simple water pumps to keep the screens damp, and the loo did the rest. Down the streets of the town and out into farmers' fields, the hot wind would be stirring branches of fruit trees: mango, guava, amla, jamun, papaya, pomegranates, and mulberry. Wooden bullock carts would be rumbling down dirt roads, hooves clopping along like living clocks keeping time, their drivers bundled under their cotton chadars against the wind and dust. Soon monsoon winds would bring rain to nourish fields and provide relief from hot days, and temple bells would herald the miracle of Krishna's creation. That was the world he had left behind to come here, to the slums of New York, hoping against hope that someone might listen and understand Krishna's message.

What a ragtag group they were, these young people around him. Intelligent, most of them, but certainly not the dignitaries he had imagined reaching in America. How strange that he had set his sights on older, more mature candidates for Krishna consciousness and that Krishna had chosen to send him alienated innocents. Their sense of identity had been held hostage by the opinions of others for so long that he could surprise them with the simplest of revelations: You are not your physical bodies, God is a person. Still, they were sincere, and who could judge what would come of it? "A million stars cannot light up the night sky," he told them. "But one moon can light up the sky. I do not want thousands of star-like disciples. Find me one moon, and I will sit under a tree and teach all about Krishna."

He felt affection for them, these mixed-up New Yorkers with their harmful habits and odd ways, and they in return felt affection for him, but they did not all stay. The strain of abandoning the past, of losing one identity and embracing another, was overwhelming for some. "I'm not meant to sit in a temple and chant on beads!" a tall young man railed one evening, waving his arms. "I'm meant to run on the beach and breathe in big breaths of air . . ."

"Then do it!" the Swami interrupted in a loud voice. "Do it!" and the tall young man shrank away. The Swami knew how to handle stubbornness. A father may alert his child, "Do not put your hand in the fire," but if the child insisted on touching fire, well, "Then do it!" and the child learned the hard way. The tall young man stayed at 26 Second Avenue for some time, but then he left and was not heard from again. When anyone went away, Swamiji felt the loss. Sometimes he wept and admitted to his students, "We could not save the soul."

For Carl Yeargens and his girlfriend, the notion of giving up drugs and sex was offputting. So were the changes they saw occurring at Matchless Gifts. Meetings in the Bowery loft had been intimate and mystical. Now attendance at the Swami's classes had grown, and people danced with an abandon the couple found disturbing. Another regular, Carol, was also wary of how some guests became wild during kirtans, flailing their arms and jumping up and down, and she concluded that chanting was an excuse for them to act out personal frustrations—not her scene. Other attendees saw things polarizing into two camps—those who were ready to make a serious commitment to the Swami and those who were not—and they, too, distanced themselves from the community. Something that had started small and communal was growing. The Swami's gatherings had begun to expand into an organization whose members were expected to clean up their behavior and shift priorities, and a number of early visitors disappeared.

"I WOULD LIKE TO CHANT IN PUBLIC," the Swami announced one morning. His students shook their heads in awe: They never knew what he was going to do next. "Perhaps in a park," he said. "You decide where." The small group that constituted his regular attendees hesitated on two counts. One was over breaking laws governing public assembly. Any gathering that drew attention in those days of violent protest against the war in Vietnam meant trouble with the police. The other hesitation was on principle. Until then, they had never chanted outdoors. Wasn't chanting their private thing? What did the Swami think he was doing? Did he really believe he could convert all of New York? It would be embarrassing to go public like the Salvation Army.

"You won't be afraid when you start chanting," the Swami reassured them. "Krishna will help you."

The following Sunday the Swami set out across Third Street and walked ten blocks west to Washington Square Park. A dozen regulars followed behind. Keith Ham, duly chastened from his insistence that something impersonal spoke through Krishna, had shaved his head and wore a saffron cloth wrapped around his waist. Cars slowed down. A driver poked his head out the window. "Hey!" he yelled at Ham. "You forgot to change your pajamas! Get a job!" Bikers and pedestrians gawked, pointing and shaking their heads.

"We're making public spectacles of ourselves," Wheeler thought and kept his eyes riveted on the Swami, who floated along, oblivious to stares and jeers. Wally Sheffey had voiced similar hesitations over painting his forehead like the Swami did, or bowing down or in any way becoming Indian. "I am not asking you to become Indian," the Swami had reassured him. Krishna consciousness was a culture, he said, not a religion.

They arrived at the park and walked under the ten-story marble arch that flanked the entrance. The Swami slid out of his pointy white shoes and sat down on the grass next to a sign that read KEEP OFF THE GRASS. He took out his kartals and began to chant "Hare Krishna, Hare Krishna, Krishna Krishna, Hare Hare . . ." A teenager with bongos walked over and tapped out a beat. A crowd congregated around them. A sailor ground out a cigarette with his shoe. "What the hell is this?" he muttered. A few minutes later police arrived and pointed to the sign. This was it, Wheeler told himself. Prison. The Swami read the sign, nodded, rose, moved off the grass, sat down on the hot asphalt sidewalk, and resumed chanting. The police shrugged and walked on, and the Matchless Gifts regulars beamed at their teacher's deft handling of authority. The crowd around them grew. This public chanting wasn't so bad, the regulars thought. It was cool.

A half hour later, the Swami stopped, opened his *Bhagavatam* to the preface, and handed the book to Wheeler. "Read," he said.

Wheeler stood and looked around the crowd, wondering if any of his university colleagues were watching. "Disparity in human society," he read aloud, "is due to a Godless civilization. There is God, or the Almighty One, from whom everything emanates, by whom everything is manifested, and in whom everything is merged to rest. Material science is trying to find the ultimate source of creation very insufficiently, but it is a fact that there is one ultimate source of everything that be. This ultimate source is explained rationally and authoritatively in the beautiful *Srimad Bhagavatam*."

As he read, he hardly recognized himself. It felt, he later described, as though some larger voice was speaking through him, something ancient and wise, and the sensation was strangely exhilarating.

BACK AT MATCHLESS GIFTS, a student asked the Swami if he was pleased. "Very nice," he said with a jaunty shake of his head. "Now you may go out in the afternoons and chant in the streets and parks. This was Chaitanya Mahaprabhu's specific recommendation for the Age of Kali."

For the past several weeks, he had been telling his flock about Chaitanya Mahaprabhu and reading to them from the *Chaitanya Charitamrita*, the biography that had comforted him during his treacherous journey to America. The *Chaitanya Charitamrita* described Mahaprabhu's brilliant refutation of anti-Krishna doctrines and the massive rallies he led through the streets of Bengal in the early 1500s. Now, every Sunday, the Swami's students staged their own version of Mahaprabhu's rallies by gathering in front of the Second Avenue temple and heading out as a group, walking single file through the Lower East Side, chanting Hare Krishna and playing hand-held instruments.

EVENTUALLY EDUCATORS WOULD acknowledge A.C. Bhaktivedanta Swami's success in implanting authentic Vaishnava culture in the West.[71] But in the 1960s, people looked at his band of fledgling disciples with skepticism. No one knew Krishna chanters represented India's oldest yoga practice[72] or that they were fulfilling a prediction from the 1600s that the Holy Names of Krishna would be heard around the world.

The Swami wrote to an acquaintance in India: "Regarding a temple here in New York and other places, I have now decided to struggle for it to the end of my life. I am now trying to incorporate under the name International Society for Krishna Consciousness."

VOL. 1 NO. 22   OCTOBER 15 - NOVEMBER 1   20¢ outside nyc   15¢

SAVE EARTH NOW !!

HARE KRISHNA HARE KRISHNA KRISHNA KRISHNA HARE HARE
HARE RAMA HARE RAMA RAMA RAMA HARE HARE ...

SEE CENTERFOLD

Early accounts of his public chanting, such as this front-page story in *The East Village Other*, drew attention to the Swami's mission in the West.

CHAPTER FIVE

There is no one dearer to me than one who teaches devotional service.

—SRI KRISHNA IN THE BHAGAVAD GITA, 18.68–69

THE FIRST TIME Bruce Scharf sat on the floor across from the Swami, the twenty-three-year-old college student attempted to explain his identity crisis. He had been a star athlete in high school, but he preferred listening to jazz and reading poetry. While his macho father hunted and fished, Bruce read Plato. He had tried psychotherapy after his father's third divorce. He had seen a lot of the world while working on a Caribbean freighter. Currently, he was enrolled in a university course called "Oriental Literature." But he had no idea who he was.

"You are part and parcel of Krishna," the Swami said. "In the Bhagavad Gita, Krishna describes that all living entities are his eternal fragmental parts.[73] And Krishna is the Supreme Personality of Godhead. Being part and parcel of Krishna, your duty is to serve him, to think of him, to worship him, and to love him. Now chant Hare Krishna. As soon as the chanting stops, maya comes." Scharf noted that the Swami's eyes were looking past him with an expression of longing. He turned to see what was prompting such an emotion. On the wall hung a painting of Chaitanya Mahaprabhu dancing in kirtan.

Before the Swami's morning classes, Scharf carried a heavy Akai reel-to-reel tape recorder down the stairs from apartment 2-C, across the courtyard and into the temple room. There was a pattern to these classes. The Swami started with a ten-minute kirtan. Then he had students chant one round on their beads. He took his own beads out of their cloth bag and draped them around his neck, and students followed along as the Swami held his beads outward with both hands, closed his eyes, and chanted the Hare Krishna mantra on each bead. Occasionally, he opened his eyes to glance at the attendees and offer a nod of encouragement. Then he lectured, and Scharf recorded the class. When the class ended, Scharf carried the tape recorder back up to the apartment, and a small group of disciples sat with the Swami and listened to the lecture he had just given. It occurred to Scharf that replaying his own words was not ego on the Swami's part: He was appreciating Krishna's teachings, even if they came out in a class he himself had given.

Sometimes people attended these lectures just to challenge the Swami. "What about Camus?" a guest asked.

"What is his philosophy?" the Swami asked.

"Camus says that everything is absurd, and that the only philosophical question is whether to commit suicide."

The Swami shook his head at such a tragic view of life. "That means everything is absurd for *him*," he said, "because he does not know the soul. The soul cannot be killed. The material world *is* absurd, but there is a spiritual world beyond this one." His ability to unravel sophisticated ideas with a simple phrase aroused emotions in his students that they couldn't name. They might have described the sensation as relief from life's uncertainties, combined with reassurance in discovering their eternal spiritual nature. Discussions often ran late into the night. Most visitors came and went, but some stayed because the Swami peeled back layers of illusion and permitted them to glimpse their own immortality. Just chant, he told them, and everything will become clear. They took the message to heart and chanted while riding the subway or walking to work.

A VISITOR PUT THE SWAMI in touch with Steven Goldsmith, a lawyer who offered to help incorporate the Swami's society as a non-profit, tax-exempt organization. Paperwork in hand, Goldsmith arrived at the Second Avenue storefront one evening in mid-July 1966. At the Swami's invitation, Goldsmith explained to people who had gathered for class that their signatures and addresses were needed. The Swami called some by name, "Bill, you can give your address—and Raphael, you can give yours." Others, including Michael Grant and his partner, Jan, stepped forward to become the first trustees of the International Society for Krishna Consciousness.

For those who cared to read them, ISKCON's articles of incorporation revealed the Swami's plans for America: to educate people in "the techniques of spiritual life"; to propagate "a consciousness of Krishna, as it is revealed in the Bhagavad Gita and *Srimad Bhagavatam*"; to bring members together by developing awareness that each soul is "part and parcel of the quality of Godhead"; to teach congregational chanting; encourage "a simpler and more natural way of life"; and to achieve these many goals by publishing and distributing books and magazines. In recognition of this formalizing of the Swami's movement, followers had taken to calling Matchless Gifts "the temple." Externally, it remained a dusty storefront with a few hand-me-down decorations, but for them it had become beautiful and sacred.

A group of students came up with a plan to surprise their teacher. They took down the filthy curtains that lined the back wall, washed them at a nearby laundromat, dyed them purple, and tacked the newly cleaned and colored curtains behind the platform where the Swami sat to give class. Along the walls, they hung posters from India, tapestries, and a large painting of Radha and Krishna executed in a somewhat abstract style by one of the regulars. One visitor contributed an Oriental rug from his suburban home. By late afternoon, they had finished remodeling the Swami's platform with a wooden riser, pillows, flowers, and candlesticks. Then, when everything was ready, they waited for him to arrive for evening kirtan and class.

He entered through the side door of the temple room, stopped, looked around, and raised his eyebrows. "Oh!" he said with a broad smile. "Krishna consciousness is expanding." He stepped up onto the newly decorated platform and sat. Then he stared at them one by one, with a grave expression that acknowledged their achievement at elevating a rented storefront to a functioning Krishna temple.

Some attendees resented the changes, in particular the raised dais. It was inappropriate, they said, to elevate someone to such a place of worship. "Why can't you sit on the floor like us?" one of them groused. "It's the Catholic Church all over again."

Next to the dais was a slop sink and a toilet. The Swami pointed and said, "I can sit and speak to you here—or there, on the commode. Shall I give class sitting on the commode?"

Ten years later a professor studying the evolution of Krishna consciousness in the West would propose that the renovation of Matchless Gifts in 1966 marked a transition from storefront to formal Vaishnava math, and that the raised and decorated dais signaled the Swami's ascension from "father and friend to guru and spiritual master."[74] The impact of that shift would happen over time. For now, one year into his mission and on or off the dais, he was still their Swamiji.

THE STUDENTS DESIGNED A HANDBILL with the temple address and an invitation that read, "Practice the transcendental sound vibration *Hare Krishna, Hare Krishna, Krishna Krishna, Hare Hare, Hare Rama, Hare Rama, Rama Rama, Hare Hare*—International Society for Krishna Consciousness, Meetings Mondays, Wednesdays and Fridays." Poet Allen Ginsberg, who lived not far from Matchless Gifts, received one of the handbills in the mail and drove up unannounced in July 1966 with his partner Peter Orlovsky. Ginsberg was forty and at the peak of his fame as poet laureate of the counterculture. He had spent several months in India and was already familiar with street chanting.

Students brought Ginsberg upstairs to apartment 2-C, where he touched the Swami's feet in the customary gesture of respect in India for a holy person. Ginsberg presented the Swami with a gift: a harmonium, the hand-pumped keyboard instrument frequently used in kirtans. Students explained that Ginsberg was a prominent literary figure, and the Swami nodded in appreciation. Ginsberg droned on the harmonium and chanted Hare Krishna to a jolly melody. When he finished, the Swami smiled.

"You are an influential man," he said. "I request you to chant this Hare Krishna at your poetry readings and other public functions. Krishna says in the Bhagavad Gita, 'Whatever actions a great man performs, all the world pursues.' Chanting Hare Krishna can purify the world."

Ginsberg listened and nodded. "Do you really intend to make these American boys and girls into Vaishnavas?" He appreciated the Swami's missionary spirit but wondered whether Krishna worship might not be a little too esoteric for New Yorkers.

"Yes," the Swami replied, "and I will make them all Brahmins."

"*Brahmins?!*" Ginsberg blanched.

There had never been Western Brahmins before, in part because the role of a Brahmin had no counterpart in Western religions. More than a priest or pastoral counselor, a Brahmin in the Vedic or ancient Indian sense was a performer of sacred ceremonies, a spiritual teacher, and a conduit between God and man. To qualify as a Brahmin required years of study and mastery of ritual, beginning in childhood. So powerful were authentic Brahmins that in India's remote past some had even been warriors and kings. Ginsberg was familiar with a few of these warrior-priests from the epic story the *Mahabharata*: Dronacharya, Kripacharya, Parashurama. But these were revered exemplars from the pantheon of Vedic spiritual leaders—not stoned hippies from the streets of New York. He shook his head and marveled at the Swami's daring.

"Well. Good luck, Swamiji," he said.

SUMMER TURNED INTO FALL, and one September afternoon the Swami led his band of chanters up Second Avenue and east to the intersection of First Avenue and Avenue A. They entered Tompkins Square Park, one of the only green spaces on the Lower East Side, sat under a tall elm tree, and chanted Hare Krishna. The Swami motioned to his students to stand and dance. A tall, thin boy raised his arms and danced as the Swami had taught: left foot over right, right over left. Charles Barnett, wearing big red chanting beads around his neck and a black turtleneck against an early fall chill, followed. Bruce Scharf stood next, determined to dance for as long as his teacher sang. People strolling through Tompkins Square Park heard the music and gravitated to the circle of Krishna chanters. A few joined in with guitars, flutes, a bass drum, and orchestra cymbals.

The Swami stood and gave a brief talk. He thanked the audience of onlookers—mothers with baby strollers, old folks on benches, neighborhood residents and passersby—for joining in the kirtan. "Hare means, 'O energy of the Lord,'" he explained. "Both Krishna and Rama are names of the Lord. The chanting emanates from the spiritual platform and is the best process in this age for reviving our dormant Krishna consciousness. Thank you very much," he concluded. "Now please chant with us."

The following week Ginsberg showed up and joined them on the grass. "I had been running around singing Hare Krishna but had never understood exactly why or what it meant," he told a reporter. He was moved, he said, by the Swami's humility in choosing the Lower East Side for his Krishna consciousness mission.

ATTENDANCE GREW AT THESE SUNDAY CHANTING SESSIONS in Tompkins Square Park.[75] One Saturday, Ginsberg arrived with a group of friends including downtown notables, fellow beat poets, actors, and playwrights. The group sat on the grass and joined the chanting. A reporter from the *New York Times*, hoping for an interview, interrupted his chanting. The renowned poet declined. "A man should not be disturbed while worshiping," Ginsberg said.[76]

The public chanting prompted a spate of newspaper articles.

The New York Times, October 10, 1966

Swami's Flock Chants in Park to Find Ecstasy
by James R. Sikes

Sitting under a tree in a Lower East Side park and occasionally dancing, 50 followers of a Hindu swami repeated a 16-word chant for two hours yesterday afternoon to the accompaniment of cymbals, tambourines, sticks, drums, bells and a small reed organ.

Repetition of the chant, A. C. Bhaktivedanta Swami says, is the best way to achieve self-realization in this age of destruction.

. . . many in the crowd of about a 100 persons standing around the chanters found themselves swaying or clapping hands in time to the hypnotic rhythmic music.

"It brings a state of ecstasy," said Allen Ginsberg, the poet, who was one of the celebrants.

THE SIXTIES WERE, in the words of one commentator, "a generation given over to some of the noblest causes and some of the most indefensible nonsense in history."[77] Yet if there was one defensible byproduct of an often nonsensical time it was music, and the Swami's chanting of Hare Krishna fit right in. Thanks to his father's insistence that he receive musical training, he was a one-man band with a strong singing voice and a virtuoso's skill on the single-headed bongo, which was the temple's only drum in those early days. A New York percussionist once commented, "The Swami gets in some good licks." Visitors to the storefront temple brought guitars, horns, metal clappers, anything that made noise and added flavor to sessions that often lasted past midnight. The sound of kirtan spread as jazz musicians picked up the melodies of the Hare Krishna mantra and weaved them into club sessions. Irving Halpern, an instrument maker and frequent attendee at the Swami's kirtans, noted, "Whenever a new musician would join and play their first note, the Swami extended his arms as though he had stepped up to the podium and was going to lead the New York Philharmonic. I mean, there was this gesture—the pick-up—that every musician knows when someone else wants you to play with them."[78]

A year later James Rado and Gerome Ragni's rock musical *Hair* debuted off-Broadway with a finale that featured the Hare Krishna mantra, and the popularity of chanting grew. Some newcomers mistook the pleasure of chanting for a new kind of drug-induced high. "When I chant," one girl told the Swami, "I feel a great concentration of energy on my forehead. Then a buzzing comes through, and I see a reddish light."

"Just keep chanting," he reassured her. "It will clear up."

LIKE MANY OTHER YOUNG PEOPLE of the era, nineteen-year-old Judy Koslofsky felt estranged from most everything, and, like many in that philosophically confused era, took comfort in the popular idea that she was herself God. In her closet, she kept a few outfits that helped her feel more God-like, including a long beige dress and black cape. One Sunday afternoon, walking through Tompkins Square Park dressed in God-clothes and on the way to visit her boyfriend, Judy heard music from the middle of a crowd of onlookers. She gently pushed her way through the crowd, and there was the Swami sitting on an Oriental rug beneath a large elm tree, eyes closed, playing one half of a bongo drum and chanting. Around him, young people danced barefoot. An hour later, at the end of their chanting session, she followed the group back to Matchless Gifts, across the small courtyard, and up the stairs to the Swami's apartment. He sat on the floor behind his makeshift desk and greeted guests as they came and went. Then he turned toward Judy. It was, she recalled, "as though he could look into my very soul." Still, she thought, since she was God, the Swami was obviously just recognizing her greatness.

"Do you live near here?" the Swami asked politely.

God lives everywhere, Judy reminded herself, and drew out the words of her reply with a knowing nod. "Yeeeess," she said slowly, "I live *veeeery* near." Big mistake.

"Good!" he replied. "Then you will be able to attend our morning programs at seven a.m."

Judy lived with her parents in the Bronx, a good hour and a half by subway. Nonetheless, she came nearly every day.

Judy studied art at New York's City College. Her ability to paint earned special attention from the Swami, who looked ahead to a time when there would be temples requiring art for the walls and books requiring illustrations. Gesturing to a print of Krishna on one of the walls of Matchless Gifts, he said, "It should not be taken that Krishna is only a picture," and then he explained that a picture of God is also God, just as the sound of Krishna's name is also Krishna himself. "Krishna is appearing as a picture just to give us the facility to understand and approach him," he said.

Judy set up supplies and canvases in one of the Swami's rooms, and he guided her in creating transcendental art. One habit Judy and other early devotee artists had to overcome was a tendency to depict Krishna as muscular. "Muscular bodies are in *raja-guna*," the Swami said, using the Sanskrit term for a passionate material nature, as might be found in warriors or athletes. "A spiritual body is not muscular. Try again—less muscle and no fat. God is not fat, nor lean. Lean men look like hungry wolves hunting for sex. Krishna is perfect beauty. When we see Krishna, we will want nothing to do with the so-called beauty of the material world. Krishna's beauty attracts everyone in creation—great demigods, men, women, even plants and animals. His beauty is unlimited. What we call beauty here is but a perverted reflection."

Judy despaired over the limits of her artistic skills. Krishna deserved a better artist, she chided herself. He deserved someone more qualified to illustrate the spiritual world. The Swami dismissed her hesitations and urged her to focus not on her limits but on the limitless Supreme Being, to suspend her worldly sense of "great" and accept that something greater could guide her.

"You are already a great artist," he reassured her, referring to Krishna's promise in the Bhagavad Gita that he will accept any service, however small, if offered with love.[79] Besides, to become a famous artist would take many births. "We have to finish our Krishna consciousness in this lifetime," he said. "We should not waste a single moment for anything else."[80]

When his students faced inner turmoil or self-doubts, they turned to him not only as a teacher but as a father figure, and he looked after them as his foster sons and daughters. Busy though he was, commenting on *Srimad Bhagavatam* and making plans for an international institution, he always had time to hear their troubles or write them a letter to remind them of the healing power of Krishna consciousness. His good counsel was calming, and because he embodied love and devotion to Krishna, they took comfort in his example and were restored to action.

So Judy adjusted her posture, lifted her brush, and began painting again.

ONE OF THE SWAMI'S STUDENTS met a friend coming out of a candy shop on Second Avenue. "Your Swami is in the paper," the friend said and handed him a copy of the *East Village Other*, a recently founded anti-establishment newspaper that sold for fifteen cents. The front page was filled with a two-color photo of the Swami, standing in yellow robes in front of the big tree in Tompkins Square Park and speaking to a crowd that had gathered around him. The Swami's acolytes hurried to the storefront, where others joined him upstairs to show the paper to their teacher.

> The *East Village Other*, October 1966
> **SAVE EARTH NOW!!**
> **HARE KRISHNA HARE KRISHNA**
> **KRISHNA KRISHNA HARE HARE**
> **HARE RAMA HARE RAMA**
> **RAMA RAMA HARE HARE**
>
> An old man, one year past his allotted three score and ten, wandered into New York's East Village and set about to prove to the world that he knew where God could be found. In only three months, the man, Swami A.C. Bhaktivedanta, succeeded in convincing the world's toughest audience — Bohemians, acidheads, potheads, and hippies — that he knew the way to God: Turn Off, Sing Out, and Fall In. This new brand of holy man, with all due deference to Dr. Leary, has come forth with a brand of "Consciousness Expansion" that's sweeter than acid, cheaper than pot, and non-bustible by fuzz. How is all this possible? "Through Krishna," the Swami says.

The regulars broke out in cheers and applause. The Swami, too, was delighted with the coverage of their chanting party in the park.

"What are hippies?" he asked. Students did their best to explain.

"I'm afraid that many people would consider *us* hippies," one student said. The Swami disagreed.

"We are not hippies," he said. "We are happies. Whatever you once were, Krishna will change you."

NOT EVERYONE changed right away. "I'm higher than you are!" a wide-eyed, bearded youth told the Swami after one evening class.

"Please accept my humble obeisances," the Swami replied, bowing slightly as Bruce Scharf showed the bearded guest to the door.

"Do not let in any more crazies," Swamiji requested. "If you tell such people they are in the grasp of material nature, they will not understand. They are so accustomed to suffering that they mistake their suffering for happiness."

Allen Ginsberg apparently missed that instruction and one Sunday brought the rock group the Fugs to a kirtan at Matchless Gifts. The Fugs were the anti-Beatles: a drug-ingesting, liquor-swilling crew of chaos-and-shock musicians. The regulars could not imagine what Ginsberg was thinking, since the group's raw lyrics about radical sex hardly fit with their teacher's insistence on self-restraint. "Kill for Peace," "Slum Goddess," "Skin Flowers of the Lower East Side"—these were some of the songs on the Fugs's albums.

"Sex pleasure binds us to this material world of birth and death," the Swami told his audience that evening. He quoted the tenth-century philosopher Yamunacharya: "Since becoming Krishna conscious, whenever I think of sex—I *spit* at the thought."

The Fugs never returned.[81]

ALLAN KALLMAN, A RECORD PRODUCER, read the *East Village Other* article and showed up at Tompkins Square Park to hear the chanting for himself. Kallman's company, Happening Records, released spoken-word recordings by celebrities of the day such as LSD evangelist Timothy Leary, human rights advocate Malcom X, and civil rights activist Mark Lane. Kallman calculated that a recording of the Swami and his group chanting, along with a spoken-word explanation, would fit his catalog. He called Matchless Gifts and made an appointment to see the Swami.

"Alan told the Swami about his plan to make a recording of the chant along with an explanation, and he loved it," remembered Kallman's wife, Carol. "The Swami explained that the chanting is important but that the philosophy behind the chanting is equally important. So he would be happy to do both on the album."[82]

In December, the Swami and his followers traveled to Bell Tone Studios on Broadway and 51st Street. Inside the studio, the Swami and his students were offered cushions on the floor of the recording room. Engineers

HARE KRISHNA TREE
Tompkins Square Park

One of Tompkins Square Park's most prominent features is its collection of venerable American elm (Ulmus americana) trees. One elm in particular, located next to the semi-circular arrangement of benches in the park's center, is important to adherents of the Hare Krishna religion. After coming to the United States in September, 1965, A.C. Bhaktivedanta Swami Prabhupada (1896-1977), the Indian spiritual leader, founded the International Society for Krishna Consciousness in New York. He worked from a storefront on nearby Second Avenue that he used as the Society's American headquarters. Prabhupada and his disciples gathered in Tompkins Square Park in the fall of 1966 to introduce the East Village to the group's distinctive 16-word mantra:

Hare Krishna, Hare Krishna, Krishna Krishna, Hare Hare
Hare Rama, Hare Rama, Rama Rama, Hare Hare

On October 9, 1966, Prabhupada and his followers sat beneath this tree and held the first outdoor chanting session outside of India. Participants chanted for two hours as they danced and played cymbals, tambourines, and other percussive instruments; the event is recognized as the founding of the Hare Krishna religion in the United States. Prabhupada's diverse group that day included Beat poet Allen Ginsberg (1926-1997). Krishna adherents continue to return to the tree to acknowledge its significance.

American elm trees are known for their towering canopies, which provide abundant shade through spring, summer, and fall. It is rare today to find such a collection of American elms, since many of the mature elms planted across the country have been killed by Dutch Elm Disease. This incurable disease, a fungus carried by bark beetles (Coleoptera Sclytidae) which colonize on the branches of the elm tree, swept across the United States in the 1930s and remains a threat to the park's collection of elms. Despite having lost at least 34 of the trees, Tompkins Square Park still hosts a large assemblage of elms, which continue to this day to enchant park patrons. The East Village Parks Conservancy, a volunteer group, raises significant private funds for the ongoing care and maintenance of the American elms and other historic trees in Tompkins Square Park.

City of New York
Parks & Recreation

Michael R. Bloomberg, Mayor
Adrian Benepe, Commissioner

www.nyc.gov/parks
Text Written: April 2011

To honor the Swami's public chanting as an event of historic importance, in 1999 the New York City's Department of Parks and Recreation installed a commemorative plaque near the base of the American elm tree where he held his weekly gatherings.

positioned microphones, then they signaled the chanters to begin. Students played kartals, and the Swami sang, keeping time on a two-headed wooden drum that a temple guest had volunteered for the occasion. An hour and several takes later, the chanting came to a resounding conclusion.

"Are you tired?" Kallman asked the Swami.

"Not too tired," he replied. Engineers again turned on their recording equipment, and the Swami leaned into the microphone.

"This chanting of 'Hare Krishna, Hare Krishna, Krishna Krishna, Hare Hare, Hare Rama, Hare Rama, Rama Rama, Hare Hare' is the sublime method for reviving our dormant Krishna consciousness." He spoke carefully, knowing that his accent might be difficult for some listeners to follow. "As living spirit souls," he continued, "we are all originally Krishna conscious entities, but due to our association with matter from time immemorial, our consciousness is now polluted by the material atmosphere. Krishna consciousness is not an artificial imposition on the mind. When we hear the transcendental vibration, this consciousness is revived. This chanting is directly enacted from the spiritual platform, surpassing all lower strata of consciousness, namely sensual, mental, and intellectual. As such, anyone can take part in the chanting without any previous qualification and dance in ecstasy. We have seen it practically. Even a child can take part in the chanting, and even a dog can take part in it. No other means therefore of spiritual realization is as effective in this age as chanting the *maha-mantra* — Hare Krishna, Hare Krishna, Krishna Krishna, Hare Hare, Hare Rama, Hare Rama, Rama Rama, Hare Hare."

Then he sang *Guru-vastakam*, a prayer honoring the lineage of spiritual masters. After another half hour of performance, he stopped. "You have made your best record," he said to Kallman. The group gathered their instruments and prepared to drive back to the tiny storefront temple.

Unexpectedly, the engineers played back the recording of Hare Krishna over the studio sound system. The Swami looked up, elated by the mix of voices and instruments, and the slight echo engineers had added for effect. He smiled, raised his arms and danced, dipping slightly from the waist and swaying back and forth. His sleepy followers came alive, set down whatever they had been carrying, and joined him, right foot over left, left foot over right. The group pointed to engineers behind the glass booth and smiled. The studio technicians had raised their arms and were also dancing back and forth to the music. The first recording of "Hare Krishna" was already a hit.

THAT YEAR, interest in the Hare Krishna chant and the philosophy of Krishna consciousness expanded in a variety of ways. While visiting the United States, the Beatles heard a broadcast of the Kallman record on radio. Of the four superstars, George Harrison was most taken by the chanting. He asked the band's road manager to order copies of the album, and back in London Harrison distributed them to friends.

On his posthumous album *Om*, recorded in 1966, jazz saxophonist John Coltrane and fellow musicians opened and closed the improvised tracks by quoting Krishna from the Bhagavad Gita: "Rites that the Vedas ordain and the rituals taught by the scriptures, the oblation, the flame into which they are offered—all these am I." That was also the year Jimi Hendrix released his album *Axis: Bold As Love*, with his own face superimposed over the image of Krishna's Universal Form. Soon after, Allen Ginsberg appeared on William F. Buckley's television talk show *Firing Line* and sang the Hare Krishna mantra to a nationwide viewing audience. Not long after that, folk-singer Tom Paxton referred to the Hare Krishna chant in his song "Talking Vietnam Potluck Blues": "So we all lit up and by and by / The whole platoon was flyin' high / With a beautiful smile on the Captain's face / He smelled like midnight on St. Mark's Place / Cleanin' his weapon / Chantin' sumpin' about Hare Krishna, Hare Krishna." Author Tom Wolfe added to the momentum by including a description of the mantra in his book *The Electric Kool-Aid Acid Test*.

Before coming to America, had the Swami imagined what success would look like, he might not have foreseen such assimilation of the maha-mantra, "the great mantra for deliverance," into pop culture. If he had been told, he would not have objected. Chaitanya Mahaprabhu used to tease children into chanting by covering his ears and pretending he would not listen. Whatever it took to get people chanting was acceptable, and through a combination of jazz albums, pop songs, talk shows and divine plan, the Hare Krishna mantra spread, and the Swami's following grew.

IN SEPTEMBER 1966, THE SWAMI ANNOUNCED to his American followers that soon he would hold an initiation ceremony. Students interested in formal initiation were expected to follow the basic rules of Vaishnava behavior and chant sixteen "rounds" of the Krishna mantra each day on their beads. "I'm being 80 percent lenient," he said, "since my guru instructed his disciples to chant sixty-four rounds." There were other qualifications, he said, that he would explain in time. None of the students was sure how initiation would change things.

The day before initiations were to take place, the Swami gave class as usual. "And now," he said at the end, "I will tell you what is meant by initiation. Initiation means the spiritual master accepts the students and agrees to take charge of their spiritual life. And the students accept the spiritual master and agree to worship him as God. Any questions?" No one dared raise a hand. So the Swami stood up and left.

"*What did he just say?*" everyone asked in shock. Wally Sheffey turned to Howard Wheeler. "My mind has just been blown," he said.

"Everybody's mind has just been blown," Wheeler replied. A small group went up to the Swami's apartment. "Does what you told us mean the spiritual master is God?"

The Swami shook his head. "No," he said. "*God* is God. The spiritual master is his representative. Initiation means the spiritual master is due the same respect as God, because he can deliver God to the sincere disciple. Is that clear?"

As members of a generation that deemed most authority suspect, they were relieved to know the Swami was not positioning himself as equal to Krishna. Still, their impression from books on India was that gurus were revered as all-knowing. Did he claim to be omniscient, like Krishna?

"If you say you have full knowledge," somebody challenged, "then how many windows are in the Empire State Building?"

"How many drops of water are in a mirage?"[83] the Swami shot back. When the Vedic texts described a spiritual master as "all-knowing" or "perfect," it meant that a guru knows everything needed to be Krishna conscious, not every detail of the ephemeral material world. And a guru was perfect in the sense that his teachings were not invented.

"A spiritual master does not concoct anything," the Swami explained. "Whatever he teaches has come from *shastra* and guru," from scripture as passed down by predecessor teachers. "That makes him perfect."[84]

His explanations calmed the waters, and for students committed to Krishna consciousness, the prospect of honoring the Swami as Krishna's representative did not pose a problem. They were already doing that. What did pose a problem were the rules he expected them to follow after initiation. The behavioral restrictions for initiates—no meat, fish, or eggs in the diet; no drugs or intoxicants; no gambling; and no sex with anyone other than a life partner and only for having children—would require difficult changes of habit. If they agreed to sit before the fire and take the initiate's vows, would they regret it? Would they break the vows after some time and then have to live with that hypocrisy? Even the Swami doubted whether Westerners could follow the guidelines for initiation.

"When I first came," he recalled, "I was thinking that as soon as I say they have to give up meat-eating, illicit sex, intoxication, and gambling, they will say, 'Please go home.' But I thought, let me try."

Despite their hesitations, Michael Grant and his partner, Jan, concluded that they were already committed to the Swami and that initiation was the natural next step. So, on a crisp September evening, they walked to Matchless Gifts, crossed the small courtyard, and mounted the stairs to apartment 2-C, where the ceremony would be held. Nine other regulars were already seated on the floor around the Swami.

"Initiation means purification," he told the group. "We are all impure in this material world and therefore we suffer from birth, death, old age, and disease. To overcome these miseries, we must voluntarily accept some *tapasya*, sacrifice—some rules and regulations."

Keeping disciples to the proper standard, he said, was the duty of a spiritual master. "To accept a spiritual master is not a hobby," he cautioned. "One who is interested in hearing about the transcendental subject matter—for him, a spiritual master is needed. Not for all. We must accept a spiritual master who can teach us about God. And who is such a person? That is stated in the *Upanishads*.[85] The spiritual master comes down in disciplic succession and must be fully, firmly fixed in brahman." His words were sobering. This is serious, he was telling them. Study me. If you find me authentic, then fine, ask me to be your guru. And if I find *you* authentic and sincere, then I will accept you as my disciple and I will guide you in your spiritual life. Without our wholehearted commitment to one another, why bother?

"This initiation is called *harinam* initiation—first initiation," he said, using the Sanskrit word meaning to chant the names of Krishna. "The spiritual master gives the disciple harinam to become purified. Later some of you may receive second initiation, Brahmin initiation." His guru, Bhaktisiddhanta Saraswati, had insisted that anyone properly trained in devotional service was de facto a Brahmin. Following that principle, the Swami said, he was prepared to institute a "second initiation" for those disciples who qualified, in essence transforming them into Brahmins regardless of their caste at birth.

"Along with chanting Hare Krishna," he said, "you must follow some rules. The rules are no illicit sex life, no intoxication, no meat-eating, and no gambling. Anyone indulging in these four things cannot understand who is God or become free from conditioned life."

Many initiates considered the restriction on sex harder than the other regulations, even though his explanations for it were convincing. The soul was by nature pleasure-seeking he described, being part and parcel of Krishna. When souls forget that relationship, they looked for pleasure in relationships with other conditioned beings. Healthy partnerships could be created in this world, but without a shared sense of life's spiritual purpose, they would never be completely satisfying. Sex in this world, Bhaktisiddhanta had once described, appeared both beautiful and ugly: beautiful in terms of its promise, ugly in terms of its failure to deliver unending love.

The Swami's students admitted that was indeed their experience. How often had their hearts been broken and their mornings-after filled with regret? Still, he was asking a lot from them. They trusted his insight into their well-being, but did he expect them to change a lifetime of habits just by going through a ceremony? If what he taught them was true, then their karma, their addictions and egos had been cultivated over many lifetimes. What made him think they could change now?

"Your karma is like a revolving fan," he said. "By chanting Hare Krishna and giving up unwanted habits, you turn it off. The fan may still revolve for a while, but since it is getting no more electricity, it will soon stop."

Do not even attempt to fathom where such residual spinning originated, he advised, since karma could be very old, possibly the consequence of actions from many lifetimes before. Those lives were over and gone, and there was no point wishing for a better past.[86] Move on, he encouraged. Karma may be old, but it was not incurable. Change was possible with sincere effort because the soul was by nature spotless, unblemished by material nature. That original consciousness simply needed to be revived. How? By chanting. No need of yogic gymnastics or miracles, just sincere chanting. And he would help them. He would be their link to Krishna, as long as their effort was sincere.

These newly initiated disciples, the first Krishna devotees in the West, reached out, accepted their beads and their future, and touched their heads to the floor in appreciation.

AFTER THREE INITIATION CEREMONIES ninteen devotees had received Sanskrit names. Wally Sheffey became Umapati Das: servant of Shiva, husband of goddess Uma. Michael Grant received the name Mukunda Das: servant of Krishna, the giver of *mukti* or liberation from birth and death. Judy Koslofsky was now Jadurani Dasi: servant of Krishna who appeared in the Yadu dynasty. Steve Guarino would from now on be called Satsvarupa Das: servant of Krishna, truth personified. Jan Campanella received the name Janaki Dasi: servant of Princess Sita, daughter of the great Vedic king Janaka. Keith Ham was now Kirtanananda Das: servant of the joy of chanting Krishna's names. Charles Barnett would now be known as Achyutananda Das: servant of the bliss (*ananda*) of infallible Krishna (*Achyuta*). Bruce Scharf received the initiated name Brahmananda Das: servant of Krishna, who is the bliss of brahman, being its source; and his brother, Greg, was now Gargamuni Das: servant of Garga Muni, the guru of Krishna's Vrindavan family. Howard Wheeler received his beads and the initiated name Hayagriva Das: servant of the horse-headed avatar of Vishnu.

For each ceremony, students carried buckets of soil up from the garden outside the Swami's building and created a two-foot-square earthen mound in the middle of his apartment. The Swami lit a handful of incense sticks and placed them around the square, sprinkled on pinches of colored powder, and arranged a foot-tall pyramid of kindling in the middle. He lit a fire and chanted mantras while pouring out small ladles of clarified butter or ghee. Flames grew, and smoke filled the room. He motioned to his newly initiated disciples to take bananas and place them in the flames. While the bananas cooked, the Swami stood, clapped his hands, and chanted Hare Krishna, and the assembly followed his lead, dancing side to side, arms raised in celebration of their rebirth into the life of Krishna devotees. Mukunda later described the moment as enthralling.

"I'd gone into the initiation casually," he wrote, "but this had become more than an informal, relaxed event. It was a change from one life to another."

The Matchless Gifts initiations marked a turning point in Vaishnava history. By traditional Hindu standards, Americans and Europeans were *mlecchas* or savages who ate meat, drank alcohol, took drugs, and had sex outside marriage. Such outcastes did not qualify for diksha, the initiation ceremony that opened the door to liberation. Custom held they would have to wait until they were reborn in higher-caste families. The Swami waved these objections aside. Krishna consciousness had nothing to do with Hindu customs or caste qualification, he said. All living beings are sparks of God, parts and parcels of Krishna. He cited chapter and verse to prove that, from the Vedic point of view, anyone who sincerely chanted Krishna's names was eligible for initiation.

TO TAKE THEIR INITIATION SERIOUSLY, disciples needed to know what was expected of them. They were now representatives of Chaitanya Vaishnavism, and their behavior had to be above reproach. The Swami took out a sheet of paper and wrote a list of rules in precise script.

- All initiated devotees must attend morning and evening classes.
- Must not be addicted to any kind of intoxicants, including coffee, tea, and cigarettes.
- They are forbidden to have illicit sex-connections.
- Must be strictly vegetarian.
- Should not extensively mix with non-devotees.
- Should not eat foodstuffs cooked by non-devotees.
- Should not waste time in idle talks nor engage in frivolous sports.
- Should always chant and sing the Lord's Holy Names: Hare Krishna, Hare Krishna, Krishna Krishna, Hare Hare, Hare Rama, Hare Rama, Rama Rama, Hare Hare.
- Thank you

He posted the sheet of paper on the temple room door. The next morning devotees arrived for class and read the list of new rules with concern.

"No tea?" someone asked. "Isn't that a bit much?"

"It is slow poison," the Swami replied.

Each student would struggle in his or her own way to maintain the rigorous standards required of initiated disciples. Many considered drugs a legitimate way to expand consciousness and sex a natural urge to be freely indulged. Instead of indulging those impulses, the Swami proposed, master them. See how much more rewarding life can be when you yourself become "swamis," masters of your senses.

HAYAGRIVA, UMAPATI, and some of the other initiates sat in the Swami's room, typing away and filing pages from his manuscripts. Umapati transcribed notes from one of the Swami's recent classes, while Hayagriva edited pages of a *Bhagavatam* commentary. He read a few pages and then stopped. "Listen to this," he said and read aloud the *Bhagavatam*'s explanation of how the universe came into being.

In the beginning, all was darkness. Vishnu slept in that darkness, floating on an ocean of undifferentiated cosmic elements. From Vishnu's body, an infinity of tiny bubbles emanated. Each bubble swelled into a universe, and each universe resembled a gigantic coconut shell half filled with the waters of causality. Vishnu entered into each of these newly created universes and reclined on Sesa Naga, a thousand-hooded serpent that undulated with the cosmic waves, while Lakshmi, the goddess of fortune, massaged her beloved Vishnu's lotus feet. From Vishnu's navel sprouted an immense lotus flower, and from the whorl of the lotus, Brahma, the first being, appeared.

Brahma stared into the darkness. He did not know who he was, or where he was, or why. He looked at the lotus and climbed down its stem, hoping to discover the source of his being. Brahma traveled past raw, unfinished worlds awaiting completion and found no end to them. Despondent, he turned and climbed back. On the way, he heard two syllables: "*ta-pa*," meaning "sacrifice something of yourself." Upon returning to his sitting place on the lotus whorl, Brahma closed his eyes, and for a thousand celestial years he meditated on the mystery of his existence, shedding ego and surrendering himself to an impulse to serve.

At last, looking up, he watched layers of darkness part. Coverings over the material universe peeled away one by one to reveal the eternal world, filled with light and an infinity of self-luminous planets. On the highest planet, Brahma observed Krishna seated under a tree, and around him were cowherds boys and girls of many colors, some white as snow, some black as cobalt, others opal, strawberry red, deep russet, wild green — a kaleidoscope of children.

Krishna rose, came before Brahma and took his hand. Thank you, Krishna said, for your sincere searching. Then Krishna imparted the Vedic wisdom into the heart of Brahma, making him the first in a lineage of teachers charged with safeguarding the wisdom that frees souls from the cycle of repeated birth in the material world.

Ages passed. Brahma completed the work of creation and populated the many worlds with living beings according to their karmic allotment. His work done, Brahma next conveyed the Vedic teachings to his son, Narada, who in turn taught them to his disciple, Vyasadev. It was Vyasadev who compiled the teachings into written form and entrusted various divisions of those writings to his disciples. Those disciples in turn taught their disciples, and the teachings were passed down through the ages.

The *Srimad Bhagavatam* answered the "who" and "why" questions asked by children before education dulled their curiosity. Who are we? We are eternal souls living in temporary bodies. Why does the world exist? Because we wanted it. We eternal souls harbor dreams of glory, and we transmigrate from body to body, from planet to planet, universe to universe until we realize the futility of those dreams and reawaken to our immortal selves. The initiates at 26 Second Avenue were learning that the world was a playground where souls acted out fantasies until the day they met a guru, set out on their yoga path, and prepared to go back to the spiritual world. See the world, the Swami taught them, not with telescopes or mathematical calculations but with the eyes of your soul. It is more mysterious than it seems.

As he listened to this brief history of everything, Umapati reached a conclusion regarding their guru's identity: A.C. Bhaktivedanta Swami was no ordinary teacher but the current link in an unbroken chain of enlightened beings, dating from the dawn of creation, when God revealed the deepest secrets of the universe to Brahma—and those secrets had now arrived in America, in the Swami's books.

"If that's true," he said with a very straight face, "it's far out."

IN NOVEMBER, THOMAS J. HOPKINS, professor of religious studies at Franklin & Marshall College in Pennsylvania, arrived at Matchless Gifts with a question burning to be answered. Could it be that the Swami he had read about in the *East Village Other* actually belonged to the Chaitanya lineage? Hopkins had done his Ph.D. thesis on the *Bhagavata Purana* (what the Swami called *Srimad Bhagavatam*) and knew something about devotional movements. But the Chaitanya tradition with its emphasis on public chanting and dancing was obscure even by Indian standards. He stepped into Matchless Gifts, and there on a table by the front door he saw three books titled *Srimad Bhagwatam*.[87]

"This may not warrant excitement today," he commented years later, "but when I did my dissertation research in the late 1950s there were only two English translations in any U.S. library, one at Yale and the other at Harvard. I had come to assume that translations of the *Bhagavata* were rare and precious items—and here was one sitting on a table in a storefront where anyone could come in and pick it up."

Hopkins flipped through one of the volumes and admired its thorough presentation of original *devanagari* Sanskrit verses, English transliterations, word-for-word synonyms, English translations, and elaborate commentaries. It was masterful. But the mystical glory of the book was its jacket. The image was at once idealized and highly realistic. Information on the jacket flaps explained the image's various elements. The top half of the illustration consisted of a lotus flower with pink petals, representing the highest place in the eternal world: Vrindavan, Krishna's village. Inside the lotus-like village, the artist had painted Radha and Krishna dancing as Krishna played his flute. In the background, Hopkins noticed a second Krishna, this one sitting with the cowherd women of the village, called gopis. Krishna, it seemed, could be in more than one place. The lotus-like planet emitted rays of light in all directions. In that light were other planets, and within each was a Krishna with four arms. These, the jacket copy explained, were Vishnu "expansions" from the original two-armed Krishna. In the lower right corner of the jacket floated a dark cloud. This, the jacket said, was the material world, and it occurred to Hopkins that he was staring at a visualization of the entire creation in a single image.

By the time of Hopkins's visit, Brahmananda and his brother, Gargamuni, had assumed a large share of the administrative duties of the Matchless Gifts storefront. Brahmananda was now the official temple president and did paperwork at a desk by the front door. Next to the display window sat two mimeograph machines on which his brother, Gargamuni, printed the Swami's *Back to Godhead* magazine. This was a hand-stapled version of the magazine the Swami had written and printed periodically in India between 1944 and 1960. The New York version contained transcripts of the Swami's classes along with articles and poems by students. One disciple typed the transcripts onto thin paper stencils, and another disciple aligned the stencils onto pegs across the top of the press. He then added ink to a recessed well that distributed the ink evenly across the stencil, threw the on-switch, and supervised while printed pages came out the other end. Gargamuni stacked the pages in numerical order, collated them one by one, and stapled them together. Then he loaded copies into bags hanging from the handlebars of his bicycle and rode around New York, delivering finished copies of *Back to Godhead* to neighborhood shops where they sold quickly at fifteen cents each. Collections after the

Swami's classes rarely amounted to more than a few dollars, and the additional income helped cover the costs of rent and groceries.

It took Hopkins a while to adjust to the idea of a Vaishnava temple replete with a printing operation in the middle of the Lower East Side of New York City. "It's an astonishing story," he reflected. "If someone told you a story like this, you wouldn't believe it. Here's this person, seventy years old, coming to a country where he's never been before. He doesn't know anybody, he has no money, no contacts, none of the things you would say make for success. He's going to recruit people not on any systematic basis but just picking up whomever he comes across—and he's going to give them responsibility for organizing a worldwide movement? You'd say, 'What kind of program is that?' There are precedents perhaps. Jesus of Nazareth went around saying, 'Come follow me. Drop your nets, leave your tax collecting, and be my disciple.' But in Jesus's case, he wasn't an old man in a strange society dealing with people whose backgrounds were totally different from his own. He was dealing with his own community. Bhaktivedanta Swami's achievement, then, must be seen as unique."[88]

IT WAS A QUIET OCTOBER NIGHT, and some of the initiated devotees decided to chant in the courtyard between Matchless Gifts and the Swami's apartment building. They sat on a bench and looked up into a clear night sky.

"It's a beautiful moon," said one devotee.

"That's maya," said another, "an illusion," sparking a debate about whether anything material could be beautiful. The group decided to bring the question to the Swami.

"For devotees," the Swami explained, "this world is as good as Vaikuntha," using the Sanskrit term for the eternal world: the place that is without (vai) anxiety (kuntha). "In the Bhagavad Gita, Krishna says the sun and moon are his eyes. When a devotee looks at the moon, he sees Krishna."

Nonetheless, a disciple suggested, the perceivable world was subject to change, so there had to be some differences between matter and spirit. "Is it our consciousness, then," the disciple asked, "that determines whether something is material or spiritual?"

"Yes," the Swami acknowledged. "For one who has attained higher stages of spiritual realization, there is nothing material. Such a person sees everything as brahman. Still, Krishna speaks of having 'superior' and 'inferior' energies. How is that? Because without the touch of spirit, matter cannot work. Therefore, it is called 'inferior.' But in a higher sense, it is not inferior, because matter also emanates from the Supreme. Just like electricity can run a cold refrigerator or a hot stove. One who knows the nature of electricity knows that the same energy is working, whether hot or cold, inferior or superior. So on the platform of real knowledge, there is no distinction between matter and spirit."

The world itself, from that perspective, was spiritual, and he had come to America to teach how to see Krishna, the Supreme Spirit, in the details of the everyday world. "Krishna consciousness" meant recognizing that commonplace events held as much importance as peak experiences—that Krishna could be found in everything. He dwelled not only in a faraway eternal realm but in each atom and between each atom.[89] That one lesson could radically change the way people related to the world around them, since respecting the Earth and the environment, from this Krishna-conscious perspective, became a spiritual imperative.

Everything was God's energy. Hayagriva remembered being in the Swami's apartment recently and making room by shoving the typewriter aside with his foot.

"Don't touch that with your foot," the Swami scolded. "It is spiritual."

"Well, aren't my feet spiritual?" Hayagriva asked.

"Yes," the Swami acknowledged, "in the service of Krishna everything is spiritual. But even with your spiritual foot you should not disrespect a spiritual typewriter. You will understand this in time."

THE SWAMI RESTED FROM 11 p.m. until 2 or 3 a.m. Then, while the city slept and before his students woke, he rose and spent several hours commenting on the Bhagavad Gita using a handheld Dictaphone. His schedule reminded students of Krishna's teaching: "What is night for others is the time of awakening for the self-controlled. What is the time of awakening for others is night for the introspective sage."[90]

Later in the day, Satsvarupa typed out the dictated tapes and handed the pages over to Hayagriva. "Edit for force and clarity," the Swami told him. "You are a qualified English professor. You know that grammatical mistakes will discredit us with scholars. I want them to appreciate this Bhagavad Gita as the definitive edition. All others try to take credit away from Krishna. Therefore, I am presenting the Gita 'As It Is.'"

Hundreds of pages were piling up, ready for publication. Meanwhile, collections were negligible. There was no money to print anything.

Poet Allen Ginsberg frequently visited Matchless Gifts in the 1960s for chanting sessions and talks with the Swami.

CHAPTER SIX

My devotees derive great satisfaction and bliss enlightening
one another and conversing about me.

—SRI KRISHNA IN THE BHAGAVAD GITA, 10.9

MUKUNDA AND JANAKI DECIDED the time had come to see India. Meeting the Swami, getting married, taking initiation—events, they agreed, pointed in the direction of a visit to Krishna's homeland. When they told the Swami their plans, he was concerned. India tended to play havoc with naïve foreigners. Would they fall prey to mayavadi philosophies and come back thinking they were God? With *ganja* (marijuana) so easily available, would they go back to old habits? His affection for them was palpable, and Mukunda, not knowing how else to say goodbye, mentioned that they would be driving to California before flying to India. California, Mukunda said, would be a good place to open a temple.

"There's lots of interest in India and spirituality in that part of the country," he said. Then he bowed to his teacher and turned to leave.

"Mukunda," the Swami said. "Just see if you can start one center in California. It would be a very great service." It was not the farewell Mukunda had planned.

"Okay," he mumbled, wondering what he had gotten himself into. Had he remembered that the Swami received a similar instruction almost fifty years before from *his* guru, he might have recognized the message: "Go West. Spread Krishna consciousness. It will be a very great service."

When Mukunda returned home, Janaki had their bags and their cat ready to go. They loaded them into a rented station wagon and drove out of New York, chanting in the warm autumn breeze. Four days later they crossed into Oregon and arrived at the tiny city of Sisters, population 250, where Mukunda's college buddy, Sam Speerstra, lived with his girlfriend, Melanie, on a wooded hilltop. All four had attended Reed College and kept in touch after graduating. Mukunda and Janaki described their recent initiation into Krishna consciousness and the Swami's encouragement to open a Krishna temple in California.

The proposal came at a moment of transition for the Oregon couple. Sam and Melanie had been reading *Autobiography of a Yogi* and felt themselves drawn to spiritual journeys. Sam's job as a fire-spotter in Deschutes National Forest for the U.S. Forest Service was about to end, and he and Melanie had no firm plans for what do to next. They sensed an adventure in Mukunda's proposal and offered to help. Mukunda and Janaki cashed in their tickets to India, and the four set out for San Francisco.

In November 1966, they arrived in Haight-Ashbury, the epicenter of hippie culture. They were joined by Roger Siegel, who had been an organizer in the South for Dr. Martin Luther King's freedom marches. The group formed a smoothly functioning team, with their sights set on opening a Krishna temple. Roger and his girlfriend, Jan Campanella's sister, Joan, suggested they organize a benefit concert and invite Allen Ginsberg as special guest.

The group put the plan in motion. Sam had contacts in the music world and convinced the Grateful Dead and Big Brother and the Holding Company to participate. Mukunda reserved the Avalon Ballroom, where a number of local groups such as Quicksilver Messenger Service and the Steve Miller Band had had their start. Friends from the area pitched in and blanketed San Francisco with thousands of psychedelic posters and flyers announcing the upcoming Mantra-Rock benefit concert. The group sent the Swami a ticket for his first airplane ride: New York to San Francisco.

Meanwhile, Mukunda found a ground-floor store for rent on Frederick Street not far from Kezar Stadium, home of the San Francisco 49ers football team. The storefront was like the one he had found for the Swami in New York, but with a bigger plate-glass window. The landlord also showed him two apartments on the fourth floor of a nearby building. Mukunda rented everything that same day. Krishna, he prayed, would figure out the financing.

ON AN OVERCAST DAY in January 1967, the Swami left New York on a United Airlines flight bound for San Francisco. The plane rose from the

The jacket of Prabhupada's edition of *Srimad Bhagavatam*, published in 1962, depicts the entirety of creation in a single image. The flap of the jacket also includes portraits of Prabhupada's spiritual master (bottom left) and of a young Abhay and an older Prabhupada (bottom right). Prabhupada repeatedly emphasized that books were the basis of his spiritual mission.

The Prime Minister of India Sri Lal Bahadur Shastri

RECOGNISES SRIMAD A. C. BHAKTIVEDANTA SWAMI FOR HIS VALUABLE WORK ELABORATE ENGLISH VERSION OF "SRIMAD BHAGWATAM" AND RECOMMENDS IT FOR PURCHASE IN ALL LIBRARIES OF GOVERNMENT INSTITUTIONS.

TOP: In 1964, after printing the second volume of *Srimad Bhagavatam*, Prabhupada approached India's Prime Minister, Lal Bahadur Shastri, for an endorsement.

BOTTOM: With financial help from Sumati Morarjee, head of Scindia Steamship Company, Prabhupada was able to print the third volume of *Srimad Bhagavatam*. Morarjee also agreed, reluctantly, to provide him passage to America.

TOP: "If you ever get money," Prabhupada's guru, Bhaktisiddhanta Saraswati, said, "print books." And he did so, by the millions. In this photo, Prabhupada lectures from the first volume of *Srimad Bhagavatam* in Butler, Pennsylvania, in 1965.

BOTTOM: Prabhupada conducted the Western world's first Vaishnava initiations, and awarded diksha to men and women regardless of their social background.

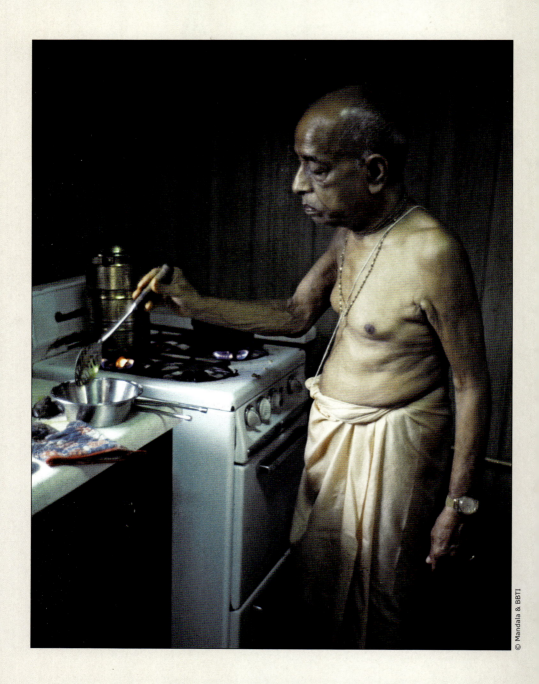

Prabhupada, a skilled cook in his own right, stressed the importance of prasadam, or food offered to Krishna with devotion, and trained his disciples in the practice of consciously prepared food. The Krishna consciousness movement is popularly known for its delicious vegetarian meals, and was sometimes referred to as "the kitchen religion."

KRISHNA CONSCIOUSNESS COMES WEST

SWAMI BHAKTIVEDANTA · ALLEN GINSBERG
THE GRATEFUL DEAD · MOBY GRAPE
BIG BROTHER & THE HOLDING COMPANY

MANTRA · ROCK DANCE

SUNDAY JAN. 29 AVALON BALLROOM 8PM

SUTTER & VAN NESS #250 BRING CUSHIONS, DRUMS, BELLS, CYMBALS
PROCEEDS TO OPENING OF SAN FRANCISCO KRISHNA TEMPLE
LIGHTS BY BEN VAN METER AND ROGER HILLYARD

© BBTI

To raise funds for their fledgling San Francisco temple, disciples enlisted rock artists of the day and packed
the Avalon Ballroom for a Mantra Rock Concert in 1967.

Despite building an international movement, Prabhupada never failed to rise early each morning to continue his translation and commentary of *Srimad Bhagavatam* and other devotional texts. In addition, during the twelve years of his mission, he wrote more than six thousand letters, offering personal encouragement to people in their spiritual lives.

TOP: In 1969, Prabhupada visited the publishing operation established by disciples in Boston and astonished them by bowing before the printing press.

BOTTOM: Prabhupada taught his artist-disciples that a painting, like a deity, becomes the Divine made manifest if the work is executed according to scriptural guidelines and with a mood of devotion.

The late singer-songwriter George Harrison played a critical role in helping to spread the chanting of the Hare Krishna mantra. He is pictured here with Patti Boyd, his wife at the time.

runway, and he watched skyscrapers and bridges shrink away to the size of matchboxes. The plane merged into a dark bank of rain clouds, and for several minutes nothing was visible. We are like that, he reflected: small, our vision easily covered by clouds of maya. He chanted on his beads and waited. Then suddenly the plane lifted up over the cloudbank into a bright sky. "Krishna is compared to sunshine and maya to darkness," he recited. "Wherever there is sunshine, there cannot be darkness."[91]

Six hours later, his flight touched down in San Francisco. Allen Ginsberg was there with a handful of devotees and friends to greet the Swami on his arrival.

San Francisco Chronicle
Swami in Hippie Land
Holy Man Opens San Francisco Temple

A holy man from India, described by friend and beat poet Allen Ginsberg as one of the more conservative leaders of his faith, launched a kind of evangelistic effort yesterday in the heart of San Francisco's hippie haven.

"Conservative?" the Swami asked on reading the article. "How is that?"

Mukunda suggested the reporter might have been referring to their restrictions on sex and drugs.

"Of course, we are conservative in that sense," the Swami agreed. "But we accept everyone into this movement, regardless of sex, caste, position, or whatever. Everyone is invited to come chant Hare Krishna. No, we are not conservative."

Kirtans in the San Francisco temple were lively. Each evening the storefront was packed with young people sporting long hair, exotic clothing, Indian beads, and painted cheeks, and their dancing was free and vigorous. From the temple, the Swami walked to his apartment on Frederick Street. A window faced east, filling the room each morning with bright sunlight. Two storefronts and a few dozen long-haired young Americans were hardly the worldwide movement predicted by Chaitanya Mahaprabhu. But it was a start.

ON SUNDAY, JANUARY 29, 1967, the Avalon Ballroom was packed with more than 500 ticket-holders for the Krishna Mantra-Rock Concert, which one commentator on the Sixties dubbed "the ultimate high of that era."[92] There were a handful of San Francisco temple regulars by now, and everyone attended in their Sixties best. Men wore Merlin-style gowns, women dressed in colorful saris, and the hippie crowd cheered appreciatively as the devotees took to the stage. Mukunda picked up a drum; others readied kartals, *tambura*, and harmonium; and the group opened with a mellow kirtan. From the balcony, technicians turned on strobe lights that projected pulsating rainbows of color onto walls and ceiling.

An hour later, the Swami and Allen Ginsberg entered the hall, and there was a drum roll and spontaneous roar of approval from the audience. The crowd parted as devotees onstage brought the kirtan to an end. The guests of honor mounted the stage and sat on cushions. Technicians positioned microphones. The Swami was dressed in fresh saffron silks and wore a fragrant gardenia garland around his neck. He studied the audience and would later remark, "Hippies are our best potential. Although they are young, they are already dissatisfied with material life and frustrated. Not knowing what to do, they turn to drugs. So let them come to us, and we will show them spiritual activities. Once they engage in Krishna consciousness, all these *anarthas*, unwanted things, will fall away."

Ginsberg adjusted the microphone. "When I was in India," he told the audience, "I got enthralled with the mantra we're going to sing. The mantra is called the maha-mantra, literally 'the great mind-deliverance mantra.' Sometimes you can have a bad acid trip, and I want you to know that if you ever do, you can stabilize yourself on reentry by chanting this mantra. Now I want to introduce you to Swami Bhaktivedanta, who brought this mantra to the place where it was probably most needed, to New York's Lower East Side—to the dispossessed, to the homeless, the lost, the anarchists, the seekers." The crowd cheered.

"He left India, where life is peaceful," Ginsberg continued, "where he could have remained happily chanting in a holy village where people never heard of war and violence, where life is slow and meaningful. But instead, he's here with us tonight, his first time in this city—his first time in America! And he's come to share with us something precious, something to treasure, something serene." He gestured to the Swami, and the crowd went silent.

Prabhupada closed his eyes. "This chanting," he said, "will lead us to the spiritual world. The mantra is not only for Indians. Hare Krishna is for all people because Krishna is everyone's father. God is God for all human beings, beasts, aquatics, insects, trees, plants—all varieties of life. That is God. This sound is the sound-representation of the Supreme Lord.

Everything has emanated from the Supreme Absolute Truth." After a few more minutes of explanation, he thanked Ginsberg, and the audience again burst into applause.

Ginsberg pumped his harmonium. "Everyone sing loud," he urged. "And dance, if you feel like it."

The devotees onstage joined Ginsberg in a slow, hypnotic repetition of the words. The audience caught on, the kirtan began, and everyone sang, swaying as the tempo slowly picked up. The drummer from Moby Grape took his place behind the drum kit. Guitarists from The Grateful Dead plugged their guitars into amplifiers and were joined by guitarists from Big Brother and the Holding Company. The audience screamed with excitement as the celebrity rockers took to the stage. Moved by the inclusiveness of the scene, janitors, stage managers, security guards, and firemen clapped and danced.

Ginsberg chanted faster, sweat cascading down his face. Young people in the audience jumped and stomped their feet. On the wall behind the musicians appeared a towering image of Krishna, flute in hand, peacock feather in his hair. Incense burned in ceramic pots around the room, sending clouds of smoke drifting out over the scene, and through the billows of smoke the Swami watched as the throngs of young people danced and screamed out "Hare Krishna! Hare Krishna!"

In his memoir, Mukunda described the unusual spectacle of serene dancers interspersed with hippies on LSD, squirming on the floor "like wounded snakes, while others shook, pranced, spun, shrieked, laughed, and cried." Without warning, the Swami stood up from his pillow and raised his arms, dancing left foot over right, right foot over left, as he had taught followers to do in New York. Soon a thousand arms were waving in rhythmic unison. Ginsberg removed his microphone from its stand and held it in front of the Swami, and for several minutes the Swami's voice filled the auditorium as he lead the chant. When Mukunda saw beads of perspiration streaming down the Swami's face, he brought the chant to a crashing halt by raising his arms and motioning for devotees to bow to the audience.

The Swami descended from the stage, and the audience parted, cheering and applauding as they made room for him to pass. Girls more or less clothed bowed before the Swami and threw flowers at his feet.

"This is no place for a brahmachari," he murmured to a disciple, referring to celibates like themselves, as they carefully made their way through the crowd of undulating young women.

THE NEXT MORNING after little sleep Kirtanananda and Hayagriva drove
their teacher to the beach. In those halcyon days of his mission, before a
movement grew into an institution and a trickle of disciples swelled into
a tidal wave, A.C. Bhaktivedanta Swami could take a morning stroll on a
beach with just a few students. It was a cool January day, and wind blew
across the boardwalk that paralleled the ocean. The Swami stopped and
looked out over the water. Then he sang a song in praise of Krishna that the
two disciples had not heard before: "Govinda jaya jaya, Gopala jaya jaya,
Radharamana Hari, Govinda jaya jaya."

Hayagriva would later remember that he chanted slowly, with the
ocean waves rushing back and forth on the sand. The Swami came to the
end of the song and explained its meaning for the two young men.

"Govinda is a name for Krishna," he said, "meaning he gives pleasure to
go, the cows and the senses. Gopal is another name for Krishna, meaning the
cowherd boy. Radha-ramana means Krishna is the *rama*—the ecstasy—of
Radha. These are the words of this mantra." Then he again began singing,
walking slowly along the boardwalk, wind blowing the bottom of his robes.
He stopped again and watched the waves roll in and out.

"There is a verse in Bengali," he said. "Oh, what is that voice across the
sea, calling, calling, Come here, Come here . . ."

Then they sat on a bench and looked out across the Pacific Ocean, and
in intermittent bursts he sang a line from one song, then another, and translated. "Oh, Gopinath—Krishna, beloved of the gopis—please sit within the
core of my heart. Subdue this mind, and thus take me to you. Only then will
the terrible dangers of this world disappear." After a few more moments, the
Swami stood up.

"Back to the temple," he said.

He had come to them as a stranger, less than three years before, to
give them a startling vision of themselves as eternal beings, and that
alone had been sufficient to change their lives. Then he gave them
recipes to cook, songs to sing, deities to worship, books to study. He
encouraged them to open temples, establish farms, and travel around the
world to teach Krishna consciousness to others. He helped them build a
community of brothers and sisters, more family than many of them had
ever known, and with simple examples showed how to see Krishna in
everything and every moment. He revealed for them the face of God as
described in scripture: youthful, joyful, a playful Supreme Being unlike

the wrathful divinity of institutional religions. He taught them verses from the prayers of Brahma:

> *I worship Govinda, the primeval Lord,*
> *Who is adept in playing on His flute,*
> *With blooming eyes like lotus petals,*
> *His head decked with peacock feathers,*
> *The figure of beauty tinged with the hue of blue clouds,*
> *His unique loveliness charming millions of cupids.*

Then, at moments such as this, on a boardwalk with the sun rising behind them, he showed them his heart and invited them to witness his love for Krishna, to inspire them on their own often difficult journey. You are eternal and your soul is pure, he reassured them. Nothing can take that from you. Chant Hare Krishna and erase all karma. Just keep going, he told them. Don't go away.

His disciples knew they did not measure up to his high standards. They loved him for accepting them with all their failings, and being with him was greater than any blessing they could imagine.

DESCRIPTIONS OF THE EARLY DAYS of the Swami's movement frequently mention his response to emotionally unstable visitors. Not only was he attempting to institute Vaishnava standards of behavior, but he was doing so in the most psychologically stressed neighborhoods of the era such as the Lower East Side of New York and Haight-Ashbury in San Francisco. Followers protected him as best they could from confrontations with irate guests and young people on drugs, but they were unavoidable.

In the middle of one of the Swami's lectures, a disoriented young woman suddenly blurted out, "What are you going to do now? Are you just going to sit there? *Who are you?*"

The Swami waited quietly while students escorted her out. He seemed saddened by the outburst, and those sitting close by reported hearing him whisper, "It is the darkest of darkness."

Some guests chose to add their own, often incoherent comments to his lectures. The Swami would handle such tense moments with reserve and calm, acknowledging the soul in the intruder's body and responding with respect and reason. Still, he never compromised the teachings, and when warranted he could be severe if it helped shock someone out of an illusion. Sometimes a guest would say, "I am God," a fantasy which frequently occurred to people on LSD. "What do you mean?" he would say, challenging their impudent claim. "Do you have the attributes of God? Are you all-knowing? Did you create the universe?"

"I used to watch how the Swami would handle things," recalled Haridas, a disciple from the early days of the San Francisco temple. "He would turn their energy around so that before you knew it they were calm, like when you pat a baby and it stops crying." His management of these moments was a combination of "superior intelligence and a lot of compassion," Haridas described. "When I saw him do these things, I realized he was not only a great teacher but a great human being."

CHALLENGES TO BHAKTIVEDANTA SWAMI'S MISSION were not limited to the ravings of distressed temple visitors. Journalists as well, encountering street-chanting parties, had no clue what his disciples were doing and usually handed in weak stories about robes and incense. Writers did not care to spend time studying the movement's philosophy, and its distinguished history simply held less appeal for readers than puff pieces about shaved heads and tambourines.

Two hundred years before, observers of Indian culture such as British evangelical Charles Grant (1746–1823) and German Orientalist Max Muller (1823–1900) had made similar assessments of Krishna devotees. They concluded, as American reporters would in the 1960s, that bhakti yogis were naïve sentimentalists who had taken refuge in a life of religious emotion. In a word, Hare Krishna people were crazy. In his classes and books, Bhaktivedanta Swami challenged the criteria by which outsiders to bhakti tradition judged who was crazy and who was sane. Knowing yourself to be nonmaterial consciousness was sane, he said. Believing yourself to be the product of matter was total madness. In an article titled "Who Is Crazy?" he quoted the Bhagavad Gita:

> "The Supreme Lord is situated in everyone's heart, O Arjuna, and is directing the wanderings of all living entities, who are seated as on a machine, made of the material energy." (Bg. 18.61) These various bodies are like cars, and they are all moving . . . Should we then think that when we [die] the personality no longer exists? This is another kind of craziness. The void philosophy, which maintains that after death

we become nothing, is also a craziness that has been contradicted. We are not void but spirit. . . . "As a person puts on new garments, giving up old ones, similarly, the soul accepts new material bodies, giving up the old and useless ones." (Bg. 2.22) Although the soul takes on new bodies, the soul does not select the bodies himself, the selection is made by the law of nature. However, the mentality of the soul does affect the selection, as indicated by Krishna in the following verse: "In whatever condition one quits his present body, in his next life he will attain to that state of being without fail." (Bg. 8.6) As one's thoughts develop, his future body also develops. The sane man understands that he is not the body, and he also understands what his duty is: to fix his mind on Krishna so that at death he can attain Krishna's nature. . . . By ardently following the instructions of Krishna in Bhagavad Gita and following in the footsteps of the great acharyas, teachers of Bhagavad Gita in the line of disciplic succession, we can spiritualize the Earth and restore its inhabitants to sanity.

If outsiders to Bhakti tradition chose to judge his students' sanity by how they dressed or how enthusiastically they sang, that was their prerogative, but more thoughtful persons knew truth was about inner significance, not outward appearance.

"Let the dogs bark," the Swami would say. "The caravan passes on."

SHORTLY BEFORE LEAVING SAN FRANCISCO to return to New York, the Swami was in his apartment when Melanie — now initiated as Malati Dasi — arrived. She took a small wooden sculpture out of a shopping bag and set it on the desk for inspection. While shopping in an import store, she had found the three-inch-tall figurine in a barrel of objects labeled MADE IN INDIA. The small wooden doll had a triangular head, rounded torso, and no feet.

"What's this, Swamiji?" she asked.

The Swami's eyes grew bright, and he quickly joined his hands together in the traditional *namaste* greeting. "You have brought Jagannath," he said with a smile, "Krishna in his form as Lord of the Universe."

He described the joy he had known as a child worshiping his own small Jagannath deity. But usually, he explained, Jagannath was accompanied by two other figures: his brother, Balaram, and sister, Subhadra. Yes, Malati confirmed, she had seen similar dolls in the import store. Malati called her husband, Shyamsundar — formerly Sam — and they returned to the store to purchase the other figures. The Swami asked Shyamsundar to carve three-foot-tall versions of the Jagannath deities and install them in the San Francisco temple. It would be most appropriate to have Jagannath in San Francisco, he explained, since Jagannath's compassion extended to "the most fallen," such as hippies. One day, when his students were qualified, he would teach them how to worship deities of Radha and Krishna.

By March 1967, the Jagannath deities were ready. Shyamsundar fastened a seven-foot-long redwood plank to two thick pillars and positioned the three deities on the plank high above the altar. At night, a few devotees raided Golden Gate Park and returned with boxes of flowers for the installation.

The next evening the temple room filled to capacity as rumor circulated that something new was happening at the Krishna temple. The Swami signaled for kirtan to begin, then he instructed a disciple to place a lit candle on a brass tray. Next he invited guests to offer the candle's flame to the Jagannath deities by making circles with the tray in a clockwise direction. This was a simplified version of the traditional arati ceremony that had been performed in Krishna temples throughout India's history. Every invading force from the twelfth-century Moghuls to twentieth-century British, as well as every Hindu reform movement in recent times, had wanted such worship of stone and wood "idols" to disappear. God is not stone or wood, the Swami told the audience.

"If all you see is a stone statue," he cautioned, "then the deity of Krishna will remain stone to you forever. People ask, 'Have you seen God?' Of course! You can see God at every moment. But you must have the qualification. What is that qualification?" He closed his eyes and sang a verse from *Brahma Samhita*, the prayer of Brahma, the words of the poem lifting upward with the melody: "Premanjana-cchurita bhakti-vilochanena, santah sadhaiva hridaiyeshu vilokayanti . . ." The room went quiet. He opened his eyes and said, "That qualification is unalloyed love—that's all."

"Unalloyed love," or pure love, meant love for love's sake, unqualified, without wanting any personal benefit in return. Because such love for the Supreme Person was natural, it could be awakened with practice. Krishna was self-sufficient, he explained. He didn't need anything. Still, if a devotee offered him a candle's flame with love, he gladly accepted it. Anything offered with love, under the guidance of a qualified guru, constituted bhakti or devotional service.

"When you come to the temple," he said, "I request that you bring a fruit or a flower and offer it to the deity. It does not have to be costly. Whatever you can afford."

Devotees and guests took his request literally. Over the next several weeks, many brought whatever they could afford and placed it on the altar before Jagannath. One person left a stalk of wheat. Someone else left a half a loaf of bread. Another guest offered a piece of fudge. Others deposited cans of baked beans and loose feathers. One person presented Jagannath a box of Saltine crackers. Two of the more imaginative guests arrived after a shopping trip and offered their purchases, calculating Jagannath would agree to sanctify their new shirts and pants. The Swami encouraged them all. They were trying to establish a relationship with Krishna, however awkwardly, and no offering was too outrageous. "If one offers me with love a leaf, fruit, a flower, or some water," Krishna declared in the Bhagavad Gita, "I am happy to accept it."[93]

In years to come, authorities on the art of *archana*, deity worship, would acknowledge the standard in ISKCON temples as the highest in the world. In 1967, it began with feathers and a box of Saltines.

Room conversation:

BARBARA: Have you ever seen Krishna?

PRABHUPADA: Yes. Daily. Every moment.

BARBARA: But not in a material body.

PRABHUPADA: He has no material body.

BARBARA: Well, in the temple here they have pictures of Krishna and deities . . .

PRABHUPADA: That is not a material body. Because your eyes are material, you cannot see the spiritual form. Therefore, he appears to be in a material body so that you can see him. However, because he has made himself just fit for your seeing, that does not mean he has a material body. Suppose the president of the United States comes to your house. That does not mean his position and your position are the same. It is his kindness. Similarly, because we cannot see Krishna with our present eyes, Krishna appears before us as a painting, as a deity of stone or wood—and Krishna is not different from these paintings or stone.[94]

IN APRIL 1967, the Swami returned to New York. Devotees had spruced up the storefront, painted the walls white, and hung new paintings by

Jadurani. "In my absence, things have improved," he said as he surveyed the changes and examined the art. He was seventy-one years old and walked with a steady step, but they would soon discover that his body could display the symptoms of aging.

So far Brahmananda's efforts to find a publisher for the Swami's *Bhagavad Gita As It Is* had failed. Swamiji had put the manuscript in his hands and said, "You must get this published," but Brahmananda knew nothing about publishing. He met with editors, explained as best he could who his teacher was, and the importance of his edition of the Gita, but the editors shook their heads.

"There's just no money in swamis," they cautioned. "Risky. Very risky."

On arriving back in New York, the Swami told Brahmananda that publishing the Gita could not wait any longer. If necessary, the Swami said, he would find the money himself somehow and have it printed in India. Brahmananda pleaded for a little more time.

Alan Kallman's recording of the Hare Krishna chant, popularly known as "The Happening Album," was released in January 1967. Devotees placed ads in the *Village Voice* and filled orders for the album as they came in by mail. One envelope carried the return address of Macmillan, one of the world's largest publishing houses. An order from Macmillan for the Swami's album seemed like a direct intervention by Krishna. Brahmananda showed the order to his teacher.

"Deliver the album in person," the Swami advised. "Tell them that you are a disciple of a guru from India and that he has translated the Bhagavad Gita. They will publish it. Do not worry."

Brahmananda dressed for the occasion in a suit and tie. He arrived at the Macmillan offices, "The Happening Album" in hand, and was brokenhearted to learn the order had come not from one of the company's publishing agents but from a clerk in the mailroom. Still, Brahmananda knew unseen forces swirled around everything the Swami did, so the hefty devotee engaged the clerk in conversation, and a young executive happened by as they were talking. The clerk made introductions.

"This is James O'Shea Wade," he said, "our senior editor."

Brahmananda took a deep breath and repeated verbatim what his guru had told him to say. Wade was stunned.

"We've just published a full line of spiritual books," he said, "but we've been looking for a Bhagavad Gita to fill out the set." The two stared at each other in silence.

"Bring the manuscript tomorrow," Wade said. "We'll publish it—sight unseen."

Brahmananda quickly returned to the temple on Second Avenue and told the Swami about his miraculous meeting. Miraculous indeed, the Swami agreed.

"When I was alone in your New York," he wrote a few years later, "I was thinking who will listen to me in this horrible, sinful place? All right, I shall stay a little longer. At least I can distribute a few of my books, and that is something. But Krishna was all along preparing something I could not see. He brought you to me, one by one, sincere American boys and girls, to be trained up for doing the work of Lord Chaitanya Mahaprabhu. Now I can see that it is a miracle. Otherwise, New York, an old man with a few books to sell for edibles—how he can survive, what to speak of introducing a God-consciousness movement for saving humankind? That is Krishna's miracle. Now I can see it."[95]

BY THE MID-TWENTIETH CENTURY, more than a dozen editions of the Bhagavad Gita by other authors had been published in English, and by the end of the century that number would jump to more than 300.[96] Only the Bhaktivedanta edition provoked "Krishna's miracle" of transforming Westerners into devotees. Most others promoted the idea of "oneness," of merging with all-pervading brahman, over devotion to the personal Supreme Being. Love for a personal divinity might be a good place to start, the other editions proposed, but personhood was an illusion, and aspiring yogis would eventually have to give up their attachments to form and personhood in order to realize oneness with God. The Swami called the temptation to become one with God "maya's last snare," a final hurdle on the path to awakening knowledge of the self as an eternal, individual soul capable of loving and being loved.[97] His edition of the Gita would educate seekers about the dangers of this last snare.

The next day the Swami took a bus with Brahmananda to the Macmillan offices on Fifty-second Street and personally delivered the 1,000-page manuscript of his Bhagavad Gita. "I vividly remember the stir caused in our rather sedate and boring office the day the Swami came to visit," senior editor James Wade later recalled.[98] "The Swami was special. That was clear. I remember him as a rather tall man, physically imposing—yet he wasn't, being rather small in stature and not at all daunting.[99] Quiet, modest, and surrounded by a kind of stillness, a peacefulness that was, well, welcoming. I can't think of a more precise word. He was in the world and at the same time not of it. He knew that we live in a world of illusion—something science has also taught us, as we go from subatomic particles and quantum mechanics to string theory."[100]

The Swami's mission seemed to be going well. He now had a book with a major publisher, a record that was getting airplay on alternative radio stations, and reporters were showing up regularly looking for interviews.

Newspaper interview: [101]

REPORTER: Do you have children?

PRABHUPADA: Yes, I have grown-up boys.

REPORTER: You just—left them?

PRABHUPADA: I have no connection with them, wife, grandchildren—they are going their own way. My wife is entrusted to the elder boys.

REPORTER: Well, is that—I mean, I find that sort of difficult to assimilate, to give up your family and just sort of say, "See you later"?

PRABHUPADA: That is the Vedic culture. One should not remain forever in family life up to death—that is not good.

REPORTER: Can you explain that?

PRABHUPADA: First, a boy is trained in spiritual life. If he is unable to remain celibate, then he can marry. At age fifty or so, the husband and wife leave home and travel to places of pilgrimage, to detach from family affection. When the man is a little more advanced, he asks his wife, "You take care of the family, and our grown-up sons will take care of you. Let me take sannyasa." Then he becomes independent and teaches the knowledge which he has acquired. That is Vedic civilization. If the whole family is Krishna conscious, then it is helpful [and there is no need of sannyasa], but that is very rare.

REPORTER: From a practical standpoint, do you think your movement has a chance to make it here in America?

PRABHUPADA: So far I've seen, it has a great chance. What do you think?

ON SUNDAY, MAY 28, 1967, Achyutananda climbed the stairs to the Swami's apartment. Swamiji was scheduled to lecture, and it was time to prepare. He found his teacher lying down, his face pale.

"Feel my heart," the Swami said weakly.

Achyutananda placed his hand on his teacher's chest and felt a quivering. The Swami made circular motions with his hand. "Rub my chest," he asked, and for two days students took turns caring for him. Achyutananda was sitting with him when suddenly the Swami twitched, his eyes rolled, and he threw himself backward into his disciple's arms. "Hare Krishna!" the Swami gasped. Acyutananda called for help. Other disciples crowded into the room.

"Hold kirtan," the Swami told them. "Pray to Krishna that your spiritual master has not yet completed his work. Please let him finish."

Brahmananda called an ambulance and took him to Beth Israel Hospital, where doctors diagnosed his condition as critical. Jadurani telephoned the San Francisco temple, then she called a small center that had recently opened in Montreal and begged the devotees to chant round the clock for Swamiji's health. The men and women who had moved into these centers had no illusions about their future. They knew they were still spiritually immature, and that without his guidance their link with Krishna would be severed, and chanting began in earnest. News spread quickly down Haight Street, and the San Francisco temple overflowed with well-wishers and friends who joined the chanting for Swamiji's recovery. Around 2 a.m. devotees emerged from the kitchen with trays of sliced fruit. Someone lit candles, and the chanting continued in flickering shadows. Fourteen hours later, people were still chanting.

After two days in the hospital, a call came from the New York temple. The Swami was slowly regaining strength. He survived, the Swami told them, because Krishna wanted him to carry out his spiritual master's order to spread sankirtan in America. When news of the Swami's improvement reached the other centers, followers cheered and embraced, and many sobbed the way people did when a child was born. They had come far in building their faith and had learned to live without public approval. But they could not live without him. The tears were not only because Krishna had spared their guru's life, but because he had spared theirs as well.

DEVOTEES PLANNED TO HOLD A BIGGER THAN USUAL KIRTAN in Tompkins Square Park on June 4, 1967. The Parks Department had authorized them to use a loudspeaker system as well as the park's outdoor stage. A disciple stood before the microphone and looked out on a crowd of several hundred. "The Swami is in the hospital," he said, "and is not able to attend today. But he wrote a message for us." Then he read:

> My dear young, beautiful boys and girls of America, I came to your country with great hope and a great mission. My spiritual master, Bhaktisiddhanta Saraswati Goswami, asked me to preach the cult of Lord Sri Chaitanya Mahaprabhu in the Western world. That was the seed-giving incident. From within, Krishna dictated that I should go to America, and after arriving here I perceived that some of the youngsters were being misled. They were confused and frustrated, although it is they who are the flower and future hope. I thought to myself that if they join with me in this movement, then it will spread all over the world and all problems will be solved. The process is very simple: chant, hear the philosophy taught by Lord Krishna, take a little prasadam, and you will find a new chapter of your life. It is not very difficult. If you just chant *Hare Krishna, Hare Krishna, Krishna Krishna, Hare Hare, Hare Rama, Hare Rama, Rama Rama, Hare Hare* — that will save you. Thank you very much, and God bless you.

Against doctors' advice, the Swami checked himself out of Beth Israel Hospital a few days later. His health was still precarious, but he found no advantage in a sterile hospital room or the mechanical probings of allopathic physicians, over his modest apartment and the attentions of young people who loved him.

"They were only sticking needles," he said of the hospital stay.

The Swami had grown up with a Vedic program for good health: properly spiced vegetarian prasadam in modest portions, daily chanting of Hare Krishna, a steady routine, and, when needed, plant-based ayurvedic medicines. As a chemist, he had no objection to allopathic products for extreme situations but urged followers to avoid invasive surgery and aggressive medicines as far as possible. For Vaishnavas who understood how to interact with the natural world, there were simpler and much less costly ways to stay healthy. The Bhagavad Gita offered a number of practical hints: don't eat too much or too little and only foods from the category of sattva-guna, "goodness," meaning vegetarian and fresh. Don't sleep too much or too little. Go to sleep early and get up early—there were dozens of such recommendations in the Gita, and the sooner he could return to the routine of devotional life, the sooner he could regain his health.

Disciples drove him to Matchless Gifts and helped him into the temple room. He lowered himself slowly to the floor and extended his arms in homage before Jadurani's paintings of his spiritual master, Bhaktisiddhanta Saraswati, and his spiritual master's father, Bhaktivinode Thakur. Then disciples drove him to Long Branch on the New Jersey shore, where they had rented a house for his convalescence.

"How are you feeling?" a student asked as the Swami settled in.

"The windows are broken, but the light inside is shining," he joked, looking to reassure them. The Swami viewed heart attacks, as he did everything, from a Krishna-conscious perspective. "If I go to the doctor and my heart is beating," he told the roomful of anxious students, "but the doctor says, 'My dear sir, you are dead'—is this not a crazy diagnosis? Similarly, just see the signs of life in this universe. The sun is rising on time, the planets are all moving in their orbits—there are so many signs of life. The universe is God's body. They are seeing all these symptoms and yet they declare God is dead. Is it not foolishness? They are rascals. I challenge them. Simply rascals." The show of philosophic strength fueled his disciples' hopes that he would not be leaving them anytime soon.

On June 10, 1967, he wrote to disciples in San Francisco, announcing that he was returning to India for his health. "Although I am practically on the path of death," he told them, "still I cannot forget about my publications. I wish that if I live or die, you will take very serious care of my publications." He had had a near fatal heart attack, yet his only concern was to see the books printed. He would gladly have relinquished any plans for returning to India—staying in America to finish the *Srimad Bhagavatam* took precedent over everything—but the odds of recuperating were better in Vrindavan, where he would have access to ayurvedic doctors and medicines.

Still, before risking such a long trip there was yet one more important project that required his attention. With Jagannath deities presiding over the San Francisco temple, now was the time to inaugurate the Rathayatra festival. What an achievement that would be: to mount the massive public festival celebrating Krishna, Lord of the Universe, in America, just as it was done in Puri, India. Once that was accomplished, he could leave.

"At present, I am on the seashore in New Jersey for recouping my health," he wrote to Sumati Morarjee, president of Scindia Steamship Company. "I am thinking of going back to India as soon as I get sufficient strength." He would turn seventy-two in September, he wrote, but the work he had begun in the West was not yet completed. He described wanting to open a temple in Vrindavan, where his students could be trained in the higher principles and behavior of Krishna devotees. "I do not know when death will overcome me," he wrote, "but I must train some of my disciples in Vrindavan."

More books, a Rathayatra festival, and now a temple in Vrindavan — nothing, it seemed, could slow him down. Least of all the the risk of dying.

"ARRANGE A PROCESSION down the main street," he told the San Francisco devotees. "Do Rathayatra nicely, so that it will attract many people." He drew a sketch showing a flatbed truck with four pillars holding up a cloth canopy topped with a triangular flag. Here is where the deities will sit, he described. Bring the Rathayatra cart to the beach with everyone chanting, as it has been done in Puri for thousands of years.

"I couldn't believe the Swami was thinking about the Rathayatra so soon after almost dying," Mukunda wrote in his memoir. The San Francisco devotees had all but forgotten about the festival in the turmoil of the Swami's stroke.

The New York devotees urged their San Francisco brothers and sisters to find a suitable place for him to recuperate. He was still weak, they explained, and he needed peace and quiet to adequately recover. The West Coast disciples took the suggestion seriously and found a ranch-style house on Stinson Beach, a small town in Marin County north of San Francisco. His second day in the rented house, the Swami was chanting on his beads when Mukunda entered to give a report on progress with Rathayatra.

"How are you feeling, Swami?"

The founder of the Krishna consciousness movement — which at that time comprised storefront temples in New York and San Francisco, a converted bowling alley in Montreal, and a few dozen initiated students—continued to chant on his beads, and at first he said nothing. After a few minutes, he put down the beads and stood up. He stretched out his arms, palms up, and with a curled lip, replied, "What is this body?"

Mukunda later reflected that the Swami's tone suggested disgust over inhabiting an ephemeral form. Embodied life was an embarrassment, he would occasionally say in classes. It was the eternal soul and the soul's service to Krishna that mattered, and a spiritually progressive person cared little how soon or how long it took for death of the body to come. "This material world," his guru, Bhaktisiddhanta, used to say, "is no fit place for a gentleman."

Mukunda retired to the kitchen where he spoke with other students about what the Swami had said and what it might mean for the future of Krishna consciousness. The Swami had already endured two heart attacks on the Jaladuta and a third in New York. What would happen to the movement if he were no longer there? It was a sensitive issue but one they agreed needed to be addressed.

Mukunda returned to the Swami's room. With as much courtesy as he could muster, he asked, "When you die, what will happen to the movement? Will you have a successor from India who will continue your work and look after our spiritual education?"

The Swami sat silently looking out the window at dunes and water and gulls gliding to a halt on the sand. Then he said softly, "Actually, it is an insult to the spiritual master," and he turned to Mukunda with a pensive expression as though hurt by the question. The Swami closed his eyes, and a trickle of tears flowed down his cheeks. He slowly wiped them away.

"My spiritual master," he said, his voice choking, "was no ordinary spiritual master." He paused and then whispered, falteringly, "He saved me."

"I'm sorry. I'll go now," Mukunda said, too overcome himself to say more. He walked out of the beachfront house and sat, dejected, on the porch to reflect on what had just happened. The Swami's answer was, he wrote later, "crystal clear. There was no question of replacing the spiritual master. His potency to teach would not end with his death but would continue even in his physical absence."

Two days later the Swami made clear to his students that, should anything happen to him, he would not call any of his godbrothers to take over as head of his movement. "If another person speaks just one word different from what I am speaking," he explained, "there will be great confusion among you."

His concern was not over disciples of Bhaktisiddhanta Saraswati helping to spread Krishna consciousness—that had been Bhaktisiddhanta's wish, and Prabhupada had written several letters urging just that. His concern lay in the risk of his disciples becoming confused by someone else's recommendations for presenting Gaudiya Vaishnavism in the West. Like his predecessors, Bhaktisiddhanta Saraswati and Bhaktivinode Thakur, Prabhupada was an innovator. Might members of the Gaudiya Math object to some of his innovations? And if that happened, would his students become disenchanted and go away?

In India, where Krishna worship had a long and rich history, followers of different lineages lived and interacted peacefully, with mutual respect and a sense of common purpose. The Vrindavan community, for example, included followers of Chaitanya Mahaprabhu; followers of Mahaprabhu's contemporary, Vallabha, founder of Pusti Marg, the "path of grace"; followers of Hit Harivams, founder of the Radhavallabha sampradaya; descendants of the Goswamis of Vrindavan; and men and women initiated by Bhaktisiddhanta or raised in other sampradayas. There were more than 5,000 temples in Vrindavan, and the diverse congregations all worshiped Krishna according to their particular heritage and without acrimony. One day his students would understand the importance of such inclusiveness—and one day, he told them, they, too, would initiate disciples of their own—but in 1967, their devotion was still precarious.

THE SWAMI DID NOT HAVE THE strength to attend Rathayatra, but he enjoyed the reports by disciples at its conclusion about the perfect weather, the five hundred people who followed Jagannath's chariot to the ocean and about Yamuna Devi's beautiful singing, and how everyone danced and jumped for the flowers devotees threw from the chariot, and the huge feast at the end with thousands of bananas and apples and piles of chapatis.

"That was but the beginning," the Swami told them. "We will inaugurate many such celebrations all over the world, one by one. I will show you." Unlike austere monastic traditions, Vaishnavas celebrated their life with Krishna. There were so many occasions in the Vaishnava calendar, he said, that they could hold a celebration every day of the year.

Over the next several days, he awarded initiation at his beachfront retreat, without the formality of a fire ceremony. He held a brief discussion with each candidate, chanted on their beads, and gave them a Sanskrit name.

"Are you going to take initiation and go away?" he asked, for it was not the fire ceremony but the dedication of their hearts that formed the essence of initiation.

GRADUALLY, he regained strength for the journey back to India. "I wish to go to Vrindavan," he announced. "For good health, more sun is required—and Vrindavan is the only place in this universe where Krishna consciousness is automatically revealed. You will see. You can become more Krishna conscious in one day in Vrindavan than in a year in America."

"Please don't speak of leaving us now," a student said.

"The spiritual master never leaves the disciple," he said, for there were two ways disciples could interact with their teacher. One—*vapuh*—was the teacher's physical presence. The other—*vani*—was the teacher's presence through sound or teachings. While vapuh was not always available, vani continued always. "Not once have I felt that my Guru Maharaj has left me," he said, "because I am always following his teachings."

The night before the Swami's departure, disciples drove him to the San Francisco temple for a last lecture before he boarded a plane for New York and then India. A hundred people crowded into the Frederick Street storefront. Where once there had been only a handful of devotees, there was now a room filled with faces the Swami had not seen before. He entered, and the kirtan stopped. The crowd fell silent and parted to form an aisle. He slowly crossed the room and climbed onto the dais.

"It was on the order of my spiritual master that I came here," he told them. "I left home thinking that I was giving up my children. I had only five children then. Now I have come to your country, and suddenly I have hundreds of children. And you are all taking care of me. Now I am going to India—for a little while—but I will return when I have fully recovered."

A recently initiated disciple entered the storefront. The young man loved the Swami, but honoring vows of self-restraint had proved beyond his ability, and he had come to say goodbye. He fell to his hands and knees and crawled sobbing toward his teacher.

"Come here, my boy," the Swami said. "What's wrong, my son? You don't have to be so unhappy." Tears trickled down the Swami's cheek as he stroked the boy's head. His tears mingled with those of the boy, and the scene provoked an outpouring of emotion in the crowded room. The young people in San Francisco had come to him, as they had in New York, attracted by his assurances that they were beautiful, spiritual beings. He planted in them a vision of themselves they had never known, but the price for sustaining that vision was a voluntary end to harmful habits. Caught in that tension between his heart and his desires, the boy's desires had won out. He stood and looked silently for a moment at the Swami, then turned and walked slowly out of the temple.

In the moments that followed, many in the room asked themselves whether the boy's fate would be their own. It took only a few classes to see that devotional life consisted of more than chanting and dancing and street festivals, and that initiation was not a fad. Discipleship meant entering a permanent relationship with a teacher who could bring them to Krishna—provided they respected the strict standards of devotional life. Contemplating such self-discipline was more than many could bear. He knew they struggled with the task of self-reform and urged them not to give up.

"I am an old man," he told the crowd. "I may die at any moment. But please, you all carry on this sankirtan movement. As Lord Chaitanya said, be humble as a blade of grass, more tolerant than a tree. You must have enthusiasm and patience to push on this Krishna conscious philosophy. In this material world, everything comes and goes. I beg you not to waste your lives with these material things. Don't throw your lives away."

If he was going back to India to die, these might be his final instructions, and they analyzed every word. "Be humble." Don't think you are more advanced than you are, for wisdom begins with humility. "Be tolerant." The world will judge you by appearances and attack you for your beliefs, so look kindly on those who may be frightened by something they do not understand. "Be enthusiastic." Keep the fire burning and your spiritual practices strong, for regular chanting and proper behavior will be your assurance of progress. "Be patient." Good things take time, and the best thing—to be Krishna conscious, to love God—could take even longer. You have a chance to regain your soul, he was telling them. Does that not merit some patience and perseverance?

The Swami climbed carefully off the dais, and the assembly rose to their feet and followed him out the door. Dozens of men and women crowded around Mukunda, who held a clipboard with names of candidates for initiation, and begged him to add their names to the list. Traditionally, as it was done in India, candidates spent years studying the philosophy, cultivating devotional character, and earning the approval of senior community members. This final series of San Francisco initiations before the Swami's departure would be a wholesale measure, since there might not be another chance. There were no forms to fill out, no examinations or lengthy trial periods. The Swami was taking what he described as "a transcendental gamble," offering the greatest gift to the least qualified on the chance that some would take initiation seriously.

The crowd followed him to his apartment building and waited anxiously outside for their name to be called. A frequent visitor, John Carter, had been holding back from making the commitment to devotional life, but the Swami's precarious health had erased his hesitation. Carter went up to Mukunda.

"Please put my name on the list," he asked.

Mukunda obliged, and Carter waited as people were called one by one to walk upstairs and receive their beads. An hour later, the crowd had dispersed. His name had not been called. "He's going to India," Carter realized, "and then he's going back to Krishna—and I just lost my chance. What's the point in living anymore?" He turned and started walking toward Golden Gate Bridge. "I'll just jump off," he told himself.

One of the recently initiated women, Harsharani, saw the sadness in his face and grabbed him by the arm. "Come with me," she insisted and raced with him up the stairs. Without knocking, she burst into the Swami's room and held Carter's hand in the air.

"Swamiji," she pleaded, "you have to initiate this boy." Carter stood by her side, on the edge of tears.

The Swami took in the melodrama of the moment and chuckled warmly. "Don't cry," he said and reassured Carter that Krishna would not neglect such a sincere soul. He lifted a set of beads from his desk, chanted on them one by one, and handed them to Carter. "Your name is Jivananda Das," he said, "servant of Krishna who gives ananda, bliss, to the soul."

The following morning, before the Swami's departure for the airport, older disciples stepped forward to reassure him they were determined to help open new centers. One group said they would drive to Santa Fe and try their best there. Dayananda and his wife, Nandarani, said they would go to Los Angeles and look for a place to rent.

"Go to as many cities as possible," the Swami urged them. "By spreading this movement, you render the greatest service to humanity."

They vowed to remember his instruction that as long as they chanted Hare Krishna, he would always be with them.

"You will be chanting here," he said, "and I will be chanting there, and this vibration will encircle the whole planet."

HE ARRIVED IN NEW YORK for a one-day stopover before taking the flight back to India with Kirtanananda, who would serve as his aid. Disciples drove him to 26 Second Avenue.

"He came into the storefront," Brahmananda remembered, "and went over to the paintings of Srila Bhaktisiddhanta, Srila Bhaktivinode, Srila Gaura Kishore Das Babaji," the Swami's predecessors in the lineage of Vaishnava gurus. The Swami put his head on the feet in each painting, then turned to his students.

"I'm leaving you in the care of your grandparents," he said, indicating the paintings. "Grandparents are kinder than parents."

After a day of rest, he was ready for the long flight. Disciples feared it would be his last, given his state of health. "I'll never forget when Prabhupada got in the car to go to the airport," recalled Gargamuni. "I held his ankles and wouldn't let him go. He patted me gently on the back, saying, 'That's okay. It will be all right.' My heart was breaking to see him go. He had come all this way."

In the Air India waiting room of John F. Kennedy International Airport, the Swami sat with his wool chadar draped over one shoulder. His hands rested on an umbrella, and he looked at disciples sitting on the floor near him. One disciple turned on a battery-operated phonograph and played the Hare Krishna mantra. The Swami nodded his head in time to the kirtan, and devotees sang along quietly. The time came to board. He patted the women on their heads and embraced the men.

"He hugged me tightly," remembered Rupanuga. "For me, someone who always had difficulty loving another person, Swamiji's leaving forced a lot of love from my heart that I didn't even know was there. I was becoming a spiritual person."

The Swami and Kirtanananda made their way down the aisle, out the door, and across the tarmac to the waiting Boeing 707. In the Swami's pocket were the forty rupees he had brought to New York less than two years before. Rupees were not accepted as international currency, and he had never been able to exchange them. In effect, he had arrived in America with no money at all. His anxiety then had been how long he would have to remain in such a hellish country. His concern now was how soon he could return. The journey to America by boat had taken him thirty-five painful days. The journey back to India by plane, with stopovers, would take only two.

THE PLANE ARRIVED IN DELHI on July 25, 1967, at two o'clock in the morning. The seventy-one-year old teacher was feverish. He was coughing and had not slept well, but coming home felt good.

"When we stepped out of the plane," he wrote to students the following day, "I knew it was India. It was like walking into a solid wall of heat. But that's what I've been wanting." He asked them to continue the work they had begun together. "I have always said," he wrote, "that if I could get American boys and girls to take up this movement, the rest of the world would join us. Now my theory is being proven. So I am depending on you all to carry on this great mission in my absence. Chant and Krishna will bless you."

The Swami picked a taxi from the airport queue and instructed the driver to take them to the Chippiwada neighborhood of Old Delhi. They would stay one night in his room on the roof of Sri Krishna Pandit's temple before leaving for Vrindavan. The taxi weaved in and out of nighttime traffic, past streets from days gone by when the Swami had sold *Back to Godhead* door to door and in cafes. They arrived at the temple, and a porter unlocked the gate, escorted them upstairs to the Swami's old room, and turned on the light.

The room was bare and dusty, and things were more or less as he had left them two years before. Kirtanananda found a collection of printed pages and jackets from *Srimad Bhagavatam* stacked in the closet, alongside a pile of form letters to prospective members of the defunct League of Devotees.

"I slept over there," the Swami said, pointing to a corner, "and over here was my typewriter and cooker. I would sleep, type, cook, type, sleep, type . . ."

By mid-afternoon of the following day, his cough had worsened. His fever had gone up, and his breathing was labored. An elderly Sikh doctor arrived and administered an injection of penicillin, and the Swami rested for the first time since his departure from New York. Word of Bhaktivedanta

Swami's return spread, and old acquaintances came by, hoping he would agree to speak at their homes or temples.

"Take *him*," the Swami suggested, pointing weakly to his young American disciple.

Kirtanananda visited homes, played the Hare Krishna mantra on his portable record player, and gave brief speeches. Pious Hindus were fascinated to see a white man wearing a dhoti and displaying lines of tilak on his face.

Six days later the Swami was well enough to make the journey by train to Vrindavan. They booked seats on the Taj Express and arrived two hours later at Mathura station. A brief tanga ride brought them to Radha Damodar Temple, and the combination of warm days, ayurvedic medicines, daily massage, and proximity to the temples and deities he loved worked their magic. Gradually, his energy returned. By mid-September, he declared himself fit to return to the United States. He was anxious to see his Bhagavad Gita finally published by Macmillan and to move forward with the commentary on *Srimad Bhagavatam*. Coming back to India had served its purpose, but the interlude had slowed down his all-important mission in America.

His students worried that he had gone to Vrindavan to die and that his death would mean the end of the International Society for Krishna Consciousness. They needn't have. He had gone back to Vrindavan to regain his health and prepare for the work ahead. The journey to Vrindavan was not the end of the Krishna consciousness movement.

It was just the beginning.

In the early 1960s, while living as a mendicant in the Radha Damodar temple in Vrindavan, the Swami would find inspiration by looking out his window onto tombs of the sixteenth-century Goswamis.

KRSNA

The Supreme Personality of Godhead

His Divine Grace
A.C. Bhaktivedanta Swami Prabhupāda

George Harrison funded and wrote a preface for *KRSNA: The Supreme Personality of Godhead* (the *Krishna Book*), which was first published in 1970.

CHAPTER SEVEN

If you cannot practice Bhakti Yoga, then just try to work for me.
By working for me, you will come to the perfect stage.

—SRI KRISHNA IN THE BHAGAVAD GITA, 12.10

THE SWAMI STEPPED OFF the plane at San Francisco International Airport. When he emerged from the customs area, devotees and friends stared in disbelief. He looked younger than when he had left. He was tanned from his six months in India, energetic, and beaming. They escorted him to a waiting car, and the driver brought him to Frederick Street. The Swami stepped out and took stock of the storefront temple. Nothing had changed. Without funds, his students had maintained but not expanded.

"All the brahmacharis may get jobs," he advised, referring to the unmarried students living in the temple. "Our temples are not meant for simply eating and sleeping. We are not afraid of work. Whatever our engagement is, by offering the results to Krishna, we become Krishna conscious." Come to morning kirtan and classes, he said, have a prasadam breakfast and then go out, work, and donate money to help support the temple. Then in the evening, come back together again for more kirtan and classes.

"What is the difficulty?" he asked, the wording he frequently used when challenging his students to do more. If he at age seventy could start a worldwide mission, why should there be any difficulty for twenty-somethings to get a job?

Disciples often heard him say that working in a spirit of devotion could lead to self-awareness—a hard concept for them to grasp, since it seemed counterintuitive: coming to know oneself as an eternal being through dedication to one's job? At first, it made no sense. Gradually, through classes and discussion, they came to respect the proposal that working like "normal" people could also lead to spiritual progress. "Not by merely abstaining from work can one achieve freedom from reaction," explained the Bhagavad Gita, "nor by renunciation alone can one attain perfection . . . Perform your prescribed duty, for doing so is better than not working."[102]

Still, this was the first time they heard him encourage them to find secular jobs. There was no shame in earning a living, he said, and he reminded them that Krishna favored working with devotion over withdrawing from the world. More emphatically, Krishna recommended work as a path to liberation for beginners in devotional life. Don't reject the world or your duties in it, Krishna told Arjuna, for they are the tools of your enlightenment.[103]

Some of the Swami's disciples took his suggestion to heart. Twenty-one-year-old Tamal Krishna Das found a job at a Kodak photo lab and submitted to the repetitious shuffling of films between drying racks. Another disciple, a former musician whom the Swami had named Vishnujan Das, carved bamboo flutes and sold them to hippies and tourists. Tamal Krishna's total weekly income after taxes was less than $50 a week, and Vishnujan's was not much more. Meanwhile, attendance for meals at the temple was increasing and so were monthly expenses.

The Swami assessed their dilemma and proposed an alternative strategy. Rather than working for such small compensation, depend on Krishna. Go out on the streets as they did in New York, chant Hare Krishna, and see what happens. Resigning from paid secular jobs to take up devotional service effectively meant rising from karma yoga to bhakti yoga, which was a higher stage of spiritual action. Karma yoga involved working in the world, generating income, and donating a portion of the income for devotional purposes. Higher than karma yogis, Krishna explained in the Bhagavad Gita, were bhakti yogis whose only motive was to love and serve him. That level of unqualified devotion had been the ideal for Vaishnavas throughout history.

Besides, he told his disciples, your life will be less stressful if you don't have to commute to jobs elsewhere. "In your country, people have to drive to an office fifty miles off. And because you have a car to get there, you think, 'I am advanced.' This is maya, illusion, thinking, 'I'm happy. I have this car.' These poor fellows have to rise early in the morning, and make so much haste—*zoom, zoom, zoom*," he said, imitating morning traffic. "Don't you feel botheration? We have created a civilization that is so painful, but we are thinking we are advanced. Better to give up this job and just depend on Krishna."

"Then," he said, anticipating objections, "the question comes, 'How shall I live?' The answer is given in the *Srimad Bhagavatam*: 'Happiness derived from sense enjoyment is obtained automatically in course of time, just as in course of time we obtain miseries even though we do not desire them.'[104] You don't aspire for misery: it is forced upon you. Similarly, happiness also will be forced upon you, whatever you are destined to receive. So don't try for getting happiness or for discarding distress. That will go on. You simply try for Krishna consciousness. God has supplied for everyone. Why not for you?"[105]

ON THE FIRST DAY OF SANKIRTAN, devotees assembled at the intersection of Market and Powell, the busiest intersection of downtown San Francisco. As manager of the sankirtan party, Tamal Krishna signaled Vishnujan to begin singing. Mukunda tapped out a beat on a mridanga, while Yamuna, Gurudas, and others followed on kartals. The line of devotees swayed to and fro, as they did in temple services. A crowd grew around them. Tamal Krishna had brought a conch shell, which he blew from time to time to flavor the music. Inspired by the moment, he moved among the crowd, extended the conch shell and requested donations, and the white bone conch filled with coins. To anyone who made a donation, he handed a copy of *Back to Godhead*. By the end of the day, he had collected $12 and distributed two dozen magazines. Excited by the exchange, the sankirtan crew added other locations to their itinerary, and donations climbed to $40 a day. With some of the money, the devotees purchased yellow dhotis for the men and colorful saris for the women, and the impression on passersby was one of a well-organized, well-appointed street performance.

The Swami had not yet witnessed them in action. One morning, the eight-person crew assembled in front of his building, and when he came down for his daily walk, they broke out in a rousing kirtan. He looked on with a smile and nodded in time to the music. It was not yet much of an international society, but these young people had heart, and that was their advantage. With Krishna's help, his little fledgling group could learn and grow, and one day they might indeed become something grand and make a mark on the world. The Swami beamed, perhaps seeing a bit of himself in their willingness to jump up and down for the right cause. He lifted his arms and danced along, sending the sankirtan crew into overdrive. The devotees spun in circles, drums blaring, kartals harmonizing with the San Francisco cable cars. It was, in its modest way, a version of the chanting and dancing Chaitanya Mahaprabhu had inspired five hundred years before:

> Chaitanya Mahaprabhu signaled the kirtan to begin and fourteen drums played at once. Mahaprabhu danced and the sound of the chanting was tumultuous. The Vaishnavas came together like an assembly of clouds and as they chanted the Holy Names in great ecstasy, tears fell from their eyes like rain. The sankirtan chanting resounded, filling the three worlds. Indeed, no one could hear any sound other than the sankirtan.[106]

San Francisco radio interview:

INTERVIEWER: We are talking with Swami A.C. Bhaktivedanta, head of the International Society for Krishna Consciousness. Your Grace, what is the basis of your teachings?

PRABHUPADA: The basis is *Bhagavad Gita As It Is*. It is very old, at least five thousand years. The speaker is Lord Krishna. Krishna means "All-Attractive," the perfect name for God. And the subject matter is our relationship with God. There is life after death. Unfortunately, people do not believe in a next life. Even though every day they can remember their childhood, you were a child, I was a child. Then we became boys, then youths. Now I am becoming old, and when this body will be useless, we will have to take another body. This information is available in the Bhagavad Gita. That is the preliminary study, and if one studies this book nicely he goes to other books. I am preparing *Srimad Bhagavatam*, but the project is very great and will take sixty volumes. It is no trifling thing, no blind faith, this Krishna consciousness.

INTERVIEWER: What is the significance of your robe?

PRABHUPADA: I am a sannyasi. According to Vedic culture, there are four divisions of human society. Brahmachari, student life. Then grihastha, household life. Then vanaprastha, retired life. And then sannyasa, which means preaching transcendental knowledge to the society from door to door. In Vedic culture, there are different dresses for each division. So this saffron dress means he is understood to be a man of transcendental knowledge.

INTERVIEWER: You also have a garland of flowers around your neck.

PRABHUPADA: That is offered by the disciples as a matter of respect for the spiritual master.

INTERVIEWER: You have some paint down your forehead and your nose—and so do all your followers who are here in the studio.

PRABHUPADA: These marks mean the body is a temple of Krishna. We mark twelve parts of the body. The idea is that we are being protected by God from all sides.

INTERVIEWER: When I went to shake hands with everybody, I found that all your right hands were wrapped. What is the significance of that?

PRABHUPADA: It is not exactly wrapping. It is a bag for our beads. The beads are for chanting Hare Krishna. They are sacred and therefore we keep them in a bag so they won't touch the dust.

INTERVIEWER: Must one renounce his religion to join Krishna consciousness?

PRABHUPADA: No, religion is a kind of faith. Krishna consciousness is transcendental to religious faith. Faith can be changed, but you cannot change the nature of the soul. That is your actual constitutional situation: part and parcel of the Supreme. That cannot be changed.

INTERVIEWER: Is there conflict with other Eastern religions?

PRABHUPADA: The only conflict is between atheists and theists. We are not trying to replace Christianity or Judaism with something Indian. In one sense, Krishna consciousness is the post-graduate study of all religions.

INTERVIEWER: The whole world has heard of Maharishi Mahesh Yogi. Many people go to him for meditation. Is meditation part of your philosophy?

PRABHUPADA: Meditation means to search out who I am. Unless you come to that point, there is no meaning of meditation. And once you know who you are, then meditation ends, and the activities after meditation begin. We take our understanding of who we are from Bhagavad Gita: eternal souls, parts and parcels of Krishna. And the activity after meditation is called bhakti, devotional service.[107]

IT WAS IN MAY 1968 while in Boston that the Swami explained to disciples that "Swamiji" was not a particularly respectful title for a spiritual master. "The spiritual master is usually addressed by names like Gurudev, Vishnupada, or Prabhupada," he said.

"May we call you Prabhupada?" his secretary, Govinda Dasi, asked.

It took a few moments of reflection, weighing the consequences of adopting a title that had always referred to his guru, Bhaktisiddhanta Saraswati. No doubt, some of his godbrothers back in India would object. Still, it was his disciples' request, and if they were to make further progress in their spiritual life, then honoring their guru in this way would help. If such an important change in title were to take effect, he recommended that they publish an article in *Back to Godhead* explaining its significance. The word had two meanings, the article described: first, the master (*prabhu*) at whose feet (*pada*) other masters gathered; second, one who was always found at the lotus feet of Krishna, the Supreme Prabhu. The article specified that there had been other Prabhupadas in Vaishnava history, such as Rupa Goswami Prabhupada and Swamiji's guru, Bhaktisiddhanta Saraswati Prabhupada. Now, the article concluded, the followers of A.C Bhaktivedanta Swami wanted to follow that tradition and henceforth would address their guru with this honorific title.

DISCIPLES FANNED OUT ACROSS AMERICA, chanting Hare Krishna, distributing magazines, and opening temples. Dayananda, who worked for IBM in San Francisco and earned a decent salary, found a showroom for rent in an office building on Hollywood Boulevard, directly across from the famed Grauman's Chinese Theater. It was an ideal location for a Krishna center: a ground-floor space with a floor-to-ceiling display window in the heart of the city. At night, with the other offices closed and dark, the brightly lit showroom glittered like a movie set and attracted crowds of curious tourists. Following Prabhupada's recommendation that they avoid commuting to work, all the devotees had to do was head out the door and begin chanting.

The honeymoon lasted about a week. Occupants on upper floors protested the smell of incense, the loud singing, and the traffic of oddly dressed young people through the lobby of their office building. Management issued a twenty-four-hour eviction notice, and Prabhupada's students found themselves on the sidewalk with their sleeping bags, knapsacks, drums, and cymbals. For the next several months, they bedded down wherever invitations could be had, in garages and living rooms and whatever other shelter they could find around the city.

Don't be discouraged, Prabhupada told them, and he described his own experience in India as a sannyasi with no fixed residence and no money for food and how in retrospect he valued those difficulties as spiritual assets. Material comforts evaporated sooner or later for everyone, he reminded them, and until the soul goes back to Godhead, it never has a permanent address. This was just one more change of location. The practitioner fixed in knowledge of the soul viewed a change of residence like a change of body—nothing more than a minor disturbance.[108]

After weeks of searching and careful financial planning, devotees purchased a building on La Cienega Boulevard. The two-story former church featured a chapel room with a high ceiling, full-length windows, a stage where the altar had stood, office rooms, kitchen, two bathrooms, and a meeting hall—enough room to accommodate hundreds of guests. The building also stood apart from its neighbors: There would be no complaints about loud kirtans.

For devotees accustomed to working out of curio shops, derelict store-fronts, and, in Montreal, a former bowling alley, this bit of news carried the aura of fantasy. A church building projected institutional authority: Maybe the Hare Krishnas would finally get a little respect.

Tamal Krishna's crew of brahmacaris took up the renovations. They stormed in wielding brooms, paintbrushes, and hammers, and every room received a fresh coat of paint. A devotee construction engineer, Nara-Narayan, built an altar. Then, inspired by the stature of their new church-temple, he crafted a gargantuan *vyasasan*—the elevated seat where Prabhupada would sit as representative of Vyasadev, the avatar who had compiled the Vedic wisdom into written form thousands of years before. In other temples, the vyasasan was a simpler affair, and Prabhupada had never asked for more than that. Nara-Narayan set himself the task of creating something royal, rich, and magical, with gold-leafed metal filigree borders; a large, ornate seat with wide silk-covered cushions; a five-foot-tall padded circular back; and carved lion's paws for feet. When light filtered down onto the vyasasan from the room's high windows, the overall impression was less like a piece of furniture than an enchanted creature that might upend itself and start chanting.

The Los Angeles congregation was not prepared for Prabhupada's reaction when he arrived in the newly renovated temple and saw what awaited him. He had not hesitated when, two years before, disciples had made a seat for him in Matchless Gifts, but that was little more than a pillow on a wooden bench. This was a throne as one might have imagined in a king's palace. When he finally overcame his surprise and climbed slowly onto the elevated vyasasan, his voice faltered. He was not at all worthy of such an offering, he said with tears in his eyes, but he would accept it on behalf of his Guru Maharaj, Bhaktisiddhanta Saraswati.

Without calling it by name, the literal elevation of their teacher to a higher level marked a third transition in the trajectory of his mission.[109] He had begun four years before in New York as Swamiji, their teacher and friend. Then students had taken to calling him Prabhupada, "the master at whose feet many gather," the guru and head of their Society. Now they had created for him a seat such as had been reserved throughout history for great acharyas, heads of the Vaishnava lineage — or for a *saktyavesha avatar*, a soul empowered by God to bring holiness back into the world.

PRABHUPADA'S BHAGAVAD GITA had finally found a publisher in Macmillan, and now he could concentrate on completing his edition of the *Srimad Bhagavatam*. Still remaining was *Chaitanya Charitamrita*, the principal biography of Chaitanya Mahaprabhu. It was Chaitanya who had inaugurated the chanting of Hare Krishna and demonstrated the character of a Vaishnava: "humbler than a blade of grass, with all respect for others."[110] And it was Chaitanya who had embodied the love of Radha for Krishna, a unique contribution that revealed the heights to which love for God could grow. When Mahaprabhu left the world in 1533, His Goswami followers created a library of devotional texts and diaries. Based on these, Krishnadas Kaviraj Goswami wrote his biography, *Chaitanya Charitamrita*, in eleven thousand verses.

It was crucial that his students understand Mahaprabhu's teachings. The Krishna consciousness philosophy was grounded in Mahaprabhu's principle of *achintya-bhedabheda-tattva*: the soul's simultaneous and inconceivable oneness with God and difference from God. In this one idea, all the anomalies surrounding personal divinity were resolved. How could God be a person in one place and everywhere at the same time? Is God in his creation, or is he separate from his creation? And if souls were sparks of God, did that not make them God?

Mahaprabhu's principle of "simultaneously, inconceivably one and different" reconciled the apparent contradictions. All living beings were one with God in quality, just as a gold ring shared the qualities of a gold mine. Yet a ring was never quantitatively as great as the mine. In the same way, souls shared God's qualities but in minute quantity. All of creation was "one with God," as the mayavada impersonalists were fond of saying, but the oneness was one of quality and interest, not quantity. Souls were eternal individuals, just as Krishna was an eternal individual, and with the permanent individuality of Krishna and souls came the capacity to give and receive love. For hundreds of years, this critical distinction had been lost on mayavada or impersonalist seekers of truth. Mahaprabhu's biography would clear up the confusion.

If Prabhupada prepared an edition of *Chaitanya Charitamrita* with the same degree of detail as *Srimad Bhagavatam*, with synonyms for each word, transliterations, translations, and commentaries, the project would fill more than a dozen volumes. There was no guarantee he would live long enough to finish both the *Bhagavatam* and another multivolume work, so he set aside his work on the *Bhagavatam* and wrote a summary of Mahaprabhu's life called *Teachings of Lord Chaitanya*. When disciples realized the depth of Prabhupada's concern to see it published, they raised the funds and presented him with finished copies.

"You do not know how pleased I am," he wrote on learning of its publication. The impersonalist missions, he said, had nothing substantial to offer people for their spiritual well-being, but because Vedanta centers had money and published so many "rubbish literatures," impersonalism had gained a following. "You are all God," the mayavada yoga teachers pontificated. "You are moving the sun, you are moving the moon." And as soon as they had a toothache, Prabhupada chided, they went to the dentist God for repairs.

"You can just imagine how powerful our society will become," he predicted, "when we have published as many *substantial* literatures."[111]

WHEN CONTEMPLATING THE ENORMITY of the *Srimad Bhagavatam*, the same thought occurred to him: A summary could serve as an insurance policy for future generations. Sage Vyasadev had divided the *Bhagavatam's* eighteen thousand verses into twelve cantos, a graduation of subject matter intended to prepare readers for entrance into the tenth canto, which described Krishna's private life. The nine earlier cantos described the structure of the universe, the nature of matter and spirit, the avatars of God, and the lives of exemplary devotees throughout history. These preliminary topics would prepare readers for understanding the tenth canto's descriptions of Krishna's lilas or pastimes. The first two cantos were compared to Krishna's lotus feet. Cantos three and four were compared to his legs, five and six to his middle, seven and eight his arms, and nine his throat. The tenth canto was compared to Krishna's lotus face.

"I don't want to pass away before my disciples are able to see Krishna's face," he explained. He would call this summary *KRSNA: The Supreme Personality of Godhead*. It would come to be known by its popular name, the *Krishna Book*.

Among the many detailed descriptions contained in the tenth canto, it was Krishna's *rasa lila*, his loving exchanges with the gopis—the cowherd women of Vrindavan—that posed the greatest risk of misinterpretation. Krishna's body and those of the gopis were pure spirit, yet the tenth canto's descriptions of Krishna embracing and caressing the gopis bore resemblance to sexual relationships between conditioned, embodied men and women. To avoid that misunderstanding, a proper commentary was needed.

> The rasa dance takes place one autumn night when the scent of jasmine flowers fills the air over Vrindavan, and the moon illuminates its forests. Seven-year-old Krishna plays his flute, and the young cowherd girls hear. They leave their homes and run toward the music, leaving their families behind and milk boiling over on wood-burning stoves. In the forest under the moonlight, the gopis assemble. Krishna attempts to reason with them. Why have you come here? Your families must be anxious. Go and take care of them. We will still be together, as I am wherever my devotees chant my glories and meditate on me. Go home.
>
> His words break their hearts, and they scratch the ground with their toes. Tears stream from their eyes and smear their makeup. Don't speak like this, they say. We have given up everything for you. You are the real dharma of our lives, not our families. Our hearts are breaking. If you refuse us, we will die.
>
> As the source of creation, Krishna is *atma-rama* or self-satisfied: He does not need the company of young girls. But he is also compassionate and cannot bear to see those who love him distressed, and so he walks with the gopis to the banks of the Yamuna River and embraces them. Such is his mystic power that each gopi thinks she alone is with Krishna in the moon-

light, and each thinks herself the most fortunate girl in the world—and in that moment, when pride enters their hearts, Krishna disappears.

The gopis are driven mad by this sudden separation and beg trees and flowers to tell them where he has gone. They find his footprints in the sand. Next to Krishna's footprints they see a second set of prints, those of a young girl. After a brief search they find her, Radha, abandoned like them and grieving. Together they continue the search until the moonlight fades, and they return to the riverbank. Krishna is not there, but they rebuke him as though he were. You who have always protected us, they say, you who are the witness in the hearts of all beings—you made promises to us. If even your flute can enjoy the nectar of your lips, why not we? Husbands, sons, brothers—we have forsaken them all to be with you. And the gopis weep.

Krishna hears their lament and returns to the bank of the river. The gopis disguise their anger as philosophic inquiry. What, they ask, do you think of someone who ignores the love of others? Krishna acknowledges their troubled hearts. You have given up the world for me, he says, and it was out of love for you that I became invisible. If I were to make myself too easily available, then our love for one another would be cheap. You deserve better than that. I am unable to reciprocate love as deep as yours. The Supreme Person, whom no one can defeat, stands helpless before the gopis' love.

The gopis forget their heartbreak, and the rasa dance begins. They form a circle. Denizens of heaven appear in the sky, playing instruments and singing. As Krishna and the gopis dance, their bracelets and ankle bells add to the celestial music. Krishna smiles. He multiplies himself, and each gopi thinks she alone is dancing with her beloved.[112]

The *Srimad Bhagavatam* consisted of a week-long discussion between Pariksit, last of the great Vedic kings, and his spiritual adviser, the sage Sukadev. Krishna was the source of dharma or righteous behavior, Pariksit said. How could he permit himself to perform the rasa dance—an act which, if performed by anyone else, would be seen as immoral and condemned? Sukadev replied that Krishna's actions may sometimes appear to contradict dharma, but they have purpose and are without flaw. He dwells in the heart of all as the paramatma, Supersoul, the witness within. If he chooses to step out of the gopis' hearts to embrace them, where is the impropriety? It is no more unethical for Krishna to dance with his own energies than for a child to play with his own reflection in a mirror. The rasa lila was not licentious, Sukadev explained, only misunderstood.

"This world," Prabhupada explained, "is a relative manifestation of the spiritual world. Just like a photograph, where you find the details of your beautiful face. The photo is not the reality, but still, you can understand a notion of the actual thing by scrutinizing the photograph. Here, when boys and girls mix, there are so many distressful things that create material bondage. There, in the spiritual world, it is the highest. So everything is there in the spiritual world. Just like the love between Radha and Krishna. They are not married, but from childhood they were friends, and Radharani ['Queen' Radha] could never forget Krishna. But there was no inebriety. Here, the so-called love is lust — the same thing but only a perverted reflection. Like the reflection of a tree, where the topmost part becomes the lowest. In the spiritual world, love is pure.

"The impersonalists," he continued, "think that because the material varieties are abominable, therefore the spiritual world must be void. That is a material calculation. They cannot imagine that in the spiritual world also there is love because here, in this world, the so-called love — lust — is frustrated and followed by so many calamities. In one sense, their idea is right: How can these nonsense things exist in the spiritual world? But their conclusion is to erase variety and make the spiritual world impersonal. They cannot understand that the photograph is a reflection of the actual person. The real explanation is that the spiritual world is the fountainhead of all emanations. These things are not understood in the beginning."[113]

"Almighty Lord" (Maha-Vishnu), "Creator of the Universe" (Jagannath), "Supreme Being" (Adi-Purusha) — these were descriptive titles. Who was the person behind the titles? Who was the person behind the functions of God? The *Krishna Book* would reveal the answer.

Los Angeles was an ideal place for Prabhupada to write the *Krishna Book*. Devotees there appeared capable of maintaining temple programs on their own now. He had installed deities of Radha and Krishna, and the daily services were going smoothly, and for the first time since arriving in America, he was free from the distractions of management. Within a half-hour drive of the temple, students rented him an apartment on Hayworth Avenue, a long residential street of two-story buildings. In his second-floor apartment, Prabhupada chose a quiet room in the rear, and in December 1968, he began work on the *Krishna Book*. How this one publication proved to be a turning point in the fortunes of the Krishna consciousness movement would become clear within the next two years.

HE WOKE EACH MORNING at about two o'clock and wrote, just as he had done in Vrindavan. The routine was more or less the same now, transposed to Los Angeles. He opened the weighty tome of commentaries by acharyas from centuries past, raised the microphone to his lips, and spoke. "By reading this one book, *KRSNA*, love of Godhead will fructify." Starting with those words in his preface, Prabhupada described that Krishna came into the world to reestablish the proper functioning of society, yet despite the sobriety of that mission he always remained the darling of Vrindavan village, the adorable divine child who made mischief and won hearts.

One by one, the little metal clicker on the side of Prabhupada's Dictaphone registered how many pages he recorded. By mid-morning, he was done for the day. While he showered and dressed, an assistant quietly entered the room, released the tape from its housing in the recorder, and noted down the number of clicks. Disciples who came to cook and clean asked, "How many clicks did Prabhupada record last night?" and challenged one another to calculate how many more clicks it would take before the *Krishna Book* was finished.

From time to time, he would break from writing to show assistants how to cook a dish. Often the recipe required a trip to the local Indian grocery for vegetables they had never heard of before, such as *karella* (bitter melon), *bhindi* (okra), or *lauki* (bottle gourd). He was as good at cooking as he was at any of the other roles he played for them and would demonstrate for his young assistants how far to press down on a melon to test for ripeness, how to measure spices in the palm of the right hand, and the proper way to prepare several dishes simultaneously using a brass three-tiered cooker: dal soup on the bottom, steam rising through holes in the second tier to cook the vegetables, then rising again through holes in the top layer to steam rice.

Two or three times each week, he visited the temple. La Cienega is a major arterial road that runs north from El Segundo Boulevard to Sunset Strip in West Hollywood, a wide stretch that in the late 1960s was home to film studios and restaurants, and disciples anticipated healthy attendance for services and meals. Prabhupada walked through the temple and nodded in approval at the scraping and painting and other improvements. People were visiting Krishna centers now not only one-by-one but in twos and threes, as couples and families, and he reminded his disciples to receive guests properly. There are small, everyday kindnesses that some people seldom knew in the rest of their lives: a warm welcome, a friendly smile, a fresh meal. At least in Krishna's temple, they should be greeted respectfully, given a tour, and a clear explanation of Krishna philosophy. He wanted his students to remain sensitive to a central fact of the human condition: Without knowledge of their souls, people suffered. It took many lifetimes for them to find Krishna, and when they finally did, they deserved a warm welcome.

Nor should devotees neglect to extend such courtesies to one another. His students were to always address one another as prabhu, "master," and bow to them, for all devotees were worthy of respect. He gave them a prayer to say to one another each day:

vancha-kalpatarubhyash cha
    kripa-sindhubhya eva cha
patitanam pavanebhyo
    vaishnavebhyo namo namaha

I offer my respectful obeisances unto the Vaishnava devotees of the Lord. They are just like desire trees and can fulfill the desires of everyone, and they are full of compassion for the fallen conditioned souls.

Then he returned to his apartment to continue work on the *Krishna Book*.

BY MARCH 1969, Prabhupada's presence in Los Angeles had attracted new followers. What had been an abandoned church became the largest of ISKCON's centers. Still, at least by U.S. government standards, his mission had not yet acquired the imprint of an authentic religion. Prabhupada never referred to Krishna consciousness as a religion—it was the inherent quality of all life, without a point of origin in historic time—yet government recognition would provide several advantages. For one, government authorization would help his disciples circumvent accusations that they followed a weird cult. For another, this was a time when young American men were being drafted for Vietnam, and membership in a recognized religious institution could save lives. "In the spiritual world," Prabhupada reassured his disciples, "there are no draft boards."

His students did not know how to react to the politics swirling around the Vietnam conflict. Should they join a picket line? Would university

students react more favorably to Krishna consciousness if they saw devotees marching with them against an unjust war? Prabhupada responded
that protesting U.S. aggressions in Vietnam would not change the government. Rather, their position should be that devotees were Brahmins, whose
job was to provide people with spiritual education. The *varnashram* system
of traditional India—what had come to be erroneously called the "caste"
system—prescribed work according to vocational skills. By this standard,
wars should be conducted by *ksatriyas*, qualified soldiers acting under
orders issued by a just government. The Brahmins' duty was to assure that
the government was indeed just, and its actions defensible.

The Selective Service had never heard of Prabhupada, whom male
devotees listed as their teacher on applications for religious deferment. In
March 1969, an assistant area coordinator for the Selective Service visited
Prabhupada at his Hayworth Avenue apartment. Prabhupada received him
cordially and explained that Krishna consciousness was a spiritual culture
that derived its authority from ancient Sanskrit scriptures. He outlined
the rules for initiation and impressed the agent with the authenticity of the
Vaishnava faith.

"You can expect to hear from us," the Selective Service agent said.

Prabhupada received a letter on March 14, 1969, declaring that before
the government would grant ISKCON religious status, he needed to provide
further details of its religious and administrative standards. The Selective
Service letter specified that he would need to provide names and locations
of all his churches, copies of his society's curriculum, a list of requirements
for a diploma with the requisite courses to be mastered, an outline of the
rules of conduct and personal standards required of his ministerial students,
and a roster of ISKCON's faculty with their degrees and accomplishments.

Prabhupada sent copies of the letter to his eldest disciples, and together
they created a curriculum that would lead to a final examination and, on successful completion, *bhakti-shastri* certification, signifying a *shastri* or expert in
bhakti scriptures. This was the West's first residency program for Vaishnava
ecclesiastical certification, and despite the monastic conditions, long hours,
and rigid studies, Prabhupada's disciples loved it. There was excitement in
learning bhakti theology under the tutelage of its leading exponent, a teacher
who embodied bhakti, devotion to God, in his every word and deed.

With five classes per day and written exams at the end of the week,
devotees found themselves in constant philosophical discussion. They

held mock debates in which teams responded to conflicting points of view such as those from reductionist scientists, fundamentalist Christians, and impersonal Vedantists. People voiced objections to Prabhupada's society for all sorts of reasons, and the bhakti-shastri curriculum prepared devotees to respond with rational explanations and scriptural references.

Of all the objections to Prabhupada's movement, the most frequent was also the most predictable: People mistook it for a kind of blind faith, a refuge for lost souls in need of something to shore up their intellectually impoverished lives. Since the days of Voltaire and other Enlightenment *philosophies*, people averse to divinity had declared the death of God and the irrelevance of faith. Truth, the thinking ran, was not a matter of faith but the product of good science and meticulous experiment. Any benefits religious faith might once have offered such as art or ethics or morality could be achieved with the right combination of physics, mathematics, biological evolution, and the unlimited potential of human intelligence. Hare Krishnas, scarred or bruised early in life — who knew what trauma had pushed them to such emotional extremes — had nothing to offer.

Yet by mid-1969, it was clear that Prabhupada had come not only to give refuge to lost souls. He had come to form a cadre of Brahmins capable of spearheading a revolution that would lead to a God-conscious world, and the bhakti-shastri candidates trained with that goal in mind. Each morning, they rose and attended services before the deities of Radha and Krishna, followed by classes on the *Srimad Bhagavatam* and other bhakti texts. Students chanted verses and studied the English synonyms for each word, which helped concretize the verses' meaning. The word *nirguna*, for example, in its simplest translation meant *nir*, "without," and *guna*, "qualities." According to followers of the mayavada or impersonalist schools, *nirguna* described the Absolute as impersonal, an undifferentiated energy devoid of qualities and form. From the bhakti perspective, *nirguna* was translated as "without material qualities," meaning that God's form was completely spiritual. Candidates for the bhakti-shastri degree learned to identify and address such differences of interpretation.

Still, noticeably absent from their curriculum were formal classes in the Sanskrit language. The conceit in university departments of Eastern Religions had always been to take seriously only scholars with command of the source language, and in India learning Sanskrit grammar alone was a twelve-year commitment. Prabhupada dismissed such concerns. He had come to raise a class of devotees, not academics. Until his books were published, any English translation of the original texts could do, as he had shown by using Radhakrishnan's Gita in the early days. Besides, a formal knowledge of Sanskrit offered no guarantee of accurate understanding. Word meanings changed over time: Who could say whether a current translation conveyed the same meaning that was intended thousands of years ago? Even more important, a word in Sanskrit could have many meanings—atma could mean, soul, body, senses, humanity—and the guidance of a qualified guru was critical for mastering the devotional content of scripture. It was the Vaishnava commentaries that took precedent in training candidates for Krishna-conscious life.

Once they had mastered the basics, devotees set out to spread Krishna consciousness elsewhere. In 1969, Prabhupada's disciples opened nearly one new temple in America each month. Some disciples traveled abroad to open centers in Europe, South America, Africa, and the Far East. Uniting these nascent communities was the experience of kirtan. Chanting bonded people across ethnic, religious, and national borders.

Interview with historian A.L. Basham (1914–1986)

INTERVIEWER: You mentioned earlier that you had taken part in a Chaitanya kirtan in Calcutta. Can you describe that experience?

BASHAM: It was about twenty years ago. I got off a train in Sealdah station just about sunset and noticed a kirtan taking place in one corner of the station yard. I was in no hurry and had time to spare. The devotees had erected a decorative tent in which they had set up a statue of Krishna and numerous brightly colored pictures of Krishna and Chaitanya and various saints of the order. They were chanting "Hare Krishna, Hare Rama," and a few began to dance. I don't think I got as far as dancing, but I joined in the chanting and was really carried away. I was there for at least two hours. That is an evening I will never forget—the intense exhilaration and relief, the feeling of security and safety and inner happiness which came from it. And it was so clear that all the people were feeling it—mostly working class people from the buildings and tenements of the surrounding area. No doubt, they worked hard and hadn't much to look forward to materially. But there was such happiness, such relief from tension and strain on their faces as one could hardly imagine.

INTERVIEWER: Do you think there is anything artificial about Westerners taking to the path of bhakti?

BASHAM: Two or three hundred years ago, nobody in Europe or in the Western world could have become a Hare Krishna even if he wanted to, because he wouldn't have known anything about it. Very few people had visited India, and those who had knew next to nothing about Indian religion. Now that this is known and understood, it's bound to have some effect.[114]

FROM THE OUTSET, Prabhupada had planned to have at least fifty paintings in the *Krishna Book*, and even before starting to write, he had sent out a request for painters. The "art department" charged with creating this collection of transcendental work began as nothing more than a room in the Boston temple, a three-story residential structure with an unfinished basement. Jadurani had relocated from her native New York, and soon other artist-disciples joined her, each with particular skills to offer and a captivating story to tell about how life had brought them to Krishna consciousness. Most of them had never met before, but there emerged a bright spirit of fellowship. Men and women who under other circumstances might never have so much as exchanged a word talked with the familiarity of old acquaintances and discussed how they would go about depicting the spiritual world on canvas.

In a fifteen-by-fifteen-foot room brightened by daylight filtered through tall bay windows, the artists set up shop. At strategic points around the room they positioned boxes containing tubes of paint, brushes, and tins of turpentine. A tape recorder sat in one corner, and as they worked they listened to recordings of Prabhupada singing, lecturing and dictating the text for the *Krishna Book*. The room was so small that the half-dozen men and women sat facing away from one another, a human wheel with arms extended like so many spokes toward canvases propped against the walls. It had always been this way, artists against the world, laboring to penetrate to the essence of life with brushes and palettes, though it was doubtful there had ever been such a collective of unseasoned novices charged with depicting the eternal world portrayed in the *Puranas*.

Given the *Krishna Book*'s target publication date of early 1970, their task was daunting: at least one finished painting per day. The only way to do that was by working in an assembly line. In a rare spirit of cooperation, the devotee-artists collaborated on one another's paintings. When Prabhupada sent a letter with the general description of a scene, they discussed as a group how it should be visualized. Inevitably, there were points needing clarification. What did Brahma, the first being, look like? What directions did his four heads face? Was the "swan carrier" that he rode an actual swan? If he was the oldest being in the universe, did he have a long white beard? What did the Bhagavad Gita mean by comparing the material world to a banyan tree? What do souls look like? Do they have hands and feet? Prabhupada replied promptly and patiently to their letters, and the artists translated his answers into paintings that would illustrate the *Krishna Book* and other publications.

"He had this vision," explained Ramesvara, former head of the Bhaktivedanta Book Trust, ISKCON's publishing office, "that people would be stunned seeing these beautiful illustrations — 'This blue cowherd boy is *God*?' — and that the paintings would compel them to read the philosophy in the books."

By popular agreement, Baradraj served as designer for the paintings. The young artist and former member of a Canadian rock band grasped the essence of their task: What the world judged as myth, they were to depict as reality. What history had relegated to shelves of folklore and non-Christian religions, they were to illustrate as the cosmology of real people inhabiting real worlds: tangible places accessed via pathways of yoga. Baradraj sketched out each composition on canvas and urged the others to strive for a vivid palette. Jadurani came next, filling in color and refining forms. Murlidhar came last, a classicist with an eye for textures, reflections, light, and detail. He would be the one to add finishing touches to their paintings.

BY THEIR OWN ASSESSMENT, the first dozen canvases were primitive, naïve, and childlike, and left them wondering how they could ever do justice to such an esoteric assignment. Prabhupada had a lifetime of devotion through which to visualize scenes from the Bhagavad Gita and *Srimad Bhagavatam*. They, on the other hand, knew nothing of the spiritual world. Some had artistic training, but not one among them had ever made a living at art or exhibited professionally. Even professional artists in India, where stone-etched chromolithographic "God prints" had been in circulation since the 1890s — even they, artists born to the culture, had never tackled anything more than simple portraits of Krishna and the demigods. An illustrated tenth canto *Bhagavatam* was a monumental undertaking, and Prabhupada's artists judged themselves unqualified for the task.

Don't worry, Prabhupada told them. These were not material paintings, and the artists did not need to go to art school to do their work. If
they chanted Hare Krishna, the inspiration would come from within and
their paintings would be "like rain after the drought of mundane art," he
said. "Everyone will become attracted."

"We knew the inspiration had to come through our hearts if we were
going to paint these transcendental personalities and places," Baradraj
recalled. "But we were not advanced devotees, and the full meaning of
the subject was not clear to us. What Prabhupada helped us see was
that our shortcomings and lack of skill or realization would not be an
impediment if we worked sincerely under his direction."

PRABHUPADA ARRIVED IN BOSTON to monitor progress in December
1969. A full press was now operating out of the 40 North Beacon Street
temple. Apart from the second-floor art studio, there were rooms for
transcribing, editing, and typesetting. In addition to the printing press,
the basement production area housed long wooden tables for stacking
and folding printed signatures. The building was ideal for their purposes:
The previous tenant manufactured funeral caskets and had installed a
small elevator that rose from the basement to a loading dock at the back
of the house. Devotees chuckled at the irony of a former funeral parlor
churning out magazines about God and reincarnation.

The press that devotees had purchased was a used Chief 29 offset.
Among the Chief 29's many jobs were several booklets summarizing
Prabhupada's position on yoga. The impression of yoga as an exercise fad
had concerned him since his arrival in America four years before, when he
observed students at New York yoga studios. Classes consisted of physical
postures and little or no instruction in the philosophy behind yoga. Almost
without exception, gurus in America had framed yoga as valuable for physical and mental well-being but minimized the study of yoga philosophy.

"No theories ever made men higher," one popular yoga teacher had
asserted. "No amount of books can help us to become purer. The only
power is in realization."[115] Yoga teachers took that idea at face value:
Few ever bothered to study the philosophical background to the practice they presumed to represent. In the 1960s and 1970s, most yoga
students labored under the misconception that yoga's philosophical
background was more or less irrelevant and possibly detrimental to yoga

practice. "The mind escapes into knowledge," wrote another, "into theories, hopes, imagination; and this very knowledge is a hindrance . . . . To know is to be ignorant; not to know is the beginning of wisdom."[116]

Many yoga teachers who came to America in the 1960s calculated that the physical postures were all that Americans could understand, and so that was what they taught. The consequence had been that many students misunderstood yoga as exclusively a technique to relax the mind and improve the body. This physical variety of yoga was easy and exhilarating. Yet five minutes after leaving their yoga class, students found themselves lapsing back into the same anxieties and stress. Without reforming behavior and opening the heart to God, Prabhupada insisted, the benefits of yoga would remain woefully brief.

"Yogic meditation is possible when there is first *yama, niyama*," he said, referring to the beginning steps of yoga as described by sage Patanjali's *Yoga Sutra*: morality and ethical living.[117] Integral to these basics, Patanjali had included *iśvara pranidhana*: surrender to God.[118] That lesson usually fell through the cracks in yoga classes. Among the yoga teachers of the Sixties, Prabhupada was the one who emphazied that yoga was for knowing the soul and awakening the soul's love for Krishna, the Supreme Being. The message came across in booklets rolling off the Chief 29, with names like *The Perfection of Yoga* and *Krishna Consciousness: The Topmost Yoga System*.

WHEN PRABHUPADA ARRIVED FROM THE AIRPORT, it was the Chief 29 he wanted to see first. His spiritual master's presses had been the pride of his mission. Bhaktisiddhanta had even included an image of a printing press in the logo of the Gaudiya Math. Prabhupada entered the workshop surrounded by disciples and stared at the seven-foot-tall, ten-foot-long machine. For the past many weeks, the press devotees had tended to it the way workers bees might tend to a queen, oiling her many cogs, lubricating her many wheels, polishing her many sides and parts. The Chief 29 chanted a mantra-like *click-clack-click-clack* as rubber grippers fed two-foot-wide sheets of paper down a metal slide and into a vertical bank of rollers one after the other. Out the other end gushed printed pages to be folded and stapled into *Back to Godhead* magazines and pamphlets such as *Krishna, the Reservoir of Pleasure* that were then boxed and shipped to temples. Without saying a word, Prabhupada lowered himself carefully to his knees and stretched out, full-length on the cold concrete floor, arms extended in homage. His disciples were stunned: Their guru was giving thanks to a printing press.

By the end of 1969, devotees were distributing hundreds of *Back to Godhead* magazines daily, and the Boston press operation was no longer capable of keeping up with the demand. In his search for a bigger supplier, Brahmananda contacted Dai Nippon in Japan, one of the world's largest printers, and ISKCON raised its monthly printings of *Back to Godhead* to twenty thousand copies.

In October 1969, the Boston press completed layouts for the long-awaited *Krishna Book*. Brahmananda carefully packed the cardboard layouts into a suitcase and flew from Boston to Tokyo. We are very sorry, Dai Nippon officers told him. You are behind in payments for your *Back to Godhead* magazine. We will only print this book if you pay us $19,000 in advance.

For the impoverished Hare Krishna movement, $19,000 was a fortune. As often happened in Prabhupada's mission, help would come from an unexpected source.

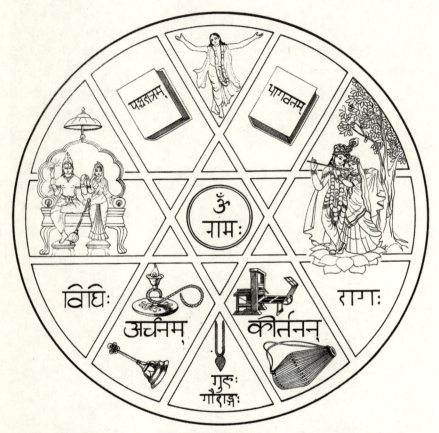

Printing books was so important to Bhaktisiddhanta Saraswati that he incorporated the image of a printing press in his institution's logo (seen at lower right), along with a drum signifying that books were the "Brihat Mridanga," or the "big drum," that could be heard around the world.

In 1970, George Harrison (left) produced an album of devotional music at Apple Studios with devotees from the London Radha Krishna Temple. The author is behind Harrison with arms raised.

CHAPTER EIGHT

For those who worship me with devotion
I carry what they lack and preserve what they have.

—SRI KRISHNA IN THE BHAGAVAD GITA, 9.22

LONDON, 1969

The three devotee couples who had opened the San Francisco temple—Mukunda and Janaki, Yamuna and Gurudas, Shyamsundar and Malati—went to London with big plans, and there wasn't anything bigger in 1968 than the Beatles. Wouldn't it be grand, they agreed, if the Fab Four took to Krishna consciousness? And why not? The Beatles had already visited Maharishi's ashram in India, and George Harrison was experimenting with sitars and yoga. Reaching them with Prabhupada's message was at least worth a try.

GEORGE HARRISON was born in Liverpool in 1943. He began playing guitar at age twelve, and by the time he was seventeen, he was a Beatle, one of four musicians who permanently changed the landscape of popular music history. By the time he was twenty-five and committed to spiritual pursuits, Harrison was to pop music what Picasso was to art or Thomas Edison to science: an astounding talent, an important example of what an innovative mind could bring to his craft. A generation raised in the turmoil of war and hungering for a more enlightened way to live appreciated not only his music but his thinking. What he did—both as a Beatle and as an independent singer-songwriter after the group's dissolution—got people excited.

Shyamasundar attended a Christmas reception at Apple Studios dressed in dhoti and tilak, which drew strange looks from the crowd. The Beatles were in an adjoining room holding a press conference about their upcoming *Abbey Road* album. John peeked out from the press room, scanned the crowd assembled for the reception, and made a quick exit out of the building. Ringo peeked out and did the same, followed by Paul. George peeked out, looked around the room, and spied the shaven-headed Shyamsundar. George had seen a photo of him with the other devotees in a *Times of London* article titled "Krishna Chant Startles London." The article reported on the devotees' arrival in England and their plans for opening a temple. George walked over and said, "Where have you been? I've been waiting to meet you."

And so began a friendship that led to an invitation for Shyamsundar to live with George at his manor home and an invitation for devotees to record the Hare Krishna mantra on the Apple Records label. "I can see it now," Harrison told them. "The first Sanskrit tune in the top ten."

In April 1969, the devotees arrived at Abbey Road Studios. Guards escorted them into a large, soundproof room filled with equipment. Paul and Linda McCartney waved from behind a glass control booth. Mukunda, who had been a jazz pianist before joining Krishna consciousness, took his place behind a grand piano, and George worked with him on a melody line. Technicians positioned microphones around the room. One take, two takes—then on the third try the maha-mantra flowed: "Hare Krishna, Hare Krishna . . ." Yamuna's strong voice led the chorus, commanding and pure, slightly nasal as Indian singing often tended to be. The music swelled, gained momentum, and spiraled for three-and-a-half minutes of pure transcendental sound, until—*Bonnng*! Malati hit a gong and brought the show to a spontaneous, rousing end. George and Paul went back to finishing work on the *Abbey Road* album, while the devotees crowded into their tiny van and drove off wondering what would become of the Hare Krishna mantra set to a rock drum beat and electric guitars.

In August 1969, "Hare Krishna Mantra" was released and received favorable reviews in the British papers and constant airplay on U.K. radio. On the first day of its release, the record sold 70,000 copies and entered the charts at number 20. Within two weeks, it rose to the number twelve spot, selling 20,000 copies a week in London alone. England's most popular television show, Top of the Pops, twice broadcast devotees chanting Hare Krishna surrounded by go-go dancers and swirling clouds of dry-ice mist.

George watched the nationally televised show with glee. It was, he later remarked, "one of the greatest thrills in my life."

THE APPLE STUDIOS RECORDING of the "Hare Krishna Mantra" track climbed the charts in Holland, France, Germany, Czechoslovakia, Sweden, Australia, South Africa, and Japan. Devotees found themselves signing autographs and posing for photos wherever they went. George had his staff book the London devotees at outdoor rock concerts, on television shows, and in nightclubs across Europe. They traveled, sang with Joe Cocker, played with the band Deep Purple in Amsterdam and with The Moody Blues in Sheffield. They headlined at the Midnight Sun Festival in Stockholm and appeared at the Star Club in Hamburg, where the Beatles had begun their career. The phrase "Hare Krishna" earned constant airplay on radio and television. It poured out of speakers in clubs and restaurants and found its way into newspapers, magazines, movies, and comedy routines. Other bands incorporated the mantra into their records and concerts. Sometimes in earnest, sometimes in jest, the chanting of Hare Krishna spread around the world.

When The Beatles sang "All You Need Is Love" on a live satellite broadcast in June 1967, the worldwide transmission reached more than 500 million television viewers. Now, barely two years later, George Harrison was reaching an even larger audience with the Hare Krishna mantra, and in doing so helping to fulfill a prophecy dating from the sixteenth century.

"One day," Chaitanya Mahaprabhu had predicted, "the chanting of the Holy Names of Krishna will be heard in every town and village of the world."

And so they were.

THE FIRST TIME I HEARD "Hare Krishna Mantra" was at the American Center for Students and Artists, a two-story building in Paris's Latin Quarter that catered to visiting jazz musicians and ex-pat lecturers. On Saturday nights, the American Center sponsored a *boom*—French for "dance party"—and a former New York recording engineer named Wally worked as the DJ. After classes at the Sorbonne, I hung out at the American Center and helped Wally with the Saturday dances. The turntable and controls filled the front row of a balcony that overlooked the dance floor. Stacks of vinyl 45 rpm records sat in boxes. My job was to hand Wally the records so he could position them on the turntable.

Every half hour or so, he played one record that started slow, then gradually the beat speeded up, and the song ended with a big *bonnng*. The lyrics repeated over and over: "Hare Krishna, Hare Krishna, Krishna Krishna, Hare Hare, Hare Rama, Hare Rama, Rama Rama, Hare Hare."

"Wally," I asked, "why do you keep playing that pop song?"

"It's not a pop song," he said. "It's a spiritual sound, a mantra." He pointed to the couples gyrating on the dance floor below. "When they dance to this record, they get spiritual benefit." I had no idea what that meant.

After the boom, we went out to a café. Wally ordered hot milk and stared at the porcelain cup for a minute or two, like he was having a conversation with it.

"What are you doing?" I asked. Everything about this guy was unusual.

"I'm offering the milk to Krishna," he said. "Even drinking a cup of milk can be spiritual if you do it right."

Wally always wore two things: a benign smile and a cap. "What's with the cap?" I asked.

"My head is shaved," he said. "The cap is so people won't be too distracted when they talk with me. When I was initiated as a Krishna devotee, my teacher, Prabhupada, gave me the name Umapati, and I shaved my head so I wouldn't get trapped in the ego of hair."

"Oh," I said, running a hand through my long hair.

"You're welcome to join me and my roommate for dinner," he offered.

We went back to the tiny hotel room he shared with another Krishna devotee named Hanuman, a French Canadian with dramatic facial expressions. While Umapati prepared rice on a little bunson burner stove, I picked up a book from a shelf. The title on the jacket was *Srimad Bhagwatam*. I opened the book and started to read a page at random. "Oh the king . . ." Hanuman reached out and gently closed the cover.

"That is too advanced for you," he said. "But you are a great soul. Someday you will appreciate this book—and you will go back to Godhead *in this one lifetime!*" His eyes grew big.

"That's great," I said, backing up, clueless as to what he was talking about. For a secular liberal like me, anything with the word God in it was suspect. I was there for dinner. Umapati put a portion of rice on a plate and put the plate on a small table in front of a photo of an elderly man with a stern expression.

"Who's that?" I asked.

"That's our teacher, Prabhupada. He's in London just now, staying with John Lennon. Why don't you go visit?"

A swami staying with a Beatle—and I've been invited to join them. I said I'd think about it.

The next day I took the boat-train from Paris and arrived in London. The temple was an elegant five-story building on Bury Place just off Little Oxford Street and a block from the British Museum. Inside the temple entrance and to the left was a hand-carved wooden door with a small circular window, like on cruise ships. Through the window, I could see deities, three-foot-tall marble versions of the same Radha and Krishna I had seen in posters Wally had hanging in his hotel room. Downstairs a dozen or so people sat on the floor sharing lunch. One of them, dressed in robes, waved me over. I sat next to him and dug into a mound of steaming rice.

"My name is Tamal Krishna," he said. "What's yours?"

When he learned that I played organ in a college band, he invited me to join them that afternoon for a recording session. We piled into a Volkswagen minivan with trays of steaming vegetables and rice and headed out.

"Where are we going?" I asked.

"You'll see," Tamal Krishna said. "Welcome to Krishna's band."

About fifteen minutes later, we turned onto Savile Row. Up and down the street were tailor shops displaying fancy men's clothing in fancy display windows. We parked in front of a building with the number 3 on the door. Something about the address rang a bell, but I couldn't place it. We walked in, and on the wall across from the receptionist was a huge photograph of a green apple. Then I remembered. Three Savile Row was Beatles headquarters. The receptionist waved us in, and I followed the devotees downstairs to a recording studio. There was George Harrison, thin as a stringbean, hair down to his waist, beads around his neck and buttons of Krishna and Prabhupada decorating his cotton vest. He hugged a few of the devotees and set us up to record. They pointed to me and said something. George walked over and handed me a harmonium.

The session began with Yamuna singing, "Govinda jaya jaya, Gopala jaya jaya, Radharamani Hari, Govinda jaya jaya." I picked up the melody on the harmonium, thinking, "If I stay with these people, I get to hang out with the Beatles—and I can also realize God. Okay, I'm in." This was still the Sixties. Monumental decisions didn't take long.

After the session, we returned to the Bury Place temple. George had signed the lease as guarantor, an act of generosity that prompted Prabhupada to begin calling him "Hari's son," Hari being another name of Krishna meaning "one who takes away all miserable conditions."

"NEVER MIND THAT HE IS NOT INITIATED," Prabhupada told Shyamsundar during his follow-up visit to the London temple in early 1970. "That is a little awkward for him." Initiation would have obliged George to follow basic rules of devotional life. He lived the life of a rock star and was not prepared for that degree of austerity. There was a saying in Bengal: Every year a snake slides easily out of its old skin, but if you try to cut the skin off, the snake will die. That was an important lesson that took me years to learn: Don't pretend to be more spiritually advanced than you are. It will just land you in trouble. George picked up on the teachings a lot faster than most people and never tried to hide his rocker habits from those closest to him. Early on he had understood the verse from Bhagavad Gita that explains how material habits fall away naturally as you progress in Krishna consciousness and experience a higher taste.[119]

"I have told him there is no need to change his name or shave his head," Prabhupada said, "just carry on serving Krishna. That is the perfection of life."

Shyamsundar mentioned that he would be seeing George the following day. George and his friend, David Wynne, Britain's sculptor laureate, had offered to select a slab of marble for the temple's altar. Prabhupada nodded and contemplated a photocopy of the *Krishna Book* manuscript sitting on his desk. He handed it to Shyamsundar, who thumbed through the massive work and blanched, intuiting what Prabhupada would say next.

"Kindly ask George to publish this book," Prabhupada said. "It will cost $19,000 to print 5,000 copies." The *Back to Godhead* printing bill was still overdue at Dai Nippon printers, and payment for the *Krishna Book* would have to be made in full and in advance.

Shyamsundar's shoulders slumped, and he stared at his hands. Nineteen thousand dollars might not have been a lot of money for someone as wealthy as George, but there was a higher principle involved. "Prabhupada, we must be very careful with George. We never ask him for anything. We just try to give to him, not take anything from him. If he gives, it's something he offers on his own."

Prabhupada nodded in appreciation. From the outset of his mission in the West he had followed the same formula: He taught and never asked for payment. But this was a unique opportunity to bring an important scripture to Western readers, and he was offering George a chance to take part.

"You may inform him that it is my personal request. Krishna will help you. You will see."

THE FOLLOWING NIGHT, rain pounded the roof of David Wynne's Wimbledon home while George, Shyamsundar, and the Wynne family finished a vegetarian dinner. The renowned designer, his wife, and two teenage children barraged their American guest with questions. Shyamsundar smiled and remained cordial, but George noted an uncharacteristic discomfort in his friend that night. Thunder echoed in the night sky. They would have to leave soon.

"George," Shyamsundar said abruptly, "do you remember I was telling you about that book Prabhupada wrote, the *Krishna Book*? He was saying that now everyone is hearing Krishna's name, but no one knows anything about Krishna's pastimes or what he looks like. That's what the *Krishna Book* is about."

George tilted his head, wary that his friend might be turning out like so many who wanted something from him.

"Prabhupada asked me to ask you something," Shyamsundar said. He took a breath and rushed ahead. "He wants you to publish the *Krishna Book* for $19,000. That will print 5,000 copies with lots of color paintings and—"

Bam! The houselights blazed hot, then exploded like bursts from a strobe. The house shook. Lightning had hit the roof. Everything went black. The darkness continued for several long moments. Then, just as abruptly, power returned. George leaned back in his chair, eyes wide, grinning from ear to ear.

"Well," he concluded, "there's no arguing with that, is there?"

"Prabhupada said Krishna would help me," Shyamsundar said, "but that was a little much."

The Wynnes and their guests couldn't stop talking with excitement over the magical display. Finally, George and Shyamsundar said goodnight and set out for their separate homes, dazed by the mini-miracle. George had his staff transfer $19,000 to Prabhupada's printing fund the following week, and the *Krishna Book* went to press.

IN EARLY 1970, THE FIRST COPIES of the *Krishna Book* arrived from Japan, and they were magnificent. The jacket featured a bright silver border framing an image of Radha and Krishna in brilliant colors.

"Everybody is looking for Krishna," began George Harrison's preface. "Some don't realize that they are, but they are. Krishna is God, the Source of all that exists, the Cause of all that is, was, or ever will be. God is not abstract. He has both impersonal and personal aspects to his personality, which is supreme, eternal blissful, and full of knowledge. As a single drop of water has the same qualities as an ocean of water, so has our consciousness the qualities of God's consciousness. But through our identification and attachment with material energy (physical body, sense pleasures, material possessions, ego, etc.) our true transcendental consciousness has been polluted, and like a dirty mirror it is unable to reflect a pure image."

Harrison concluded his preface to the *Krishna Book* with the maha-mantra:

> *Hare Kṛṣṇa, Hare Kṛṣṇa*
> *Kṛṣṇa Kṛṣṇa, Hare Hare*
> *Hare Rāma, Hare Rāma*
> *Rāma Rāma, Hare Hare*

He then signed it with a handwritten note: "All you need is love (Krishna). Haribol. George Harrison, March 3, 1970."

When devotees received the shipment of books, they were stunned by the detailed accounts and lavish illustrations that brought Krishna to life. They also confronted a dilemma. This was not a magazine or brochure that could be easily presented to people on the streets. It stood nearly a foot tall and weighed more than two pounds. Business people hurrying to work, parents rushing home to children and chores, pedestrians in the swarm of traffic—why would anyone stop long enough to consider purchasing such a heavy hardbound book?

In their first attempts, devotees managed to sell no more than a few copies a day—mostly by pointing out George Harrison's preface—and soon they fell back on selling incense for a donation and giving away magazines. In the evenings, they returned to the Los Angeles temple for a hot prasadam dinner and tallied the results. On good days, they distributed two hundred magazines. The income was hardly enough to pay for groceries. The story was more or less the same in all ISKCON centers. Collections barely covered rent.

When temple leaders in New York or Seattle or San Francisco sat down at the end of a month to send their reports to Prabhupada, they described in glowing terms the community's success in selling fifty or a hundred magazines. He saw through their spin on a bleak situation, but they needn't have been concerned. Poverty never bothered him. The active principle of devotional life was gratitude for the honor of serving God, whatever the circumstances.

Besides, he had been trained by Bhaktisiddhanta Saraswati, who operated on the understanding that God was no pauper and could turn things around in a second. When asked where the money would come from for his many ambitious projects, he replied, "I will take one brick from a temple in Vaikuntha [the spiritual world] — and that should more than cover the costs."

WITH THE *KRISHNA BOOK* FINALLY PRINTED, Prabhupada returned to completing his translation of the *Bhagavatam*'s twelve cantos. Financed by sales of the *Krishna Book*, every few months, a new volume arrived from Dai Nippon Printing Company, packaged in cardboard boxes stacked onto wooden pallets. Devotees greeted these deliveries the way they might once have greeted a new album by the Beatles: as a life-changing event, something bound to contain surprises and revelations. With each new canto, their way of seeing the world expanded.

In the first canto — an improved edition of the three volumes Prabhupada had printed in India — disciples learned the story of Vyasadev, who compiled the Vedic wisdom in written form at the dawn of Kali Yuga. Vedic cosmology divides the lifespan of the universe into a cycle of four *yugas* (ages), each cycle lasting 4,320,000 years. The *Bhagavatam* describes the first age, Satya Yuga — the Age of Truth or Golden Age — as a time of bucolic contentment and prosperity, of long life and wise governance. After 1,728,000 years, Satya Yuga came to an end and Treta Yuga — the Silver Age — began. By the end of Treta Yuga, a quarter of the world's population had turned away from religious practices. After 1,296,000 years, Treta Yuga ended and the Dvapara Yuga or Bronze Age began. During this age, only half the population remained interested in spiritual pursuits, primarily construction of temples and worship of deities.[120] After 864,000 years, Dvapara Yuga ended, and Kali Yuga, the fourth and most degraded yuga, began.

Kali Yuga, the current Iron Age or time of quarrel and confusion, started 5,000 years ago and according to the *Bhagavatam* will last 432,000 years, after which the cycle of yugas will begin anew. This age is character-ized by wars and disease, by deteriorating natural conditions, uncivilized human behavior and a lifespan of, at most, one hundred years. As a spiri-tual guide for the people of Kali Yuga, Vyasadev transposed the oral Vedic teachings into written texts. First, he divided the original Veda—the *shruti* or "heard" text, spoken directly by the Supreme Person—into four parts. Then he compiled the *smriti*, "remembered" texts or commentaries. Most of these writings addressed technical issues of philosophy and ritual, and Vyasadev felt dissatisfied with his work. His spiritual master, Narada Muni, sensed his unrest.

"No wonder you are unhappy," Narada said. "Philosophy and ritual do not touch people's hearts. Immerse yourself in devotion, in bhakti yoga, and describe the glories of Sri Krishna."

The path of bhakti follows two parallel lines: scriptural study (*bhaga-vata-marg*) and contemplative practices such as yoga, deity worship and meditation (*pancharatrika-marg*). Scriptural study undertaken without such practices remains abstract theory. On the other hand, those who attempt to perform yoga or meditation without an understanding of the philosophical grounding risk seeing their spiritual life deteriorate into sentiment or, in the extreme, fanaticism. Vyasadev took his guru's advice and wrote the *Srimad Bhagavatam*, which illustrated Vedic philosophy with histories of the avatars, of the enlightened beings, and even spiritually aware animals who brought Vedic philosophy to life.

THE FIRST CANTO tells the story of Pariksit, last of the great Vedic kings, who had been cursed to perish in seven days. "What is the duty of someone preparing to die?" the king asks the renowned teacher, Sukadev, who has come to guide him in his final days. Sukadev advises Pariksit to focus his mind exclusively on the Supreme Being, for thoughts at the moment of death become the chariot that carries the soul to its next destination.

In the second canto, Sukadev teaches Pariksit how to meditate on Vishnu or paramatma, the "supersoul" who dwells in the heart of all beings. The sages who have assembled in the forest to hear their discus-sion are moved by Sukadev's description of four-armed paramatma—not as an imaginary "God is in you" sentiment, but an actual incarnation of the Supreme Being, whom advanced yogis perceive in *samadhi*, or yogic trance. Sukadev explains that this same Vishnu at the dawn of creation brings the elements of material nature into existence. The elements coalesce into universes. Meditation on Krishna as the source of these unlimited material universes, Sukadev concludes, forms the first step toward realization of higher realities.

In the third canto, Sukadev describes scales of time, which vary according to the orbits of planets within the universe's fourteen planetary systems. In the early days of our universe, the sage says, Earth fell from its orbit into the cosmic ocean and had to be retrieved. The Supreme Being appeared as the giant boar avatar Varaha and lifted the Earth from its watery grave with his gigantic tusks. Once reinstated in its orbit, Earth received many souls. Among them was Devahuti, daughter of Emperor Svayambhuva Manu. Devahuti married the powerful yogi Kardama Muni, and their child was the avatar Kapila. In his youth, Kapila taught his mother esoteric details of yoga practice.

PRABHUPADA EXPLAINED THE MEANING of these histories in "purports" that occasionally included stylized vocabulary he had acquired as a student in British-run schools: words such as "sinful," which he used to describe behavior contrary to scriptural guidelines, and "demon," signifying an abusive, selfish individual who defied or denied the existence of a Supreme Being. Despite the occasionally awkward language, his writing was conversational and conveyed insight into complex subjects, as in his fourth canto commentary on Dhruva, a child prince whose stepmother stands between him and the affections of his father. Angered by this injustice, young Dhruva travels deep into a forest to mediate on Vishnu, whom he is convinced will award him a kingdom greater than his father's.

In the forest, Dhruva's spiritual master, Narada Muni, challenges the young prince's resolve. "Go home," Narada tells Dhruva. "Even advanced yogis are not all capable of following the arduous path of God realization. When you grow up, maybe then you will be ready for such austere practices and obtain the kingdom you seek." Dhruva refuses to back down and when Narada sees his young disciple's determination, he relents and teaches him how to meditate on the form of Vishnu in his heart. Dhruva follows his guru's directions and after many years does have the darshan, or vision, of Vishnu, who blesses Dhruva and awards him the kingdom he covets.

In his purport to the Dhruva story, Prabhupada commented that unenlightened people think childhood should be spent in sports and play, that youth is for exploring sexuality, and that only in old age does it make sense to consider God and spiritual life. "This conclusion is not for devotees who are actually serious," he wrote. "It is the duty of the spiritual master to test the disciple to see how seriously he desires to execute devotional service." A qualified spiritual master is able to "observe the psychological movement of [the disciple] and thus train him in a particular occupational duty." In coming to the West, Prabhupada wrote, his mission was to train disciples in the "particular occupational duty" of the Brahmin order, so that they might "raise human society to the highest standard of spiritual consciousness."[121]

WHILE THE FIRST FOUR CANTOS of the *Srimad Bhagavatam* delivered an unfamiliar and exotic description of Earth's history, the fifth canto stretched devotees' understanding of reality to an extreme. According to the cosmology of the fifth canto, the Earth is contained within a flat, disk-shaped construct called *bhu-mandala* comprised of a series of *dvipas* (islands). On the center island stands a cone-shaped mountain, Meru, which forms the *axis mundi*: the pillar connecting Earth to higher realms. This entire galactic structure revolves not around the sun but around the Earth. In essence, the fifth canto proposes that the Earth is both a globe and also part of a larger flat plane at the center of the universe.

The contradiction between the scientific explanation of the universe and that of the fifth canto baffled Prabhupada's students. As long as Krishna consciousness consisted of chanting and dancing and tasty prasadam all was well, but the fifth canto upended an understanding of reality they had been taught since childhood.

"Is there a difference," one disciple asked cautiously, "in the quality of service between a person who just accepts Krishna outright and one who wants to scrutinize him more and more?" Said differently, did Prabhupada really expect his students to embrace strange notions such as a flat Earth and a geocentric universe? Were they disqualified from devotional life if they did not?

"For neophytes, it is necessary to know about Krishna," Prabhupada replied, and he reminded them that reality was deeper than what their limited senses could perceive. How often throughout history had scientific calculations, based on imperfect senses and ever-changing evidence, been proved wrong? Look around you, he said. Miracles abound. He recounted the parable of a frog in a well—a frog that could not imagine the expanse of a great ocean. If you wish to love God, Prabhupada counseled, then first study his creation with an open mind.

"Still," Prabhupada said, reassuringly, "love for Krishna does not depend on knowledge of His greatness. Real love is without any such consideration of what He is or is not. In Bhagavad Gita, Krishna explains himself, 'I am the light of the sun and moon, and I am the controller of all planets,' and so on. But those who are advanced devotees do not care whether He is great or small. They simply love Him. The gopis and cowherd boys of Vrindavan are playing with Krishna. The Bhagavad Gita describes that one comes to such an elevated place only after many lives of acquiring knowledge.[122] But one does not attain love of Krishna merely through study. One must also receive the grace of Krishna or Krishna's devotee. Therefore, Chaitanya Mahaprabhu recommended *sadhu sanga*: the company of devotees."[123]

Don't look at reality with limited material eyes and intellect, he advised. See reality with *shastra-chaksus*, the "eyes" of scripture. Material eyes see imperfectly. Some day the deeper reality will be revealed to you. Until then, stay in the company of fellow devotees and keep chanting.

PEOPLE WERE ATTRACTED TO BHAKTI LIFE for many reasons. The Bhagavad Gita grouped them under four general headings: *arta*, those who were distressed and needed shelter; *jijnasuh*, the inquisitive; *artha-arthi*, people hungry for material gain who saw opportunities in becoming a devotee; and *jnanis*, those seeking knowledge of the Absolute.[124] Whatever their reason, the majority of initiates report that their initial contact with Krishna consciousness came through Prabhupada's publications. From a handful of publications sold daily during the early days of his movement, sales grew steadily to hundreds, then thousands, and then overseas in foreign languages. People received a book or magazine from a sankirtan devotee and, made curious by what they read, visited a temple. Others picked up books that had been abandoned in buses or subways. Some people discovered a Bhagavad Gita on a friend's shelf or found a *Back to Godhead* packed away in someone's basement. A woman in Canada had had a near-death experience at age eight. In her forties, she received a copy of Prabhupada's Bhagavad Gita from her son. She read about the difference between the body and the soul and stepped forward for initiation later that year. The personnel director at a hospital for chronic diseases in New York witnessed the harsh reality of material life every day and could make no sense of it. His assistant came in one day and handed him a small book he had bought from a devotee in a bus terminal, titled *Beyond Birth and Death*. The personnel director started chanting soon after. Books about Krishna showed up everywhere and some accounts of how people became devotees bordered on the miraculous. A bookkeeper in France described that one day, feeling depressed, he went fishing. From his rowboat on the calm waters of a pond, he cast his line and asked the universe for guidance. He felt a tug and there on the hook, in a waterproof plastic wrapper, was a copy of the French edition of *Bhagavad Gita As It Is*.[125]

DR. RICHARD L. THOMPSON, PH.D., did not discover Krishna at the end of a fishing line but at the end of a long line of questions about the world around him. He grew up among people who had eliminated God from their lives. His parents went to church but didn't believe what they heard there, and their indifference to religion rubbed off on him. By the time he was in high school, Thompson was drawn to science. The more he heard science's explanation of life, the more science, too, lost its allure. The notion that consciousness could be explained by patterns of oscillating molecular balls and springs made no sense to him. He looked forward to college. "That's where I'll find satisfying knowledge," he thought.

In college, things got worse. The professors seemed even more convinced that all natural phenomena could be described by mathematical laws. The universe and life itself, according to them, were products of a cold, impersonal natural order. Tall, studious, and gifted with a keen intellect, Thompson looked at problems from unusual angles. He was convinced modern science was wrong to define life in purely mechanistic terms and set out to find a better explanation of how reality operated. If traditional institutions of higher learning had no satisfying answers for life's grand questions, there had to be other places he could turn.

In 1969, while earning his master's degree in mathematics at Cornell University, Thompson read books on Indian philosophy, including a copy of Bhaktivinode Thakur's biography of Chaitanya Mahaprabhu. Each individual soul, the book described, was a spark of nonmaterial energy, simultaneously one with and also different from Krishna, the Supreme Person. That struck a chord with Thompson. The idea that consciousness originated not from matter but from a higher order of energy appealed to him.

He next came upon a book with the intriguing title *Easy Journey to Other Planets*, first published in India in 1960, and was fascinated by its origins.

TOP: Prabhupada's Puspa Samadhi Mandir, a temple located in Mayapur, was built in Prabhupada's honor, and the flower garland that he wore upon leaving his body was placed within the foundation of the temple.

BOTTOM: Chaitanya Mahaprabhu, known in his youth as Nimai Pandit, spent his time teaching and instructing his students on the theology of devotion. His lessons were held on the banks of the river Ganges. Nimai was known for his ability to refute the best scholars and logicians of the Nadia district, which was the seat of Sanskrit learning at the time.

Krishna-Balaram Mandir, located in Vrindavan, Uttar Pradesh. The temple was built in 1975, during Prabhupada's lifetime and under his guidance.

Along with other devotional activities, Prabhupada taught his followers the art of kirtan, or devotional singing. His voice had a distinctive and recognizable sound, and Prabhupada's kirtan was known to inspire listeners.

In 1971, during the Cold War and when non-indigenous religions were outlawed in the Soviet Union, Prabhupada traveled to Moscow. There he met and instructed a young man who later became his first Russian disciple.

TOP: When attending a public sankirtan chanting party, Prabhupada would, even at his mature age, frequently join his disciples in chanting and dancing in the processional kirtan.

BOTTOM: The daily distribution of prasadam, sanctified vegetarian food, is a prominent component of ISKCON temple activity. Prabhupada aimed to ensure that no one within ten miles of an ISKCON temple should go hungry.

TOP: Two of Prabhupada's earliest disciples, Gurudas and Yamuna, met with India's Prime Minister Indira Gandhi in 1972.

BOTTOM: In 2013, the Dalai Lama visited the ISKCON temple in Bangalore and placed a commemorative flower garland around a deity of Prabhupada.

TOP: In 1995, Nelson Mandela was the chief guest at ISKCON's Food for Life inauguration in South Africa. Mandela enjoyed a close friendship with Prabhupada's sannyasi disciple, Bhakti Tirtha Swami (far left).

BOTTOM: Prabhupada met with Apa Pant, the Indian Commissioner to the United Kingdom, in 1968.

TOP: First-generation disciples in front of Matchless Gifts, New York, 1967.

BOTTOM: Second- and third-generation disciples in front of Matchless Gifts, New York, 2014.

The author, A.C. Bhaktivedanta Swami, had read in an October 1959 issue of the *Times of India* that two physicists from the University of California had received the Nobel Prize for a startling discovery. Some particles, the physicists announced, were coupled with other particles spinning in reverse orbit. The physicists concluded there must exist an anti-material world parallel to our own world. They further theorized that, as pure energy, anti-material particles might prove to be an ideal fuel for interplanetary travel.

As a former pharmacist, Bhaktivedanta Swami understood the value of science on its own terms. After all, doctors did good work without having to invoke supernatural forces. Still, the *Times of India* article prompted the thought that contemporary scientific language might serve to convey to Western audiences the Vedic perspective on consciousness. Terms in the article suggested poetic equivalents: souls as "anti-material" particles, the spiritual universe as an eternal realm "spinning" opposite to the world around us, mystic yoga as a path to "interplanetary travel." The Swami wrote a thirty-eight-page essay called "Easy Journey to Other Planets," later published as the book Thompson found in his university library.

"The latest desire man has developed," Thompson read in *Easy Journey*, "is the desire to travel to other planets." Such a desire was natural, since the soul originally belonged to an "anti-material world," where life is eternal, blissful, and fully self-aware. The desire for interplanetary travel could be fulfilled by the process of bhakti yoga—the highest of all yogic processes.

The book went on to explain that, like antimatter, the "anti-material world" of the soul could only be understood by moving past realities felt and seen to realities intuited. The secrets of creation would not be found with electron microscopes or orbiting optical telescopes, tools hampered by the limitations of human perception and thought, but by inner experiment.

Farther down, below the realm of short-lived subatomic particles, on the most fundamental levels of creation, lay an indestructible reality. This was the realm of consciousness, that part of life that was never annihilated. The *Svetasvatara Upanisad* gave an exact measurement: the dimension of the soul was "one ten thousandth part of the tip of a hair."[126] Too small to ever be perceived by material tools, this indestructible particle of nonmaterial energy was so powerful that it illumined the entire body with consciousness. "The scientists' conception of antimatter," *Easy Journey* continued, "extends only to another variety of material energy, whereas the real antimatter must be entirely anti-material and free from annihilation by its very nature."

Easy Journey quoted the Bhagavad Gita's description of two forms of energy: one inferior (*apara-prakriti*) and the other superior (*para-prakriti*). The soul is formed of superior or anti-material energy and can never be destroyed. "Because of the presence of this anti-material particle, the material body is progressively changing from childhood to boyhood, from boyhood to youth to old age, after which the anti-material particle leaves the old, unworkable body and takes up another material body."

Easy Journey then described that, "as material atoms create the material world, so the anti-material atoms create the anti-material world with all its paraphernalia." By using what astrophysics might later describe as black holes, master yogis "give up their material bodies at will at a certain opportune moment and can thus enter the anti-material worlds through a specific thoroughfare which connects the material and anti-material worlds."

From the Vedic perspective, the book concluded, interplanetary travel depended not on technology but on mental preparation. "Scientists who explore outer space in an attempt to reach other planets by mechanical means must realize that organisms adapted to the atmosphere of the Earth cannot exist in the atmospheres of other planets. One can attempt to [inhabit] any planet he desires, but this is only possible by psychological changes."

Easy Journey cited the Bhagavad Gita's prescription for travel between worlds: "That upon which a person meditates at the time of death, quitting his body absorbed in the thought thereof, that particular thing he attains after death."[127] Such transfer to other worlds takes place instantly at the speed of mind, and for a master yogi, it is "as easy as an ordinary man's walking to the grocery store. By the grace of God, we have complete freedom. Because the Lord is kind to us, we can live anywhere — either in the spiritual sky or in the material sky, upon whichever planet we desire. However, misuse of this freedom causes one to fall down into the material world and suffer the threefold miseries of conditioned life."[128]

Easy Journey concluded that "Bhakti Yoga is the eternal religion of man. At a time when material science predominates all subjects — including the tenets of religion — it would be enlivening to see the principles of the eternal religion of man from the viewpoint of the modern scientist."

IT WAS CLEAR TO PROFESSOR THOMPSON that the book was a semantic exercise, but it was one that had required a bold, intuitive leap on the author's part. Bhaktivedanta Swami, it seemed to him, had discovered a way to make use of scientific terminology to show the relevance of Vedic teachings. The book even alluded to the multiverse, a theory of infinite universes that had only recently made its appearance in scientific circles in 1960 when *Easy Journey* was first published.

On an emotional level, Thompson found *Easy Journey* exciting. Intellectually, however, he was torn. Was the Swami just trying to validate religious myths with science? "How could this stuff possibly be true?" Thompson wondered. "Life on other planets? Mystic space travel? This is so different from what I've been trained to believe all my life."

Thompson was of that generation of twentieth-century scientists who had begun asking new questions since, for all practical purposes, science had reached the limits of its ability to see past the very small or penetrate beyond the very distant. What lay on the other side of those limits? Something more than the empiric picture of the universe was going on, but for fear of being marginalized or losing their jobs, none dared call it divinity. Twenty-two-year-old Richard Thompson walked the streets of Ithaca, New York, displaced from the world he knew yet uncertain about the world he had discovered.

"Just thinking science wrong and the Vedic view right—that's not sufficient," he concluded. "There has to be a way to reconcile the two. That would be important. If I'm feeling this way, there must be others who are torn by the contradiction between modern science and Vedic knowledge. If I can put those two things together, maybe I can help them, as well as myself." Eventually, he approached the book's author, A.C. Bhaktivedanta Swami Prabhupada, for initiation and received the name Sadaputa Das. Over the next thirty years, Sadaputa dedicated himself to defining the relationship between science and religion.

"Some see it as one of inevitable conflict," he wrote in the introduction to a collection of his essays, "others see it as harmonious, and still others see differences that they hope to reconcile. For many years, I was one of the latter. However, I have come to realize another potential relationship between religion and science. Both can cross-fertilize one another with inspiring new ideas that may ultimately culminate in a synthesis that goes beyond our understanding of either."

In his career as a devotee-scientist, Sadaputa emulated his teacher, Prabhupada, in pointing out the shortcomings of attempting to explain consciousness and complex biological forms in purely mechanistic terms. He would go on to write several acclaimed books that reconciled prevailing scientific perspectives with the Vedic viewpoint.

"I liked the third chapter of [Thompson's book] *Mechanistic and Nonmechanistic Science* very much," wrote Eugene Wigner, a theoretical physicist who had won the Nobel Prize in 1963 for his contributions to the study of elementary particles. "In particular, it acquainted me with the Bhagavad Gita. I learned that the basic philosophical ideas on existence are virtually identical with those which quantum mechanics led me to." Another Nobel laureate, Brian Josephson, best known for his pioneering work on superconductivity and quantum tunneling, admired Thompson's "cogent arguments against the usual scientific picture of life and evolution." Like his guru, Prabhupada, Sadaputa managed to shine a light on scientific anomalies while maintaining utmost respect for good science. "Because he loves science," wrote a reviewer, "he is pained by its contradictions and seeks its intelligibility in a larger context."

BY 1973, Prabhupada had initiated several scientist-disciples and founded the Bhaktivedanta Institute, whose mission was to establish the Vedic viewpoint as scientifically defensible. "Our worship of Krishna," he told them during a morning walk in Los Angeles,[129] "is our internal affair. The external affair is to establish that life comes from life. Otherwise, atheistic scientists will misguide society. Because it is truth, you will come out triumphant, no doubt, but your work is to determine how to present it in a modern way." Encouraging—and initiating—scientists became a seminal component of Prabhupada's campaign to establish the Vedic viewpoint in the West.

Among Prabhupada's many visitors were some scientists who admitted their inability to explain the anomalies in the scientific model. There were too many holes in mechanistic theories, they described, too many loose ends. For them, Prabhupada had only words of praise. Scientists who were unwilling to admit their limitations earned his scorn. He called their predictions of someday uncovering an ultimate theory of everything "dishonest" and "dangerous."

"They are not even gentlemen," he said. "A gentleman would be ashamed to speak such nonsense. A gentleman thinks twice before saying anything. You all," he said, indicating his scientist disciples, "must write very strongly, vehemently. Even if it is a little offensive, these rascals should be taught a good lesson. They are misleading others. As soon as you say 'God created,' immediately they become arrogant. That is our protest. We don't deprecate their intention of advancing in knowledge, but we protest against their defying the authority of God."

A COMPETITION ENSUED for a place near him on these morning walks. Wherever he was in the world, at around 6 a.m. he took up his cane and led students on a brisk one-hour walk. Disciples enjoyed hearing his insights and jokes and jostled to occupy a place close enough to take part in the discussion. His personal assistant, carrying a recorder and microphone, commanded a spot up front. Next came sannyasis and heads of ISKCON departments, followed by whoever was able to tag along. Those up front had the privilege of launching points for debate.

"Proponents of Darwinism say that the first living organism was created chemically," one student argued on a walk along the beach outside Los Angeles.

"And I say to them that if life originated from chemicals," Prabhupada replied, "and if your science is so advanced, then why can't you create life biochemically in your laboratories? You cannot even create a blade of grass—and I have to believe such a rascal?"

The group passed by a dead tree. Prabhupada stopped and pointed with his cane. "Now here is matter. Why leaves and twigs are not growing now? Formerly, they were growing. What is the difference? Let scientists explain this." One of the great pleasures of these morning walks was his commentaries on the commonplace. No detail, however small, escaped his scrutiny.

"They would say the tree's chemical composition has changed," a student suggested.

"All right, inject the chemicals," he replied, challenging science to bring a dead tree back to life. He pointed to the sprinkler system watering a nearby garden. "They are supplying water to those green trees—why not to this dead wood and make it green again? The chemicals are already there. But that particular individual living entity," referring to the soul that had previously inhabited the tree body, "has left. He has simply changed bodies."

"We don't say it is useless for scientists to study the laws of nature," he added. "We say go further. *Na hanyate hanyamane sarire*: The individual soul does not die, nor is he born.[130] He simply changes from one body to another, just as one changes garments. In the Gita, Krishna makes the presence of life within the body easy to understand: 'As the embodied soul passes in this life from childhood to youth to old age, the soul similarly passes into another body at death.'[131]

"In these two lines," Prabhupada concluded, "Krishna solves the whole biological question of what is life."

Look at the world around you, he taught them. Open your eyes. Even the tiniest thing means something. When you see a dead tree, there is a message there. Krishna is telling you things don't last in this world, but you, the eternal soul, will not die. Maybe you don't see Krishna speaking to you at first, but if you look closer—there he is.

DEVOTEES LEARNED OF THESE SCIENCE-RELATED TALKS through various channels. Prabhupada's publishing company, the Bhaktivedanta Book Trust (BBT) in Los Angeles, printed booklets of his conversations and classes. Newsletters circulated among temples. And every month, *Back to Godhead* featured articles and photos of his travels. Achyutananda, one of Prabhupada's first disciples from the early days in New York, had been living in India for nearly three years when he received a box of *Back to Godhead* magazines by air parcel. The cover featured a full-page photo of a Rathayatra festival in San Francisco with thousands of people chanting and dancing around the colorfully decorated chariot. In the center of the photo stood Prabhupada, leading the dance with his arms raised high in the air.

Achyutananda showed the magazine to Prabhupada's godbrother Madhav Maharaj. The elder sannyasi stared, and his eyes opened wide. Their guru, Bhaktisiddhanta Saraswati, had given his life to see Chaitanya Mahaprabhu's mission go abroad—and there was Abhay Babu, before a Rathayatra chariot—in America!—with Americans chanting and dancing around him. It was the fulfillment of Mahaprabhu's prophecy, the harbinger of a golden interlude within the tragic Age of Kali. Madhav Maharaj had spent years with Abhay in the Gaudiya Math. They had shared their guru's dream of witnessing the Holy Names leave India and circle the globe. Travel had been an enormous enterprise in those days, expensive and dangerous. Yet there was Abhay Babu, arms raised, white people all around him—

"*Go, Swamiji!*" Madhav Maharaj yelled at the photo, arms raised.

"*Go! Go! Go!*"

In San Francisco in 1967, Prabhupada inaugurated the Western world's first Rathayatra, modeled after the centuries-old festival in Puri, India.

PART THREE

THE
WORLD

TOP: In August 1973, a pointed discussion about whether animals have souls took place between Prabhupada and renowned Jesuit Cardinal Jean Daniélou.

BOTTOM: That same week, the Deputy Mayor of Paris invited Prabhupada to an official reception in Paris's Hotel de Ville.

CHAPTER NINE

One who is a friend to others and free of ego, who is tolerant and whole-heartedly engaged in acts of devotion—such a soul is very dear to me.
—BHAGAVAD GITA, 12.13–14

INDIA, 1970

Embedded in the geography of Mahaprabhu's prophesy that the names of Krishna would be chanted "in every town and village" was India itself. With his global mission sufficiently underway in America and Europe, the time had come for Prabhupada to return and revitalize Krishna consciousness in its homeland. In early 1970, he instructed leading students to prepare for an all-India tour.

Word spread that A.C. Bhaktivedanta Swami was arriving in Calcutta with Western disciples. Reporters, godbrothers, friends from his younger days, and a crowd of enthusiastic bystanders assembled at the airport to greet them. When Prabhupada disembarked, a kirtan group from the Calcutta Chaitanya Math chanted Hare Krishna, and well-wishers piled garlands of gardenias and marigolds around his neck until his face was nearly covered by the fragrant flowers.

Then garlands were offered to his students, and the VIP reception took them by surprise. Some had visited India before, but they had been tourists then. Within the first few moments of their arrival dressed as devotees, it was clear they were part of something extraordinary. Not only was the crowd greeting them enthusiastically, but people were looking at them with awe. For a thousand years, foreigners had come to India to conquer and exploit. Prabhupada's disciples were standing that history on its head. They had come to honor India's spiritual culture, and the onlookers applauded and cheered, crying out, "Sadhu! Sadhu!" and stepped forward to touch their feet.

A reporter asked what advice Prabhupada wished to give India.

"I have been around the world," Prabhupada said, "and I have found that happiness and peace cannot be established by materialistic advancement. My advice to the Indians is that if you advance only in science and technology, then you will remain backward forever. Chant the Holy Names of Krishna. All animosity, all problems will be solved if they take this advice."

A supporter who had offered to be their host escorted them to waiting cars. At the supporter's home, Prabhupada's sister, Bhavatarini, was on hand to greet him and his disciples. It was past midnight, but Prabhupada would not allow his students to rest without first accepting the dishes of prasadam Bhavatarini had prepared.

"Whatever my sister cooks, we have to eat," he told them and then added with affection, "and we must eat everything. This is her favorite activity."

The following day, *Amrita Bazar Patrika* ran a front-page story about the Calcutta native who had brought Krishna to the West and his triumphant return to India. "Many VIPs have come to Dum Dum Airport before," the article reported, "but never before have we seen gaiety and celebration of this magnitude."

Other disciples arrived in the days that followed, and the entourage swelled to forty men and women. They moved cross-country by train, bus, and rickshaw, and everywhere they went Prabhupada presented his Western students as evidence that Chaitanya Mahaprabhu's message was indeed universal. Stay pure, he told his young followers. Here in India you will be judged by people who know devotional culture and who will be skeptical whether Westerners can maintain such a high standard of behavior.

They arrived in Bombay. One of the first people to greet him there was Sumati Morarjee, who had given him his ticket to America five years before. "I did not think you would come back alive!" admitted the head of Scindia Steamship Company.

Invitations for Prabhupada's disciples to appear at public events flooded in. One program billed itself as a gathering of holy people. Organizers ushered the devotees into a hall furnished with long rows of wooden tables. Sitting on the tables at one end of the hall were yogis and sadhus in various stages of dress and undress. Some wore elaborate robes; others were covered with nothing but ashes and armbands. Many sported scraggly beards and matted hair that reached to the ground. A few held tall metal tridents. The devotees stared at them, and the sadhus stared back, each group thinking the other to be the strangest thing they had ever seen. Not knowing what else to do, the devotees broke out in kirtan, and the audience responded with ecstatic clapping and dancing. In his enthusiasm, one of the organizers led them out of the hall and onto the streets of the city, and many in the audience followed along, singing and dancing in delight over Westerners performing like natives.

Now it was they who were strangers in a strange land, yet in a sense they had also come home, and each day compounded the feeling, until whatever residue remained of life before Krishna began fading into memory. One evening, when the devotees returned to their quarters and gave their report, Prabhupada encouraged them to take the chanting to the streets, as they did in America.

The following morning, a dozen male disciples in crisp robes and heads freshly shaved, and as many female disciples in colorful silk saris, worked their way down crowded marketplaces in the center of the city. Their voices synchronized with the drums and kartals and the entourage proceeded in unison, left foot over right, right foot over left. Pedestrians hurrying to work stopped and gawked, not quite believing their eyes. Patrons in food stalls put down their *samosas* and blinked in disbelief. Customers exited shops to congregate on the sidewalk and stare. For their part, the devotees did their best to not get distracted by the crowd that swelled around them, and to stay fixed on keeping step with the kirtan leader.

After a few days of such sorties down the main thoroughfares of Bombay, the press took notice. Radio commentators, photographers, and journalists followed them wherever they went. A reporter for the *Times of India* wrote, "Can the materialistic West, or at any rate, a microscopic part of it, have turned at last to embrace the spiritualism of the East? I met several of the kirtan-chanting Americans and was at once struck by their sincerity and utter surrender. The Vaishnavas of Mathura [the city outside Vrindavan where Krishna first appeared five thousand years before] could not be so guileless, I thought, as this band of Bhakti enthusiasts."[132]

The *Times* journalist followed Prabhupada and his disciples to a program on Bombay's Chowpatti Beach, where cool breezes stirred clouds over the Arabian Sea and the sand was fine and soft underfoot. Several thousand people had assembled before a raised stage for talks by popular swamis. After two hours of dry philosophy by mayavada teachers, it was Prabhupada's turn. He did not utter a word but simply looked at his disciples.

"Begin chanting," he said.

The devotees launched into an enthusiastic kirtan with mridangas and kartals. Shyamasundar and Malati's two-year-old daughter, Saraswati, pirouetted across the stage. The impersonalist swamis rose and walked off, uninterested in the ecstasies of devotion. The devotees jumped into the audience. The crowd rose from their seats, chanting and clapping and dancing along. Devotees lead a joyous chorus line back and forth from one end of the huge tent to the other. Some people cried, others laughed. Police joined in, dancing along with the best of them. Finally the kirtan came to an end. The crowd was buzzing.

"I do not feel that I have to say very much," Prabhupada said into the microphone. "You can see the result of Krishna consciousness. It is not something artificial. It is there in everyone. We simply have to revive it."

The next day the *Times* journalist wrote, "One greying reporter whom I had always regarded as a particularly unsentimental person said to me in an emotion-choked voice, 'Do you realize what is happening? Very soon Hinduism is going to sweep the West. The Hare Krishna movement will compensate for all our losses at the hands of *padres* through the centuries.'"[133]

Some readers did not share the reporter's enthusiasm. One letter to the editor of a local paper summed up the feelings of many traditionalists: "These foreign Hindus of the Hare Krishna movement cannot be equal to the native original Brahmins. They will have to be relegated to the lower castes." Another reader wrote that the movement was "just a sporadic fad of sentimentalists." Prabhupada was incensed and wrote to the editor, "Lord Krishna says that anyone who comes to him is eligible to be elevated to the highest position of going back to home, back to Godhead. How can the bhakti movement be guilty of being 'sporadic' when this science was taught in the Gita five thousand years ago—when our activity is *sanatan-dharma*, the eternal occupation of the living entity?"[134]

By responding to critics in the Indian press, Prabhupada drove home for his Western disciples something startling: Even people who should know better, people born and raised in India, did not understand their own devotional culture.

DESPITE THE HECTIC TRAVEL SCHEDULE, Prabhupada never failed to rise early to work on his books, and his consistency amazed everyone around him. He never slowed down. Aging merely fueled his determination. Krishna had given him a chance to set humanity back on track, and the price for such an honor was non-stop effort. Growing old was no excuse.

"I want to travel around the world with two dozen boys and girls," he announced one morning. "Let us impress Krishna consciousness into every country of the world." Round-the-world tours were a young person's adventure, but he lived in a place beyond consideration of age or discomfort. Since his first contact with Bhaktisiddhanta, Prabhupada had trained himself to minimize physical needs and sleep. It was well known among followers that he rested at most four hours at night, then rose to write and chant. They had never met anyone like him. He was seventy-five years old and gave people less than half his age a run for their money.

Traveling with him through India opened their eyes to something quite unexpected. Back home in the streets of New York, Los Angeles, or San Francisco, the public saw them as an anomaly, a curiosity, something alien and suspect. Here they were heroes led by an elderly guru who was quickly becoming one of the most renowned spiritual figures in the nation.

To be adored for chanting Hare Krishna—what a change that was.

IN SURAT, GUJARAT, the entire city turned out for Prabhupada and his "dancing white elephants," as he had affectionately dubbed his Western disciples. Thousands of people lined the streets to watch them perform sankirtan. Crowds cheered and threw flower petals from windows and rooftops. The turnout was so large that after the third day the mayor closed schools and proclaimed a citywide holiday. Signs posted around town read: WELCOME TO THE AMERICAN AND EUROPEAN DEVOTEES OF KRISHNA.

Throngs of locals assembled outside the home where Prabhupada and his students stayed. The crowds blocked traffic as they cried out to see the saint who had brought Krishna to the world. Relenting, Prabhupada walked out onto the balcony of his room.

"Hare Krishna!" he called down. The crowd roared, arms waving in the air.

"Practically, there is no credit for me," he would often tell reporters. "If there is any credit, it goes to my spiritual master, Bhaktisiddhanta Saraswati

Goswami Prabhupada, who is helping me by sending so many good souls to this movement. My business is just to carry out his order. That is the way of the disciplic succession."[135]

ONE OF THE DEVOTEES with the India traveling party from its outset was an African-American renowned for his melodious singing and expert mridanga playing. In 1969, while on shore leave from the U.S. Navy, nineteen-year-old Donald Brawley had met devotees on the streets of Los Angeles and accepted their invitation to meet Prabhupada at the temple on La Cienega Boulevard.

"What are you planning to do with your life?" Prabhupada asked from behind his desk. The young sailor replied that he intended to become a doctor.

"How many people graduate with a degree in medicine each year?" Prabhupada asked.

"Thousands," the young man replied.

"How many graduate with a degree in the science of the self?" Prabhupada challenged. "We need doctors of the soul. First be a doctor for yourself, then you can be a doctor for others."

Prabhupada initiated the sailor in March 1969 and gave him the name Dinanath Das.

"IN INDIA we were received like demigods," Dinanath recalled. "It was very surreal, all these people touching our feet, garlanding us, and anointing our face with sandalwood pulp. People were constantly inviting us to their homes and serving us feasts and insisting, 'Eat more! Eat more!' Prabhupada laughed and reminded us that in India it was considered an insult to refuse a gift. When he spoke at these receptions, he reiterated for our hosts that this worldwide chanting was Chaitanya Mahaprabhu's prophesy and that everyone born in India had the duty to help fulfill it."

Invitations arrived from all parts of India for Prabhupada and his "dancing white elephants" to visit homes, temples, schools, and community centers. He took advantage of these offers to introduce his students to places of pilgrimage such as Kurukshetra, where Krishna spoke the Bhagavad Gita; and Rama Tirtha Sarovara, where, in the Satya Yuga, Sage Valmiki, author of the epic *Ramayana*, had established his ashram. They traveled outside urban centers to bring the chanting of Krishna's names to villages where white people had never been seen before and entire populations turned out to greet them. The devotees arrived back at their quarters after fifteen-hour days, exhausted and ready for sleep. Prabhupada would be at his desk, chanting, translating, energized, and ready for more. The next day they rose, packed, and traveled on across the subcontinent.

Interview, Bombay, November 7, 1970:

> PRABHUPADA: I went to America and remained with a friend's son in Pennsylvania for three weeks. I had no money, and my philosophy was completely different [from the American way of life]. I asked the Americans to cease from four kinds of sinful activities: illicit sex, meat eating, intoxication, gambling—these were their daily affairs.
>
> REPORTER: Then why were they attracted to Hare Krishna?
>
> PRABHUPADA: You are taking Krishna as Hindu. That is your mistake. He is God. I am not interested to preach Hindu dharma. Krishna consciousness is not Hindu. Don't misunderstand the philosophy. We are teaching love of Godhead. First stage is brahma-jnana, knowledge of God as light, just like seeing sunlight. Then paramatma-jnana, knowledge of God in the heart. Then bhagavad-jnana, knowledge of Krishna, the Supreme Personality of Godhead. That is pure bhakti. We are not talking of Hinduism or any 'ism.' We are talking about the science of God.[136]

IN JANUARY 1971, they arrived in Allahabad at the campgrounds of the Ardh Kumbha Mela, held every six years after the even bigger Maha Kumbha Mela. There, the three sacred rivers converged: the Ganges, Yamuna, and Saraswati. To prepare for Kumba Mela's fifteen million pilgrims, the Indian Army had erected a sprawling city of wood and canvas dwellings. Prabhupada's entourage staked tents, set up a corrugated tin kitchen, lined the floor with hay and burlap rugs, stoked wood fires, and began cooking. Each day during Kumbha Mela, they distributed hundreds of plates of vegetables, fried flatbread *puris*, and sweet semolina *halava*. Prabhupada ranked distributing prasadam as equal in importance to chanting Hare Krishna, and in years to come disciples would feed fresh, nutritious prasadam lunches to more than one million indigent children across India every day.[137]

For miles on either side of their tents, the pageantry of Kumbha Mela was on display. Devotees met yogis, some of them rumored to be five hundred years old; naked *fakirs* on elephants; wizened sadhus, their arms atrophied from remaining upraised for years; and "sky-clad" (naked) *naga babas*. For some devotees, accounts of mystic yogis in books such as Paramahansa Yogananda's 1946 memoir *Autobiography of a Yogi* had been the impetus to their own spiritual journey. Prabhupada understood their fascination with mystic displays, and he regaled them with stories about yogis he had known growing up at a time when such things were commonplace. Trailanga Baba, a friend of Yogananda's grand-guru, Lahiri Mahasaya, had lived not far from Prabhupada's childhood home and passed away when Prabhupada was still a boy. Rumors held that Trailanga had been more than three hundred years old at the time. Visitors reported seeing him levitate, drink poison without harm, and shrink himself down to the size of a pea.

Prabhupada described that as a boy he had witnessed mystic powers on display when his father took him to the circus. They walked the fairgrounds holding hands and watched as one popular yogi proved his resistance to rusty nails and another made a syrupy *gulab jamun* sweet appear from thin air. "That mystic power is worth about two paise," young Abhay's father, Gour Mohan, told him. Two paise was the price of a gulab jamun in sweet shops.

Despite the fascination of such mystic performances, at the 1971 Ardh Kumbha Mela it was Prabhupada's disciples who created the greatest buzz.

WORK BEGAN THAT MONTH to prepare for yet another public event. This time, ISKCON would be the organizer in Bombay, and devotees drew on their American savvy to promote and advertise. Thirty-foot-wide colored banners hung at major intersections and large posters appeared on the sides of office buildings. A twenty-foot-wide hot air balloon floated over the fairgrounds, with the words HARE KRISHNA emblazoned in bright colors.

The first day of the festival, ten thousand people attended. Word spread, and attendance on the second day doubled. Later that month, Prabhupada sent Giriraj and Tamal Krishna to Calcutta to organize a similar pandal program, which ended up drawing more than twice the attendance of the Bombay program. On the final day, forty thousand people packed into a huge tent erected on Calcutta's Maidan field near the city center. By now the Hare Krishna movement had begun attracting young Indian men and women. Prabhupada held initiations, and his traveling sankirtan party swelled.

Politicians and business people also felt drawn to Prabhupada's movement, but they were cautious about trusting its authenticity. Many of these business people came from India's wealthier and more influential families. They had seen gurus try to revive India's spiritual culture before, and fail. Most of these swamis were self-appointed "incarnations" who recited Sanskrit verses or performed a few mystic tricks to prove their "divinity," but nothing much had come of it.

But in Prabhupada, these influential men and women of Indian society found a devotion to Krishna they had not witnessed in others. In his discussions with members of the nation's elite, Prabhupada invited them to judge Krishna consciousness by the evidence before them: Europeans and Americans who had set aside worldly pursuits to live as bhakti yogis and as aspiring servants of Krishna.

"India's culture is Krishna conscious," he reminded a group of Bombay civic leaders, "but we have forgotten that culture and are becoming too much materially absorbed. I have now forty-two temples in the West, and in each there are fifty to one hundred disciples." It was a good start, he concluded, but there was more to do. "Please help me with this movement," he asked.

The guests agreed: The Krishna consciousness movement was something unprecedented. Some became his initiated disciples and helped build temples, print books in local languages, and fund prasadam distribution programs. Others who were not yet ready for initiation paid a fee to become "Life Members" of ISKCON, which entitled them to sets of books and overnight privileges in the growing number of temples worldwide. With the help of these well-to-do supporters, Krishna consciousness in India spread.

DESPITE THEIR CONSTANT TRAVEL, Prabhupada insisted that his disciples not compromise their daily devotional practices. Each morning they showered and dressed and marked their foreheads with tilak. Often they stayed in homes that featured a temple room, and in the morning devotees gathered before the altar. One or another among them would volunteer to serve as pujari and perform the arati ceremony as Prabhupada had taught. Over time, disciples had improved their standards of deity worship, and pujaris followed the strict protocols outlined in the traditional texts, purifying their hands with drops of water, then presenting the deities a stick of incense and offering it in seven circles around the whole body of the deity, then a flower, conch, handkerchief, and other items, while the assembly sang prayers.

After arati, devotees chanted their daily sixteen rounds of beads. They put their hands in their bead bags and murmured the maha-mantra quietly to themselves: "Hare Krishna, Hare Krishna, Krishna Krishna, Hare Hare, Hare Rama, Hare Rama, Rama Rama, Hare Hare." Some sat on cushions, eyes closed, listening intently. Others wrapped a wool chadar around their shoulders and strolled quietly around the neighborhood as they chanted.

Assembling again in the temple room, the devotees bowed down when Prabhupada entered to lead discussion on the *Srimad Bhagavatam*. Often his explanations connected stories from long ago with the world around them. In one such morning program, he spoke from the sixth canto of the *Bhagavatam*, relating the life of Ajamila, a young man with a good heart but little resistence when a beautiful woman came between him and his family.

"You will find many Ajamilas at the present moment," Prabhupada said. "It is the Age of Kali."

Ajamila left his family and fathered ten children with his new love, occasionally resorting to illegal means for securing the money to maintain them. After a long life, he lay dying and regrets haunted him. Death approached, and in fear Ajamila called out for his young son, Narayan, whom he had named after Krishna, the shelter (*ayan*) for all humans (*nara*). By calling out the name of the Supreme Being at the moment of death, Ajamila's soul was liberated from further material births. The story recalled for Prabhupada his own situation as a child.

"I was not at home when my father was dying," he said. "He was living for one more day just to see me — always inquiring whether Abhay has come back."

The story of Ajamila had meaning for them, he cautioned. If you choose to marry, he said, don't become an Ajamila. Take your responsibility as spouses and parents seriously. Love one another and raise your children to always think of Krishna. "What is learned early in life," he reminded them, "is never forgotten," and it would have occurred to disciples there that surely he was the living proof.

PRABHUPADA TRAVELED ON, one country after another. In June 1971, he flew from Delhi to Moscow to meet with an Indologist at the Academy of Sciences. After checking into their hotel, his assistant, Shyamasundar, went looking for some of the city's scarce vegetables. Two teenage Russians watched, surprised to see a tall American with shaved head and cotton robes crossing Red Square. Shyamsundar stopped and invited the young Muscovites to meet Prabhupada. Within twenty years of that first encounter, there were more than 100,000 Krishna followers in Russia. For people isolated so long by a government that denied them access to spiritual knowledge, Krishna consciousness fell like a healing rain.

He would not stop traveling, and one round-the-world journey became two, then three, then four. Occasionally, he admitted retirement appealed to him, since it meant he could concentrate on completing the *Srimad Bhagavatam*. "This body is old," he would say. "It is giving warning." But then he would dismiss retirement as impractical, since his students still had not convinced him they were capable of managing ISKCON on their own.

IN OCTOBER 1971, he drove with disciples to Vrindavan. Twenty years before, he had lived there penniless and unknown. Now he was returning as a renowned spiritual ambassador who had made Vrindavan famous around the world. Civic leaders greeted him with words of admiration, calling him the "great preacher of Vedic culture." He had been "one of us" in the early days of his mission, they proudly declared, and by his efforts "all the people of the world are becoming very intimately related with Vrindavan-dhama."[138]

Despite the warm reception, Brijbasis harbored reservations about his disciples. On social grounds, many residents viewed the foreigners as mlecchas, meat-eaters and outcastes, impure and unfit for devotional worship. On emotional grounds, they viewed them as uncouth strangers who simply did not fit in with Vrindavan life. They had some cause for concern, since this early generation of Krishna devotees had not yet mastered the habits of proper Vaishnavas. Some persisted in eating with their left hand, others chewed their fingernails or allowed their prayer beads to touch the ground, and Brijbasis feared such behavior would bring shame on Krishna's holy dhama.

"Suppose after you and I are gone, they become a nuisance and make a disturbance," one Brijbasi said. Prabhupada objected to this insinuation.

"You are putting blame on my disciples. It is not good for you. My disciples are really devotees of God, and you are saying like that. I cannot tolerate this thing." His students were doing their best, he said, maybe imperfectly, but the effort deserved the encouragement of Vrindavan's residents, not their disdain.

"If you have any suggestion for them," he said, "you tell it to me, not to my disciples. My students are very new, and if they hear others discouraging them, they may become weak. I am trying hard to save them, so confidentially we can speak of these things, but not in front of them."[139]

When certain Brijbasis refused to eat prasadam cooked by Prabhupada's disciples, Vishwambhar Goswami, mayor of Vrindavan, spoke on the Westerners' behalf. He had known Prabhupada from the early days and proudly defended his disciples' legitimacy. "They have left all maya to come here and chant Hare Krishna," Vishwambhar Goswami argued. "We can accept *anything* from the hands of such devotees."[140]

PRABHUPADA AND HIS STUDENTS TOURED VRINDAVAN, walking from one holy place to another, and at each stop he recounted Krishna's pastimes. "Just over there," he said, pointing to a hilly spot at Varsana, the village where Radha was raised, "Krishna used to come down that hill." Pointing to another spot nearby, he added, "Radha would come down this hill, and they would meet in the middle." They came to another spot, and Prabhupada described that this was where child Krishna played with his cowherd friends. One day he ate dirt and his friends tattled on him to Mother Yashoda.

"Oh, your son is eating dirt!" they said.

"Krishna!" Mother Yashoda scolded. "You are eating dirt?"

"No," the child replied. "Those cowherd boys are my enemies. This morning we had some quarrel, so now they are telling lies about me."

"No! No!" the cowherd boys cried out. "He ate dirt! He ate dirt! We saw him!"

"All right, we shall see," Mother Yashoda concluded. "Open your mouth."

When the Supreme Being was so ordered by his mother, he obediently opened his mouth—and in her child's mouth Yashoda gazed upon the entire creation. She saw outer space in all directions, mountains, oceans, planets, the moon, and stars. She perceived eternal time, the totality of elements, and all forms of life. In that one cosmic vision, she beheld the infinity of existence. She saw herself as well, holding child Krishna on her lap, and Yashoda wondered if perhaps she had gone mad.

"Or else," she thought, "I am mistaken in thinking he is my child. Surely, Krishna is the Supreme Personality of Godhead. And if so, then it is only an illusion to think I am his mother and that Nanda Maharaj is my husband."

Rather than see her love for him weakened by preoccupation with his identity as the Supreme Being, child Krishna used his mystic skill to erase all such thoughts from her mind, and Yashoda once again knew herself to be Krishna's mother.

"Well, whatever is done is done. Just don't do it again," she told Krishna with a wag of her finger, and off the cowherd children went to resume their play.

Prabhupada and his disciples resumed their tour of Vrindavan.

A PIOUS VRINDAVAN COUPLE, Kashi Prasad Saraf and his wife, Gita Devi, owned a parcel of land in the area called Raman Reti, a few miles from the center of Vrindavan. The quiet, pastoral acreage sat at the end of a tree-lined dirt path that bordered a dense forest. Peacocks and deer wandered about, and at night, tigers and wildcats rummaged for food and stalked four-foot-tall horned nilgai antelopes. The Sarafs had no children and announced they had chosen to gift the land to Prabhupada for construction of an ISKCON temple. The deed for the 4,800-square-yard property was signed on March 12, 1972. Prabhupada directed students to build a temple that would honor Krishna and Balaram, for it was here in Raman Reti that the Supreme Person and his brother, Balaram, herded cows and played as children five thousand years before.

Some devotees volunteered to clear the land and secure building materials, but they soon left, complaining that the brutal heat and lack of drinking water made life unbearable. Older devotees stepped in and reassured Prabhupada they would carry out the work. This core team included Gurudas and Yamuna, who had helped found the London temple; a Dutch devotee-architect named Saurabhi; and a British assistant, Gunarnava. None of them had ever built anything like the proposed Vrindavan temple, let alone under such conditions, and every day they survived development of the Krishna-Balaram Mandir was like a year of survival anywhere else.

In those pioneer days, there were moments when being a devotee felt like living in an adventure movie. Just getting up in the morning could be life-threatening, especially when a scorpion crawled over someone's sleeping bag or a snake slithered out from under a pile of clothes. As always,

Prabhupada found just the right words to keep his disciples encouraged. You are on the front line for Chaitanya Mahaprabhu, he told them, and great sacrifices were to be expected. Are you convinced, he asked them, that Krishna consciousness is the most important thing for setting the world back on track?

"As far as I am concerned," he said, "I am convinced. Therefore, I am pushing on, because it is fact, not fiction. Whenever someone says, 'Do you believe in Krishna?' I say, 'No, not belief. It is fact.' But are *you* convinced? It was my plan to give Krishna consciousness to the world, with your help. But you have to be spiritually strong."

To remain "spiritually strong," the Western devotees charged with building Vrindavan's most prestigious new temple gathered together at the end of a day's work. They took up seats on piles of sand and bricks and other construction remnants, and for several hours as the sun slowly dropped below the horizon of trees, they read passages from the *Srimad Bhagavatam* and recited verses from the Bhagavad Gita. This evening sanga relieved the stress of days spent dealing with shortages of everything and the complaints of laborers whose language they did not speak. Sanitation was non-existent. They lived in mosquito-infested mud huts and bathed by squatting on planks of wood and dousing themselves with water from rusty tin buckets. Prabhupada shared their austerities and demonstrated the devotional quality of *samatvam*, equipoised, in all circumstances. "The nonpermanent appearance of happiness and distress, and their disappearance in due course," said the Gita, "are like the appearance and disappearance of winter and summer seasons. They arise from sense perception, O scion of Bharata [Arjuna], and one must learn to tolerate them without being disturbed."[141]

Prabhupada's old friend and godbrother, O.B.L. Kapoor, visited the construction site and offered words of praise. "I can hear Sri Rupa Goswami, Sri Jiva Goswami, and others," he said, referring to Chaitanya Mahaprabhu's leading disciples, "saying, 'Long Live Prabhupada!'" Another one of Prabhupada's godbrothers, Ananda, came to cook for the devotee crew and care for their health with homemade remedies. These elder Vaishnavas understood better than others how difficult a task Prabhupada had undertaken. Since the days of the Goswamis and their sixteenth-century renovation of Vrindavan, few had ever tried as hard to resuscitate Krishna consciousness. Even among Prabhupada's disciples, not many grasped just how difficult a job it was for him to spearhead the International Society for Krishna Consciousness.

To become Krishna conscious, candidates had to overcome the effects of thousands, if not millions, of births in material bodies. The cumulative karma of so many lifetimes ran deep, and old habits died hard. Even stalwart disciples could succumb to sex, drugs, and other allurements of secular life. The BBT archives house more than six thousand letters written by Prabhapada, mostly to disciples, offering words of encouragement.

"Once, in the mid-seventies," senior disciple Ravindra Svarup wrote to Prabhupada in a commemorative offering, "a devotee showed me something I was probably not supposed to see: your correspondence files for a few years, filled with all the letters you had received. I was shocked by the volume of problems within our movement, by the maya bedeviling your followers, not excluding many leaders. It seemed not a day went by without your mail delivering to you setbacks, perplexities, quarrels, and failures. The combination of the world's resistance and the movement's weaknesses seemed to present an overwhelmingly fatal obstacle. It was a disillusioning and discouraging few hours of reading for me. . . . I understood then more of your greatness. . . . You knew with chilling clarity of vision all the shortcomings and failures of your followers and your institution. You corrected as much as possible and kept on advancing Lord Chaitanya's mission with whatever flawed and imperfect instruments came to your hands."[142]

IN HINDSIGHT, THE MOST DECISIVE YEAR in the growth of Prabhupada's movement was 1972. Spurred by the conviction that nothing pleased him more than seeing books about Krishna distributed, that December Los Angeles sankirtan devotees conducted a bookselling "marathon." Teams of devotees set out in vans to try their luck in shopping malls during the holiday period. The heavy volume of Christmas traffic combined with the mood of gift buying, and the result was magical. Devotees sold one *Krishna Book*, then another and another, and in the three days leading up to Christmas, the Los Angeles crew sold more than eighteen thousand books and magazines.

When results of the Los Angeles marathon reached Prabhupada, he was incredulous. Eighteen thousand books and magazines—about Krishna—in three days? "It is scarcely believable," he told his secretary, and he requested that telegrams be sent to the other temples informing them of what had happened. Officers of his publishing company, the Bhaktivedanta Book Trust (BBT), made projections based on the three-day pilot program and realized ISKCON's financial problems were over.

"That's when ISKCON's fortunes turned around," commented Ramesvara Das, former BBT director. "The 1972 marathon changed everything."

Prabhupada saw his disciples' enthusiasm for selling books and encouraged them to continue. "There is no literature throughout the universe like *Srimad Bhagavatam*," he declared in a morning class soon after the marathon. "Every word is for the good of human society. Somehow or other, if a book goes in someone's hand, he will be benefited."

Vaishnavas honored sacred texts such as the Bhagavad Gita or *Srimad Bhagavatam* as "literary incarnations" of God. Even holding such a scripture could be the beginning of someone's spiritual journey. "Therefore we are stressing so much," Prabhupada continued, "please distribute books, distribute books." Receiving weekly reports of book sales gave him strength, he told them, and made him feel "like a young man."

Inspired by his appreciation for book sales, entrepreneurial distributors expanded their outreach to include shopping malls, rock concerts, airports, and other public venues. "The results showed us he had been right," concluded Ramesvara, "namely, that a global society for Krishna consciousness could be supported through books. What drove us was knowing he had given his life to create these books for the benefit of the world. His health was so precarious, the least we could do was let him see results while he was still alive."

RECEIPTS FROM DISTRIBUTION of BBT publications soared from $100,000 in 1972 to more than $1 million in 1973, and Prabhupada issued a directive for how the movement's newfound revenues should be spent. Fifty percent was to be used for printing more books and the other fifty percent was to be made available as loans for purchasing land and building temples and farms.

"He had no interest in accumulating large sums of money for himself," Ramesvara explained. "He reminded us that a true Vaishnava could receive a million dollars in donations in the morning and be a pauper again by night. Everything was meant to be engaged in Krishna's service, not hoarded. So he instructed us to make sizeable loans to help purchase properties and construct temples all over the world—and that was how the Hare Krishna movement was built."

ON AUGUST 9, 1973, Prabhupada entered Paris's City Hall, the fabled Hotel de Ville. The five-block-wide landmark had been commissioned in 1533 by King Francis I and completed in 1628 during the reign of Louis XIII. From its balconies in 1870, the establishment of the French Third Republic had been declared. During the liberation of Paris from the Nazis in August 1944, president Charles de Gaulle had greeted cheering crowds from atop one of its many guilded balustrades.

Prabhupada strode across the marble-arched hallway and noted the elaborate frescoes, gold-leafed columns, and carved inlaid furniture. If the purpose of such ostentation was to remind heads of state that they were guests of the world's artistic and cultural capital, the message bounced off him like raindrops. Later and in private, he would express appreciation for the caliber of workmanship, but in the moment he was impervious. He strode through the corridors with an expression both somber and purposeful. He knew that official receptions in the Paris City Hall were reserved for France's most distinguished visitors—in 1961, ten years before Prabhupada's reception, John and Jacqueline Kennedy had been received in the same room he now entered—and he intended to make the most of the occasion.

The chief of protocol, a handsome woman wearing a black Chanel dress and pearl necklace, invited him to sit on a nineteenth-century gold-leafed wing chair, the seat of honor for visiting dignitaries. She invited me to sit in a more modest chair next to him.

"Yogesvara," Prabhupada said, leaning toward me. "You translate."

That the reception was happening at all fell just short of miraculous. The elegant chief of protocol would forever be blessed, I thought. She had met devotees in Charles de Gaulle airport the month before. Both she and they were there to greet the mayor of Bombay. The devotees described Prabhupada's preeminence as an ambassador of Indian spiritual culture, and the chief of protocol commented that Prabhupada, too, deserved a proper reception when he came to Paris.

Just before the reception was to begin, the woman explained in French the procedure for an official reception. As she spoke, I translated softly into Prabhupada's ear.

"When the deputy mayor arrives," I said, "you are supposed to stand up. He will give a greeting in French. Then you will be invited to respond."

Prabhupada pulled back, and with the signature sideways tilt of his head that signaled a challenge, he asked, "I'm supposed to stand—for who?"

Uh-oh, I thought. Trouble. No one in the history of France, as far as we knew, had ever remained seated during an official reception. It was unheard of. Wars had been waged over such a break with tradition. There were bound to be repercussions.

Deputy mayor Jacques Dominati arrived in a three-piece suit, flanked by guards carrying gold-tipped spears and wearing plumed metal helmets. The deputy mayor stood before Prabhupada's chair and waited. Nothing happened. Prabhupada stayed seated and stared at him, hands resting casually on the carved lion head of his walking cane. Dominati looked anxiously at his head of protocol as if to inquire, "Has this Hindu not been told the rules?" The head of protocol glowered at me. I pretended to make notes, not daring to look at her. Dominati's expression changed from cordiality to disgust. If slow-burning coal had a face, it might have looked like Dominati's expression at that moment. The photographers snapped away, single clicks accelerating into machine-gun rapid fire with each passing second. This was front-page stuff.

Prabhupada remained motionless, as though sitting for one of the six-foot-tall paintings of French kings adorning the walls. He continued to look at Dominati with unblinking eyes, silent and grave. It was a lasting image, one captured on film by Yadubara, who had worked as a photo-journalist before becoming a devotee. He and his photographer-wife, Vishakha, had arrived earlier in the day to position lights on tripods that flanked the scene. Vishakha clicked away with abandon on her Nikon. There was no way this confrontation would escape filmed immortality.

After a long silence, Dominati admitted defeat. His face softened into a smile, and he began his welcoming address, elaborating on the many dignitaries who had been received in this same room over the centuries and how appropriate it was to receive Bhaktivedanta Swami, since France had honored spiritual values throughout its distinguished history. Vishakha's photo of the moment — Dominati standing, hands outstretched, Prabhupada seated majestically before him — formed an iconic image of Krishna consciousness penetrating the world beyond India's borders. At last Dominati finished, and Prabhupada slowly rose.

"You have spoken very nicely about France as a place that recognizes spirituality," he said. "Let us examine what is spirituality. There is a soul in the body. Any government unaware of this simple fact is demonic. Your Napoleon once said, 'I am France.' Well, France is still there. Where is

Napoleon? The soul is gone. *Where* has it gone?[143] That is the subject of education which world governments must support."

"He spoke in a perfectly structured way," recalled Jyotirmayi Dasi, head of the French editions of Prabhupada's books, "so it was easy to translate his talk. The points were logical. But this was strong even for him."

After delivering a ten-minute response, Prabhupada approached Dominati with a broad smile and did something unusual. He shook the deputy mayor's hand. That in itself stood out. Prabhupada rarely shook anyone's hand. On this occasion, it was a gesture of conciliation, as if Muhammad Ali had put an arm around the shoulder of Sonny Liston after defeating him in the 1964 World Heavyweight Boxing Championship.

The gesture carried another meaning as well. Prabhupada had remained seated not because he had taken twenty-two flights that year and needed to rest, but because Dominati and other inhabitants of the political stratosphere needed reminding that the nation's spiritual well-being came before its politics. Good governance was not fulfilled by solely meeting the animal needs of citizenry, and leaders who ignored their constituents' higher needs—their eternal dharma—were a menace to all they served. Throughout history, learned acharyas had counseled politicians in India regarding this higher dharma. Why not in France?

Around the same time as the reception in City Hall that afternoon, Prabhupada's sankirtan devotees were arrested by the Paris police for selling magazines without a permit—one more irony in a movement of constant contrasts. The Paris police called devotees *les foux de Dieu*, "God's mad people," unaware that their leader had just been received in City Hall like a head of state.

THE BALANCE OF HIS TIME IN PARIS was absorbed by meetings with French intellectuals and religious leaders. One of the meetings was with a renowned cleric, Jesuit cardinal Jean-Guenolé-Marie Daniélou (1905–74), who occupied a distinguished place in twentieth-century Catholic theology. Along with Pierre Teilhard de Chardin, Hans Küng, and Joseph Ratzinger (later to become Pope Benedict XVI), Daniélou was leader of a controversial movement called New Theology, which sought dialogue with other religions on such topics as scripture and mysticism.

Beneath the surface of Prabhupada's meeting with Daniélou lay shifting tectonic plates of French politics. Since World War II and, more vividly,

since the student revolution of May 1968 barely five years before the
Prabhupada-Daniélou dialog, the French Catholic church had been under
siege by socialist ideologues looking to move France's government away
from centralization of authority—any kind of authority, but particularly
religious. Daniélou had taken it upon himself to balance the scales by rekin-
dling the French people's pride in their church. Christianity was "a more
advanced stage of evolution," he wrote. "I believe this idea to be absolutely
essential if we are to understand how Christianity completes other religions
and other civilizations, summed up in God's design of giving His spiritual
creatures a share in the life of the Trinity."[144] The term "spiritual creatures"
did not include animals, since church doctrine held that only humans possessed a true soul with which to enter into the mystery of the Word-made-
flesh, Jesus Christ. It was an issue that animated Prabhupada's discussion
with Daniélou on August 9, 1973.

THAT MORNING, disciples drove him to Daniélou's residence in central
Paris. The renowned cardinal was dressed in black robes. He greeted
Prabhupada and they sat in armchairs facing one another as disciples
recorded the encounter. Glasses of water were offered, and Prabhupada
wasted no time getting to essentials.

"May I ask you one question?" he said. "Jesus says 'Thou shalt not kill.'
Why are you Christian people killing?"

Daniélou might have expected this to be a dispassionate talk on comparative religion, but from the beginning Prabhupada's blunt inquiry signaled there would be a showdown.

"It is forbidden in Christianity to kill, surely," the cardinal said, "but
there is a difference between the life of man and the life of beasts. The life
of man is sacred because man is the image of God. We do not have the
same view relating to the beasts. Animals are at the service of man. What is
forbidden is to kill a human person."

"But Jesus does not say 'human person,'" Prabhupada replied. "He just
said generally 'Thou shalt not kill.' You think that to kill an animal is not
also a sin?"

"It is not the words of Jesus," Daniélou countered, "but from Leviticus,
a part of the Ten Commandments which God gave to Moses."

"But one of the commandments is 'Thou shalt not kill,' is it not?"
Prabhupada cautioned.

Daniélou shook his head. "It is surely the killing of man," he said. "I have a great difficulty to understand why in Indian religion animals are not allowed for food."

"Humans can eat grains," Prabhupada replied, "Fruits, milk, sugar, wheat."

"Yes, yes. I understand," Daniélou interrupted, "but grains and plants are also living beings."

"That's all right," Prabhupada said, "but if I can live on fruits and grains, why should I kill an animal? How can you support that animal killing is not a sin?"

"We think there is a difference of nature between the life of man, life of spirit, and biological life," Daniélou replied. "Animals and plants are not real beings. They are part of the world of appearance. Only the human person is a real being, and, in this sense, the material world is without importance. It is a question of motivation. There could be a bad reason to kill an animal, but if the reason is to give food to children who are hungry . . ."

Daniélou's frustration showed in his face and hand gestures. He had dedicated his entire religious career to proving that the French Church was not an anachronism, and that Catholicism had an important contribution to make, particularly when it came to extending compassion to the less fortunate—by which he meant less fortunate humans.

"Why is it forbidden in India," Daniélou continued, "to kill cows, if doing so will feed children who are hungry?"

"According to the Vedic vision," Prabhupada explained, "we have many mothers: our original mother, the wife of the spiritual master, the wife of a teacher, the Earth, the wife of a king—and also the cow. We drink the cow's milk, and therefore she is like a mother, is it not? And when she is old and cannot give you milk, should she be killed? How can we support the killing of our mother?"

I had seen Prabhupada exercise this strategy before, in other meetings with clerics and religionists. If Daniélou could at least agree that this one peaceful animal—the cow, whose milk sustained life—deserved compassion, then perhaps they could reach an agreement on the larger issue of whether animals had souls.

"In India," Prabhupada said, "meat-eaters are advised to kill some lower animals like goats, even up to buffaloes. Don't kill cows. It is the greatest sin, and so long as one is sinful, he will not be able to understand what is

God. A human being's main business is to understand God and to love him. But if he remains sinful, he cannot. Therefore, this cruel maintenance of slaughterhouses must be stopped."

"The importance is to love God," Daniélou agreed, "but the practical commandments can be various. God says to Indians that it is not acceptable to kill animals, but then he says to the Jews and others that it is."

Prabhupada had little patience for dismissal of a principle central not only to a religious life but to an ethical one as well. "Whether you call Jesus Christ God or confidential representative of God," Prabhupada said, "when the instruction is, 'Thou shalt not kill,' why should we interpret it in another way to our convenience?"

"Jesus ate the Passover lamb," Daniélou argued.

"That's all right," Prabhupada conceded, "but Jesus Christ never maintained slaughterhouses. In certain circumstances, when there is no other food or a life must be saved—that is another thing. In wartime, they ate hogs and dogs. But why maintain slaughterhouses just for the satisfaction of the tongue? Our Krishna says, 'Vegetable, fruits, milk, grains—these things should be offered to me with devotion.'"[145]

"Soul means human soul," Daniélou repeated with a shake of his head. "In animals, you have some psychological existence but not a life of spirit with freedom and a mind. You Hindus also admit there is a difference in nature between spiritual creation and the material world. The material world is not of the same essence as the spiritual world. And man is a part of the spiritual world."

Prabhupada shook his head. "Our Bhagavad Gita says, 'In all species of life the spirit soul is there.'[146] This outward body is just like a dress. You may have a very costly dress, and I may have a very shabby, poor dress, but both of us are living entities. Similarly, these different bodily forms of living entities are just like different types of dress." He pointed to Daniélou's robes.

"You are in black dress, and I am in saffron dress. This is external. Within the dress, you are a living being, and I am also a living being. The Vedic literatures have calculated there are 8,400,000 forms of living entities, but they are all part and parcel of God. Say that one man has ten sons, not all equally meritorious. One may be a High Court judge, and another may be an ordinary clerk. For the father, there is no distinction that this son—the High Court judge—is very important, but the clerk son is not. If the High Court son says, 'Father, your other son is useless. Let me kill and eat him,' will the father allow?"

Daniélou shifted uneasily in his chair. "The difficulty for us," he said, "is metaphysical. The idea that *all* life is part of the life of God? This is difficult for us to admit. There is a great difference between the life of man, who is called to partake of the eternal life of God, and animal life, which is temporary."

"That difference is due to development of consciousness," Prabhupada replied. He pointed out the window of Daniélou's office. "That tree is also a living entity, but its consciousness is not yet developed. If you cut the tree, it resists but in a very small degree. That was shown by Jagadish Chandra Bose, a scientist in Calcutta.[147] When you cut a tree, it feels. And for an animal, we see it resists being killed. It cries and makes a horrible sound. So it is a question of development of consciousness—but the soul is there."

Daniélou would not relinquish the point. "Why," he asked, "would God make animals that eat other animals? Is it a fault in the creation?"

"No," Prabhupada said. "God is very kind. If you want to eat animals, then he will give you good facility. You can become a tiger and eat animals unrestrictedly. God will give you the body of a tiger in your next life so that you can very freely eat. Why bother to maintain a slaughterhouse? 'I give you nails and jaws. Just eat.' Meat-eaters are awaiting that life."

The finger pointed at Daniélou made him uncomfortable. "I am very joyful to speak with you," he said, checking his watch, "and if I can, tomorrow I will visit your temple. Yes, yes. I hope I can come tomorrow." And with that, the meeting was over.

As we drove back to the Paris temple, I struggled to understand why my teacher had chosen to debate vegetarianism rather than find points of agreement with a dignitary from the French church. Surely there was more to be gained by establishing common ground. Daniélou's movement—New Theology—proposed that religion could transform modern culture. His advocacy of that cause had earned him an appointment to the Académie Française along with an invitation from Pope John XXIII to serve as consultant to the Second Vatican Council. Would it not have been advantageous to win him over as a friend of Krishna consciousness?

I leaned over from the back seat and said to Prabhupada, "His point was that Christianity sanctions meat-eating based on the view that lower species do not have souls, but still . . ."

"That is foolishness," Prabhupada replied. "First of all, we have to understand the evidence of the soul's presence within the body. Then we can see whether the human being has a soul, and the cow does not. What are the different characteristics of the cow and the man? If we find a difference in characteristics, then we can say that in the animal there is no soul. But if we see that the animal and the human being have the same characteristics, then how can you say that the animal has no soul? The general symptoms are that the cow eats, and you eat. The cow sleeps, and you sleep. The cow mates, and you mate. The cow defends, and you defend. Where is the difference?"[148]

My confusion dissipated. If Prabhupada stuck so firmly to this one point, that a divine spark animates all life, it was not from an unwillingness to cooperate with religious leaders. Rather, he understood that religious leaders would never have the impact on modern culture that Daniélou wanted if they failed to understand the basics. Without acknowledging the sanctity of life in all its forms, good intentions alone would not improve the human condition. In dozens of such discussions during his European tour, Prabhupada was obliged to defend this basic concept of Vedic philosophy, the sanctity of all life. Many of these dialogues took place among highly educated guests. Some were acclaimed authors and educators. Yet almost without exception their intellectualism was tainted by the same assumption Daniélou had made, namely that only human life deserved respect.

HIS ROOM IN THE PARIS TEMPLE was on the second floor of a four-story triangular building in the Fifth Arrondissement, an exclusive quarter near the famous Arc de Triomphe. The building had originally been designed as a residence for an aristocratic family of four. We were an ashram of forty. Due to the added traffic, polished oak floorboards buckled, dainty boiserie bookshelves collapsed, one-hundred-year-old plumbing gave out, and wealthy neighbors scowled. In the flush of income from selling books, the devotees in charge had simply picked the wrong neighborhood to set up shop. It was the Hollywood Boulevard fiasco all over again, and eventually we would also be asked to leave, but it was fun while it lasted. I slept on the floor of the upstairs publications office and opened the window one morning to find Princess Grace of Monaco standing on the terrace of her apartment across the street. It was 8 a.m., and she wore a tiara. Another morning I draped a wool chadar over my head and walked along the main avenue chanting on my beads. Ladies of the night sometimes took up positions on this elegant tree-lined boulevard, waiting for customers. In the shadowy pre-dawn light, a car slid up, and the window came down. A man leaned over, assessed my robes and covered head, and asked, "*Combien?*" How much?

Poor fellow. I smiled, pulled off the chadar to reveal my shaved head, held up my beads, and answered, "C'est gratuit!" It's free!

He groaned in disgust and drove off at a clip.

The week after Prabhupada's meeting with Daniélou, a group of Theosophists arrived at the elegant Paris temple off Avenue Foch. The visitors described themselves as "esoteric Christians" who believed Jesus possessed certain secret doctrines of which the public was unaware. These doctrines, they said, surpassed the power of natural reason. They acknowledged reincarnation and were curious to know what other secret doctrines Hinduism held.

"What is your deepest truth?" one of them asked once they were settled in Prabhupada's room. "What are your mystic practices?"

From childhood, Prabhupada had known such people: *jnanis*, in Sanskrit. They sought knowledge but often failed to recognize that the road to transcendence began with humility and with respect for all life, which meant abstaining from animal slaughter and eating meat. This had been his message to Daniélou and other religionists, but these Theosophists had no interest in such preliminaries. They wanted the bottom line.

"Vaishnavas do not eat meat," Prabhupada said. "They do not have sex outside of marriage. They do not take intoxicants or gamble."

"Yes, yes," a spokesperson for the group said dismissively, "these are no doubt important. But we mean to say, what are the *greater* truths of your faith?"

"There is no meat-eating, no illicit sex," Prabhupada repeated, as though they had failed to hear him.

"But these things are external," the man protested. "They are of the body. It is of no importance spiritually if one eats meat or not."

Prabhupada shook his head with a mixture of sadness and concern. "Do you accept that killing is a sin," he asked calmly, "and that Jesus *died* for your sins?" The guests looked at one another as if confused by this detour away from the topic.

"Well, yes, of course."

"Then why do you continue to sin?" Prabhupada demanded. "You are not Christians," he said, and a tear fell from the corner of his eye onto his saffron dhoti. His reaction was so unexpected that the guests made their excuses and departed. I sat there, unsure why the discussion had taken such a turn. It took a while before the thought crossed my mind that here was a person who knew something about Jesus and giving one's life for others, and about the heartbreak of seeing that sacrifice cheapened by armchair mystics collecting souvenirs. Meetings with mayors and talks with dignitaries had their value, but it was moments such as this, when we caught a glimpse of his heart and the depth of his concern for others, that lingered in memory.

FOR YEARS he had announced plans to build three centers in India: a large, beautiful temple in Vrindavan, where pilgrims would be welcomed when they came to worship Krishna in his homeland; a hotel complex in Bombay, where business people could visit in comfort and leave inspired; and an edifice in Mayapur, the birthplace of Chaitanya Mahaprabhu, such as had not been seen in India for hundreds of years: a mecca to Vaishnavism that would include a 400-foot-high domed temple housing a planetarium of Vedic cosmology. The Vrindavan temple was at last nearing completion, and construction had begun in Bombay and Mayapur, but every inch of progress was earned at great effort. Negotiations for land and supplies were endless and occasionally life-threatening when criminal elements plotted to steal devotees' money. Serving on these huge projects was not for the faint of heart.

"I'm so disturbed by these dealings that I can't chant my rounds properly," one disciple confided to Prabhupada after a particularly difficult struggle for land in India. "But I can see that I am making spiritual advancement. I used to think about how to avoid difficult situations. Now I think I should not run away from them."

Prabhupada agreed. "We should welcome difficulties," he said. "They give us an opportunity to advance."

Some time later a renowned athletic instructor made a similar complaint. The gold medalist had begun reading the Bhagavad Gita and occasionally spoke to clients about the benefits of Krishna consciousness. His well-intended gesture backfired when a multimillion-dollar deal fell through after a financial partner connected him with chanting, dancing devotees. Despondent, the instructor related the incident to his spiritual master.

"Do not be upset with the instrument of your karma," Prabhupada advised. He compared karma to a spinning fan: dangerous. Then he compared the practice of bhakti yoga to unplugging the fan. The fan did not stop spinning immediately. Some residual spinning—leftover karmic reactions to past deeds—continued. Still, the fan was slowing down and would eventually stop, provided the disciple remained vigilant in habit and devotional practices. So when leftover karma created difficulties, he advised, see them as a thin residue of past deeds. Things could be a lot worse.

As we were soon to discover.

PRABHUPADA WAS APPROACHING EIGHTY, yet he continued to tour, spending two days here, a week there as needed, rising early each morning to write and conduct morning classes, then spending the balance of his day answering letters, resolving disputes, recording albums of devotional music, officiating at the opening of new temples and the installation of deities, meeting with guests, and initiating anyone with even a modicum of sincerity. Those of us privileged to observe him during these busy times marveled at how consistently he kept to a daily schedule. No matter how radical the change in time zone, he acclimated without missing a beat. Nor did the meteoric growth of his movement diminish his sensitivity to detail. Some examples come to mind.

The building in London leased by George Harrison for use as a temple was elegant but small. To create a separate space for his assistant, we put up a lightweight dividing wall in Prabhupada's bathroom. A few of us were huddled in the narrow space and talking about recent events when we heard him call out, "Who is responsible for this?" Prabhupada was peeking around the wall and pointing to a tiny plant perched on the edge of his sink. The plant had shriveled from neglect. "You should take care," he said, and then he turned on the faucet and splashed a few handfuls of water into the pot.

Later that morning we accompanied him on a walk through Hyde Park. He pointed to a willow tree and asked his assistant to break off a few twigs. Usually Prabhupada brushed his teeth with twigs from neem trees, which contained medicinal qualities, but no neem trees grew in London and willow twigs worked almost as well. His assistant reached out, broke off a twig, then a second. When he reached out to break off a third, Prabhupada held up his hand and said, "No, do not disturb the tree more than necessary." Then he walked off, quietly reciting a verse from *Sri Isopanisad* that began "ishavasyam idam sarvam . . ." "Everything animate or inanimate that is within the universe is controlled and owned by the Lord. We should therefore accept only those things necessary, which are set aside as our quota, and not accept more, knowing well to Whom they belong."[149] His mind was no doubt preoccupied by the daily challenges of an international society, but the fate of a neglected houseplant and the comfort of a willow tree held his attention.

"What do you see when you look at a tree?" I asked him when we were back at the temple. He was patient with my often impertinent questions.

"A pure devotee," he began, not wanting to take such credit for himself, "does not exactly see the tree. He sees the soul who has taken up residence in the tree body. Then again, he does not only see the soul in that tree body. He sees the Supersoul also dwelling there. So a pure devotee does not just see the tree. He sees the soul and Krishna simultaneously."

Poet William Blake once wrote: "To see a world in a grain of sand / and a heaven in a wildflower / Hold infinity in the palm of your hand / and eternity in an hour."[150] That's as close as we might have come in those days to describing what it was like to watch Prabhupada interact with the world around him.

HE HAD BEGUN, HE ONCE DESCRIBED, "in a hopeless way, a helpless way," and now Krishna was showering his mission with success. Books were going out, money was coming in, land was being purchased around the world, temples and farms were opening, and communities were flourishing. Things seemed to be going well. Maybe he could finally retire and dedicate himself to completing his beloved *Srimad Bhagavatam*.

Were the hard times finally over?

Govinda Dasi, an early disciple, is shown walking with Swami Prabhupada.

The New York Times

© 1977 The New York Times Company   NEW YORK, FRIDAY, MARCH 18, 1977   25 cents beyond 50-mile zone from New York except Long Island, Higher in air delivery cities

Judge Dismisses Charges in Hare Krishna 'Brainwashing' Case

By MURRAY SCHUMACH

The Hare Krishna movement was called a "bona fide religion" yesterday by a State Supreme Court Justice in Queens who threw out two indictments against officials of the movement. The indictments had charged them with illegal imprisonment of two members and attempted extortion from the father of one of the believers.

"The entire and basic issue before this court," said Justice John J. Leahy, "is whether or not the two alleged victims in this case and the defendants will be allowed to practice the religion of their choice—and this must be answered with a resounding affirmative."

The indictments, handed up last year, were the first of their kind against the Hare Krishna movement. They charged that Angus Murphy, the president of the New York temple of the religion, and Harold Conley, the supervisor of women at the temple, held Edward Shapiro and Merylee Kreshour in the temple illegally, by brainwashing them.

Mr. Murphy was also accused of joining Mr. Shapiro in an attempt to extort $20,000 from Mr. Shapiro's father. The allegations were denied by the younger Mr. Shapiro and by Miss Kreshour.

After determining that Miss Kreshour and the younger Mr. Shapiro had lived voluntarily in the temple at 340 West 55d Street and that there was no case for attempted extortion, Justice Leahy said:

"The Hare Krishna religion is a bona fide religion with roots in India that go back thousands of years. It behooved Merylee Kreshour and Edward Shapiro to follow the tenets of that faith and their inalienable right to do so will not be trammeled upon.

"The separation of church and state must be maintained. We are, and must remain, a nation of laws, not of men. The presentment and indictment by the grand jury was in direct and blatant violation of defendants' constitutional rights."

The judge pointed out that the prosecution, during the hearing last month, had conceded that no physical force had been used by the defendants against Miss Kreshour or the younger Mr. Shapiro, adding:

"The said two individuals entered the Hare Krishna movement voluntarily and submitted themselves voluntarily to the regimen, rules and regulations of said so-called Hare Krishna religion, and it is also conceded that the alleged victims were not in any way physically restrained from leaving the defendant organization."

On the allegation of brainwashing, he said:

"It appears to the court that the people rest their case on an erroneous minor premise to arrive at a fallacious conclusion. The record is devoid of one specific allegation of a misrepresentation or an act of deception on the part of any defendant."

Justice Leahy, who stressed that his decision was intended as a "dire caveat to prosecution agencies throughout the length and breadth of the land," cited the constitutional guarantee of freedom of religion and said:

"The freedom of religion is not to be abridged because it is unconventional in its beliefs and practices or because it is approved or disapproved by the mainstream of society or more conventional religions.

"Without this proliferation and freedom to follow the dictates of one's own conscience in his search for and approach to God, the freedom of religion will be a meaningless right as provided for in the Constitution.

"Any attempt, be it circuitous, direct, well-intentioned or not, presents a clear and present danger to this most fundamental basic and eternally needed right of our citizens—freedom of religion."

Legal and ethical questions have arisen from intensive efforts to "deprogram" members of Hare Krishna and other movements. The main method is to separate the follower from the group and to subject him to long periods of counter-persuasion. Among the controversial and well-known deprogrammers is Ted Patrick, a Californian who was released recently from prison on kidnapping charges resulting from a deprogramming case.

The grand jury was drawn into the Hare Krishna case last September when Miss Kreshour alleged that she was kidnapped by her mother, Edith, and a private investigator in Queens and subjected to four days of a treatment called "deprogramming."

Newspaper headlines announce a landmark decision by the New York Supreme Court: Krishna consciousness is a bona fide religion.

CHAPTER TEN

Armed with yoga, stand and fight.
—SRI KRISHNA IN THE BHAGAVAD GITA, 4.42

1976

ALONG WITH THE GROWTH OF THE HARE KRISHNA MOVEMENT came a proliferation of psychologists who delighted in diagnosing why the movement was growing at all. Solemn discussions and learned symposia were held to discuss what could possibly be fueling young people's passion for such an exotic faith. Why did followers chant for so long and shave their heads? What compelled them to leave their homes and schools for life in a bizarre and foreign culture? A battery of researchers descended on ISKCON temples with analytical tools and the vocabulary of their trade: "subversion mythologies," "cognitive dissonance," "alienation." By such assessments, Prabhupada had not created a Western world branch of Chaitanya Vaishnavism so much as a "revitalization movement" that exploited disenfranchised youth with "abasements, degradations, and profanations of self."[151]

Professors of Hinduism, as well, raised doubts over the legitimacy of Krishna consciousness. "Adherents of the Krishna movement here are not really engaged in the same religious worldview or place in the culture as those in India," wrote one purveyor of Eastern philosophy.[152] Another academic wrote that Krishna consciousness was "one of the clearest examples of what was wrong with traditional Hinduism: emotional rather than rational; steeped in polytheistic mythology; laden with rituals centered on material images. . . . One might admire its rich tradition of stories for literary purposes, but few among the educated classes . . . give it credence as a religion worthy of serious attention."[153]

"They fall into this easy rhetoric," proclaimed Sanskritist Leopold Fischer (Agehananda Bharati) at Syracuse University, who condemned Prabhupada's followers as "hopping ISKCON Hare Krishna jokers."[154] Most such pronouncements were based either on outright ignorance of Vaishnava history or else on interviews conducted in only one or two ISKCON temples, not on rigorous research. That did not stop journalists from quoting them in articles portraying ISKCON as a "cult."

Prabhupada walked an ideologically thin line. On one side stood academics accusing him of inventing his own version of Vaishnava faith and on the other reporters depicting his students as mentally confused hippies with prayer beads. Military commander that he was, he took the offensive and instructed disciples to prepare a pamphlet titled "The Krishna Consciousness Movement is the Genuine Vedic Way," containing the transcript of a correspondence with Dr. J.F. Staal, professor of philosophy and South Asian languages at the University of California, Berkeley. Staal had refused to accredit a devotee-organized course on the UC Berkeley campus, telling reporters from the *Los Angeles Times* that devotees spent too much time chanting to develop an actual philosophy. He proceeded to challenge the very legitimacy of Prabhupada's Krishna-centered interpretation of the Bhagavad Gita. In their exchange of letters, Prabhupada responded to Staal with a volley of scriptural references to substantiate the practice of chanting as the prescribed yoga for the modern age[155] and Krishna as the goal of the Gita's philosophy.

Some of the strongest antipathy toward Prabhupada's movement came from irate parents. Confused and frightened by the changes Krishna consciousness had imposed on their families, a growing number of mothers and fathers pinned hopes for their children's redemption on a radical cure.

IN 1971 TED PATRICK, "THE FATHER OF DEPROGRAMMING,"[156] was appointed California's Special Assistant for Community Affairs. Two months later, Mrs. Samuel Jackson contacted Patrick about her missing son, Billy, who was involved with a cult known as the Children of God. Patrick pretended to join the group to learn how they operated and developed an aggressive method for breaking members' convictions: kidnapping, sleep deprivation, and verbal confrontation. Patrick's successes quickly spawned a mini-industry of deprogrammers, willing for the right fee to retrieve wayward sons and daughters from the hands of cultists. In part due to their visibility on the nation's streets, Krishna devotees often ranked at the top of deprogrammers' hit lists.

Twenty-one-year-old Merylee Kreshour met devotees during her summer break from college in 1974 and decided to move into the Brooklyn temple. Her mother hired deprogrammers to "liberate her daughter's mind and to restore her free will" and brought suit against ISKCON of New York, charging that her daughter was the victim of "mental kidnapping."[157] In September 1974, the grand jury instructed the New York district attorney's office to investigate any alleged illegal activities of the International Society for Krishna Consciousness. D.A. Michael Schwed concluded that, although Merylee had voluntarily accepted the diet and lifestyle of the Hare Krishna religion, the charge of brainwashing held up. The case made headlines worldwide. "The very survival of our movement was at stake," wrote Tamal Krishna, who was in the thick of the proceedings. "The theological legitimacy of both our beliefs and praxis was being legally challenged."[158]

The deprogrammers had not targeted Krishna devotees alone: Any new religious movement in America was fair game. But Prabhupada's movement posed a more dire threat, since devotees had begun appearing on college campuses and at youth events, which were the traditional arenas for mainstream Christianity. It was this direct challenge to establishment values that precipitated legal proceedings against ISKCON. In newspapers across the United States and Europe, front-page headlines announced that the International Society for Krishna Consciousness was under indictment for unlawfully seducing young people into accepting devotee life.[159] In effect, the reports rejected Krishna consciousness as a valid religion and condemned bhakti yoga as mind manipulation. News of the trial reached Prabhupada in Vrindavan in November 1976.

"Parents are saying we should be investigated," said Gopal Krishna, one of his leading disciples in India. "They say we are not real Hindus." That was not a bad thing, Prabhupada replied, if properly understood. "Krishna says, 'In all forms of life I am the seed-giving father.'[160] Why should he be simply for Hindus? In the pictures, Krishna is embracing the calf," he argued. "He does not embrace only the gopis. He is equal to everyone. We are not Hindu." The Bhagavad Gita described the soul passing from childhood to youth and then to old age and from there into a new body. Was this journey of the soul limited to Hindus?

"We embrace everyone," he said, "otherwise we would not have come to Western countries. We are actually spreading universal brotherhood. Krishna is the father, and everyone is our brother. We include even the animals, trees, plants—we are claiming all our fallen brothers to become Krishna conscious."[161]

In addition to branding devotees' lifestyle as brainwashing, the case sought to discredit Krishna worship itself as an invention and without roots. "Now that we have become important, our enemies are trying to suppress us," Prabhupada said. "We should not be afraid. Krishna advised Arjuna to fight, and we shall fight to the best of our ability. Take signatures from Indians that this is a genuine Indian cultural movement. It is based on Bhagavad Gita, which was spoken many years before other religious literature. The Buddhist or Christian or Jewish literature cannot be counted more than two thousand years or a little more than that. Krishna's movement is coming from millions of years ago. But even in recent history, it is five thousand years old.[162] Present this in the court. You have to fight."

His assistant, Hari-sauri, later described that up to this time, Prabhupada wanted to retire and write and had been delegating management responsibilities to his Governing Body Commissioners, "but on this court case he was not going to take a backseat. His began exhibiting a vigor and enthusiasm I'd never seen before."[163]

Prabhupada asked that all leaders of the movement assemble in his Vrindavan quarters. He would not allow ignorance or prejudice to stop his mission, and the leaders of his society needed to rally. The real issue, he told them, was that a devotee's life of "simple living and high thinking" challenged capitalism's propaganda for consumption and indulgence.

"Their whole Western civilization is threatened," he said. "Theoretically, if people give up meat-eating, smoking, gambling, intoxication, and illicit sex, then their whole civilization is finished. And the most dangerous point is that young people are taking part." This wasn't brainwashing, he said, just common sense. He asked Hari-sauri to tell the gathering about similar charges brought against the movement in Australia.

"The Sydney city council tried to have us banned," Hari-sauri said, "but they lost the case after spending thousands of dollars and hundreds of hours trying to get rid of us. A newspaper reporter interviewed a psychiatrist and asked why there had been such strong reactions to a few people singing and dancing in the street. The psychiatrist said it was because city-dwellers felt threatened by our simple lifestyle."

"Just see," Prabhupada commented. "This whole Western civilization is threatened. So you have to fight with all the resources that we have got. Brainwashing? Actually, you have no brain. We are giving you a good brain. That is our mission. Tell them like that. Expose them."

Prabhupada derided the charges as ludicrous. He had not kidnapped anyone. He presented Bhagavad Gita "as it is," and people were responding. Why paint him with the same brush as scammers and false prophets? As a child growing up in Calcutta, he had witnessed such pretenders take advantage of his father's charitable nature by begging alms in the name of God but then using the money to support their sex and drug habits. The science of bhakti lived at the opposite extreme from such hypocrisy.

"It is not a so-called religion," he said. "It is a culture for the benefit of the whole human society. That was Chaitanya Mahaprabhu's mission. People are in darkness. The Vedic injunction is *tamaso ma jyotir gamayah*: Come to the light.[164] The first ignorance is thinking this one lifetime is everything, one hundred years at most, so let us eat, drink, and be merry because then everything is finished. The professors think like that, the politicians think like that—so our first business is to convince people: Your life continues after death."

Krishna consciousness was nothing he had invented, he repeated. The knowledge has been there all along in the ancient Sanskrit texts. "Therefore I am working so hard on these translations. This is my life and soul, according to the order of my Guru Maharaj. Hold a meeting among the Gaudiya Vaishnavas here in Vrindavan, and I will explain the position."

THE ODDS OF WINNING THE NEW YORK CASE were stacked against him. He was taking on powerful adversaries, a tidal wave of negative press, and a State Supreme Court wary of "cults" masquerading as religions. Even Indians who grew up with Krishna worship all around them struggled to differentiate between true devotion and its shadow.[165] A proper grasp of bhakti theology took years of study, so how could even the most dispassionate of courts be expected to recognize its authenticity? Since his arrival in America twelve years before, Prabhupada had struggled to legitimize devotion to Krishna. The success or failure of that effort, at least in the eyes of the New York Supreme Court, came down to this one litigation, and despite failing health, he rallied his energies.

Residents of Vrindavan entered his room in the Vrindavan temple compound, bowed respectfully, and sat. "Come with me and fight," he told them, "because there is a world fight now. The liquor manufacturers, gambling houses, cigarette factories—theoretically, if this movement is successful, then the whole civilization is finished. This is not a bogus movement. It is taking a stand. These young people have taken it seriously, so our opponents are making a strong party to fight us."

He had started alone and without help, he said, but his credit was presenting the Bhagavad Gita without change. He urged everyone to chant Hare Krishna because chanting revived awareness of the immortal self. Nothing more than reviving this knowledge of the soul was needed to set the world back on track. But entrenched powers were conspiring against him, since that message threatened to derail the entire apparatus of consumer culture.

"Combine together in Vrindavan," he urged. "Fight. Without fight, where is life? Krishna's whole life was fighting from the very birth. His father carried him across the river to Gokula," he said, "and he fell down in the Yamuna."

THE STORY WAS TOLD in the *Krishna Book* that despotic King Kamsa had heard a prediction: His sister Devaki's eighth child—Krishna—would bring him down. Kamsa imprisoned Devaki and her husband, Vasudeva, and murdered each of the newborn babies. When their eighth child was born, Vasudeva escaped and carried baby Krishna in a basket across the Yamuna River. Raging winds blew the divine infant into the water. Vasudeva struggled to rescue Krishna and brought him to safety on the other side. Once across, he sheltered his son in the home of Nanda and Yashoda, leaders of the cowherds.

"Just born," Prabhupada said, "and the struggle had already begun. Then at Yashoda and Nanda's house, so many demons came daily to kill baby Krishna. So this fighting means they are feeling the presence of the Krishna consciousness movement. Had it been an insignificant thing, there would be no question of fighting."

From the outset, his purpose had been to present bhakti yoga, devotion to the Supreme Being, not as a religious sentiment but as the inherent nature of all life. "Try to convince them that it is not just a kind of faith," he wrote to a disciple in Egypt. "In every religion there is a glimpse of the idea of God. This movement is explaining what God is."

ADI KESHAVA, the twenty-two-year-old president of the New York Krishna temple, was co-defendant in the New York Supreme Court case against ISKCON. His mother, who was secretary of the New Jersey State Bar Association, put him in touch with American Civil Liberties Union board member William Kuntsler (1919–1995), whose defense of the Chicago Seven[166] in the late Sixties had prompted the *New York Times* to label him "the country's most controversial and, perhaps, its best-known lawyer."[167]

"Kuntsler and his crew were pretty much useless for our purposes," Adi Keshava recalled. "There was already enough controversy without adding his reputation to the case." It was Gene Harley, a young lawyer in the ACLU offices, who drew Adi Keshava's attention.

"Harley had a righteous sense of justice. He sat me down and said, 'This case is virtuous.' He saw clearly that no one had the right to interfere with a person's freedom of religion. But that was the challenge: to establish Krishna consciousness as a bona fide religion."

The irony of proving Krishna consciousness to be a religion, when Prabhupada was emphatic that it was not, prompted discussion. On the one hand, bhakti yoga was the only yoga that did not end with the body: Devotion was the inherent nature of the soul. It had no point of origin in historic time, as did the world's many religions. On the other hand, zealots seeking to destroy the Krishna consciousness movement based their prosecution on that very assumption: The movement, they argued, had no standing in history. It had no provenance as did authentic religious traditions and was therefore an invention.

While bhakti defined the eternal nature of life, evidence thousands of years old attested to bhakti's antiquity in India. It was this dimension of his movement—its antiquity in historic time—that would be their best defense. Once his movement gained historic legitimacy, devotees would be empowered to speak about its deeper dimension: the part that originated in transcendence.

Prabhupada, always ready with an apt analogy, compared their game plan to using a thorn to remove another thorn. They would use bhakti's history to prove it lived outside history.

LAWYERS FOR THE PROSECUTION leaked a rumor to the New York police that Adi Keshava was a flight risk, and on the pretext of needing information, police called him in. He arrived in devotee garb. Once inside the door, two police officers pushed him to the floor, braced his neck with their boots, handcuffed him, and threw him into a holding tank. Over the next several days, police moved the young devotee from one jail to another to avoid detection by the press. As they escorted him into one downtown facility, an enterprising photographer snapped away. A photo of Adi Keshava in orange robes and handcuffs ran in the next edition of *Time* magazine. In prison, he met Big Mac, a sympathetic guard with a big stomach and blond Afro.

"You don't want to be in that funny dress," Big Mac told him. "Not in here. Tell 'em you're concerned for your safety, and you want your own cell."

Adi Keshava managed to get himself transferred to a cell closer to a phone. He placed a few calls, and Harley and other ACLU lawyers secured his release on bail. The next day he booked a ticket to Delhi and arrived in Vrindavan to consult with his spiritual master.

PRABHUPADA'S ENERGY HAD BEGUN TO ABATE, age and constant travel beginning to take their toll on an octogenarian, but seeing Adi Keshava revived him, and they launched into a discussion about how to defend Krishna consciousness in court. There were two options: attack the charges on their legality or pursue a first amendment defense of freedom of religion. The choice was obvious. Adi Keshava was to wear full devotee dress, with shaved head and tilak face marking, and he was to appear in court with the entire library of Prabhupada's scriptural commentaries.

"This will be a high point for our movement," Prabhupada predicted.

Adi Keshava described that the press were attempting to bias public opinion against Krishna worship by saying devotees were austere zombies who spent nothing for their own comfort. Prabhupada took it as a compliment.

"They are correct," he said. "We don't go to restaurants, we don't go to cinema, and we don't spend lavishly for dress." Then, looking around the room at disciples sitting on the floor, he added, "Or furniture," eliciting a chuckle from his audience. "We live very simply. Whatever funds we have, we print books. Which point do they find faulty? Our only business is to establish Krishna as the Supreme Personality of Godhead."

DISCIPLES AROUND THE GLOBE rallied to build a defense by securing documents of support from scholars and dignitaries. Giriraj, president of the Bombay temple, enlisted Indian industrialists and prominent citizens to write letters certifying that Prabhupada's movement was genuine. In America and Europe, other disciples solicited the academic world, and sympathetic professors responded with endorsements, appreciations, and positive reviews of his books. Before leaving India for the West, Prabhupada had persistently approached heads of state, educators, and leading industrialists for such endorsements. In those days, reponses to his letters were few and far between. Now, responses poured in by the hundreds. It seemed that all the letters he had been waiting for since the 1940s were descending in a flood. Excerpts from some of the best endorsements were compiled into a brochure, "The Krishna Consciousness Movement Is Authorized."

"There is little question," wrote Professor Thomas Hopkins, who had first met Prabhupada when he was still "Swamiji" in 1966, "that this edition is one of the best books available on the Gita and devotion. Prabhupada's translation is an ideal blend of literal accuracy and religious insight." Scholar of South Asian languages and civilization, Edward C. Dimock at the University of Chicago, commented, "By bringing us a new and living interpretation of a text already known to many, he has increased our understanding manifold." Regarding Prabhupada's *Srimad Bhagavatam*, Professor Garry Gelade wrote from Oxford University, "This is a work to be treasured. No one of whatever faith or philosophical persuasion who reads these books with an open mind can fail to be both moved and impressed." Bruce Long of Cornell University's Department of Asian Studies wrote that publication of the Bhaktivedanta edition of *Chaitanya Charitamrita* was "a cause for celebration among both scholars in Indian studies and lay-people seeking to enrich their knowledge of Indian spirituality." Lawrence Shinn, professor of religion at Oberlin College, summed up the sentiments of many by writing that "the best feature of the Hare Krishna movement is that it is providing scholars with excellent translations of the rarest books on Krishna Bhakti."

Nice words from a few scholars did nothing, however, to appease irate parents whose offspring had taken to Krishna consciousness. The father of a Chicago temple devotee incited his friends to harass book distributors in O'Hare International Airport and petitioned the city council to withdraw ISKCON's permit for public assembly. Reverberations were felt nationwide. Devotees who had bid on a property in San Diego found their offer summarily rejected. There were reports of devotees being beaten up in Montreal and Chicago. Deprogrammers celebrated.

NEW YORK TIMES REPORTER Francis X. Clines established his reputation as a literary journalist in the mid-1970s as the author of a long-running column, "About New York." Born in 1938 of second- and third-generation Irish stock, Clines's working-class worldview captured the colorful and varied life of city-dwellers, the rich and the poor, the unknown, and the influential. His feature titled "Religious Freedom vs. Parental Care" appeared on November 1, 1976. He began by laying out particulars of the case against Krishna consciousness, explaining that the Queens district attorney, Michael Schwed, had charged that Merylee Kreshour was brainwashed by her religious leaders, a victim of "mind control" at age twenty-four.

"The case is an extraordinary one," Clines wrote, "because . . . it poses one of the country's founding issues, religious freedom, against one of its perpetual concerns, parental care. And in the process it seems to get at whatever disturbing suspicions ordinary passers-by might have at the sight of the distracting, monkish, bands of religious believers who stand like happy aliens in the middle of the city's great commercial tides of pedestrians."

Clines quoted Schwed as saying, "The thing that frightens me is that a group like this or any other group can use mind control to create an army of zombies or robots who could undermine the government and law enforcement."

But, Clines observed, "one era's 'captive' can be a later era's saint," noting that Francis of Assisi and Thomas Aquinas stirred resistance from disappointed parents when they launched their saintly careers. Clines closed his column with a statement by Merylee Kreshour herself. "I've never felt healthier or happier," she said. "The purpose of life is to inquire into absolute truth. That's what I'm doing."

In late November 1976, Prabhupada spoke with disciples in his room at ISKCON's Krishna Balaram Temple in Vrindavan. How tragic, he said, that their opponents failed to ask why the great souls of history encouraged the building of character and not the building of skyscrapers. Were they brainwashed to choose a simple life over ostentation and wealth?

"So-called educated people," he said, "are thinking how to get money and enjoy life. And to get money, they'll do anything—black money, white money, yellow money." He smiled, remembering the poverty and isolation of his early days in New York and the controversy his mission was now generating. "In the beginning I was hopeless, thinking who will hear this movement?"

The bottom line was simple. It didn't take a university degree to understand the difference between the body and the soul. But acknowledging a soul meant acknowledging at least the possibility of a Supreme Soul, and many people found that threatening to their sense of an independent existence. The fact that Krishna was not a threatening divinity was irrelevant: People's experience of religion was so tragic that even a heartless, purposeless universe seemed preferable.

BY FEBRUARY 1977, deprogrammers had extended their power base to include Christian and Jewish organizations. Krishna consciousness was draining churches and temples of future members, deprogrammers warned, and conservative religionists listened. In one city, 500 rabbis convened in a show of unity against Krishna consciousness. In Phoenix, an angry father donated $100,000 to help build a citywide deprogramming center. Similar deprogramming offices were opening in Canada, England, France, Australia, and South America. A center in Tucson prompted a long article in *Newsweek*, favorable to the cause of "rescuing" devotees from their own "religion." Two states legalized the practice of deprogramming and awarded tax-exempt status to its offices. By early 1977, at least one devotee had been kidnapped from each of the many Krishna temples across America.

Prabhupada's disciples fought back and won an injunction in California against abductions, but despite the occasional victory in battle, they were losing the war. Prabhupada's movement had been implicated in court cases before, but those had mostly been about the legality of methods. For example, did distributing books in airports constitute a First Amendment privilege? This was the first time a suit was being brought over the content of bhakti philosophy.

IN FEBRUARY 1977, Adi Keshava again flew to India from New York to report on developments in the case and explain for Prabhupada why deprogramming had gained legal status. The courts were comparing his disciples to addled old people, he said.

"When a man gets old and becomes senile," Adi Keshava described, "he may have money but not be competent to use it. So the courts have sanctioned a law that empowers family members to take charge of such a person. The law says anyone who is of unsound mind or body and who may consequently be fooled by artful and designing persons can be put under conservatorship. Now they are applying this law to us."

"This is their new tactic," Tamal Krishna added, "getting the courts to declare that *their* kidnapping is legal."

"If it is legal," Prabhupada said, "then what can I say? America's liberty is gone."

"That's why certain other lawyers are alarmed," Tamal Krishna said. "It's becoming like Russia." Krishna devotees had been portrayed as a sect in the distasteful company of Moonies, Children of God, Jews for Jesus, Charles Manson, Patricia Hearst, Scientologists—the smorgasbord of Sixties fanaticism—and public sentiment was growing against them.

Adi Keshava had undergone physical abuse by police and humiliation in the press. Prabhupada examined the orange robes that hung down over his disciple's thin frame. "Don't go into court with any other dress," Prabhupada said. "Preach there with this dress. First of all, make them understand the living force. That can be practically experienced. A machine may be complicated, but without a person to push the button, it has no value. Everything is done by a living being. *Yayedam dharyate jagat.*[168] The universe is like that. Krishna is maintaining. Who can deny it?

"The spirit soul is invisible to our material eye, atomic in size," he continued. "After the destruction of the gross body, which is made up of the senses, blood, bone, fat, and so forth—the subtle body of mind, intelligence, and ego goes on working. So, at the time of death, this subtle body carries the small spirit soul to another gross body. The process is just like air carrying a fragrance.[169] Nobody can see where a rose's fragrance is coming from, but we know it is being done. Similarly, according to the condition of the mind at the time of death, the minute spirit soul enters the womb of a particular mother through the semen of the father. And when the soul develops a particular type of body given by the mother, it may be human, cat, dog—anything.[170] According to the infection of the different modes of material nature, we are creating a good or bad body for our next life. But these laws of nature are unknown to the foolish society. They think this life is everything, and when we present the real solution, they say it is brainwashing. It is not brainwashing; it is heartwashing. Our heart is stacked with so many dirty things, so we are trying to wash it. That is our movement: to cleanse the heart.

"And you are helping me," he said to the devotees around him. "Without your help, I cannot do anything. Thank you very much."

"This is an opportunity to differentiate ourselves," Adi Keshava said. "Some people suggested we should stand in alliance with religious groups to concentrate our strength. But I'm not in favor of that."

"No," Prabhupada agreed. "We should keep our purity."

"The judge handling this case," Brahmananda said, "well, his reputation is that he is the toughest judge in the state. The district attorney deliberately arranged for this judge. It will be a little difficult."[171]

"That is our success," Prabhupada said, "when there is opposition. They don't oppose other movements, but here they see it as venomous poison: no illicit sex, no meat-eating . . ."

"They didn't realize your intentions when you first came in 1965," Tamal Krishna said.

"All their charges are replied in these books," Prabhupada said, holding up a volume of the *Bhagavatam*. "Tell our lawyer he must read these books and argue on that. Bring Bhagavad Gita. Bring the entire set of *Bhagavatams*. From a legal point of view, what I have to say, you have to hear. Then they can give their judgment."

THE DISTRICT ATTORNEY'S OFFICE arguing the case against ISKCON had misjudged Justice John J. Leahy to be a malleable appointment, someone who would arrive at an expedient verdict of guilt. They had not counted on Leahy's sharp mind or his commitment to due process. In his modest way, Leahy advocated the Hellenic ideal of the "shining deed," a heroic act of noble intentions and righteous purpose. From the outset, he sensed something amiss in the prosecution's arguments and took seriously the massive documentation presented by the defense: The dossier of endorsements attesting to the legitimacy of Krishna worship had reached encyclopedic proportions. There were hundreds of letters, petitions, and telegrams voicing outrage over the charges.

Arguments began. The prosecution introduced experts in the fields of psychiatry, medicine, social work, and religion, along with disgruntled former Krishna devotees and their parents and relatives. Based on their testimony, the prosecution argued that the religious rituals, daily activities, and teachings of the Hare Krishna movement constituted a form of intimidation to maintain control of its members. Members were coerced, the prosecution said, into handing over their freedom of thought along with their worldly possessions.

Adi Keshava arrived in court, and his entrance raised eyebrows. His head was freshly shaved, he wore crisp saffron robes, carried a six-foot sannyasa bamboo staff, and was wheeling a table filled with eighty-four volumes of Sanskrit commentaries. For the next three weeks, he and the defense team presented their evidence and arguments. Then it was over and there was nothing left to do but await the verdict of the court.

PRABHUPADA'S HEALTH continued to deteriorate. As the end of his life approached, he thought of the wife and children he had left behind. He and Radharani had stayed married for thirty-six years, during which time she bore him eight children. Three had died at birth, not an uncommon occurrence at a time when prenatal care was rudimentary and the infant mortality rate was high. Their first child, Sulakshmana, was born in 1921. In her teens, she married, had children, and lived with her family in Calcutta. Their second child, Prayagraj, was born in 1924. During his college years, he became mentally unstable. Prabhupada paid to have psychologists attend to his son in the expensive British wing of a local hospital. For some time, treatments seemed to help, but Prayagraj's condition returned and he died, homeless, on the streets of Calcutta around the age of thirty. Prabhupada's middle son, Mathura Mohan, was born in 1932. When Abhay left home in 1951, Mathura Mohan grew resentful of having to assume responsibility for the family's well-being and broke off contact with his father. The fourth child, a daughter named Bhaktilata, was born in 1937. She, too, resented her father for leaving home, never married, and eventually moved in with her younger brother, Vrindavan Chandra. Unlike his siblings, Vrindavan Chandra, born in 1939, never expressed resentment over his father's mission. When asked what his reaction had been when his father left for America, he said, "I felt so proud of him."[172]

Now, in his final days, Prabhupada requested that his former wife and children receive a monthly stipend, the equivalent then of a middle-class income. The allocation was added to his last will and testament.

TAMAL KRISHNA hurried to Prabhupada's room. He bowed down, then stood up with a huge smile and held aloft a copy of *The Times of India*. The front page displayed an article that had appeared the day before in the *New York Times*.

"Shall I read it?" he asked. Prabhupada nodded.

Hare Krishna Movement is a Bona Fide Religion

The Hare Krishna movement was called a "bona fide religion" yesterday by the New York High Court Justice who threw out two charges against the officials of the movement of "illegal imprisonment" and "attempted extortion." The charge had been preferred by an angry parent that his son, as well as another disciple, had been held by the movement illegally and that they had been brainwashed. "The entire and basic issue before the court," said the Justice in dismissing the charges, "is whether the two alleged victims in this case and the defendants will be allowed to practice the religion of their choice, and this must be answered with a resounding affirmative." Said Mr. Justice John Leahy, "the Hare Krishna movement is a bona fide religion with roots in India that go back thousands of years. It behooved Merylee Kreshour and Edward Shapiro to follow the tenets of that faith, and their inalienable right to do so will not be trampled upon. The separation of church and state must be maintained. We are and must remain a nation of laws, not of men. The presentment and indictment by the Grand Jury was in direct and blatant violation of defendants' Constitutional rights."

The Justice said that it appeared to the Court that "The People rest their case on an erroneous minor premise to arrive at a fallacious conclusion. The record is devoid of one specific allegation of a misrepresentation or any act of deception on the part of any defendant." The Justice said, "The freedom of religion is not to be abridged because it is unconventional in its beliefs and practices or because it is approved or disapproved by the mainstream of society or more conventional religions. Without this proliferation and freedom to follow the dictates of one's own conscience in this search for the approach to God, the freedom of religion will be a meaningless right as provided for in the Constitution. . . . The Hare Krishna movement has been under pressure from various groups, and this judgment is expected to stop some of the harassment to which it has been subjected in recent months.

"This is on the front page, Prabhupada," Tamal Krishna said.

"A big headline?" Prabhupada asked.

"Yes," Tamal Krishna said, holding up the paper. "You couldn't pay for an advertisement this good."

It had been more than a half-century since Prabhupada's guru, Bhaktisiddhanta Saraswati, had asked him to go to America. Now he was back in Vrindavan, having fulfilled that order and ready to die. He had said as much to disciples. The signs were clear to him.

"So," Prabhupada said, "my mission is now successful. In 1965, I went to New York, loitering in the street. Nobody cared for me, alone, carrying books."

Prabhupada turned to the guests assembled in his room and asked, "Why should people be kept in darkness? What kind of civilization is that? The knowledge is there, and people should be educated. India should now stand up: 'Stop this nonsense.' That is Chaitanya Mahaprabhu's mission. We are not expecting everyone to do it, but the ideal should be there. Am I right?"

Swarup Damodar, one of his leading scientist-disciples, came from Manipur, a historically religious part of the country. "Most educated people in Manipur accept Krishna consciousness," he said. "I have seen in the airport — the policemen have tilak."

"Tilak!" Prabhupada exclaimed. That appealed to him: police displaying their faith on their faces and defending God's devotees instead of attacking them. "I want to have a small Vaishnava state," he said. "Let's have a small, ideal state. If respectable gentlemen take it, oh, it will be a great success, an ideal throughout the whole world. Show their policemen, all with tilak, and marching. 'Hare Krishna, Hare Krishna, Krishna Krishna, Hare Hare, Hare Rama, Hare Rama, Rama Rama, Hare Hare' — we shall train them. Military march."

They sat and watched in awe of this diminutive volcano of a person who would not stop, even now, envisioning new ways to bring Krishna to the world.

"So let us go, our whole party. I have no other desire. There is no end of it. Work is our life. There is no question of how long. As long as possible. Krishna is giving us good opportunities. It is not a joke: 'Hare Krishna Movement is Bona Fide Religion' — New York High Court decision."

"And that senior man in the courts is very old and conservative," Tamal Krishna said.

"Send him a letter of congratulations," Prabhupada said. "May God bless you for such righteous judgment." Then he turned to his disciples.

"Now, work very strenuously," he said. "You are all young men. Somehow or other, this dead horse, you have given life. Otherwise, the last fortnight I was thinking I am dead now. Life can be finished at any time. That is not wonderful. To live, that is wonderful."

"Krishna is wonderful," Tamal said.

"Krishna is wonderful always," Prabhupada said. His hand never left his bead bag. Between sentences, he chanted, the beads clicking gently, the words coming softly, "Hare Krishna Hare Krishna . . ."

THE SUPREME COURT DECISION not only vindicated his movement in America but by extension overturned eighteenth- and nineteenth-century Orientalists' claims that bhakti was the remnant of a crude and undeveloped period in India's history. What had taken foreign invaders hundreds of years to bury, Prabhupada had resurrected in less than twelve. Still, he did not think in terms of having completed a mission. Kali Yuga was not over. Science still signed blank checks, promising to soon deliver the formula for consciousness, or a solution to old age and death. People believed the pronouncements and held out hope for a brighter future that would never come.

He had trained his disciples to expand what he had started, yet none felt qualified to do so. They saw clearly that Prabhupada's love for Krishna was *prema* bhakti, spontaneous and unselfish. They were beginners who practiced *vaidhi* bhakti, regulated devotional service, taking baby steps, running behind his giant leaps.

"You can overcome this," Brahmananda said, voicing the thoughts of all present that surely he could postpone death if he chose. Krishna would help him live longer. "You have all the mystic powers. You can go on living, if you wish to."

"That is fanaticism," Prabhupada replied, his voice uncharacteristically soft in these final days. "That is not my magic. My magic is different. Why are you sitting here?" he asked of the disciples assembled around his bed. "Why do you feel a love for this person, Krishna, whom you haven't even seen? That is my magic—what is in your hearts today."

WORD WENT OUT TO TEMPLES within hours of his passing on November 14, 1977. My work on French editions of his books had taken me to New York, where some of the press operations were housed. The call from India came in just as snow began settling on the city, the first snowstorm of the year. Trees, scattered around Manhattan like emaciated sentries, sprouted white icy crests. Slick streets made for treacherous driving, and cars slowed to a crawl. New Yorkers being who they were, pushed on, complaining and drenched but resolute. Devotees and congregants arrived at the twelve-story temple on Fifty-Fifth Street—things had grown since the days of Matchless Gifts—bundled against the cold. By the time they unpacked themselves from coats and scarves and assembled into the temple room, the impact of Prabhupada's passing began to sink in. Some people fainted, others collapsed weeping, and not a few like myself wandered around aimlessly, not knowing what to do. Devotees seated by the altar chanted Hare Krishna, but the pace was slow, and their dolorous voices only added to the weight of the moment. It was not until a few days later that we learned details of his final moments.

HE ASKED TO SEE HIS GODBROTHERS, and several arrived from various maths. His voice had grown weak, and the sannyasis leaned closer to hear what he had to tell them.

"Our Srila Prabhupada," he whispered, referring to their spiritual master, Bhaktisiddhanta Saraswati, "said that we should preach in Europe and America. I tried my best. It is my desire that you all forgive me for my mistakes. When we preach, there may be some disputes, some misunderstandings. Maybe I also committed some offenses like that. Please forgive me."

"These are all trivial things," one godbrother replied. "Whatever you did, you did for the well-being of the entire human society. You never did anything wrong."

"I am a little temperamental," Prabhupada replied. "I used words like rascal and so on—the *Bhagavatam* in one hand, a club in the other. Please forgive my offenses."

Another godbrother reiterated the feelings of all. "You were never offensive. You have saved millions of people around the world. You are savior of the most fallen."

Disciples arrived in Vrindavan from all parts of the world, and he instructed that everyone be allowed to come into his room, to chant and share these final moments together. By now, his eyesight had failed, and he had not eaten in days. He lay on his bed, no longer able to move—yet even now he continued work on the *Srimad Bhagavatam*, and all who came witnessed something unforgettable. Pradyumna, his Sanskritist, read verses from the tenth canto out loud. Jayadvaita, head of Prabhupada's publications office, held a microphone close to Prabhupada's mouth and captured his whispered commentaries. Prabhupada's final words came part-way through the tenth canto, at the place where Brahma, the first being, offers prayers to child Krishna.

> "Your transcendental body is dark blue, like a new cloud," Brahma said. "Your garment is brilliant, like lightning, and the beauty of your face is enhanced by your gunja earrings and the peacock feather in your hair. You wear garlands of forest flowers and leaves. Holding a herding stick, buffalo horn and flute, you stand, beautifully, with a morsel of food in your hand . . ."

More than a translation of Sanskrit words, in these final moments Prabhupada described what he was seeing, what he was witnessing in *samadhi*, in trance of love. Disciples watched and chanted for days until the final breath left his body.

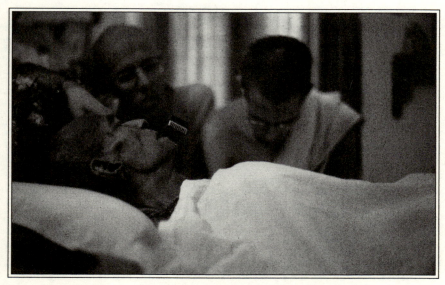

Even on his deathbed, Prabhupada never stopped working on his edition of the *Srimad Bhagavatam.*

Prabhupada in a Paris airport, preparing to continue on his world tour in 1972. He is watching appreciatively as disciples chant.

EPILOGUE

BY THE BEGINNING of the twenty-first century, Prabhupada's mission had had a dramatic impact on Vrindavan. Pilgrims were visiting from every country. Developers had built guesthouses and apartment buildings on farmland where previously cows and peacocks wandered. Cellphone towers rose up over Govardhan Hill. Traditional robes and sandals had yielded to blue jeans and designer sneakers. Vendors were doing a brisk commerce in digital recordings of temple songs. The Brijbasis watched with surprise as their little village transformed into an international city for Krishna worship. Shopkeepers in Loi Bazaar received customers from every continent, and the streets buzzed with languages they had never heard before.

Yet some things about Krishna's village will never change. If you visit today, you will still hear peacocks trumpet, and Brijabasis will still greet you with shouts of "Jaya Radhe!" and "Radhe Shyam!" And if you wake early enough and climbed to the roof of your Wi-Fi–equipped hotel and look out across the landscape before the sun rises, or if you wander down to the shores of the Yamuna before the crowds arrive, you just might hear echos of Krishna's flute or catch a glimpse of his yellow cloth. You just might have a fleeting vision of the divine cowherd boy with a peacock feather in his hair and a garland of forest flowers around his neck, beckoning, smiling, as Prabhupada had always promised, inviting you back home, waiting to welcome you at your journey's end.

CHANGES HAD OCCURRED ELSEWHERE in the world as well. Embarking on a spiritual path used to mean leaving others behind and going to a remote place to achieve enlightenment. But by the time Prabhupada passed away, the world had become a global village, and a spiritually productive life meant not removing oneself from others but working with them, as a collective exercise, to help humanity progress. When I think about the many gifts Prabhupada brought to the West, that one stands out: awareness that my spiritual progress is dependent on the contribution I make to others.

Krishna consciousness — God realization — is an active proposition. We see examples in devotee-organized projects such as Midday Meals, a food relief effort that serves fresh prasadam lunches to a million or more indigent children across India every day. Devotee doctors operate mobile hospitals and offer cost-free cataract surgeries in remote villages. We see Prabhupada's style of engaged devotional service in the programs of hospice caregivers, whose work demystifies the death experience for those approaching the end of this life and the beginning of another. In researching this biography, I spoke with a lawyer whose service on behalf of Native Americans was inspired by reading Prabhupada's edition of the Bhagavad Gita. I interviewed a government officer who serves as a "Track II" diplomat:[173] a negotiator operating behind the scenes in areas of armed conflict. She credits her effectiveness in mediation to bhakti guidelines for *niskama-karma* or unselfish action. Another follower of the bhakti path runs one of the world's most renowned wildlife shelters. His inspiration comes from a verse in the Gita that speaks of seeing all life, human and other than human, as equal.[174] One of the most memorable examples of Prabhupada's mission in action came in the form of an email back in 2008.

"One of my buddies died in my arms," a soldier wrote from Baghdad. "We had been practicing yoga together for some time, and he was chanting when he expired. That gave him and me both some solace. I make the best of the situation by teaching yoga to the men and women on my team."

War had been as difficult for him as it had been for everyone else in his unit. "We've been hit with a lot of IEDs [improvised explosive devices]," he wrote. "I took a round and lost some hearing, and I'm only five months in. There was a massive casualty event recently — this was after several suicide attacks in the North — and I credit the Gita with giving me enough strength to lead my team through that.

"In this town," he continued, "we had to treat more than sixty men, women, and children. Really gruesome material-world stuff. There's nothing more sobering then having to put some little child's brain back in her head while speaking soothing words before she dies. I carried sacred objects with me from India, and I showed them to her and told her stories. She smiled before she left her body. It's such a powerful thing, this process of bhakti yoga. How special this life is, however hard it gets. And there's always something you can do, even here."

That realization—"there is always something you can do, even here"—lies at the heart of Prabhupada's teachings. We may not control destiny, but we can always do something to improve the situation if we remember two things. First, that our material eyes only see the surface of reality—the story is deeper than it seems. Second, as immortal sparks of the Supreme Being, we can do more than we imagine. No battlefield is too big.

In Krishna's words, "Get up and fight."

TIMOTHY KIERNAN was born in 1961 into a family with roots dating back to chieftains of the MacTighearnan clan in eighth century Ireland. His cousin, Kitty Kiernan, portrayed by Julia Roberts in the 1996 movie *Michael Collins*, was engaged to the founder of the Irish Republican Army. At age thirteen, Timothy checked out a book from the local library titled *The Republic*, expecting to read about politics, and discovered it was about philosophy. On the shelf were other philosophic writings such as the *Buddhist Sutras*, the *Holy Qur'an*, and the *Tao Te Ching*. He read them all.

Over the next few years, Timothy visited monasteries, attended meditation sessions, and tried macrobiotic food. One day he met "a chap in strange clothes" who invited him to visit the Dublin Krishna temple. "The senior disciple served me a multicolored sweet called carrot *halvah*," he recalled. "My mind couldn't grasp the idea of a dessert made of carrots, but when he spoke, it was obvious he had mastered a lot of philosophy." Timothy decided to study Krishna consciousness "not to leave Christianity," he explained, "but to better serve God."

The next day Timothy noticed a photo of Prabhupada and asked his host who this person was. The senior devotee fell silent for several moments and then said quietly, "I'm so sorry. The fact that you have to ask means I haven't explained Krishna consciousness sufficiently. Everything I know spiritually comes from him. He was a pure servant of God, and my whole life is about trying to help him serve God."

The senior devotee's humility touched Timothy and inspired a hope that perhaps he, too, could do something to serve God. Timothy eventually received initiation and the name Shaunaka Rishi.

That was the early 1980s, when the Irish Republican Army was fighting a fierce battle for independence from Britain, and tensions between Northern Ireland's Protestant and Catholic communities were strained. On a visit to Belfast, Shaunaka asked a pedestrian for directions to the city center. The man was from Protestant East Belfast and took Shaunaka's Southern Irish accent to mean he must be Catholic.

"Go home, sonny," he told Shaunaka with a look of pity. "This is no place for the likes of you. Just go home."

Shaunaka had a shaved head and wore the bright orange robes of a Vaishnava, "but the man didn't even see that," he recalled with surprise. "His mind was so preoccupied with me being Irish-Catholic that all he could say was 'go home.'"

Shaunaka described the encounter to the senior disciple. In reply, the senior disciple described a conversation he had with Prabhupada in India.

"I would like to open a temple in Belfast," he told Prabhupada.

"Why do you want to do that?" Prabhupada asked.

"There's conflict there between Catholics and Protestants," the disciple explained, "and devotees can help."

"I see," Prabhupada replied. "So now there will be Catholics, Protestants—and Hare Krishnas? Is that your idea? Three religions?"

"What an utterly brilliant analysis of the situation," Shaunaka commented. "He knew his disciples believed everyone should come over to their way of seeing the world, which wasn't going to work. Particularly in conflict zones, no one wants to hear that. To be effective in defusing conflict, the desire to help must be selfless. Then maybe we can contribute something. Bhakti, devotion, the kind that works as a tool of reconciliation, must be free of sectarian thinking."

After thirteen years, Shaunaka moved out of ashram life to practice his faith in the larger world. One of his contacts at that time was Reverend Kenneth Cracknell, interfaith secretary for the British Council of Churches. Shaunaka brought Reverend Cracknell to a Krishna farm where a cow was giving birth. The devotee-farmer who delivered the calf placed the newborn on the altar, signifying that this animal would be honored as a child of God. Cracknell was moved.

"I find so much devotion, so much love of God practiced here," he told Shaunaka. "It challenges me to look deeper into my own tradition." Experiences such as this inspired Shaunaka to found the Oxford Centre for Hindu Studies, dedicated to preserving India's cultural heritage.

"No one has a monopoly on truth," he said. "My happiness was discovering that our Krishna tradition has the intellectual and spiritual breadth to acknowledge that. Prabhupada's character was my reference point. He gave evidence that Krishna is the Supreme Personality of Godhead, but everything else was wide open. He was very broadminded. Our strength as devotees lies in our ability to do like he did: Go into any situation with something to offer, without any conversional agenda. That understanding for me was liberating."[175]

THERE IS AN OLD SAW: God turns to the Devil and says, "I've got this really great idea. I think I'll call it religion." The Devil thinks for a minute and then says, "That *is* a good idea. Let me organize it for you." As soon as something becomes institutionalized—be it a faith community or a physics laboratory—it becomes problematic: in need of financing, administration, differentiation from other institutions, and so on. The institutional dimension of Prabhupada's mission led some people to misunderstand Krishna consciousness as a new religious movement, transplanted from India. There is certainly a historical dimension to Prabhupada's movement, but its origins are not Indian. "This knowledge is the king of education, the most secret of all secrets . . . everlasting, and joyfully performed."[176]

Most recently, this secret of all secrets was delivered by an elderly gentleman who came by cargo ship, carrying only an umbrella, a sack of cereal, and a box of books.

Wherever he traveled, Prabhupada's early morning health walk became a forum for discussing points of philosophy with disciples.

AFTERWORD

IN THE INTRODUCTION to the first volume of *Srimad Bhagavatam*, published in 1962, Prabhupada wrote, "It is admitted even in the higher circles that in fact, the whole root and background of Indian culture is wrapped in the Sanskrit language. And we know that the foreign invaders of India could break down some of the monumental architectural work in India but they were unable to break up the perfect ideals of human civilization so far kept hidden within the Sanskrit language of Vedic wisdom. . . . *Srimad Bhagavatam* is the mature ripe fruit of the tree of Vedic literature. . . . We have just begun to give it rendered into English with broader outlook . . ." He printed 1,100 copies of that first book.

In 2015, the year that marked the fiftieth anniversary of Prabhupada's arrival in the West, the Bhaktivedanta Book Trust calculated the total number of his books distributed to date: The number exceeded 500,000,000 (one-half billion).

FOR TWO REASONS, this biography focuses on Prabhupada's formative years in India and on the early days of his mission in the West. First, it was in India, under the guidance of his guru, Bhaktisiddhanta Saraswati, that Prabhupada developed the structure and goals for a mission in the West. Second, my own life as a devotee began in 1969, and I was privileged to participate in many of the incidents described here.

More than fifty disciples agreed to be interviewed for this book. As I reached out to others, it was startling to discover how many first generation Krishna devotees had passed away. Gour Govinda Swami—the person described in the introduction stirring a pot of *kitchuri* in Bhubaneshwar—was one of Prabhupada's leading *sannyasis* (monks in the renounced order). He passed away in 1996. Bhakti Tirtha Swami, another leading disciple and a friend who dedicated himself to the African and African-American communities, passed away in 2005. My London roommate in the early 1970s, Tamal Krishna Goswami, became a respected Vaishnava scholar in his later years. He passed away in 2010. With us in London was our godsister, Yamuna Devi, author of the award-winning cookbook *Lord Krishna's Cuisine*.

She passed away in 2011. While proofreading the manuscript for this book, I received notice that Brahmananda Das, another pillar of Prabhupada's movement, had passed away in Vrindavan. He was followed a few weeks later by Saurabha Das, the architect of Prabhupada's Vrindavan and Juhu temples. It was a joy serving with these first-generation devotees, and fortunately many of them left memoirs. So it was not necessary to imagine the conversations readers will find here: They were available from primary sources. Occasionally, I have abridged, edited, or combined these discussions to make their meaning clearer for readers.

An important reference for the work at hand was *Srila Prabhupada Lilamrta*, the official and highly detailed biography by Satsvarupa Das Goswami. A wealth of information concerning Prabhupada's early years would have been lost if not for this herculean six-volume achievement. Other sources such as *Our Srila Prabhupada: A Friend to All* and similar anecdotal accounts were compiled by well-intended followers who did not always adhere to standard archival or interview practices. Quotes from these works were made judiciously and researched as far as possible.

ACKNOWLEDGMENTS

I OWE THANKS to many people for their help during the preparation of this book. For giving the manuscript a close read and providing important editorial insight, I thank Giriraj Swami, who led the triumphant struggle to build Prabhupada's Juhu temple complex. I also thank Achyutananda Das, one of the first disciples to receive formal training in India and author of the unforgettable memoir *Blazing Sadhus*; Daivishakti Dasi, torchbearer of Prabhupada's mission in Vrindavan; Gurudas, one of my first buddies in Krishna consciousness, former president of the Vrindavan temple, and a devotee with the world's biggest heart; literati Jayadvaita Swami, a colleague from the early days; Satsvarupa Das Goswami, the esteemed author of Prabhupada's official biography; Jadurani (Shyamarani) Dasi, another friend from the sandbox and one of the first people to illustrate Prabhupada's books; fellow jokester and editor-in-chief of the *Journal of Vaishnava Studies*, Satyaraj Das (Steven Rosen); Swarup Das, a stalwart from the Boston and New York temples; and Umapati Das, who showed me how to see God in a cup of milk. These senior disciples offered important suggestions that greatly enhanced the presentation. Others who read all or part of the manuscript and gave their advice and encouragement include Brahmananda Das (of beloved memory), Devamrita Dasi, Krishna-lila Dasi, Vraja-Vihari Das, Hari-sauri Das, Prishni Dasi, Ravindra Svarup Das, Sthitadhi Muni Das, and Tamraparni Das.

For agreeing to be interviewed and for lending their personal memories and perspectives on various topics, I thank, among others, Abhirama Das (John Sims), Adi Keshava Das (Prof. Angus Murphy), Ambarish Das (Alfred Ford), Baladev Vidyabhusan Das, Baradraj Das (Marek Buchwald), Bhakti Marga Swami, Bhakti Vijnana Swami, Srila Bhakti Bibudha Bodhayan Maharaj, Dinanath Das, Haripuja Dasi, Hridayananda Goswami, Kalindi Dasi (obm), Kirtiraj Das, Peter Leggiere, Ramesvara Das (Robert Grant), Saunaka Rsi Das, Sri Nathji Das (Narendra Desai), Subhananda Das (Steven J. Gelberg), Sujitendriya Das, Tejiyas Das, Tosan Krishna Das, Vaisesikha Das, and Prabhupada's son Vrindavan Chandra. Jyotirmayi Dasi, who dedicated her life to Prabhupada's French translations and to the care of young devotees, and with whom I shared many wonderful years in devotional service, deserves special mention. I am indebted to Arya Dasi for generously sharing her own research and interviews. I am grateful to Professor David Haberman for his memories of Vrindavan and his insights into the correspondence between bhakti and the environment.

I owe special thanks to Devi Deva (Dave Dobson) who not only saw value in this project from its outset and provided critical support and encouragement, but who also inspired me with his many important community service projects. Prabhupada would have been proud to see a disciple extending such compassion to the homeless and destitute.

I wish to thank the disciples and followers of Bhaktisiddhanta Saraswati—those who are with us and those who have passed away—for their contributions to Chaitanya Mahaprabhu's movement. Prabhupada taught his disciples to honor all Vaishnavas, whether formally part of his ISKCON institution or not. We are all privileged to be members of the same devotional family.

This book would not have been possible without the friendship and enthusiasm of Mandala Publishing's founder, Raoul Goff (Ramdas). His vision of a new generation of devotional publications has been an inspiration. It is my pleasure to work with him on a variety of books, including a series for young readers. I also owe a debt of gratitude to Pandita Wong and Courtney Andersson at Mandala Publishing, whose utter dedication to a complex manuscript was a source of constant inspiration.

Swami in a Strange Land and many of my other books would not be worth reading without the radical makeovers, seismic rejiggerings, and painful exorcisms performed by my editor for nearly twenty years, Kyra Ryan. She is a master of her craft.

Since all writing is ultimately autobiographical, I would be remiss in not thanking Adele Greene, Cara Greene, Emmanual Greene, Sundari Greene, Radhika Greene, Brian Greene, Susan Greene, Wendy Greene, Rita Greene and my late father Alan Greene. It is my good fortune to have always had their love and support.

Periodically throughout the narrative, I permitted myself to step in as a participant in the story. I hope readers enjoy these "insider" moments, but I realize that they may leave an exaggerated impression of the role I played in Prabhupada's mission. He initiated nearly five thousand disciples in twelve years, and since his passing, tens of thousands of others have taken up Krishna consciousness. There are many great souls among them who deserved mention—particularly women disciples, who are underrepresented here. My only excuse is that there were, regretfully, limitations in writing a brief biography.

Finally, from the bottom of my heart I thank my wife, Esther Fortunoff-Greene, for her infinite patience, wry humor, and unwavering love. Some guys have all the luck.

ISKCON STATISTICS

AUGUST 13, 1965

A.C. Bhaktivedanta Swami Prabhupada departs Calcutta, age seventy.

Total net worth: 40 rupees ($7 U.S.) plus 200 three-volume sets of first canto, *Srimad Bhagavatam*

AUGUST 18, 2015[177]

Fifty years later, his movement, the International Society for Krishna Consciousness, included:

602 temples

65 farms and eco-villages

54 educational institutes including primary schools, secondary schools and colleges

110 Hare Krishna restaurants

75,000 initiated devotees

7,000,000 guests and worshippers attending ISKCON centers each year

2,000 home study groups meeting weekly (30,000 enrolled students)

516,000,000 books and magazines distributed

3,000,000,000 (3 billion) plates of sanctified vegetarian meals (prasadam) served

1,200,000 food relief meals served daily

1,000 *sankirtan* chanting parties worldwide each week

6,000 Vaishnava festivals held (e.g. Rathayatra)

Total net worth: in excess of $1,000,000,000

A BRIEF BIOGRAPHY OF BHAKTISIDDHANTA SARASWATI

"PEOPLE EITHER LOVED BHAKTISIDDHANTA [1874–1937] for his saintly qualities and strength of character," writes one of his biographers, "or hated him for his uncompromising critique of Vedantic monism . . . and archaic caste structures."[178] In his brief life, the tall, austere Bengali scholar created the first institution for Gaudiya Vaishnavism and paved the way for the global expansion of Krishna bhakti. Intimidated by his forceful and uncompromising style, adversaries nicknamed him "the Lion Guru."

Bhaktisiddhanta developed his reputation from necessity: Nothing less than ramrod leadership could resurrect the Gaudiya culture—what Prabhupada called Krishna consciousness—from three hundred years of slanderous misrepresentation. Within a generation of Chaitanya Mahaprabhu's demise in 1533, tantric opportunists had begun propagating deviant sexual practices in the name of Radha-Krishna worship. The Gaudiya community's ecumenical acceptance of lower castes—often sincere people but lacking education—added to its tarnished reputation. His father, Bhaktivinode Thakur, head of the Gaudiya Vaishnava community, trained him from an early age to reverse that image by enrolling him in Bengal's finest schools and introducing him to exemplars of progressive thought.

Bhaktisiddhanta admired his father's vision for spreading Chaitanya Vaishnavism and throughout his teen years served as his assistant and organizer. Bhaktivinode's Visva Vaisnava Raj Sabha, the Royal World Vaishnava Association, which he began in 1885, brought together intellectuals of the day, including reformist publisher Sisir Kumar Ghosh and Sanskrit scholar Bipin Bihari Goswami; and by the time Bhaktisiddhanta was twelve he was taking part in their discussions. By age thirteen he was proofreading his father's monthly magazine *Sajjana-tosani* and cultivating publishing skills that would play a critical role in the worldwide expansion of Krishna consciousness.

At age seventeen, after only a few years of training in mathematics and astrology, Bhaktisiddhanta managed the impressive feat of starting his own school of astronomy, the Sarasvata Chatushpati, which held sessions in his father's Calcutta home. The school prepared students for application to the city's prestigious Sanskrit College and operated for nearly ten years until disagreements with the College over technicalities of astronomical calculation forced Bhaktisiddhanta to shut it down. College administrators simply could not keep up with his prodigious mind. From that experience emerged a facility for debate that became a hallmark of Bhaktisiddhanta's pedagogy.

The young scholar's reputation attracted the attention of Tripura's royal family, and from 1895 to 1905 he served on retainer to the king, editing the royal family's history and teaching Bengali and Sanskrit to the king's sons. The post gave him access to the palace library where he researched his first book, *Bonge Samajikata*, "The Structure of Society in Bengal," published in 1900, an analysis of Bengali history, which successfully rebutted European accusations that Vaishnavism lacked history, morality, and philosophical structure. By approaching the tradition's history from both indigenous and European perspectives, Bhaktisiddhanta revealed the morality implicit in a life of devotion and established the universal structure of Chaitanya's philosophy of divine love. This was the first in a continuous stream of books and articles that the scholarly celibate would complete in his lifetime.

As heir to his father's place as head of the Gaudiya community, Bhaktisiddhanta enjoyed a more intimate relationship with Bhaktivinode than his twelve siblings. Until Bhaktivinode's demise in 1914, father and son would plan and execute publications, organize gatherings of scholars, give joint lectures, and travel to places of pilgrimage. By turns dramatic and prosaic, their constant efforts to bring devotion into the twentieth century occasionally took unexpected form. Within a hundred yards of Radhakund, a bathing ghat in Vrindavan where Radha and Krishna are reputed to have met for nighttime play, Bhaktivinode purchased a small brick residence for use when he and his son went there on pilgrimage. In that house, in the holiest of Vaishnava holy places, surrounded by medieval temples and sacred spots dating to remote antiquity, Bhaktisiddhanta installed the town's first flush toilet: a ceramic bowl, wooden seat, and flush system with rubber float and metal chain. No plaque marks the achievement. History books do not mention it. Yet as an indicator of a modernist's mindset for India's most ancient devotional community, the functioning commode provides a vivid image among Bhaktisiddhanta's more erudite achievements.

Both father and son must have shared a sense of historical imperative. Chaitanya's prediction that "in as many towns and villages as there are on the surface of the Earth, the Holy Name will be heard"[179] was well known from available hagiographies. To prepare himself for such a historic mission, in 1905, at age thirty-one, he began the austere practice of chanting 300,000 names of Krishna daily—roughly twelve hours of prayer each day. He slept on the ground, never used a pillow, and observed severe dietary restrictions. Even his initiating teacher, Gaura Kishore Das Babaji, himself a renowned ascetic, marveled at the young man's staunch behavior.

By 1906, Bhaktisiddhanta had begun initiating disciples of his own and, true to Chaitanya's example, accepted qualified candidates from both Brahmin and non-Brahmin families. Stung by this threat to their control of religious authority, in August of 1911, orthodox Hindu leaders organized a conference intended to reassert the superiority of family succession. As head of the Vaishanva community, Bhaktivinode would have given the response, but the Thakur was bedridden with severe rheumatism.

Beside himself over his inability to rebut the caste Brahmins' spurious claims, he roared out in frustration. "Is there no one in the Vaishnava world capable of presenting the logic of scripture and putting an end to their lowly activities!?"

At this outburst, Bhaktisiddhanta sat down and wrote a paper titled "Brahmana o Vaisnava" ("Brahmin and Vaishnava") in which he condemned brahminical birthright and presented scriptural evidence of brahminhood based on personal qualities and behavior. The paper gave compelling arguments for the preeminence of *daiva varnashrama* (divinely ordained social structure) which encourages social authority according to ability and character and disqualifies arbitrary caste claims. Bhaktisiddhanta read the paper aloud to his father, and at its conclusion the elder devotee sat up in bed.

"Saraswati," he said weeping, "truly, truly Saraswati.[180] You are the acharya sun [the shining embodiment of sacred teachings] illuminating the face of the Vaishnava world."

Two weeks later, on September 11, 1911, Bhaktisiddhanta presented his paper before several hundred religious leaders who had come from across India to attend the conference. After two days of discourses and debate, his concluding remarks were followed by stunned silence. The presentation had been masterful—and an embarrassment to program organizers.[181]

With each new stance on such polarizing issues as religious ecumenism and the right of non-Brahmins to enter restricted temples, the Gaudiya Math's reputation for controversy grew. As a result, it was mostly in progressive urban centers such as Calcutta that the mission found a warm reception and collected the largest donations for publishing and temple construction. It was in the cities as well that Bhaktisiddhanta's organization found its leadership: twenty celibate men whom Bhaktisiddhanta deployed across India and Europe charged with finding ways to introduce Chaitanya's teachings among mainstream audiences.

It is reasonable to assume that the imperative to fulfill the "every town and village" prophesy factored in Bhaktisiddhanta's decision to take formal initiation and eventually enter the renounced order (sannyasa), since the enhanced prestige would serve to bolster his authority when presenting a mature understanding of Chaitanya ideology. Bhaktisiddhanta was the only initiated disciple of the late ascetic Gaura Kishore Das Babaji, and consequently there was no one physically present who was qualified to award him sannyasa status. On March 29, 1918, he made the controversial gesture of awarding himself sannyasa status before a photo of his late spiritual master. From that time, he was known as Sri Bhaktisiddhanta Sarasvati Goswami Maharaja.

By the time he was fifty, he had published Bengali editions of such classics as *Chaitanya Charitamrita*, *Bhagavata Purana*, and *Chaitanya Bhagavata*. He had also established printing presses, a daily newspaper, a weekly magazine in Bengali, a monthly magazine in English and Sanskrit, and a number of smaller magazines in local languages. In addition to this aggressive calendar of writing and publishing, he frequently lectured and organized a series of exhibitions modeled on world fairs and popular science expos.

It is no wonder that Abhay Charan found his future spiritual master so appealing when they first met in 1922.

GLOSSARY

BELOW ARE A FEW of the more important terms found in this book, with definitions intended to provide a deeper look into their meaning as understood within the Gaudiya Vaishnava (Krishna consciousness) tradition.

•••

acharya

Literally, "one who teaches by example." More than an academic instructor, an acharya embodies scriptural teachings in personal habits, relationships, and community affairs. Men and women are equally eligible to become an acharya, since criteria detailed in the *Upanishads* specify not gender but authenticity of instruction and impeccable personal character. Qualified acharyas are so dear to Krishna that he declares in the *Srimad Bhagavatam*, "As my ideal representative, the acharya should be accepted as my very self" (11.17.27). This accounts, in part, for the formality visitors sometimes witness when disciples in ISKCON temples receive their guru, which may include bowing down, offering a flower garland, or showing other forms of respect.

atma (often atman)

In its most frequent usage, atma refers to the jiva soul, the individual eternal being who is the source of consciousness animating the material body and mind. Because Sanskrit terms have multiple meanings, depending on context, atma can also refer to the body, the senses, the mind, the Supreme Being, humanity, or the essence of a thing. The *Srimad Bhagavatam* explains that selfless, loving service to Krishna satisfies all the atmas (1.2.6–7).

avatar

The common definition is an "incarnation," which is about as informative as describing poetry as "a collection of words." Most often "incarnation" is meant to imply that the Supreme Being is formless energy and when he wishes to come into the world, he becomes embodied, taking on material form. This anthropomorphic understanding of avatars is misleading. Avatars from the category of the Supreme Being do not take on material bodies. Rather, they appear in their original, eternal, non-material form. In the Bhagavad Gita, Krishna warns about confusing his eternal form with temporary material form (9.11). The word avatar more accurately translates as a "descent into the world." One particular category of avatar is not a descent of the Supreme Being. These are the shaktyavesha avatars, jiva souls empowered to implement God's plan in the world. By the Gaudiya Vaishnava estimation, Jesus Christ is to be honored as such an avatar. Prabhupada's followers honor Prabhupada as also from this category. For a more detailed outline of avatars, see Chaitanya Mahaprabhu's explanations to Sanatan Goswami in *Chaitanya Charitamrita*, Madhya Lila, volume 8.

bhakti

From the root *bhaj*, meaning "to share," bhakti is the ultimate goal of all yoga practice, as described in the Bhagavad Gita: "Of all yogis, those who always abide in me with great faith, worshiping me in transcendental loving service, are most intimately united with me in yoga and are the highest of all" (6.47). Bhakti culture was strong in India throughout its history but suffered a decline during the centuries when Buddhism rose to prominence, and then later when Shankara's mayavada doctrine attracted a wide following. Some scholars argue that bhakti culture arose as a response to the brahminical hierarchy that dominated this medieval period. India was suffering from a malaise of social stratification, the argument goes, and a religion of the people—Krishna bhakti—was needed to help balance the social scales. This historic assessment of bhakti, however, overlooks bhakti's a-historic role as the very nature of all souls.

brahman

Brahman is the energy of which all creation is made, the single binding unity behind everything that exists. In monistic schools, brahman is identical to the atman. In essence, these schools declare, we individual living beings are ourselves the brahman energy of everything, or simply put, we are God. This perception of the self as *nirguna* (devoid of form and personhood) has dominated the world's impression of Indian religion for centuries. Bhaktisiddhanta, his father Bhaktivinode, and his disciple Bhaktivedanta Swami Prabhupada sought to remedy the misunderstanding by emphasizing brahman's dimension of *saguna* (with-form and personhood). They did so by surfacing elements of Vedic wisdom that had been sidelined by the monistic teachers.

Brahmin (also spelled Brahmana)

According to the Bhagavad Gita, a Brahmin is someone who exemplifies ideal character and who understands the true nature of brahman (the Supreme Being). "Peacefulness, self-control, austerity, purity, tolerance, honesty, wisdom, knowledge, and religiousness—these are the qualities by which the Brahmins work." (18.42) There is no evidence in the Sanskrit scriptures to support the caste notion that only someone born into a Brahmin family qualifies as a Brahmin.

darshan

The most frequent use of "darshan" is in reference to "a vision of truth" by seeing the guru or the temple diety, as in "I had darshan of my guru today," or "I had darshan of the deities this morning." The other frequent use is *sad-darshan*, which refers to the six principal schools of Indian philosophy. These are *nyaya*, the philosophy of logic and reasoning; *vaisesika*, atomic theory; *sankhya*, nontheistic dualism; *yoga*, self-discipline for self-realization; *karma-mimamsa*, elevation through the performance of duty; and *vedanta*, the conclusion of the Vedic revelation.

dharma

The root *dhr*, means "to hold or maintain." The Sanskrit Monier-Williams Sanskrit-English dictionary defines dharma as that which is established or firm; a steadfast decree, statute, law, practice, custom, duty, right; and also justice, virtue, morality, ethics, religion, religious merit, good works, nature, character, quality, or property. The commonly held meaning is "righteous action," meaning behavior that maintains the well-being of society.

diksha

The word is derived from the verb *diks*, meaning "to consecrate." Diksha refers to a formal commitment between a guru and his or her disciple. The relationship is intended to be lifelong (or longer, should the disciple not achieve full liberation from further births). In some instances, as when a guru falls from proper behavioral standards, there are allowances for a disciple to accept a new guru and to be re-initiated by that person. The initiation occasion is usually formalized by the guru giving a mantra to the disciple along with a Sanskrit name. For ISKCON members, the first initiation is called harinam initiation and includes a fire ceremony. Grains, fruit, and ghee are placed on an open fire, which is considered the mouth of Vishnu, who receives the offerings and in exchange blesses the initiation.

Hindu

The word Hindu is not found in any of the Sanskrit literature. Toward the start of the fifteenth century, the word appeared as the name for India's indigenous people: non-Muslims who lived by the river Indus. "Hindu" had no religious significance until the late nineteenth century when British census-takers required local inhabitants to state their religion. Prabhupada was emphatic that he had come from India not to convert anyone to "Hinduism" but to establish the eternal identity of all living beings as "parts and parcels" of Krishna, the Supreme Personality of Godhead.

ISKCON

International Society for Krishna Consciousness, incorporated in New York City, 1966. While each of the hundreds of ISKCON temples, farms, and restaurants around the world is individually incorporated, all follow standard ecclesiastic and administrative regulations, originally set down by Prabhupada and implemented by his Governing Body Commission.

Jagannath

In the Vedic era of India's past, devoted King Indradyumna wished to worship deities of Krishna and his siblings. The king appointed renowned sculptor Vishwakarma to carve the deities from massive blocks of wood. Vishwakarma accepted on condition that no one interrupt him before the task was completed. He began his work behind closed doors. Two weeks later, no longer able to contain his eagerness, King Indradyumna opened the door to Vishwakarma's workshop. The master craftsman stormed from the room in disgust, leaving the deities unfinished—rough-hewn, with big round eyes and no hands or feet. Dismayed, the king prayed to cosmic architect, Brahma, for guidance. Within his heart, the king heard Brahma's reply: The images would be accepted as they were, in their unfinished form, by the world.

jnana and karma

For thousands of years prior to Chaitanya, India acknowledged three major paths which promised followers knowledge of ultimate reality: *karma-kanda*, the path of work as inculcated in the original Vedas; *jnana-kanda*, the path of knowledge as espoused in the supplementary *Upanishads*; and *upasana-kanda*, or bhakti, the path of devotion as promoted in the *Itihasas* (the epics *Ramayana* and *Mahabharata*) and the *Puranas* (histories). Chaitanya corrected and expanded the previously held view of devotion as different from jnana and karma by defining bhakti as inclusive of them. All knowledge, all work, finds its fulfillment when undertaken in the spirit of devotion, as underscored in the Bhagavad Gita: "Whatever you do, whatever you eat, whatever you offer or give away, and whatever austerities you perform—do that, O son of Kunti, as an offering to me. In this way you will be freed from bondage to work and its auspicious and inauspicious results" (9.27–28).

sadhana

To reawaken love of God, Chaitanya stressed five activities as most important in *sadhana*, or daily devotional practices: 1) keeping company with Krishna's devotees, 2) chanting the names of Krishna, 3) hearing narrations of Krishna's pastimes (as described in texts such as the *Srimad Bhagavatam*), 4) residing in Vrindavan or some other holy place, and 5) worshiping the deity of Krishna daily. It is significant that Chaitanya's community placed no restrictions on who could perform these functions and advocated equal places for men and women: "All living beings are by nature eternal loving servants of Krishna, and by chanting his names love for Krishna will be revived." (*Chaitanya Charitamrita*, Madhya, 22.107)

Vaishnavism

Most scholarly books on Vaishnavism describe four principal schools (*sampradayas*). These are the Sri sampradaya (founder: Ramanuja, 1017–1137), the Madhva sampradaya (founder: Madhva, 1197–1276), the Kumara sampradaya (founder: Nimbarka, 1125–1162), and the Rudra sampradaya (founder: Vishnu Swami, 1200–1250; also called the Vallabha sampradaya after a more recent saint Vallabha, 1479–1533). The Chaitanya School, named after its founder (1486–1533), is often associated with the Madhva sampradaya yet has grown to such importance that it is often listed separately. Vaishnava practice is called bhakti or devotional service to Krishna.

Vedic literature

Scholars divide the Sanskrit texts into two general categories. The first, *shruti*, refers to "that which is heard," or directly revealed to humanity by the Supreme Being. These scriptures are the primary source of authority for dharma, or righteous life. The *shruti* texts start with the Veda. Sage Vyasadev is credited with having divided the Veda into four parts: the Rig, Sama, Yajur, and Atharva Vedas. Little of their content relates to the contemporary world, apart from an underlying principle that all actions should be done as an offering or sacrifice (*yajna*) to the Divine. These four texts contain hymns to be recited at fire sacrifices; formulas for propitiating various gods; incantations for specific needs; mantras, songs, and spells. Vyasadev is also credited with having written the epic narrative *Mahabharata* (100,000 verses), called "the fifth Veda," as it presents a story-based depiction of Vedic social codes and philosophy. In the section titled "Book of Bhishma" we find the dialogue known as Bhagavad Gita, which distills Vedic wisdom down to a concise 700 verses.

Other texts considered shruti include the *Brahmanas*, codes for "the knowers of brahman," which discuss the details and meanings of sacrificial rituals; the *Aranyakas* or "wilderness texts," composed for recluses and meditators; and 108 *Upanishads*, "coming-closer-to-the-Divine" texts, which summarize Vedic philosophy in short verses.

Schools of Indian philosophy have taken differing positions on the Vedas. Those which cite the Vedas as their scriptural authority, such as Vaishnavas (worshippers of Vishnu/Krishna, India's largest religious community), Shaivites (worshippers of Shiva), and Shaktas (worshippers of Durga or the Goddess) are classified as orthodox. Other traditions, notably Buddhism and Jainism, do not regard the Vedas as authority and are considered heterodox or non-orthodox schools.

Smriti is the second category of Vedic literature. Scholars commonly translate smriti as "tradition." In a sense, smriti texts consist of the memories that sages have passed on to their disciples. These include ancient works such as the *Manu Samhita* ("Laws of Manu"), the epic tale *Ramayana*, and more recent commentaries by renowned teachers of Indian philosophy, such as Ramanuja, Madhvacharya, and Shankara.

Tradition credits Vyasadev with having also compiled the *Puranas*, which are historic narratives of the universe from creation to destruction, and the Gaudiya Vaishnavas consider these of equal importance as the shruti texts. The *Puranas* contain genealogies of kings, heroes, sages, and demigods and descriptions of cosmology, philosophy, and geography.

However, the earliest written versions date from the time of the Gupta Empire (3rd-5th century CE) and some scholars place the *Puranas* in this later period, identifying them as *smriti* texts.

NOTES

1. Readers will find variations in titles such as Das, Dasa, das, dasa, etc. I have used whatever form the interviewee preferred.

2. There are differences of opinion among scholars concerning what constitutes "Vedic." The prevailing attitude has been to include only the four original Vedas and their immediate supplements: the *Brahmanas*, *Aranyakas*, and *Upanishads*. Prabhupada's use of the term "Vedic" included later scriptures, which he described as "in pursuit of the Vedic version," including the *Puranas*, *Itihasas*, and commentaries. He based his understanding of "Vedic" on the writings of predecessor acharyas such as Jiva Goswami, who in *Tattva Sandarbha* argues that, particularly in the current Age of Kali, the *Puranas* rank higher in importance than the original Vedas.

3. For a thought-provoking exploration of Vaishnavism's potential impact on world affairs, see Klaus K. Klostermaier, "Will India's Past Be America's Future? Reflections on the Caitanya Movement and Its Potentials," *Journal of Asian and African Studies* 15, nos. 1–2 (Jan. and Apr. 1980): 94–103. Klostermaier argues that European religions have largely ignored the question of consciousness, which is central to the Krishna-conscious experience and thus "ahead not only of traditional Western religiosity but also of the modern sciences."

4. British census figures from 1881 and 1901 concluded that one-fifth of Bengal were Chaitanya Vaishnavas, including most of Calcutta's wealthy, influential families. Janardan Chakravarti describes Bengal Vaishnavism as "a mighty social force, released by [Chaitanya,] the greatest-ever humanist that India produced" (*Bengal Vaishavism and Sri Chaitanya*, The Asiatic Society, 1975, 29).

5. Tamal Krishna Goswami, *A Living Theology of Krishna Bhakti: Essential Teachings of A.C. Bhaktivedanta Swami Prabhupada*, ed. by Graham M. Schweig (New York: Oxford University Press, 2012), 90. From his mother, Prabhupada acquired a practical approach to problem solving, cooking skills, and faith in the traditional life of Vaishnavas. "If Gour Mohan is to be credited for encouraging Prabhupada's early

practice, solidified later through the doctrinal instruction of his guru," writes Tamal Krishna Goswami, "it is Rajani who deserves recognition for much of his enculturation vital to both practice and belief." Goswami concludes that both parents together instilled in their son "the ritual and experiential aspects of Krishna bhakti."

6.   In the Vedic era of India's past, devoted King Indradyumna wished to worship deities of Krishna and his siblings. The king appointed renowned sculptor Vishwakarma to carve the deities from massive blocks of wood. Vishwakarma accepted on condition that no one interrupt him before the task was completed. He began his work behind closed doors. Two weeks later, no longer able to contain his eagerness, King Indradyumna opened the door to Vishwakarma's workshop. The master craftsman stormed from the room in disgust, leaving the deities unfinished—rough-hewn massive blocks of wood with big round eyes and no hands or feet. Dismayed, the king prayed to cosmic architect, Brahma, for guidance. Within his heart, the king heard Brahma's reply: the images would be accepted as they were, in their unfinished form, by all the world.

7.   Alexander Duff, *India and Indian Missions, Including Sketches of the Gigantic System of Hinduism, Both in Theory and Practice* (Edinburgh: John Johnstone, 1839), 209–11. The anti-Krishna propaganda had been going on for nearly one hundred years. "The incarnations of Hinduism are the most extravagant caricatures of truth. . . . Take by far the happiest, fairest and most perfect of them; namely, Vishnu, in the form of Krishna. . . .What was the character of this incarnate divinity? In his youth, he selected sixteen thousand shepherdesses, with whom he 'sported away his hours in the gay revelries of dance and song', as well as in all the wantonness and levities of unhallowed pleasure. In a quarrel with a certain monarch respecting some point of precedency, he became so enraged that he cut off the head of his rival. He was in the habit of practicing all manner of roguish and deceitful tricks. With the most deliberate acts of falsehood and of theft he was more than once chargeable. And at his door must be laid the guilt of many abominations over which Christian purity must ever draw the veil. What a contrast to all this is the character of our incarnate Redeemer!"

8.   Sardella and Ghosh, "Modern Reception and Text Migration of the Bhagavata Purana." Chap. 12 in *The Bhagavata Purana: Sacred Text and*

Living Tradition. (New York: Columbia University Press, 2013). The statement is excerpted from an 1862 judgment against the Vaishnava community known as the Vallabhaites.

9. James Kennedy, *Christianity and the Religions of India* (Mirzapore: Orphan Schools Press, 1874).

10. Letter to Gopal Krishna, May 11, 1972.

11. Letter to Gargamuni, May 5, 1968.

12. *Mundaka Upanishad*, 1.2.12.

13. Mahaprabhu: "Great Master," an honorific title referring to Chaitanya. The preeminent work on his life and teachings is the seventeenth-century Bengali biography *Chaitanya Charitamrita* by Krishnadas Kaviraj Goswami. Prabhupada's multivolume edition was first published in the mid-1970s.

14. Condemning Chaitanya Vaishnavism with faint praise, Vivekananda told the Chicago gathering, "Is it a sin if a man can realize his divine nature with the help of an image—would it be right to call that a sin? No, nor even when he has passed that stage should he call it an error. Man passes from truth to truth, from lower to higher truth . . . Images, crosses and crescents are simply so many symbols to hang spiritual ideas on. Those that do not need it have no right to say it is wrong . . . Idolatry in India does not mean anything horrible. It is the attempt of undeveloped minds to grasp high spiritual truths . . ."

15. Eric Sharpe, "Hindu-Christian Dialogue in Europe," in *Hindu-Christian Dialogue: Perspectives and Encounters*, ed. Harold Coward (Maryknoll: Orbis Books, 1993). Sharpe offers insightful comments about the anti-Hindu history of America and Europe.

16. Antipathy toward Hindus would grow more pronounced with publication in 1927 of Katherine Mayo's notorious best seller *Mother India*, which sensationalized wife burnings and other anomalies of Indian culture. In 1929, when poet Rabindranath Tagore arrived in Los Angeles, immigration officials treated him with such disdain that he canceled his tour. "Jesus could not get into America," he remarked, "because he would be [branded] an Asiatic."

17. Abhay Charan to Narayan Maharaj, 28 September 1966, in *Letters from America*, 17.

18. In 1896, Bhaktivinode published *Chaitanya Mahaprabhu, His Life and Precepts*, a small book that portrayed Chaitanya Mahaprabhu as a

champion of "universal brotherhood and intellectual freedom." He sent the book to scholars and universities in England and North America. Copies were included in the libraries of McGill University in Montreal, the University of Sydney in Australia, and the Royal Asiatic Society of London. The book also made its way to prominent scholars, including Oxford Sanskrit scholar Monier Monier-Williams, and earned a favorable review in the *Journal of the Royal Asiatic Society*.

19. Bhakti Vikasa Swami, *Sri Bhaktisiddhanta Vaibhava: The Grandeur and Glory of Srila Bhaktisiddhanta Sarasvati Thakura*, vol. 1, 349–359.

20. Rupa Goswami, *Bhakti-rasamrita-sindhu* 1.2.255. "When one is not attached to anything, but at the same time accepts everything in relation to Krishna, one is rightly situated above possessiveness."

21. Examples of women leaders frequently cited from Chaitanya's period include Jahnavi Devi, Basudha Devi, and Sita Devi, all of whom became respected preceptors and organizers of the movement. Also noted are Madhavi Dasi, author of the Sanskrit commentary *Purushottamadevanataka*; Subhadra Dasi, author of the Bengali text *Anangakadambavali*; Vrindavati Dasi, an Oriyan Vaishnavi who composed the *Purnatmachandrodaya*; and Hemlata Dasi, daughter of Shrinivasa Acharya and an eminent scholar of the *Bhagavata Purana*. The community also raised no objections to widows remarrying nor was their choice of partners limited by caste restrictions.

22. The five primary rasas of love for God receive detailed treatment in Prabhupada's *Nectar of Devotion*, 23, 271–357.

23. Literally "the ocean of ambrosial rasa." Prabhupada titled his translation of this work *Nectar of Devotion*.

24. Bhakti Vikasa Swami, *Sri Bhaktisiddhanta Vaibhava*, vol. 1, 142.

25. Ibid, 218.

26. Ibid, 215.

27. F.S. Growse, *Mathura: A District Memoir*, part 1, 123. Cited in Chatterjee, *Srikrsna Caitanya: A Historical Study on Gaudiya Vaisnavism* (New Delhi: Associated Publishing Company, 1983), 96.

28. Quoted by Sivarama Swami: http://www.sivaramaswami.com/en/2007/03/29/prabhupada-in-vrindavan-2/.

29. Visvanath Chakravarti Thakur: *Vraja-ritti-chintamani*, cited in Mahanidhi Swami, *Vidaghda Madhava* (Vrindavan: Rasbihari Lal & Sons, 2006), 11.

30. Mahanidhi Swami, *Vidagdha Madhava* (Vrindavan: Rasbihari Lal & Sons, 2006), 37.

31. A.C. Bhaktivedanta Swami Prabhupada, *Srimad Bhagavatam*, 12 vols. (Los Angeles: The Bhaktivedanta Book Trust, 1972), 3.2.29.

32. Mulaprakrti Devi Dasi, *Our Srila Prabhupada: A Friend to All—Early Contemporaries Remember Him* (New Delhi: Brij Books, 2004), 49–50.

33. Raghunath Das Goswami, *Sri Vilapa-Kusumanjali,* verse 6.

34. A name for Krishna, meaning one who takes away all material desire and gives himself in return.

35. Rupa Goswami, *Sri Vidagdha Madhava*, Kusakratha dasa, trans. (Vrindavan: Rasbihari Lal & Sons, 2006).

36. Mulaprakrti Devi Dasi, *Our Srila Prabhupada*, 31–32.

37. Krishna's feet are described as *aravinda* (lotus-like) because they are elegantly tapered like a lotus leaf.

38. Mulaprakrti Devi Dasi, *Our Srila Prabhupada*, 33–34.

39. His Holiness Swami B.P. Puri Maharaja, *Of Love and Separation: Meditations on My Divine Master* (San Rafael: Mandala Publishing Group, 2001), 12, 44. The phrase "humbler than a blade of grass, more tolerant than a tree" comes from the *Sikshastaka* prayers of Chaitanya Mahaprabhu.

40. "The Bombing of Calcutta by the Japanese," BBC, accessed October 8, 2015, http://www.bbc.co.uk/history/ww2peopleswar/stories/50/a5756150.shtml.

41. Nathuram Godse's brother and co-conspirator in the assassination, Gopal Godse, claimed that, contrary to popular belief, Gandhi never called out "Hey Ram!" ("O my dear Lord Rama") as he was dying. This was a rumor, he said, begun by the Indian government to reinforce the image of Gandhi as a staunch Hindu who deserved to be elevated to sainthood. In an interview with *Time* magazine, he said, "Someone asked me whether Gandhi said, Hey Ram. I said Kingsley did say it"—referring to actor Ben Kingsley who played Gandhi in the Academy Award–winning movie of 1982—"but Gandhi did not. Because that [the real assassination] was not a drama."

42. Satsavarupa Das Goswami, *Srila Prabhupada Lilamrita* (Los Angeles: Bhaktivedanta Book Trust, 1980–83), vol. 1, 142.

43. A.C. Bhaktivedanta Swami Prabhupada, *Srimad Bhagavatam*, 10.88.8.

44. Satsavarupa Das Goswami, *Srila Prabhupada Lilamrita*, vol. 1, 151.

45. *Gaudiya* 20.319, cited in Bhakti Vikasa Swami, *Sri Bhaktisiddhanta Vaibhava*, vol. 1, 277.

46. Thakura Bhaktivinoda, *The Bhagavata: Its Philosophy, Its Ethics, and Its Theology* (San Jose, CA: Guardian of Devotion Press, 1985), 8.

47. Satsavarupa Das Goswami, *Srila Prabhupada Lilamrita*, vol. 1, 212–13.

48. Poem published in *Gaudiya Patrika*.

49. Mulaprakrti Devi Dasi, *Our Srila Prabhupada*, 119.

50. "Chant the names of Hari (Krishna)!" Among Krishna devotees, this is both a greeting and an expression of joy.

51. Mulaprakrti Devi Dasi, *Our Srila Prabhupada*, 75.

52. Charles R. Brooks, *The Hare Krishnas in India* (Princeton, NJ: Princeton University Press, 1989), 77.

53. Mulaprakrti Devi Dasi, *Our Srila Prabhupada*, 111.

54. *Letters from Srila Prabhupada*, 5 vols. (Culver City, CA: The Vaisnava Institute, 1987), vol. 1, 71. In the mid-1980s, several of Prabhupada's disciples established the ISKCON Prison Ministry, which continues to operate.

55. Quoted on http://www.wikiwand.com/en/Sumati_Morarjee.

56. Mulaprakrti Devi Dasi, *Our Srila Prabhupada*, 235.

57. Ibid, 205.

58. Sankirtan—"complete" kirtan—refers to congregational chanting of the Hare Krishna mantra, for the benefit of the general public.

59. "Do not stay in illusion; go to the eternal reality. Do not stay in darkness; go to the light. Do not keep taking material bodies; become immortal!" *Brihad-aranyaka Upanishad*, 1.3.28.

60. Mahaprabhu and his followers chanted and danced in the streets of sixteenth-century Bengal. When the Muslim government insisted they cease, Mahaprabhu continued his public chanting in defiance of the interdictions. Some commentators suggest these civil disobedience marches were the original model for Gandhi's campaigns. (S.C. Chakravarti, *Philosophical Foundations of Bengal Vaishnavism: A Critical Exposition* (Lewisburg: Bucknell University Press, 1985) 35. Cited in *Journal of Vaishnava Studies*, vol. 6, no. 2, 9.

61. *Letters from Srila Prabhupada*, vol. 1, 79.

62. Mulaprakrti Devi Dasi, *Our Srila Prabhupada*, 276.

63. Brooks, *Hare Krishnas*, 76. Prabhupada had spoken with similar conviction before leaving India. Anthropologist Charles R. Brooks re-

counts a conversation between a Vrindavan merchant and his family who remembered Bhaktivedanta Swami saying, in the early 1960s, "I have temples already in America, and many people worship Krishna there. Only time now hides them from vision."

64. *Sikha*, the tuft of hair left on top or at the back of a shaven head, traditionally worn by Vaishnava brahmacharis and sannyasis as a sign of their renunciation and to distinguish them from monists who shave their heads completely.

65. Dating the *Bhagavatam* has always been problematic for scholars, many of whom generalize to sometime in the past two thousand years while agreeing that the *Bhagavatam* likely reflects much more ancient teachings. Nineteenth-century Indologist Max Muller dated the *Bhagavatam* to three thousand years ago. "Since the . . . Puranas represent an oral tradition that was constantly revised over a period of several thousand years," writes Indologist Wendy Doniger O'Flaherty, "a passage actually composed in the twelfth century A.D. may represent a surprisingly accurate preservation of a myth handed down since the twelfth century B.C. — or a completely original retelling of that myth." Going by its own internal references, the *Bhagavatam* dates in written form to the dawn of Kali Yuga or about 3100 B.C. Whatever the actual date of its codification, most everyone agrees the *Bhagavatam* opens a window through which we are allowed to share an ancient way of seeing the world.

66. Indradyumna Swami, *Diary of a Traveling Preacher* (Imperial Beach, CA: Torchlight Publishing, 2012), vol. 3.

67. Kees W. Bolle, "The *Bhagavadgita* Within the Study of Mysticism," *Journal of South Asian Literature* 23 no. 2 (July 1988): 1–19. For a modernist such as Radhakrishnan, the advaitic position was a foregone conclusion, and the Gita's mysticism lay not in the specificity of knowing Krishna as the supreme lovable object but in a general oneness of all mystical experience. Radhakrishnan's philosophical assumptions imposed an arbitrary value on all mystical phenomena. Bolle has done a worthy job of exposing the risks of such generalizations.

68. Prabhupada had previously dealt with Radhakrishnan's commentary on Gita 9.34 in an essay, "Scholars Deluded," which ran in two 1958 issues of *Back to Godhead*.

69. *Bhagavad Gita As It Is* (Bhagavad Gita), 9.11. "Fools deride me when I

descend in human form. They do not know my transcendental nature as the Supreme Lord of all creation."

70. Ravindra Svarupa Dasa, "Religion and Religions," *ISKCON Communications Journal*, 1 no. 1 (Jan.–June, 1993): 35–36. "The Western youth who joined ISKCON," writes Ravindra Svarupa Dasa, "never thought of themselves as 'converting' to something called Hinduism. . . . [T]hey did not think that in adopting ISKCON's practices they were plunging into the historically conditioned forms of a particular religious sect. Indeed, they usually did not think of themselves as practicing something called a 'religion' at all. Prabhupada managed quite compellingly to convey an altogether different vision."

71. The late Indologist A.L. Basham noted that Bhaktivedanta was not one of the self-appointed swamis who glutted the market with "a streamlined kind of Hindu mysticism designed to appeal to modern, jet-age disciples: levitation . . . moksa in a few easy lessons—a Hinduism without class, without worship, without rigid taboos." Subhananda Das, "A Theology with Heart: An Interview with Prof A. L. Basham," *Back to Godhead* (November 7, 2013).

72. From a historic perspective, bhakti yoga appears in the earliest of Vedic texts, which describe *yajna* or sacrifice: a personal offering meant for the pleasure of God and the stability of the world. Chaitanya took the principle of yajna and gave it contemporary relevance and popular form in chanting. From an ahistoric perspective, bhakti (loving devotional service) is the eternal nature of the soul and does not depend on historical textual reference for its relevance in social organization.

73. Bhagavad Gita, 15.7

74. J. Frank Kenney, "The Manifestation of A.C. Bhaktivedanta as Swami, Guru and Avatar" (paper presented at the American Academy of Religions, Little Rock, AR, 1976). Given that his classes in those early days covered the ABCs of Krishna consciousness, the Swami occasionally called the storefront "a kindergarten of spiritual life." See Satsavarupa Das Goswami, *Srila Prabhupada Lilamrita*, vol. 2, 147.

75. To honor the chanting as an event of importance in the history of New York, in 1999 the City's Parks Department installed a plaque near the base of the American elm tree where Prabhupada held his weekly gatherings.

76. Satsavarupa Das Goswami, *Srila Prabhupada Lilamrita*, vol. 1, 214.

77. David Pichaske, *A Generation in Motion: Popular Music and Culture in the Sixties* (New York: Schirmer Books, 1979), xvi.

78. Satsavarupa Das Goswami, *Srila Prabhupada Lilamrita*, vol. 2, 208.

79. Bhagavad Gita, 9.26. "If one offers me with love and devotion a leaf, a flower, fruit or water, I will accept it."

80. Letters dated April 8 and 13, 1968.

81. Satsavarupa Das Goswami, *Srila Prabhupada Lilamrita*, vol. 2, 238. The visit had some impact on the music group. The Fugs recorded "Hare Krishna" with Allen Ginsberg on their 1968 album *Tenderness Junction*.

82. Satyaraja Dasa, "A Spiritual Happening on the Lower East Side," *Back to Godhead* (Mar.–Apr. 2011).

83. Achyutananda Das, *Blazing Sadhus or Never Trust a Holy Man Who Can't Dance* (Alachua, FL: CMB Books, 2012), 226.

84. Morning walk with Srila Prabhupada, Mayapur, India, April 8, 1975.

85. "To understand spiritual truths, one must humbly approach, with firewood in hand, a spiritual master who is learned in the Vedas and firmly devoted to the Absolute Truth." *Mundaka Upanishad* 1.2.12. The word *srotryam* in this verse signifies "learned in the Vedas" and also implies the disciplic succession: a teacher who has heard from a predecessor in the tradition's lineage.

86. Bhagavad Gita, 4.16–17. Krishna himself advises against attempting to understand the history of one's karma. "Even the intelligent are bewildered in determining what karma is," He tells Arjuna. "The intricacies of karma are very hard to understand."

87. The spelling changed in subsequent editions to the more familiar *Srimad Bhagavatam* or *Bhagavata Purana*.

88. Thomas Hopkins, interviewed in *Hare Krishna, Hare Krishna: Five Distinguished Scholars on the Krishna Movement in the West*, ed. Stephen J. Gelberg (New York: Grove Press, 1983), 101–161, quoted in Tamal Krishna, *A Living Theology, 36*.

89. Bhaktisiddhantha Saraswati Goswami, *Brahma Samhita* (Los Angeles: Bhaktivedanta Book Trust, 1985), 5.35. See also Bhagavad Gita, 18.61.

90. Bhagavad Gita, 2.69.

91. *Chaitanya Charitamrita*, Madhya 22.31.

92. David G. Bromley and Larry D. Shinn, eds., *Krishna Consciousness in the West* (New Jersey: Associated University Presses, 1989), 106.

93. Bhagavad Gita, 9.26.

94. Conversation with Bhakti Cohen, recounted to the author.

95. *Letters from Srila Prabhupada*, vol. 4, 2187.

96. Richard H. Davis, *The Bhagavad Gita: A Biography* (Princeton, NJ: Princeton University Press, 2014), 8.

97. "Can water quaff itself?" asked seventeenth-century bhakti poet Tukaram. "Can trees taste of the fruit they bear? He who worships God must stand distinct from Him, so only shall he know the joyful love of God. For if he says that God and he are one, that joy, that love, shall vanish instantly away. Pray no more for utter oneness with God."

98. A more detailed description of Macmillan's edition of the *Bhagavad Gita As It Is* appears in Steven Rosen's *Mentor Sublime: A Collection of Essays on the Life and Teachings of His Divine Grace A.C. Bhaktivedanta Swami Prabhupada* (Vrindavan: Rasbihari Lal & Sons, 2006), 83–89.

99. Steven J. Rosen, *Swamiji: An Early Disciple, Brahmananda Dasa, Remembers His Guru* (Badger, CA: Torchlight Publishing, 2014), 89. According to his passport, A.C. Bhaktivedanta Swami was 5'3" tall.

100. For an insightful introduction to string theory, see Brian Greene, *The Elegant Universe* (New York: W.W. Norton, 1999).

101. *Conversations with Srila Prabhupada*, 37 vols. (Los Angeles: The Bhaktivedanta Book Trust, 1988), vol. 1, 217–218.

102. Bhagavad Gita, 3.4 and 3.8.

103. Ibid, 3.6–7 and 3.19. "One who restrains the senses of action but whose mind dwells on sense objects certainly deludes himself and is called a pretender. On the other hand, if a sincere person tries to control the active senses by the mind and begins karma-yoga without attachment, he is by far superior. . . . Therefore, without being attached to the fruits of activities, one should act as a matter of duty, for by working without attachment one attains the Supreme."

104. A.C. Bhaktivedanta Swami Prabhupada, *Srimad Bhagavatam*, 1.5.18.

105. *Conversations with Srila Prabhupada*, vol. 2, 200–01. The verse in question is Bhagavad Gita, 9.22: "Those who always worship me with exclusive devotion, meditating on my transcendental form—to them I carry what they lack, and I preserve what they have." A similar assurance is offered in the Bible: "So why do you worry about clothing? Consider the lilies of the field, how they grow: they neither toil nor spin and yet I say to you that even Solomon in all his glory was

not arrayed like one of these." Matthew 6:28–29.

106. *Chaitanya Charitamrita*, Madhya, 13.33–55.

107. Compiled from 1968 radio interviews in San Francisco, March 9 and 12, and Seattle, September 24.

108. Bhagavad Gita, 2.13.

109. Kenney, "Manifestation." The paper was read to Prabhupada, who commented favorably on its content.

110. *Shik-shastaka* prayers of Chaitanya Mahaprabhu.

111. *Letters from Srila Prabhupada*, vol. 3, 215.

112. This brief explanation of the rasa dance summarizes five chapters from the tenth canto of *Srimad Bhagavatam*. For an eloquent analysis of the full text, see Graham Schweig, *Dance of Divine Love: India's Classic Sacred Love Story: The Rasa Lila of Krishna* (Princeton, NJ: Princeton University Press, 2005).

113. *Conversations with Srila Prabhupada*, vol. 1, 250–53.

114. Steven J. Gelberg, ed., *Hare Krishna, Hare Krishna: Five Distinguished Scholars on the Krishna Movement in the West* (New York: Grove Press, 1983), 181–82.

115. Swami Vivekananda, *Jnana Yoga* (New York: Ramakrishna-Vedanta Center, 1955), 216.

116. J. Krishnamurti, *Commentaries on Living*, vol. 1, 11th ed. (Wheaton, IL: Quest Books, 2001), 207.

117. The five *yamas* or guidelines to social behavior as listed in *Yoga Sutra* are *ahimsa* (doing no harm to any living creature), *satya* (truthfulness), *asteya* (not stealing), *brahmacharya* (celibacy, sometimes also translated as faithfulness to one's partner), and *aparigraha* (non-possessiveness). The five *niyamas* or virtuous habits include *saucha* (purity of mind, speech, and body), *santosha* (contentment, acceptance of one's circumstances), *tapas* (perseverance, austerity), *svadhyaya* (sober reflection in thought, speech, and action), and *ishvarapranidhana* (contemplation of God). See Edwin F. Bryant, *The Yoga Sutras of Patanjali, A New Edition Translation, and Commentary* (New York: North Point Press, 2009).

118. *Yoga-sutra*, 2.32.

119. Bhagavad Gita, 2.59.

120. Some of the temples from Dvapara Yuga remain intact to this day. See, for instance, http://www.stephen-knapp.com/antiquity_of_deity_worship_in_vedic_tradition.htm.

121. Purport to A.C. Bhaktivedanta Swami Prabhupada, *Srimad Bhagavatam*, 4.8.36.

122. Bhagavad Gita, 7.19.

123. *Conversations with Srila Prabhupada*, vol. 1, 132–34.

124. Bhagavad Gita, 7.16.

125. Conversation with the author in Paris, 1974.

126. *Svetasvatara Upanishad*, 5.9.

127. Bhagavad Gita 8.6.

128. *Adyatmik*, *adibautik*, and *adidaivic*: "miseries" provoked by one's own body or mind, by others, and by external conditions.

129. *Conversations with Srila Prabhupada*, vol. 3, 326–363.

130. Bhagavad Gita, 2.20.

131. Ibid, 2.13.

132. *Times of India*, October 10, 1970.

133. Satsavarupa Das Goswami, *Srila Prabhupada Lilamrita*, vol. 4, 130–31.

134. Ibid, 132.

135. *Letters from Srila Prabhupada*, vol. 2, 805.

136. *Conversations with Srila Prabhupada*, vol. 2, 133–34.

137. For more information about these food relief efforts, visit www.annamrita.org and www.akshayapatra.org.

138. Satsavarupa Das Goswami, *Srila Prabhupada Lilamrita*, vol. 5, 20.

139. Brooks, *Hare Krishna*, 180–81.

140. Ibid, 201.

141. Bhagavad Gita, 2.14.

142. Vyasa-puja offering, 1999.

143. Prabhupada had conducted a similar conversation the previous year with Alfred Ford, great-grandson of automobile scion, Henry Ford. "So," Prabhupada said, "you are Henry Ford's great-grandson. Where is he now?" Alfred was initiated soon afterward and received the name Ambarish Das.

144. Jean Daniélou, *The Advent of Salvation* (Mills River, NC: Deus Publications, 1962).

145. Bhagavad Gita, 9.26.

146. Bhagavad Gita, 14.4. Prabhupada's use of the phrase "our Krishna" echoed the Passover service, in which the doubting son says, "What did *you* do in Egypt," removing himself from the family circle. The Passover Hagaddah advises the father to reply, "Our God led *us* out of slavery,"

suggesting the son is still slave to his doubts, as was Daniélou to his doubts about the presence of souls in other than human forms of life.

147. Sir Jagadish Chandra Bose (1858–1937) was a Bengali physicist, biologist, botanist, and archaeologist who pioneered the investigation of radio and microwave optics and made significant contributions to experimental science. In 1926, he lectured at the Sorbonne in Paris on the nervous system of plants.

148. *Conversations with Srila Prabhupada*, vol. 5, 155–178.

149. *Sri Isopanisad*, verse 1.

150. William Blake, "Auguries of Innocence," *The Pickering Manuscript*, originally published in 1807 (Whitefish, MT: Kessinger Publishing, 2004), 18.

151. Tamal Krishna, *Living Theology*, 47. See also Anthony Wallace, "Revitalization Movements," *American Anthropologist* 58 (1956): 264–81.

152. Tamal Krishna, *Living Theology*, 50.

153. Bromley and Shinn, *Krishna Consciousness in the West*, 42.

154. Agehananda Bharati, "Fictitious Tibet: The Origin and Persistence of Rampaism," *Tibet Society Bulletin*, vol. 17 (1974). http://www.serendipity.li/baba/rampa.html.

155. A.C. Bhaktivedanta Swami Prabhupada, *Srimad Bhagavatam*, 12.3.51. For example, "Although Kali Yuga is an ocean of faults, there is still one good quality about this age. Simply by chanting the Hare Krsna maha-mantra, one can become free from material bondage and be promoted to the transcendental kingdom."

156. George Chryssides, *Exploring New Religions* (London: Continuum International Publishing Group, 1999), 346–348.

157. The People of the State of New York v. Angus Murphy and ISKCON, Inc.

158. Tamal Krishna, *Living Theology*, 53.

159. For an insightful article on representation of ISKCON in the press, see James A. Beckford, "The Mass Media and New Religious Movements," *ISKCON Communications Journal* 2, no. 2 (Dec. 1994).

160. Bhagavad Gita, 14.4.

161. *Conversations with Srila Prabhupada*, vol. 30, 69.

162. This date relates to the codification of Krishna's teachings from oral to written form.

163. Hari-sauri Dasa, *A Transcendental Diary: Travels with His Divine Grace A.C. Bhaktivedanta Swami Prabhupada* (Murwillumbah: Lotus Imprints, 2005), vol. 5, 280.

164. *Brihad-aranyaka Upanishad*, 1.3.28.

165. After the disappearance of Chaitanya Mahaprabhu in 1533, the Vaishnava community confronted misrepresentation by *sahajiyas*, who promoted sexual promiscuity in the name of *lila* or "divine play."

166. The Chicago Seven were seven defendants—Abbie Hoffman, Jerry Rubin, David Dellinger, Tom Hayden, Rennie Davis, John Froines, and Lee Weiner—charged with conspiracy, inciting to riot, and other charges related to protests that took place in Chicago on the occasion of the 1968 Democratic National Convention.

167. Victor S. Navasky, "Right On! With Lawyer William Kunstler," *New York Times*, April 19, 1970. "William Kunstler is without doubt the country's most controversial and, perhaps, its best-known lawyer period."

168. Bhagavad Gita, 7.5.

169. "Beings in this world carry conceptions of who they are from one body to another as the air carries aromas." (Bhagavad Gita, 15.8).

170. *Conversations with Srila Prabhupada*, vol. 27, 235.

171. Ibid, vol. 30, 338.

172. Interview with the author in Mumbai, April 2015.

173. Douglas Johnston and Cynthia Sampson, eds., *Religion, the Missing Dimension of Statecraft* (New York: Oxford University Press, 1994).

174. "The humble sage, by virtue of true knowledge, sees with equal vision a learned and gentle Brahmin, a cow, an elephant, a dog and one who eats dog." Bhagavad Gita, 5.18. For information about the TIGERS Preserve, a private wildlife preserve based on yogic principles, visit www.tigerfriends.com.

175. For ISKCON's position on the interfaith dialogue, see "ISKCON and Interfaith" at www.iskcon.org/wp-content/documents/Interfaith-Brochure.pdf.

176. Bhagavad Gita, 9.2

177. "ISKCON report," accessed October 12, 2015, http://www.radha.name/news/general-news/iskcon-report.

178. Sardella, Ferdinando, "Bhaktisiddhanta Sarasvati (1874–1937): Vaishnava Identity in Modern Dress," *Journal of Vaisnava Studies*, spring 2007, 95.

179. *Chaitanya Bhagavata*, Antya, 4.126. The prophesy connects to an older prediction in the *Srimad Bhagavatam*: "Whatever result was obtained in Satya Yuga by meditating on Vishnu, in Treta Yuga by performing

sacrifices, and in Dwapara Yuga by serving the Lord's deity can be obtained in Kali Yuga simply by chanting the names of Hari." (A.C. Bhaktivedanta Swami Prabhupada, *Srimad Bhagavatam*, 12.3.52).

180. Demigoddess of learning. Throughout his later life, Bhaktisiddhanta was known as Bhaktisiddhanta Saraswati.

181. Bhaktisiddhanta's success also contradicts Max Weber's assertion that "caste is the fundamental institution of Hinduism. Before everything else, without caste, there is no Hindu." From Max Weber, *The Religion of India* (New York: The Free Press, 1958), 29.

BIBLIOGRAPHY

BOOKS BY A.C. BHAKTIVEDANTA SWAMI PRABHUPADA

Beginning: The 1966 New York Journal of His Divine Grace A.C. Bhaktivedanta Swami Prabhupada, The. Los Angeles: Bhaktivedanta Book Trust, 1996.

Bhagavad-gita As It Is. Abr. ed. New York: Collier Macmillan, 1968.

Bhagavad-gita As It Is. Complete ed. Los Angeles: Bhaktivedanta Book Trust, 1989.

Easy Journey to Other Planets. Los Angeles: Bhaktivedanta Book Trust, 1970.

Jaladuta Diary of His Divine Grace A.C. Bhaktivedanta Swami Prabhupada, The. Los Angeles: Bhaktivedanta Book Trust, 1995.

KRSNA: The Supreme Personality of Godhead. 2 vols. Los Angeles: Bhaktivedanta Book Trust, 1970.

Nectar of Devotion: A Summary Study of Srila Rupa Goswami's Bhaktirasamrita-Sindhu, The. Los Angeles: Bhaktivedanta Book Trust, 1970.

Perfection of Yoga, The. Los Angeles: Bhaktivedanta Book Trust, 1970.

Sri Caitanya-caritamrita. 17 vols. Los Angeles: Bhaktivedanta Book Trust, 1974.

Sri Isopanisad. Los Angeles: Bhaktivedanta Book Trust, 1969.

Srimad Bhagavatam. 12 vols. Los Angeles: Bhaktivedanta Book Trust, 1972.

Teachings of Lord Chaitanya. Los Angeles: ISKCON Press, 1968.

BOOKS ABOUT A.C. BHAKTIVEDANTA SWAMI PRABHUPADA

Achyutananda Das. *Blazing Sadhus or Never Trust A Holy Man Who Can't Dance.* Alachua, FL: Charles M. Barnett, 2012.

Gelberg, Steven J. *Hare Krishna, Hare Krishna: Five Distinguished Scholars on the Krishna Movement in the West.* New York: Grove Press, 1983.

Gurudas. *By His Example: The Wit and Wisdom of A.C. Bhaktivedanta Swami Prabhupada.* Badger, CA: Torchlight Publishing, 2004.

Hari Sauri Dasa. *A Transcendental Diary: Travels with His Divine Grace A.C. Bhaktivedanta Swami Prabhupada.* 6 vols. Alachua, FL: Lotus Imprints, 1992–2005.

Hayagriva Das. *The Hare Krishna Explosion: The Birth of Krishna Consciousness in America (1966–1969).* San Rafael, CA: Palace Press, 1985.

Mukunda Goswami. *Miracle on Second Avenue: Hare Krishna Arrives in New York, San Francisco and London 1966–1969.* Badger, CA: Torchlight Publishing, 2011.

Mulaprakrti Devi Dasi. *Our Srila Prabhupada A Friend to All: Early Contemporaries Remember Him.* New Delhi: Brij Books, 2004.

Ravindra Svarupa Dasa. "Religion and Religions." *ISKCON Communications Journal* 1, no. 1 (Jan.–June, 1993): 35–36.

Rosen, Steven. *Mentor Sublime: A Collection of Essays on the Life and Teachings of His Divine Grace A.C. Bhaktivedanta Swami Prabhupada.* Vrindavan, India: Rasbihari Lal & Sons, 2006.

Rosen, Steven J. *Swamiji: An Early Disciple, Brahmananda Das, Remembers His Guru.* Badger, CA: Torchlight Publishing, 2014.

Satsvarupa Das Goswami. *Srila Prabhupada Lilamrita.* 6 vols. Los Angeles: Bhaktivedanta Book Trust, 1980–83.

Siddhanta das, ed. *Memories; Anecdotes of a Modern-Day Saint.* 4 vols. Culver City, CA: CH Books, 2002–10.

Siegel, Roger. *Love, Medicine and Music: The Flipside of the Sixties.* Mumbai: Tulsi Books, 2013.

Tamal Krishna Goswami. *A Living Theology of Krishna Bhakti: Essential Teachings of A.C. Bhaktivedanta Swami Prabhupada.* New York: Oxford University Press, 2012.

———. *Servant of the Servant.* N.p.: self-published, 1984.

Umapati Swami. "My Days with Prabhupada: A Young Man's Path to God in the Hare Krishna Movement." Unpublished manuscript.

Vaiyasaki dasa Adhikari. *Radha-Damodara Vilasa.* Silver Spring, MD: Sravanam-Kirtanam Press, 1999.

OTHER REFERENCES

Back to Godhead: The Magazine of the Hare Krishna Movement. Alachua, FL: Bhaktivedanta Book Trust International.

BBC. "The Bombing of Calcutta by the Japanese." Accessed October 8, 2015. http://www.bbc.co.uk/history/ww2peopleswar/stories/50/a5756150.shtml.

Beckford, James A. "The Mass Media and New Religious Movements." *ISKCON Communications Journal* 2, no. 2 (Dec. 1994).

Bhaktisiddhanta Saraswati Goswami. *Brahma Samhita.* Los Angeles: Bhaktivedanta Book Trust, 1985.

Bhaktisiddhanta Saraswati. *Prabhupada Saraswati Thakur: The Life and Precepts of Srila Bhaktisiddhanta Saraswati.* San Rafael, CA: Mandala Publishing Group, 1997.

Bhakti Vikasa Swami. *Sri Bhaktisiddhanta Vaibhava: The Grandeur and Glory of Srila Bhaktisiddhanta Sarasvati Thakura.* 3 vols. Surat, India: Bhakti Vikas Trust, 2009.

Bhaktivinoda Thakura. *The Bhagavata: Its Philosophy, Its Ethics, and Its Theology.* San Jose, CA: Guardian of Devotion Press, 1985.

Bharati, Agehananda. "Fictitious Tibet: The Origin and Persistence of Rampaism." *Tibet Society Bulletin,* vol. 17, 1974. http://www.serendipity.li/baba/rampa.html.

Blake, William. "Auguries of Innocence." *The Pickering Manuscript.* Whitefish, MT: Kessinger Publishing, reprint, 2004.

Bolle, Kees W. "The *Bhagavadgita* Within the Study of Mysticism." *Journal of South Asian Literature* 23, no. 2 (July 1988): 1–19.

Bromley, David G., and Larry D. Shinn, eds. *Krishna Consciousness in the West.* New Jersey: Associated University Presses, 1989.

Brooks, Charles R. *The Hare Krishnas in India.* Princeton, NJ: Princeton University Press, 1989.

Bryant, Edwin. *The Yoga Sutras of Patañjali: A New Edition, Translation, and Commentary.* New York: North Point Press, 2015.

Bryant, Edwin F., and Ekstrand, Maria L., eds. *The Hare Krishna Movement: The Postcharismatic Fate of a Religious Transplant.* New York: Columbia University Press, 2004.

Chakrabarty, Ramakanta. *Vaishnavism in Bengal.* Calcutta: Sanskrit Pustak Bhandar, 1985.

Chatterjee, A.N. *Srikrsna Caitanya: A Historical Study on Gaudiya Vaisnavism.* New Delhi: Associated Publishing Company, 1983.

Chryssides, George. *Exploring New Religions.* London: Continuum International Publishing Group, 1999.

Conversations with Srila Prabhupada. 37 vols. Los Angeles: Bhaktivedanta Book Trust, 1988.

Daivisakti Devi Dasi, ed. *Vrndavana Is My Home: A History of Srila Prabhupada's Sri Sri Krsna Balarama Temple.* Vrindavan, India: Bhaktivedanta Book Trust International, 2015.

Daniélou, Jean. *The Advent of Salvation.* Mills River, NC: Deus Publications, 1962.

Davis, Richard H. *The Bhagavad Gita: A Biography.* Princeton, NJ: Princeton University Press, 2014.

Duff, Alexander. *India and Indian Missions, Including Sketches of the Gigantic System of Hinduism, Both in Theory and Practice.* Edinburgh: John Johnstone, 1839.

Ellwood, Robert S., ed. *Eastern Spirituality in America: Selected Writings.* Mahwah, NJ: Paulist Press, 1987.

Ferdinando Sardella. *Modern Hindu Personalism: The History, Life, and Thought of Bhaktisiddhanta Sarasvati.* NY: Oxford University Press, 2013.

Greene, Joshua M. *Here Comes the Sun: The Spiritual and Musical Journey of George Harrison.* Hoboken, NJ: John Wiley & Sons, 2006.

Haberman, David L. *Journey Through the Twelve Forests: An Encounter with Krishna.* New York: Oxford University Press, 1994.

"ISKCON report." Accessed October 12, 2015. http://www.radha.name/news/general-news/iskcon-report.

James, Lawrence. *Raj: The Making and Unmaking of British India.* New York: St. Martin's Press, 1998.

Johnston, Douglas, and Cynthia Sampson, eds. *Religion, the Missing Dimension of Statecraft.* New York: Oxford University Press, 1994.

Kapoor, O.B.L. *The Saints of Vraja.* New Delhi: Aravali Books International, 1992.

Kennedy, James. *Christianity and the Religions of India.* Mirzapore, India: Orphan Schools Press, 1874.

Kenney, J. Frank. "The Manifestation of A.C. Bhaktivedanta as Swami, Guru and Avatar." Paper presented at the American Academy of Religions, Little Rock, AR, 1976.

Klostermaier, Klaus K. "Will India's Past Be America's Future? Reflections on the Caitanya Movement and Its Potentials." *Journal of Asian and African Studies* 15, nos. 1–2. (Jan. and Apr. 1980): 94–103.

Letters from Srila Prabhupada. 5 vols. Culver City, CA: Vaisnava Institute, 1987.

Mahanidhi Swami. *Appreciating Sri Vrndavana Dhama.* Raman Reti: ISKCON Vrndavana, 1991.

———. *Gaudiya Vaisnava Samadhis in Vrindavana.* N.p.: self-published, 1993.

Marwick, Arthur. *The Sixties: Cultural Revolution in Britain, France, Italy, and the United States, c. 1958–1974.* New York: Oxford University Press, 1998.

Memories of Vrndavana: Srila Prabhupada's Sri Sri Krsna-Balarama Temple. Vrindavan, India: Bhaktivedanta Book Trust, International, 2015.

Pichaske, David. *A Generation in Motion: Popular Music and Culture in the Sixties.* New York: Schirmer Books, 1979.

Prabhodhananda Sarasvati. *Sri-Vrndavana-Mahimamrta: The Nectarean Glories of Sri Vrndavana.* Bhumipati Dasa, trans. Vrindavan, India: Rasbihari Lal & Sons, n.d.

Rupa Goswami. *Sri Vidagdha-madhava.* Kusakratha dasa, trans. Vrindavan, India: Rasbihari Lal & Sons, 2006.

Schweig, Graham. *Dance of Divine Love: India's Classic Sacred Love Story: The Rasa Lila of Krishna.* Princeton, NJ: Princeton University Press, 2005.

Sharpe, Eric. "Hindu-Christian Dialogue in Europe." In *Hindu-Christian Dialogue: Perspectives and Encounters,* Harold Coward ed. Maryknoll: Orbis Books, 1993.

Songs of the Vaishnava Acharyas: Hymns and Mantras for the Glorification of Radha and Krishna. Los Angeles: Bhaktivedanta Book Trust, 1996.

S. Radhakrishnan. "Brihad-aranyaka Upanishad." *The Principal Upanisads.* Atlantic Highlands, NJ: Humanities Press, 1953: 149–333.

———. "Svatasvatara Upanishad." *The Principal Upanisads.* Atlantic Highlands, NJ: Humanities Press, 1953: 709–750.

Swami B.P. Puri Maharaj. *Of Love and Separation: Meditations on My Divine Master.* San Rafael, CA: Mandala Publishing Group, 2001.

Swami Vivekananda. *Jnana Yoga.* New York: Ramakrishna-Vedanta Center, 1955.

Syamarani Devi Dasi. "The Art of Transcendence." Unpublished manuscript.

Thompson, Richard L. *Mechanistic and Nonmechanistic Science: An Investigation into the Nature of Consciousness and Form.* Lynbrook, NY: Bala Books, 1981.

Wallace, Anthony. "Revitalization Movements." *American Anthropologist* 58 (1956): 264–81.

INDEX

Page references followed by *p* indicate a photograph.